A BIRDER'S GUIDE
TO
SOUTHEASTERN ARIZONA

A BIRDER'S GUIDE
TO
SOUTHEASTERN ARIZONA

completely revised by
Richard Cachor Taylor
1995

revisions to the original version by
Harold R. Holt

original version by
James A. Lane
1965

American Birding Association, Inc.

Library of Congress Catalog Number: 95-75101
ISBN Number: 1-878788-06-X

Fourth Edition
    1   2   3   4   5   6   7   8
Printed in the United States of America
Publisher
    American Birding Association, Inc.
    George G. Daniels, Chair, Publications Committee
Series Editor
    Paul J. Baicich
Associate Editors
    Cindy Lippincott and Bob Berman
Copy Editor
    Hugh Willoughby
Layout and Typography
    Bob Berman; using CorelVENTURA, Windows version 5.0
Maps
    Cindy Lippincott; using CorelDRAW version 5.0
Cover Photography
    front cover: *Painted Redstart;* Herbert Clarke
    back cover: *Costa's Hummingbird;* C. Allan Morgan
             Elf Owl; Brian E. Small
Illustrations
    Georges Dremeaux
    Narca Moore-Craig
    Terry O'Nele
    David A. Sibley
    Gail Diane Yovanovich
Distributed by
    American Birding Association Sales
    PO Box 6599
    Colorado Springs, Colorado 80934-6599 USA
    phone: (800) 634-7736 or (719) 578-0607
    fax: (800) 590-2473 or (719) 578-9705
European and UK Distribution
    Subbuteo Natural History Books, Ltd.
    Treuddyn, Mold, Clwyd
    CH7 4LN UK Tel: 0352-770581; fax: 0352-771590

A Special Note

Like all books that attempt to describe
the avian dynamics of Southeastern Arizona,
this book owes much to *The Birds of Arizona*, 1964,
by Allan Phillips, Joe Marshall, and Gale Monson,
and the subsequent *Annotated Checklist
of the Birds of Arizona*, 1981,
by Monson and Phillips.
These works are the foundation
of our knowledge
of the status and distribution
of the avifauna in this state.
They have made this book possible.

FOREWORD

After my first visit to Southeastern Arizona fifteen years ago, I knew I would return. I have lived or visited there every year since. Because of my intense interest in the area, friends often asked me to plan their visits. I started writing itineraries for them. Each year these get more detailed and numerous. Someone suggested I write a book....
— Jim Lane, 1965

These words were written for the preface of the very first edition of a little book entitled *A Bird Watcher's Guide to Southeastern Arizona* by the late James A. Lane (1926-1987). Jim dedicated most of his adult life to helping others find and enjoy the birds of all of North America. During the last two decades of his life he wrote or co-authored seven books in his popular regional *Birder's Guide* series. The first of Jim's guides was for Southeastern Arizona. It was a charming little book containing 46 pages, modest by today's standards, but a very real accomplishment in 1965. For the rest of his life, Southeastern Arizona remained Jim Lane's favorite place to bird in North America.

Soon after Jim Lane met Harold Holt in 1972, the two teamed up to co-author a Colorado birdfinding guide. Although Jim was also leading tours for the Massachusetts Audubon Society, he managed to revise the Southeastern Arizona book twice, once in 1974 and again in 1977. Meanwhile, Harold had assumed responsibility for distribution of the Lane Guides, and in 1982 he began updating all of the books. The Southeastern Arizona birdfinding guide was revised by Harold Holt in 1983, 1984, and 1986.

Jim Lane, the father of the popular modern North American birdfinding guide, was honored at the 1986 Tucson Convention with the American Birding Association's Ludlow Griscom Award for his outstanding contributions to the birding world. At the same time Jim's health was gradually failing. The North American birding community lost a great path-finder in March of 1987, but Jim's legacy continues in what have come to be known among birders as "The Lane Guides."

After Jim Lane's death, Harold Holt updated his late friend's Southeastern Arizona birdfinding guide twice, in 1988 and again in 1989.

In 1990, the American Birding Association assumed the on-going responsibility for keeping the Lane Guide series current and for adding new titles to the *ABA Birdfinding Guides*. Major new editions in an innovative format have now appeared for all but two of the books in the original Lane series.

For this edition, the ABA asked Richard Cachor Taylor to revise *A Birder's Guide to Southeastern Arizona*. Rick is a local birder with a lifetime of first-hand experience in the region, and he is also the author of *Trogons of the Arizona Borderlands,* based on a research project that he launched in 1977. Not only did Rick build on the considerable contributions of Jim Lane and Harold Holt, and capture the spirit of Jim's intentions in this book, but Rick also added extensively to the depth and coverage of the book.

It is hoped that this new version of the Southeastern Arizona guide will earn the same kind of reception as previous editions, that it will enable birders to thoroughly enjoy the birding potential in Southeastern Arizona, and that users of the book will continue to make suggestions for improving future editions.

Paul J. Baicich
Series Editor, ABA Birdfinding Guides

ACKNOWLEDGEMENTS

The list of birders to whom I am indebted for the information contained in these pages is long. I am especially grateful to the hundreds of birders with whom I've shared the oases, deserts, valleys, canyons, and mountains of this beautiful and bird-rich area. This book owes much to their companionship and their insights. It would have been impossible to write it without their help.

At the same time, this book is very much the outgrowth of the pioneer work done by the late Jim Lane and subsequently by Harold Holt. All those who helped Jim and Harold in the past versions of this birdfinding guide should be recognized: Larry Balch, Janice Bezore, Jewel Bezore, Steve Bezore, Barbara Berton, Edward Chalif, Edna Chamness, Peter Christensen, Hal Coss, Mary Dodd, Bill Harrison, Wes Hetrick, Gary Kirkreit, LaVona Holt, Glenn Isaacson, Billie Lane, Cebina Lane, Kent

Nelson, Ray Olson, Carroll Peabody, Joan Peabody, Edna Phelps, George Pilling, Noble Proctor, Eleanor Pugh, Vincent Roth, Doug Salyar, Fletcher Sillick, Larry Smith, Tom Southerland, Rich Stallcup, Jolan Truan, Bernard Weiderman, Hugh Willoughby, Bob Witzeman, and Fern Zimmerman.

Since I undertook this project in the fall of 1994, a number of people who deserve special mention have made concrete suggestions or contributed information. I would like to take this opportunity to express my deep appreciation to the following friends and fellow birders: Sandy Anderson, Chris Benesh, Tom and Debbie Collazo, Jeffrey Cooper, Alan Craig, Doug Danforth, Louie Dombroski, Shawneen Finnegan, Clive Green, Mary Jean Hage, Stuart Healy, Dave Jasper, Kenn Kaufman, Karen Krebbs, Dave Krueper, Paul Lehman, Katherine Lunsford, Terry McEneaney, Bill Maynard, Scott Mills, Gale Monson, Arnie Moorhouse, Bob Morse, Jack Murray, Jeff Price, Jay Schnell, Wayne Shifflett, Robert T. Smith, Walter and Sally Spofford, Mark Stevenson, Lynne Taylor, Dave Thayer, Thea Ulen, Jack Whetstone, Sheri Williamson, and Tom Wood.

I would also like to thank Georges Dremeaux, Narca Moore-Craig, Terry O'Nele, David A. Sibley, and Gail Diane Yovanovich for their illustrations and Herbert Clarke, C. Allan Morgan, and Brian E. Small for their cover photos. Cindy Lippincott supplied the maps and black-and-white photographs. Bob Berman and Eric Taylor provided the computer expertise necessary to bring the bar-graphs and mileage chart to life. The guide would be neither as attractive nor as user-friendly without these superb graphics and visual devices.

Finally I owe a special debt of gratitude to those people who improved the text immeasurably with their editorial patience and expertise. Every word was carefully scrutinized for accuracy and precision by Barbara Bickel, Cindy Lippincott, and Hugh Willoughby. Paul Baicich, as series editor, helped to bring disparate elements of this book together. This book would not be as good without their encouragement and teamwork.

Rick Taylor
Tucson, Arizona
June 1995

TABLE OF CONTENTS

American Birding Association Code of Ethics

We, the membership of the American Birding Association, believe that all birders have an obligation at all times to protect wildlife, the natural environment, and the rights of others. We therefore pledge ourselves to provide leadership in meeting this obligation by adhering to the following general guidelines of good birding behavior.

I. Birders must always act in ways that do not endanger the welfare of birds or other wildlife.

In keeping with this principle, we will

- Observe and photograph birds without knowingly disturbing them in any significant way.

- Avoid chasing or repeatedly flushing birds.

- Only sparingly use recordings and similar methods of attracting birds and not use these methods in heavily birded areas.

- Keep an appropriate distance from nests and nesting colonies so as not to disturb them or expose them to danger.

- Refrain from handling birds or eggs unless engaged in recognized research activities.

II. Birders must always act in ways that do not harm the natural environment.

In keeping with this principle, we will

- Stay on existing roads, trails, and pathways whenever possible to avoid trampling or otherwise disturbing fragile habitat.

- Leave all habitat as we found it.

III. Birders must always respect the rights of others.

In keeping with this principle, we will

- Respect the privacy and property of others by observing "No Trespassing" signs and by asking permission to enter private or posted lands.

- Observe all laws and the rules and regulations which govern public use of birding areas.

- Practice common courtesy in our contacts with others. For example, we will limit our requests for information, and we will make them at reasonable hours of the day.

- Always behave in a manner that will enhance the image of the birding community in the eyes of the public.

IV. Birders in groups should assume special responsibilities.

As group members, we will

- Take special care to alleviate the problems and disturbances that are multiplied when more people are present.

- Act in consideration of the group's interest, as well as our own.

- Support by our actions the responsibility of the group leader(s) for the conduct of the group.

As group leaders, we will

- Assume responsibility for the conduct of the group.

- Learn and inform the group of any special rules, regulations, or conduct applicable to the area or habitat being visited.

- Limit groups to a size that does not threaten the environment or the peace and tranquility of others.

- Teach others birding ethics by our words and example.

INTRODUCTION

Southeastern Arizona is one of the most exciting birding regions in North America. More than 400 species occur here annually, and nearly 500 species have been recorded. That is more kinds of birds than occur in any other land-bounded area of comparable size in the United States. In fact only Texas, California, and Florida have state lists that exceed the total list for the 15,000-square-mile area encompassed by Southeastern Arizona. Of these birds, 36 species are not regular anywhere else in the U.S., and another 40-plus are confined to the zone along the U.S. border with Mexico.

Not only is the birding exceptional, the scenery is spectacular. If Sabino Canyon, Sonoita Creek, Cave Creek Canyon, or any of the other southeast Arizona beauty spots, were found in any other state, they would be declared scenic wonders and set aside as national parks. Where else in the United States would you take time out from watching such dazzling birds as Magnificent Hummingbird, Red-faced Warbler, or Varied Bunting simply to enjoy the scenery?

GEOLOGY

Southeastern Arizona is usually defined as that part of the state lying south and east of Tucson, but also including the Altar and Avra Valleys west of the city. Geologically, Southeastern Arizona belongs to the Basin and Range Province, a region of comparatively small mountains oriented on a north-south axis, separated by broad alluvial valleys. Elevations range from 1,500 feet at Picacho Reservoir to 9,796 feet on the summit of Chiricahua Peak near the New Mexico border.

The drainage system of the region is both complex and confusing, since most of the water flows underground. Two rivers flow north, two flow south, and another system of streams goes nowhere. Those running north are the Santa Cruz and the San Pedro Rivers. The Santa Cruz rises in the San Rafael Valley east of Nogales, swings south into Mexico, makes a big loop, and then flows northward through Tucson. The San Pedro is born in a low pass that barely separates it from the Río Sonora in Mexico. Sycamore Canyon on the west and Guadalupe Canyon along the Arizona/New Mexico boundary in the east harbor south-flowing streams at the headwaters of Mexico's Río de la Concepción and Río Yaqui, respectively. The Sulphur Springs Valley collects a number of streams that dead-end in a large alkali basin called Willcox Playa. But there is no land barrier whatsoever between the Sulphur Springs Valley and the Río Bavispe in Sonora.

Clearly, watercourses serve as a direct conduit for tropical birds to enter Southeastern Arizona. Since 1950 Buff-collared Nightjar, Violet-crowned Hummingbird, Green Kingfisher, Thick-billed Kingbird, Flame-colored Tanager, and Streak-backed Oriole have all nested successfully in this area. And, since 1990, the list of valley and canyon vagrants has included Ruddy Ground-Dove, Cinnamon Hummingbird, Blue Mocking-bird, Crescent-chested and Fan-tailed Warblers, and Black-vented Ori-ole.

BIOMES AND LIFE ZONES

Just as important for the birdwatcher, these 15,000 square miles contain the terminae of four major biogeographical regions, or biomes: the Rocky Mountains, the Chihuahuan Desert, the Sonoran Desert, and the Sierra Madre Mountains. Each contributes a unique flora and bird fauna to Southeastern Arizona.

On the north end of the region, the Santa Catalina and Rincon Mountains mark the southern limits of the Rocky Mountain Biome. These ranges are composed largely of granite and gneiss. Vegetation is similar to that of the Mogollon Rim in Central Arizona. Both Corkbark Fir and Mountain Chickadee find their southernmost outpost in the Santa Catalina Mountains.

The Chihuahuan Desert from the southeast extends fingers of thorn-scrub and desert grassland as far west as Tombstone, particularly in areas of limestone soil. It is characterized by White-thorn Acacia, Tarbush, and Soaptree Yucca, the New Mexico state flower. This is the preferred habitat of Scaled Quail and Chihuahuan Raven.

The Sonoran Desert follows low-lying valleys into the vicinity of Tucson. Saguaro cactus—whose large, showy white blossom is the Arizona state flower—both delimits and symbolizes the Sonoran Desert Biome. Saguaros cannot withstand more than 24 hours of continuous frost. The range of the Saguaro-nesting race of the widespread Purple Martin nearly conforms to the boundaries of the Sonoran Desert in Arizona. Gila Woodpecker, the architect responsible for the majority of the martins' nest-holes in Saguaro, also follows the desert rivers upstream to exploit the cottonwood groves in all the valleys southeast of Tucson.

Of special interest to the birder are the northernmost outliers of the Sierra Madre Occidental of Mexico. From west to east along 150 miles of the frontier with Sonora, the Border Ranges (sometimes called "Mexican Mountains" or "Sky Islands") are represented by the Atascosa (Ah-tah-SKO-sah), Santa Rita, Huachuca (Wah-CHEW-cah), and Chiricahua (Cheery-CAH-wah) Mountains. Each of these four ranges is isolated by desertscrub or desert grassland. Madrean pine/oak woodland cloaks the mid-elevations of all four of the mountain islands, and provides a habitat not found elsewhere in the entire United States. This is the home of the only breeding Elegant Trogons north of Mexico.

Each biome has a somewhat different group of plants and animals. Combined, they make a long list. In addition to nearly 500 species of birds, there are some 30 fishes, 20 amphibians, 79 reptiles, 102 mammals, and about 2,500 plants. No one has counted the insects, but bugwatchers—-especially butterfly-watchers—find Southeastern Arizona an entomologist's paradise. An incredible 253 species of butterflies and skippers have been recorded in this corner of Arizona.

Southeastern Arizona can be further stratified into life zones and biotic communities. Climbing from the desert at Tucson (2,300 feet) to the boreal spruce forest on top of Chiricahua Peak (9,796 feet), one crosses five life zones: Lower Sonoran, Upper Sonoran, Transition, Canadian, and Hudsonian. The corresponding plant communities for each life zone are Chihuahuan or Sonoran desertscrub, interior chaparral or Madrean pine/oak woodland, Ponderosa Pine forest, Douglas-fir/aspen forest, and, at the highest elevations in the Chiricahua Mountains, Hudsonian stands of Engelmann Spruce, the southernmost spruce in North America.

The life zone concept was invented by C. Hart Merriam, based on his floristic studies in Arizona near the turn of the century, when he realized that for each 1,000-foot gain in elevation, the vegetative change was equivalent to a journey north about 300 miles. In Southeastern Arizona the temperature decreases an average of four degrees for every thousand feet of elevation-increase. Since cold air cannot hold moisture as well as hot air, average annual precipitation increases approximately four inches per thousand feet. Consequently the 5,000 feet of vertical elevation-change on a trip from the hot, dry mesquite thickets at Portal to the cool, moist spruce groves on Chiricahua Peak is roughly equivalent to a 1,500-mile change in latitude. For his pioneer work in describing how elevation, temperature, and moisture combine to create distinctive plant and animal communities, Merriam is generally regarded as the founder of the modern science of ecology.

Saguaro, Prickly Pear, Agave, and Ocotillo
Terry O'Nele

Both life zones and biomes have many applications for today's birder. First and foremost, if the temperature is a pleasant 75 degrees in Tucson, it will probably be a frigid 50 degrees at the 8,500-foot-elevation Ski Valley in the nearby Santa Catalina Mountains. Birders will also find that certain species are restricted to certain life zones. Cactus Wrens live in the Lower Sonoran Life Zone, in both the Chihuahuan and Sonoran Deserts. However, to locate Sierra Madrean species such as Blue-throated Hummingbird, a birder must explore the Upper Sonoran Life Zone in the Border Ranges, such as Ramsey Canyon in the Huachuca Mountains.

Together, these life zones and biomes create a rich mosaic of habitats unmatched for diversity anywhere else in the United States. Understanding how they interact will help birders to pinpoint the location of the species which they hope to find.

WEATHER

Sunshine is the most constant weather feature here. A day without sunshine in Arizona is the exception. The lowlands in the southeast corner receive approximately 300 days of sun per year. From November until May, this abundance of sun makes almost every day a perfect day in Tucson. Of course, there is that one little stretch from mid-May through October when the word "desert" takes on special significance. Most birders will want to follow the birds up into the mountains during the prolonged annual desert heat wave.

Midsummer highs around Tucson average 100 degrees Fahrenheit or more during the day, and it does not cool off much below 80 at night. The low humidity helps, but temperatures at or above the century mark are never comfortable—no matter how zealously the natives extol the virtues of "dry heat." On the other hand, the mountains are quite comfortable in summer, especially when the rains begin. After the onset of the monsoons, daily highs in Madera, Ramsey, and Cave Creek Canyons seldom run above the low 80s, and are frequently lower.

Southeastern Arizona is a land of summer rains, usually commencing in early July and ending in mid-September. Nearly two-thirds of the annual precipitation occurs in these three months. Moist air from the Gulf of Mexico moves northwestward into the area. Crossing the high mountains it rises and forms huge cumulus clouds. Every afternoon these clouds mushroom over the peaks, and then drift over the surrounding countryside. They are accompanied by intense lightning, thunderclaps, and downpours. These showers are so concentrated that you can stand at the edge of the rain and wash your hands without getting the rest of yourself wet.

During the summer rainy season, the nights and mornings are ideal. As a rule, it rains only during the afternoon, and then only for *siesta* hour. Since these showers are both cool and refreshing, you will soon be looking forward to them.

During late summer and early fall, storms called *chubascos* occasionally arrive from the southwest out of the Sea of Cortéz, and then it may rain all night. These storms are typically the outer fringes of tropical hurricanes, and they can produce unusual birds. Almost annual late summer sightings of Magnificent Frigatebirds over Tucson are a consequence of the *chubasco* phenomenon.

Winter rains generally occur about once a month, and seldom last more than a day or two. Most desert winter days are balmy, and the nights are cool, not frigid. But maximum temperatures in the mountains are likely to be 20 to 30 degrees cooler than in the adjacent valleys.

WHEN TO COME

Southeastern Arizona has plenty to offer birders every month of the year. With luck, you may discover an exotic species such as Plain-capped Starthroat, Blue Mockingbird, or Flame-colored Tanager that all North American birders covet for their life list. It is entirely possible to discover a bird so rare that everybody will call it a hybrid until they have seen it themselves! But even many of the expected species have charisma. Taken by month some of the prime attractions are:

January: Bendire's, Crissal, and Le Conte's Thrashers burst into full song, often from exposed perches. Mountain Plovers and Ruddy Ground-Doves are easier to locate during this month than at any other time of the year. Some Anna's Hummingbirds are already fledging young in Tucson. The "Wings Over Willcox" birding festival celebrates Sandhill Cranes and 14 species of raptors wintering in the Sulphur Springs Valley.

February: Numbers and species of ducks and geese peak. Inca Doves, Great Horned Owls, and Curve-billed Thrashers begin to nest. Waves of Tree Swallows pass through as they migrate north. Male Yellow-rumped Warblers assume nuptial plumage, although they remain in the lowlands, thousands of feet below their summer territories on the mountaintops. South and west of Tucson, Mexican Gold Poppies and Parry Penstemons begin to daub the desert with fields of gold and hot pink.

March: Common Black-Hawk, Gray Hawk, and Zone-tailed Hawk—the three Southwest specialty raptors—arrive almost simultaneously. Hummingbirds increase from sparse to common as the month progresses, and the population of Vermilion Flycatchers multiplies ten-fold. Lucy's Warblers and Painted Redstarts enter the southeast corner of the state en masse. Cottonwoods leaf out in all the valleys.

April: Early in the month Flammulated and Elf Owls join resident Western and Whiskered Screech-Owls in nightly choruses. Virginia's, Grace's, and Red-faced Warblers arrive. After mid-month the first Elegant Trogons begin to set up territories in Madera, Garden, Cave Creek, and other canyons in the Border Ranges. Desert mesquite trees put on their new leaves just as the Sierra Madrean oaks in the foothills drop their somber brown and orange foliage and begin to bud.

May: Common Poorwills in the deserts, Buff-collared Nightjars in thornscrub, and Whip-poor-wills in the mountains fill the hours before dawn and after dusk with their unique calls. Sulphur-bellied Flycatchers and Purple Martins arrive all the way from South America. Rose-throated Becards commence knitting their enormous, globe-shaped nests using materials salvaged from the preceding year's nursery. Many birds are nesting, and the first fledglings begin to appear. Canyon streams are now trimmed with the nodding blossoms of showy Golden Columbine.

June: Most Yellow-billed Cuckoos, Varied Buntings, and Five-striped Sparrows finally arrive. This is the best month to find a vagrant Yellow Grosbeak from Mexico. Fruiting Saguaro cacti attract White-winged Doves and a host of other Sonoran Desert species. By the end of the month the first male Rufous Hummingbirds will have begun the migration south. This is the hottest month, but distant lightning flashes on the southern horizon in Mexico herald the approach of the life-giving, midsummer monsoons.

July: The onset of the rainy season initiates the breeding season for Montezuma Quail and Botteri's and Cassin's Sparrows. Painted Redstarts and Western Tanagers launch their second clutch. Baby birds are everywhere. Owls stop calling and seem to disappear altogether by the end of the month. The mountains turn green, and the wildflowers that transform southern Arizona into hummingbird heaven begin to blossom.

August: Hummingbird numbers and diversity reach their peaks for the year, augmented by new fledglings, southward migrants, and late arriving rarities from Mexico. This last group includes much sought-after White-eared, Berylline, Violet-crowned, and Lucifer Hummingbirds, and Plain-capped Starthroat. Families of Elegant Trogons are silent but conspicuous as they move through the border canyons. By the end of the month most *Myiarchus* and Sulphur-bellied Flycatchers have vanished. This is the best month to search for Aztec Thrush. The "Southwest Wings Birding Festival" is held in Sierra Vista.

September: Astonishing numbers of Red-tails, Swainson's Hawks, and American Kestrels appear, one seeming to cap every post and pole. Hordes of migrating shorebirds transform sewage lagoons into de facto estuaries. Lines of Western Kingbirds perch on valley electric wires like clothespins. Early wintering species include Northern Harrier, Cedar Waxwing, and Green-tailed Towhee. This is the greenest month of the year, and the valley grasslands may be belly-deep in sunflowers.

October: Before the end of the month 10,000 or more Sandhill Cranes will assume their winter quarters in the Sulphur Springs Valley. Joining them are a scattering of brightly-plumaged Ferruginous Hawks. White-winged Doves become scarce around Tucson and other towns farther east. Red-naped Sapsuckers invade the canyons, orchards, and isolated valley groves. Aspens turn golden on the peaks.

November: Most of the winter birds have arrived. The early morning carols of Townsend's Solitaires flute over the juniper woodlands. Eared Trogons may descend into South Fork Cave Creek or Ramsey Canyon just as the Bigtooth Maples reach their peak autumn colors. Depending on the winter, flocks of Mountain Bluebirds in the valleys can number from a handful to several hundred.

December: Christmas Bird Count teams always discover some goodies, either on the count itself, or earlier in the month while scouting for the count. Locations are pinpointed in the San Rafael Valley for Sprague's Pipit, Bald Eagle, Baird's Sparrow, and McCown's Longspur. "Regular" rarities like Rufous-backed Robin, Black-throated Blue Warbler, and Streak-backed Oriole turn up every year, and occasionally true vagrants like Red-headed Woodpecker or Blue Mockingbird are also discovered. December in Southeastern Arizona offers some the year's most exciting birding!

WHAT TO WEAR

Western apparel is generally informal, and casual attire is acceptable nearly anywhere. Shorts, blue jeans or tough slacks are the order of the day for birding. T-shirts are both cool and socially acceptable, but long sleeves are suggested for early mornings in shady mountain canyons, and are a necessity for those who burn easily. Don't forget a warm jacket or sweater. The nights can be chilly, especially on spring owl-prowls. When it clouds over in the rarefied air above 8,000 feet in Rustler Park or on top Mount Lemmon, temperatures may plummet to below 50 degrees at high noon, even in midsummer. Winter fronts can hold daily highs below 50 throughout Southeastern Arizona. A windy November day sorting through sparrow flocks in the Sulphur Springs Valley can feel like the Arctic. Long underwear, gloves, and a wool cap will all be welcome. Vast areas of the southeastern corner lie above 5,000 feet in elevation, where the thin air can change from scorching to cold in a scant few minutes. Be prepared for sudden shifts in the weather.

If you expect to hike or take prolonged bird walks, wear the appropriate foot gear. This may translate into lightweight boots or tough walking shoes for the field, and an extra pair of house shoes in your duffel. Dinner while wearing a clean, dry pair of shoes just seems to taste better!

WHAT TO BRING

This is the skin-cancer capital of North America: do not forget a brimmed hat. The short pants and T-shirt set have a special self-obligation to invest in sunblock rated SPF 15 or higher. Sunblock is recommended every day of the year for both your face and your neck. Lip balm is a good idea for anyone. And remember to carry a canteen with you on any bird walk. Experts calculate that everyone should drink at least two quarts of water a day during the Arizona summer, a full gallon for those exercising outdoors. (You will absolutely need that full gallon if you intend to chase Five-striped Sparrows down near the border in Sycamore Canyon.)

Mosquitoes and other biting insects are seldom a problem, but some people attract what few there are. If you know that you are one of those people, dose yourself with insect repellent before every bird walk. For reasons undoubtedly related to the community of 600,000 souls who have put down roots here on the rim of the Sonoran Desert, the arid valleys surrounding Tucson frequently have more mosquitoes than the wet mountain canyons—especially in late summer. After the summer monsoons commence in July, there are chiggers. The Patagonia-Sonoita Creek Preserve is the single worst location in Arizona for encountering them, but they also occur along all the major lowland watercourses, and in lower mountain canyons. To avoid the raised, extremely itchy welts occasioned by chigger bites, simply stay out of tall grasses and weeds where chiggers lurk. If you must plunge into the rank undergrowth, first dust your clothes with sulfur powder, or spray them with an aerosol repellent. Chigger season is over by the first of October.

Hummingbird aficionados arriving in late summer may want to bring an umbrella, poncho, or at least a water-repellent wind-breaker. The likelihood of an August thundershower is pretty high on any given day in the Border Ranges. Similarly, campers will need a tent with a rain fly.

This should go without saying, but *do not* attempt to cross washes, streams, or rivers in flood. Do not ignore warning signs or attempt to circumvent barriers erected for your protection. Don't be foolhardy. Water levels usually recede in a few hours, and it's not worth losing your vehicle, or even your life, because you are in a hurry to see a Gray Hawk.

WHERE TO STAY

Many camping and lodging facilities are listed at the end of each trip loop in this book. Additional lists of motels, etc., may be obtained from the chambers of commerce of the various cities or from the numerous travel guides, such as those published by AAA. More details on camping sites in the Coronado National Forest are available from the Recreation Staff, Coronado National Forest, 300 W. Congress, Tucson, AZ 85701.

Southeastern Arizona is ideal for camping. The weather is warm and usually dry. Biting insects are few, although the hatch of new, "benign" insects in the spring and summer is what makes this a birder's paradise. Newcomers to Southwest camping may worry about snakes; however, you will be lucky to find even one during your entire stay.

In recent years Black Bears have learned that campers in the high Chiricahuas carry food. A few have developed the unsavory habit of punching out the windshields of parked cars in Rustler Park, especially after dark, as they search for edible tidbits. There have been no serious attacks on humans—not counting a Boy Scout who went to sleep with his candy bars in his sleeping bag—but campers at Rustler should be aware that simply locking up leftovers in the trunk may not be enough to deter a hungry Black Bear. With the exception of Rustler Park Campground, the history of human/wildlife interactions in Southeastern Arizona has been excellent.

CAMPGROUNDS

Location	Name	Elevation	Open
Tucson	Gilbert Ray (Tucson Mtns.)	3,000	All year
	Catalina State Park	3,000	All year
Santa Catalina Mtns.	Molino Basin	4,500	Sep-May
	General Hitchcock	6,000	Apr-Oct
	Rose Canyon	7,000	Apr-Oct
	Spencer Canyon	8,000	Apr-Oct
Madera Canyon	Bog Springs	5,600	All year
Peña Blanca Lake	White Rock	4,000	All year
Nogales	Patagonia Lake State Park	4,050	All year
Parker Lake	Lakeview	5,400	All year
Huachuca Mtns.	Reef Townsite	7,100	Feb-Nov
	Ramsey Vista	7,400	Feb-Nov
Chiricahua Mtns.	Idlewilde (Cave Creek)	5,000	Apr-Oct
	Stewart (Cave Creek)	5,050	All year
	Sunny Flat (Cave Creek)	5,150	All year
	Rustler Park	8,400	Apr-Nov
	Pinery Canyon	7,000	Apr-Nov
	West Turkey Creek	5,900	All year
Rucker Lake	Camp Rucker	5,600	All year
	Rucker Lake	6,300	All year
	Cypress Park	6,000	Mar-Oct
	Bathtub	6,050	All year
	Rucker Forest Camp	6,150	All year
Dragoon Mtns.	Cochise Stronghold	5,000	All year

RESOURCES

All birders will benefit from a visit to the Tucson Audubon Society Nature Shop (300 E. University Blvd., #120, Tucson, AZ 85705, telephone 520/629-0510, hours 10am to 4pm Monday through Saturday, 10am to 6pm Thursday) at the onset of their tour of Southeastern Arizona. This natural history book store is among the finest in the state, and it also carries field guides, checklists, binoculars, feeders, and other birdwatching accessories. Among the services provided by TAS is a listing of local bird guides, which they will furnish upon request. Interesting sightings are posted weekly on their bulletin board, or call 520/798-1005 for their taped rare-bird-alert information.

The Arizona Chapter of The Nature Conservancy has developed brochures that offer insight into the Aravaipa Canyon, Patagonia-Sonoita Creek, Ramsey Canyon, and the Muleshoe Ranch Preserves, as well as information on their hours, parking regulations, and other rules. To obtain these brochures contact them 9am to 5pm Monday through Friday at 300 E. University Blvd., #230, Tucson, AZ 85705, telephone 520/622-3861.

Two birding festivals are held annually in Southeastern Arizona. On the third weekend of January the Willcox Chamber of Commerce sponsors "Wings Over Willcox," a celebration of the thousands of Sandhill Cranes that winter in the upper Sulphur Springs Valley. This area is also one of the most important wintering areas for birds of prey in the entire Southwest. To obtain more information call the Willcox Chamber of Commerce at 520/384-2272.

During the third week of August the Sierra Vista Chamber of Commerce hosts its "Southwest Wings Birding Festival." Between the San Pedro River Valley and the neighboring Huachuca Mountains, participants are treated to an average of 12 species of hummingbirds, and at least 100 other species of birds. Information on this exciting event can be obtained by calling either the Friends of the San Pedro at 800/946-4777 or the Sierra Vista Chamber of Commerce at 800/288-3861. Activities at both of these events include lectures, birding workshops, and numerous field trips.

SOME HELPFUL PUBLICATIONS

Excellent maps produced by the Coronado National Forest can be obtained by writing to the Recreation Staff, Coronado National Forest, 300 W. Congress, Tucson, AZ 85701. Maps are available for the Santa

Catalina Mountains, the Nogales and Sierra Vista Ranger Districts, and the Chiricahua, Dragoon, and Peloncillo Mountains in the Douglas Ranger District at a cost of $3.00 each. Maps, checklists, and other information pertaining to the San Pedro Riparian National Conservation Area are available by writing the Bureau of Land Management, 1763 Paseo San Luis, Sierra Vista, AZ 85635; telephone 520/458-3559. The official state map is available from the Arizona Highway Department, 2039 West Lewis Avenue, Phoenix, AZ 85009; telephone 800/543-5432. A free travel-information kit is available through the Arizona Office of Tourism by phoning 800/842-8257. *Arizona Atlas and Gazetteer* by DeLorme Mapping ($16.95) is available at book stores and convenience stores throughout the region as well as from ABA Sales.

Very detailed topographical maps can be ordered from the U.S. Geological Survey, Denver, CO 80201. First write for the *Index to Arizona Maps*, for which there is no charge, and then order the ones that you want. Hiking maps for the Santa Catalina, Santa Rita, and Chiricahua Mountains based on USGS quadrangles are available from Rainbow Expeditions, 915 S. Sherwood Village Drive, Tucson, AZ 85710, and a hikers map for the Huachuca Mountains is available through Thunder Peak Productions, P.O. Box 121, Sierra Vista, AZ 85636.

You will need field guides that cover all of North America to identify the regularly occurring birds of Arizona, as well as a Mexico guide for many of the tropical rarities. Of special interest are *Davis & Russell's Finding Birds in Southeast Arizona*, which is published by the Tucson Audubon Society, and *Annotated Checklist of the Birds of Arizona* by Gale Monson and Allan R. Phillips, published by the University of Arizona Press. Tucson Audubon Society has also prepared a new field checklist for Southeastern Arizona. This pocket-sized checklist provides a general indication of the status of each bird species. To obtain a copy, send a self-addressed, stamped envelope and 25¢ to Tucson Audubon Society Nature Shop, 300 E. University Blvd., #120, Tucson, AZ 85705.

Numerous publications cover the natural history and ecology of this region. Some of the better ones are listed in the reference section at the end of this book. Many of these can be obtained from the American Birding Association Sales, Box 6599, Colorado Springs, CO 80934; telephone 800/634-7736. When you are in Tucson, try the Tucson Audubon Society Nature Shop, the Arizona-Sonora Desert Museum Gift Shop, or the visitor centers of Saguaro National Park, either east or west section.

Away from Tucson, natural history book stores located in some of the prime birding areas include the Santa Rita Lodge Gift Shop, the Ramsey

Canyon Preserve Bookstore, The San Pedro House at Highway 90 and the San Pedro River, Coronado National Memorial, Sierra Vista Ranger Station, Portal Store, U.S. Forest Service Portal Information Center, Southwestern Research Station Gift Shop, and Chiricahua National Monument.

THE ARIZONA BIRD COMMITTEE

The Arizona Bird Committee was created in 1972 to improve the quality of state bird records and to further our knowledge of bird distribution within Arizona. The committee would appreciate detailed descriptions to substantiate any sightings of accidental, rare, or otherwise unusual birds. Please send details to the attention of Rare Bird Report compiler, Tucson Audubon Society, 300 E. University Blvd., #120, Tucson, AZ 85705. Your detailed descriptions (preferably written at the time of sighting without reference to a field guide) will be circulated among the six members of the ABC. They will evaluate the report and (if desired) notify you of their decision. A sample report form is included at the back of this book.

Some records will be published in *National Audubon Society Field Notes*, and all records are included in the committee's annual report that is sent to all contributors. Descriptions and supplementary material (photographs, sound recordings, etc.) and the committee's decisions are filed in the Department of Ecology at the University of Arizona.

ATTRACTING BIRDS TO THE VIEWER

Many birders have tried the various squeakers and calls that are sold to attract birds. After a few days the novelty wears off, and they become too much trouble to carry around. "Hissing-at-the-villain" or "pishing" through pursed lips is still the time-proven favorite for most birders, along with the sound made by sucking on the back of the hand—which is reminiscent of a lovers' lane on a moonlit night.

However, in the Southeastern Arizona sky islands the sound that outdoes them all is the double "toot" of the Northern Pygmy-Owl. No other noise will excite the birds of the mountains nearly as much. It is not uncommon to attract 5 to 15 species at once. In valley riparian areas such as the San Pedro River and along Sonoita Creek, the descending, bouncing-ball call of the Western Screech-Owl produces similar results. During the practice period, you may be ridiculed by your family or given odd glances by your neighbors, but when you have mastered imitating these owls, you will be an Arizona bird-finder extraordinaire.

If, however, you just cannot squeak, hiss, pish, or hoot, you can still attract birds with the judicious use of a tape-recorder. Most birds will respond to an imitation of their calls, even flycatchers. *Remember, however, that any use of bird tapes is forbidden in both the Ramsey Canyon and Patagonia-Sonoita Creek Preserves, as well as in Garden, Scheelite, and Sawmill Canyons on Fort Huachuca, and in Madera Canyon and South Fork Cave Creek on the Coronado National Forest.*

During the day, small birds can be attracted with owl calls. At night, the owls themselves can be coaxed into view by playing their respective calls (no fewer than 11 species of owls occur in the southeast corner!). But birds are not hard-of-hearing. *Do not play the tapes loudly.* Most birds will come much closer if the tape is played softly, and this behavior is particularly true of owls.

BIRDER BEHAVIOR

The American Birding Association *Code of Ethics* appears following the Table of Contents in this book. Adhering to the ABA *Code of Ethics* is particularly important in this heavily birded region. There are also some special concerns for birders in Southeastern Arizona.

1. Please respect the rights of landowners. Always ask permission before entering private property. Your trespass may result in the loss of visitation privileges for all future birders. Areas of private land are always indicated in the text.

2. Please drive slowly to insure your own safety. Many of the access roads in Southeastern Arizona are not hard-surfaced, and dust clouds churned up by fast-moving cars endanger vehicles following behind, and on-coming traffic as well.

3. Avoid abrupt stops that may lead to rear-end collisions, and never park in the road. This admonition is extremely important in the small canyons of the Border Ranges where blind curves and narrow roads are the rule.

4. During the summer rainy season or after heavy winter storms make local inquiry before assuming that any road is passable. Never enter flooded washes or streams.

5. Most of Southeastern Arizona is rangeland. Watch for cattle— especially at night. Even straight-aways are often intersected by blind washes that may conceal either livestock or wildlife.

6. Remember that more nest failures can be directly attributed to photographic disturbance than from any other human cause. Canyon and river groves are often so narrow that it is impossible to set up either

a blind or even a camera without attracting undue attention from other birders, who may be less sensitive to the moods of the bird than you are. Also remember that many birds simply cannot tolerate any prolonged attention. Above all, never manipulate the actual nest or the surrounding vegetation.

7. Tape recordings or taped play-backs to lure rare birds into binocular range are inappropriate where a few birds may be exposed to a wholly unnatural onslaught of such devices at popular birdwatching locations. In Southeastern Arizona the use of tape recordings is strictly prohibited at Madera Canyon in the Santa Rita Mountains, the Patagonia-Sonoita Creek Sanctuary, Ramsey Canyon Preserve and the Garden Canyon drainage in the Huachuca Mountains, and South Fork Cave Creek in the Chiricahua Mountains.

8. Please stay on trails and established routes. Plants grow back slowly in this arid environment, and if the tens of thousands of other birders who visit Southeastern Arizona all broke branches and smashed low-growing vegetation, they could easily destroy this fragile environment.

As the number of birders grows and the special joy of birdwatching in Southeastern Arizona is better publicized, these common-sense considerations have become essential.

HOW TO USE THIS BOOK

The purpose of this guide is to help visiting birders design a custom tour of Southeastern Arizona that suits their time, energy, and budget. Resident birders in southeast Arizona should also find directions to sites, bird status, and locational information to be helpful.

The bird nomenclature in this book basically follows that of the American Ornithologists' Union (AOU) and the American Birding Association (ABA). Some recent name changes (including "splits" and "lumps" are listed on page 319.

The book is divided into three major sections. The first section includes nine chapters describing nine primary locations plus Chapter Ten which is devoted to thirteen additional sites. Listed under the title of each trip are the total mileage and the minimum time recommended to cover the area. After some locations, mileages are shown in parentheses. These represent the distance *from the last place mentioned* and *not* from the Starting Point. Whenever an outstanding site is mentioned, it is shown in **bold-faced** type. If you have a catholic taste in birds and wish to see the greatest number of species possible in a limited amount of time, stop only at bold-faced sites on the loop. Three of the sites where you will be hiking as well as birding are enhanced by special duplicate Tear-Out Trail Maps which are reproduced at the end of this book.

In the second section, under the heading of "Specialties of Southeastern Arizona," an effort has been made to give the status and to describe the habitat of every southwestern and Mexican species presently known to have occurred in Southeastern Arizona. With a few exceptions, at least three places are listed where each species has been found in the past. These sites are highly specific. *Please remember not to put undue pressure on an unusual species through prolonged observation or photography.*

The third section features a series of bar-graphs representing all of the regularly occurring birds of the region, showing relative abundance for each month of the year, as well as habitat preference. A seasonal clock divided into four "pie wedges" tells which habitats birds are most likely to use when they are present. Briefly annotated lists of the herpetofauna and mammals of Southeastern Arizona conclude the book.

Regardless of the length of your visit, I suggest a visit to the Arizona-Sonora Desert Museum at the outset of any trip. Here you will receive a solid introduction to the flora and fauna of the entire region and have an opportunity to study approximately 100 species of birds in captivity, as well as many wild birds ranging freely on the grounds. The Hummingbird Aviary features eight species of Southwest hummingbirds in a flower-filled garden.

To cover all the trips allow at least two weeks. If you have less time, it's best to read all the trip descriptions and choose the ones that suit you best, according to the season and your most-desired birds. From April 1 through October 31, be sure to visit a valley riparian area such as Patagonia or the San Pedro River, and at least one of the three principal Border Ranges: the Santa Rita, the Huachuca, or the Chiricahua Mountains. The mountains are not particularly productive from November 1 through March 31, and the upper elevations may be closed by snow. During winter, the deserts, grasslands, and valley riparian areas offer the best birding. Plan a trip to the grasslands in the San Rafael Valley or the Sulphur Springs Valley for hawks, sparrows, and longspurs.

It's impossible to savor all the delights of Southeastern Arizona birding on any one excursion. Different birds will quicken your pulse as the months change, and every year brings its new exotics, some of which may never have been seen in the U.S. before. After your first visit, you'll understand why so many birders count Southeastern Arizona as their favorite birding destination in the entire United States.

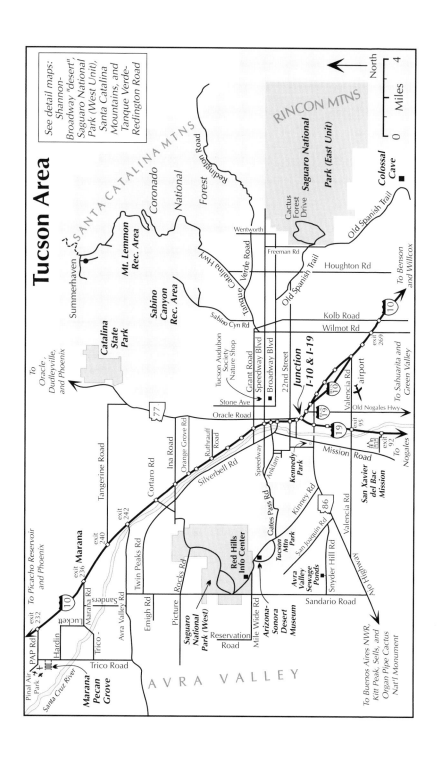

Tucson Area

See detail maps: Shannon-Broadway "desert", Saguaro National Park (West Unit), Santa Catalina Mountains, and Tanque Verde-Redington Road

North

0   Miles   4

RINCON MTNS

Saguaro National Park (East Unit)

Colossal Cave

Cactus Forest Drive

Old Spanish Trail

Wentworth

Freeman Rd

Houghton Rd

To Benson and Willcox

SANTA CATALINA MTNS

Redington Road

Coronado

National

Forest

Mt. Lemmon Rec. Area

Summerhaven

Catalina Hwy

Tanque Verde Road

Sabino Canyon Rec. Area

Sabino Cyn Rd

10

Kolb Road

Wilmot Rd

exit 269

To Sahuarita and Green Valley

Catalina State Park

To Oracle, Dudleyville, and Phoenix

77

Oracle Road

Ina Road

Orange Grove Rd

Ruthrauff Road

Grant Road

Speedway Blvd

Broadway Blvd

22nd Street

Tucson Audubon Society Nature Shop

Stone Ave

Junction I-10 & I-19

Valencia Rd

airport

10

19

Old Nogales Hwy

exit 95

exit 92

To Nogales

Tangerine Road

Cortaro Rd

Silverbell Rd

Speedway

Anklam

Kennedy Park

Kinney Rd

Mission Road

San Xavier del Bac Mission

exit 242

exit 240

Marana

exit 236

Twin Peaks Rd

Picture Rocks Rd

Emigh Rd

Gates Pass Rd

Tucson Mtn Park

Red Hills Info Center

San Joaquin Rd

86

Valencia Rd

Avra Valley Sewage Ponds

Snyder Hill Rd

Sandario Road

To Picacho Reservoir and Phoenix

exit 232

Marana Rd

Sanders Rd

Avra Valley Rd

Luckett

PAP Rd

Hardin

Trico Rd

Marana Pecan Grove

Pinal Air Park

Santa Cruz River

Trico Road

Saguaro National Park (West)

Reservation Road

Mile Wide Rd

Arizona-Sonora Desert Museum

Ajo Highway

To Buenos Aires NWR, Kitt Peak, Sells, and Organ Pipe Cactus Nat'l Monument

AVRA VALLEY

CHAPTER 1

TUCSON OASES

THE ARIZONA-SONORA DESERT MUSEUM LOOPS

This trip explores a series of oases—areas with trees and ornamental plantings and/or permanent water—that are magnets for both resident birds and migrants. En route it passes a neighborhood on the outskirts of Tucson that hosts a representative selection of the city's "backyard birds," as well as visiting the neighborhood "wilderness" in Tucson Mountain Park, and the western unit of Saguaro (pronounced Sah-WHAH-row) National Park. The highlight of the trip is the Arizona-Sonora Desert Museum, which features an excellent collection of plants and animals native to the Sonoran Desert. Many of the species are displayed in naturalistic enclosures that are true to their preferred habitats in the wild.

To conclude this loop, birders can choose between the Marana Pecan Grove (also known as Pinal Air Park Pecan Grove), a well-known vagrant-trap north of the Tucson Mountains, or turn south to the Avra Valley Sewage Ponds (also known as Snyder Hill Road Sewage Ponds) for water birds, before continuing on to San Xavier del Bac Mission, founded by the Jesuits in 1700. Both the Pecan Grove and the Mission are most productive early in the morning, and birders may well choose to run either or both of these loops in reverse sequence.

Arizona-Sonora Desert Museum Loop

(28 miles/one-half day to Arizona-Sonora Desert Museum)

The starting point is the intersection of Interstate 10 and St. Mary's Road in Tucson (exit 257A). Just 100 yards west of I-10, St. Mary's Road crosses the Santa Cruz River, which is one of the major drainages in Southeastern Arizona. Ordinarily there is no surface flow unless you arrive on the heels of a storm. However, in October 1983 a mud-choked

19

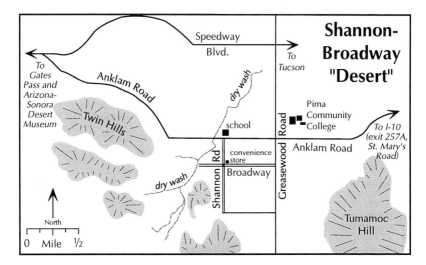

torrent closed the bridge for 24 hours and swept away other concrete spans 11 miles upstream at San Xavier Mission.

Continue straight west. St. Mary's Road turns into Anklam Road at Silverbell Road (1.0 mile), passes Pima Community College, and then climbs over a rise to a public junior high school (1.8 miles) opposite the "T" intersection with Shannon Road. Turn left (south) onto Shannon Road. Traffic is usually light in this west-side neighborhood, and there is plenty of road-shoulder to pull onto if you spot an interesting bird on the power-lines on the right, or in the undisturbed desert beyond. An abandoned convenience store at the northeast corner of the intersection with Broadway Boulevard (0.3 mile) provides a paved parking area where it is possible to get off Shannon Road altogether.

In early morning, the **Shannon-Broadway Desert** intersection abounds with birds, but in the heat of the afternoon sun, not a single bird may be visible. Permanent residents include Gambel's Quail, Mourning Dove, Greater Roadrunner, Gilded Flicker, Gila and Ladder-backed Woodpeckers, Verdin, Cactus Wren, Curve-billed Thrasher, Black-tailed Gnatcatcher, Phainopepla, Northern Cardinal, Pyrrhuloxia, Canyon Towhee, Black-throated Sparrow, and House Finch. In summer, watch for White-winged Dove, Elf Owl (night), Lesser Nighthawk (after dusk, fluttering around the mercury-vapor light overhanging the intersection), Black-chinned Hummingbird, Ash-throated Flycatcher, Purple Martin, Bronzed Cowbird, and Hooded Oriole. In winter, look for Anna's Hummingbird, Rock Wren, Northern "Red-shafted" Flicker, and White-crowned Sparrow.

Shannon-Broadway is one of the most reliable locations on the western perimeter of Tucson for Rufous-winged Sparrow. This small Chipping Sparrow look-alike differs in having a grayish eyebrow and a long, rounded tail. The rufous shoulder-patch is usually concealed. Watch for it to sing from exposed perches in small trees. If walking all four cardinal directions at the intersection doesn't turn up a Rufous-winged, try the west (right) end of Broadway (0.2 mile) where the boulevard dead-ends at a large, dry wash. This area is also good for Broad-billed and Costa's Hummingbirds in early spring. Both species patronize the hummingbird feeders in the mobile-home park on the south edge of Broadway.

Return to Anklam Road (0.5 mile) and turn left (west). Saguaro cactus becomes common along Anklam Road as it enters the foothills of the Tucson Mountains. In summer this is an excellent place to see the desert race of Purple Martin, which nests in Saguaro holes originally created by Gila Woodpeckers. Power-lines running north from just east of the intersection of Anklam and Speedway (2.1 miles) serve as an evening roost for literally thousands of Purple Martins in late August and September. After Anklam and Speedway merge and become Gates Pass Road, the pavement winds sinuously up to Gates Pass (2.7 miles; elevation 3,150 feet) and arcs steeply down into Avra Valley. Tucson Mountain Park may not match your mental image of either a mountain or a park,

Stop by the Shannon-Broadway desert early in the morning to look for Rufous-winged Sparrow on your way to the Arizona-Sonora Desert Museum.

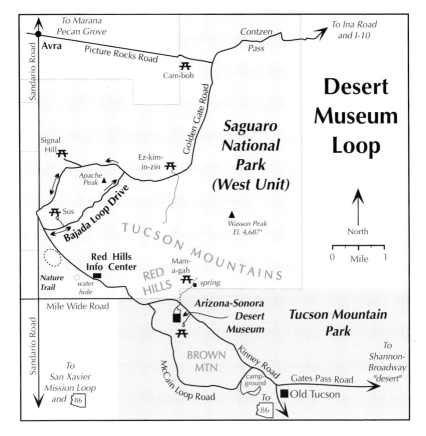

but it contains an excellent variety of desert vegetation. Plant life is surprisingly lush and varied. Before trying to key out the shrubs and cacti, wait until you reach the Desert Museum, where the plants are labeled.

Two miles west of the pass, the road swings north of a cluster of buildings on the left. This is Old Tucson, a movie set inaugurated in 1939 that doubles as an amusement park for tourists. A fire in April 1995 destroyed much of the facility and no firm date has been announced for its re-opening. Gates Pass Road ends at Kinney Road (2.2 miles). Turn right (north) toward the Desert Museum. McCain Loop Road, the turn-off to the Gilbert Ray Campground, is on the left (0.7 mile; $9 per night for RVs, $6 for tents). A pair of Great Horned Owls nests in a Saguaro near the campground. In midwinter, Gilbert Ray is often overflowing with "snowbirds"—seasonal human refugees from the north.

Another 1.9 miles brings you to the **Arizona-Sonora Desert Museum** (13.3 miles from Tucson; October-February: 8:30am to 5:00pm; March-

September: 7:30am to 6:00pm; $8.95 for those 13 and older, $1.50 for children from 6 to 12, free under 6). The word 'museum' hardly describes this institution. It is not a dusty assortment of artifacts and stuffed animals. The Desert Museum has earned an international reputation for both its outstanding collection and its imaginative presentation of the *living* plants and animals native to this region. Exhibits portray not only the Sonoran Desert, but also the Sierra Madre in northern Mexico—the continuation of the same "mountain islands" of Southeastern Arizona which are treated in this book. Since it opened in 1952, this combination of zoological park, arboretum, and research facility has been wholly funded by private donations, membership support, and public admissions.

Learning about the native flora and fauna is easy at the Desert Museum because many of the plants, vertebrates, and even arthropods are displayed in naturalistic settings. In addition, a cadre of docents—volunteer staff—are stationed at strategic points around the grounds to answer questions and explain the ecology of the exhibits. Birders will have a field day at the hummingbird house, in the aviary, and at the wheel-shaped bird enclosures, especially when they see the Mexican species that appear in Arizona only as vagrants—or have yet to arrive. Military Macaws, for example, are known to breed just 75 miles south of the border, and Black-throated Magpie-Jays are common in southern Sonora.

Here, wild birds hold their own. All the "regular" desert species are present: Inca Dove, Gila Woodpecker, Cactus Wren, Verdin, Curve-billed Thrasher, Black-tailed Gnatcatcher, Phainopepla, and Northern Cardinal. Owing to the lush plantings, the Desert Museum is also an excellent place to see Anna's Hummingbird from October through April, Black-chinned Hummingbird from May through September, Red-naped Sapsucker (primarily in the cottonwoods by the Otter Pool) during migration, Purple Martin in summer, Canyon Wren (using the artificial rock cliffs in the mountain-island exhibit), Bronzed Cowbird in summer, and Hooded Oriole in summer. The "oasis effect" of tall trees in the desert also attracts the unexpected. Over the past decade, the Museum has played host to such surprise species as Black Vulture, Lucifer Hummingbird, Sulphur-bellied Flycatcher, Rufous-backed Robin, and Indigo Bunting.

The tiny Costa's Hummingbird illustrates the dynamic impact of a desert oasis. Like Inca Dove and Curve-billed Thrasher, it has adapted to the harsh climate by nesting early in the spring. Formerly, after exploiting the desert's peak flowering period between February and April, Costa's left the lowlands before temperatures began to soar. Just within the past decade, however, Costa's Hummingbirds have learned to take

Male Costa's Hummingbird at Salvia
Narca Moore-Craig

advantage of this man-made habitat. Now, Costa's is a year-round resident at the Arizona-Sonora Desert Museum, as well as in gardens in west Tucson.

Some of the mammals that live on or near the Museum grounds include Kit Fox (night), Coyote, Rock Squirrel, Harris's Antelope Ground-Squirrel (chipmunk-like stripes), Desert Cottontail, and Desert Mule Deer. An excellent place to look for wildlife is across from the Museum parking lot in King Canyon. A parking area on the right (east) side of Kinney Road just past the Museum entrance marks the trailhead. It is a one-mile hike on an abandoned mining road to Mam-a-gah ("Deer Dancer") Picnic Area. Here, the trail intersects King Canyon at a point where water bubbles up in the wash. In winter, this is a great place to watch for Cooper's Hawk, Rock and Canyon Wrens, Ruby-crowned Kinglet, Yellow-rumped and Orange-crowned Warblers, Green-tailed and Canyon Towhees, and Chipping and Black-chinned Sparrows. Petroglyphs, just one-quarter mile downcanyon from the picnic area, date back approximately 1,000 years.

To catch bird and wildlife activity at its peak, arrive as early as possible at the Desert Museum, especially in summer. It takes no less than two hours simply to walk the grounds. If you plan to read exhibit materials, attend docent demonstrations, photograph the wildlife, or shop at the natural history book store and gift shop, count on a minimum of four hours. Even then it's hard to leave.

To continue the loop, turn north (left) onto Kinney Road and proceed to the entrance of the western unit of Saguaro National Park(1.2 miles). At Mile Wide Road, stay right on Kinney Road to the modern Red Hills Information Center (0.9 mile) to look at the exhibits and to study the map showing the roads and trails in the Park. You will also find a good selection of books dealing with local natural history.

This part of the Park was acquired in 1961 to protect one of the best stands of Saguaro in the state. Three miles past the visitor center on Bajada Loop Drive, the dense cactus "forest" averages 15,000 to 20,000 Saguaros per square mile. This is also a fine area for other plants and for birds, especially in April during the peak of the flowering and nesting season. Phainopeplas are particularly abundant on the north end of the Tucson Mountains, and breeding Harris's Hawks occur here, as well. Most birds are less disturbed in Saguaro National Park than in adjacent Tucson Mountain Park, mainly because the average tourist seldom gets past the Desert Museum.

Except in midwinter, reptiles are a common sight in the Park. The usual lizards are Common Collared, Large-spotted Leopard, Side-blotched, Regal Horned, Desert Spiny, Arizona Desert Whiptail, and the dainty little Zebra-tailed, which dashes across dirt roads waving its tail in the air. Most desert snakes are nocturnal. If you drive these roads at night, especially after a rain, you may spot such snakes as Western Patch-nosed, Glossy, Western Long-nosed, Saddled Leaf-nosed, Spotted Leaf-nosed, and Banded Sand Snakes, or Western Diamond-backed Rattlesnake. Harmless and beneficial, the Sonoran Gopher Snake is probably the most abundant snake in the Park.

This is decision time: It is a total of 23.3 miles northwest to the Marana Pecan Grove; alternatively, it is 28.6 miles southeast to San Xavier Mission. Or it is just 13.3 miles east on Golden Gate, Picture Rocks, and Ina Roads across the north end of the Tucson Mountains to Interstate 10 and Tucson. In summer, take the scenic, short route back to Tucson. But in spring and fall migration and throughout winter, there is excellent birding along the way to either the Marana Pecan Grove or San Xavier Mission.

Marana Pecan Grove Loop
(65 miles/one day to Marana Pecan Grove)

To reach the Marana Pecan Grove (also known as Pinal Air Park Pecan Grove) from the Red Hills Information Center at Saguaro National Park, follow Kinney Road right (northwest) to Sandario Road (1.8 miles), and then proceed right (north) on Sandario 6.5 miles to Marana High School on the northwest corner of Emigh Road. Between late December and early March—when they sing—it is worth the time to detour left onto Emigh Road for possible Le Conte's Thrashers. They can be anywhere along the road in the surrounding open creosote desert. Watch for them to sprint along on the ground, dodging between the shrubs like pale rodents with cocked tails.

To reach the Marana Pecan Grove continue due north on Sandario Road until it ends at a "T" junction with Avra Valley Road (2.5 miles). Turn left and proceed west to Trico Road (5.3 miles). Turn right here to follow Trico Road north, scanning for raptors. The area near the bridge over the Santa Cruz River (5.4 miles) is especially productive during winter. Aside from dozens of light- and dark- (rare) morph Red-tailed Hawks, Northern Harriers, and American Kestrels, this is an excellent place to find a gorgeous White-tailed Kite and, some years, a Rough-legged Hawk.

The signed intersection with Hardin Road (0.6 mile) signals your approach to the south access to **Marana Pecan Grove** (0.5 mile). Turn left onto the dirt road here and follow an abandoned concrete-lined irrigation ditch straight west toward the trees. Burrowing Owls are sometimes seen sitting motionless on the edge of the track anywhere between Trico Road and the grove (0.7 mile).

*The Marana Pecan Grove is private property, where birders have no acknowledged permission from the owner to bird. It isn't posted and there have been no problems, but to lose access, as has happened in other places, would be a disaster. Birders must stay out of fields, away from machinery, leave gates as they were found, and stay out of the grove if cattle are present. For a few months in 1994, the owner fenced the grove and ran cattle in it. The cattle may or may not be present when you bird there, but remember that farmers are very sensitive about having their stock spooked, even when it's unintentional. This is such an important site that birders must be on their best behavior. To lose access would be a **major** loss.*

The grove of dead and dying trees is about 0.4-mile square with a large, overgrown, earthen irrigation canal along its western boundary. Surrounded by miles of bare fields and open desert (which makes it *very* hot in summer), the Marana Pecan Grove is obviously an important resting area for migrating and wintering birds, as well as a magnet for vagrants passing through the Santa Cruz River Valley. Some of the regular wintering species include White-tailed Kite (resident in the nearby fields), Sharp-shinned and Cooper's Hawks, Inca Dove, Barn Owl, White-throated Swift (sometimes hundreds), Anna's and Costa's Hummingbirds (check the Tree Tobacco along the back irrigation canal), Gila and Ladder-backed Woodpeckers, Red-naped Sapsucker, Northern "Red-shafted" Flicker, Black and Say's Phoebes, Vermilion Flycatcher, Horned Lark, Common Raven (a major roost), House Wren, Ruby-crowned Kinglet, Black-tailed Gnatcatcher, Bendire's Thrasher, Loggerhead Shrike, Orange-crowned and Yellow-rumped Warblers, Pyrrhuloxia, Abert's Towhee, Lark Bunting, Song and Lincoln's Sparrows, Red-winged and Brewer's Blackbirds, and Lesser Goldfinch.

The list of vagrants and rarities found (1992-1995) at Marana Pecan Grove is equally impressive. These include Zone-tailed Hawk, Crested Caracara, Mountain Plover, Ruddy Ground-Dove, Groove-billed Ani, Tropical Kingbird, Greater Pewee, Chestnut-sided, Blackburnian, and Black-and-white Warblers, American Redstart, Painted Bunting, and Lawrence's Goldfinch (irruptive). In 1994 a pair of Streak-backed Orioles twice attempted to nest here, but were foiled by summer winds. In fact, a visit to the Marana Pecan Grove (particularly in the fall) may easily produce the most exciting find of your entire trip to Southeastern Arizona.

The dirt track continues west past some pipe-corrals, then turns north, paralleling a major ditch, trimmed with rank vegetation, that usually contains water. Locked gates, however, may prevent vehicle access to the west side of the grove. Another dirt road runs west from Trico Road through some open fields to the north end of the grove (0.6 mile). It is all wonderful birding.

To return to Tucson, turn left (north) onto Trico Road till it ends at Pinal Air Park Road (1.0 mile from the north entrance of the Pecan Grove). Turn right. It is 2.2 miles east to exit 232 on Interstate 10. Twenty-five miles south on the Interstate will bring you back to the starting point at St. Mary's Road.

San Xavier Mission Loop

(70 miles/one day to San Xavier Mission)

This extension of the basic tour begins by returning to Kinney Road from the Saguaro National Park's Red Hills Information Center. Turn right (north) onto Kinney Road to Sandario Road (1.8 miles). At Sandario Road turn left (south), and proceed 1.5 miles to the intersection with Mile Wide Road. The west end of Mile Wide has intermittently hosted Tucson's closest pair of Le Conte's Thrashers.

To try for this rare and irregular species between late December and early March, turn right here and follow the pavement down to the floor of Avra Valley. Barn Owls are occasionally found holed up under either the first bridge (1.5 miles), or the second bridge (1.5 miles). During winter, the adjacent Sonoran desertscrub along the roadsides is worth checking for both Sage Thrasher and Sage Sparrow. Winter raptors here often include Prairie Falcon. The pavement ends here, but Mile Wide Road continues to an "L" intersection with Reservation Road (0.5 mile). A rough and rutted power-line road runs due south through a pipe-gate opposite the beginning of Reservation Road. A sign here reads "Cocoraque Ranch–Please Close Gates". A short walk up the power-line road into Cocoraque Ranch may yield Le Conte's Thrasher. Birders using taped playbacks should be aware that Crissal Thrashers respond vigorously to Le Conte's songs, and Crissals are common here in winter. Bendire's and Curve-billed Thrashers along the same road mean that it is possible—although unlikely—to see all five species of regularly occurring Arizona thrashers at a single location.

Return to Sandario Road and continue south to Snyder Hill Road (6.0 miles). A conspicuous line of tall eucalyptus trees on the right (west) side of Sandario, opposite the west end of Snyder Hill Road, merits investigation. Vagrant warblers are always a possibility here, and careful perusal can often reveal several Great Horned Owls on concealed perches.

Cross Sandario Road and drive east on Snyder Hill Road, a wide, well-graded gravel road that floods in heavy rains. The low-growing, mesquite-dominated desertscrub here is generally unproductive, so continue to the signed turn-off to the

Avra Valley Sewage Ponds (also known as the Snyder Hill Road Sewage Pond) on the left (north) side of the road (2.5 miles). A gravel road runs 100 yards to a chain-link gate into the ponds, which are open from 7:30am to 2:00pm seven days a week. Visitors are asked to sign in at the office before birding. If the gate is locked, a dirt lane outside the fence that parallels Snyder Hill Road offers a fair view of quarter-mile-long South Pond. A spotting scope is helpful.

There are four impoundments altogether, with a total area of about 160 acres. The two largest ponds—on the left or west side of the facility—usually harbor the most waterfowl and shorebirds. The list of species that have been found here includes almost all of Southeastern Arizona's water birds. Eared Grebes are common in winter; Western and Clark's Grebes are occasional. Great Blue Herons are present year-round. Flocks of White-faced Ibis pass through during migration, as do large numbers of Least, Western, and Baird's Sandpipers, Long-billed Dowitchers, and both Wilson's and Red-necked Phalaropes. There are typically one hundred to one thousand ducks on the ponds in winter. Tiny insects in the air above the water are irresistible to Lesser Nighthawks at dawn and dusk throughout the summer; five or six species of swallows dine on the same items during migration. Spotted Sandpipers and American Pipits teeter down the shorelines in winter. At present, the Avra Valley Sewage Ponds constitute the single most important stop-over area for water-dependent species in the Tucson region.

Turn left (east) as you exit the facility. Pavement begins on Snyder Hill Road at mile 1.4; some 1.8 miles farther along, Snyder Hill Road ends at San Joaquin Road. Turn right (south) onto San Joaquin for a short distance until it comes to an end at Ajo Way (0.6 mile). Turn left (east) to return to Tucson or to continue this birding loop. Ajo Way cuts through a low pass on the south end of the Tucson Mountains before arriving at a traffic signal for La Cholla Boulevard (6.4 miles).

If time is not tight, consider turning left (north) onto La Cholla to check out the five-acre lake in John F. Kennedy Park (0.2 mile). Fishermen can ring the lake every morning by 8am, but this doesn't seem to discourage wintering waterfowl, and it has no impact on migrating swallows. For example, in April, Tree, Violet-green, Northern Rough-winged, Bank, Cliff, and Barn Swallows are all possible simultaneously.

Back on Ajo Way at La Cholla Boulevard, continue east to the next traffic light at Mission Road (0.4 mile). Turn right (south) here, and follow Mission Road onto Tohono O'odham Nation lands to San Xavier Road (5.6 miles). Glimpses of the double white domes and accompanying towers of **San Xavier del Bac Mission** telegraph your approach to the "T" intersection. Turn left (east) onto San Xavier Road.

The mission is plainly visible ahead (0.6 mile), but a brightly orna-mented cemetery on the left just beyond the turn should be inspected first. *Do not enter the cemetery under any circumstances.* Most morn-ings, at least one and often as many as a half-dozen Burrowing Owls are perched on the crosses over the graves. If they are not apparent, search for them on the monuments next to the fence on the far side of the graveyard. The mesquite desert on the south side of the road across from the cemetery is a good location to check for Bendire's Thrashers in winter and spring, and for Rufous-winged Sparrows throughout the year.

San Xavier Mission was founded by Father Eusebio Kino in 1700, but work on the present structure did not begin until 1783. Kino selected this place known as Bac—or place where the river reappears—as the site for the first church in what became Arizona and California, simply because it had the largest concentration of Tohono O'odham in the Santa Cruz Valley. The year 1797 is usually given as the completion date, but it is evident that the east bell-tower was never finished. Church historians have speculated that the padres continued to receive funds just so long as they could claim that the edifice was still under construction.

The area on the east side of San Xavier Mission usually has the best birding. Follow the low wall back past the book store and gift shop to a seed-feeder in front of a line of apartments. A long list of birds visits this feeder throughout the year. Regular clients are Gambel's Quail, Mourning and Inca Doves, Common Ground-Dove (in truth, uncommon), Cactus Wren, Northern Mockingbird, Curve-billed Thrasher, Northern Cardinal, Pyrrhuloxia, Canyon Towhee, Black-throated Sparrow, Great-tailed Grackle, Brown-headed Cowbird, and House Finch. In summer, White-winged Doves are abundant, and a Ruddy Ground-Dove appeared during the winter of 1993-1994.

Greater Roadrunner during Painted Lady irruption
Narca Moore-Craig

Winter is especially "birdy" in a patch of desert just east of the low wall. From October through March, watch for Sharp-shinned and Cooper's Hawks, Greater Roadrunner, Anna's Hummingbird, Gila and Ladder-backed Woodpeckers, Northern "Red-shafted" Flicker, Verdin, Blue-gray and Black-tailed Gnatcatchers, Ruby-crowned Kinglet, Bendire's and Crissal Thrashers, Phainopepla, Green-tailed Towhee, and White-crowned Sparrow. Wintering Rock Wrens sing from the small knoll overlooking this little patch of desert.

During the cold months, it is worth the trouble to work the edge of the fields that lie behind and to the east of the mission. Northern Harrier, Red-tailed Hawk, and American Kestrel are usually present. During most winters, there are sporadic sightings of Rough-legged Hawks and Prairie Falcons on isolated tree and utility-pole perches. Among the other open-terrain winter residents are Killdeer, Say's Phoebe, Horned Lark, Common Raven, Mountain Bluebird (irruptive), Loggerhead Shrike, Lark Sparrow, Lark Bunting, and both Eastern and Western Meadowlarks.

Follow the edge of the fields south until you are on the far (east) side of the little hill from the Mission. The old irrigation ditch between the fields and the hill usually has water during winter. Birds to look for here include Hermit Thrush, Yellow-rumped Warbler, Abert's Towhee, and Vesper, Song, and Lincoln's Sparrows. A Yellow-bellied Sapsucker, strictly a vagrant to Southeastern Arizona, wintered here in 1993-1994.

Don't forget to visit the Mission itself. The interior reflects San Xavier's origins in the Spanish colonial period, and its ornate style will inspire your respect for the unknown Native American artists of centuries past.

Little Nogales Road turns south in front of the mission and soon ties in to Community Road (0.25 mile). Turn left (east) onto Community Road, following it 1.1 miles to Interstate 19 (exit 92) south of Tucson. Go under the freeway and turn left (north) to return to Tucson.

Campgrounds, Restaurants, and Accommodations:

Camping facilities are available at Gilbert Ray Campground in Tucson Mountain Park or at Catalina State Park nine miles north of Tucson off Highway 77. Motels and hotels are abundant in Tucson, particularly along Interstate 10 and in "hotel row"—Tucson Boulevard north of Tucson International Airport.

Local-guide referrals for the Tucson area, as well as for all of Southeastern Arizona, are available from Tucson Audubon Society, 300 E. University Boulevard #120, Tucson, AZ 85705; telephone 520/629-0510.

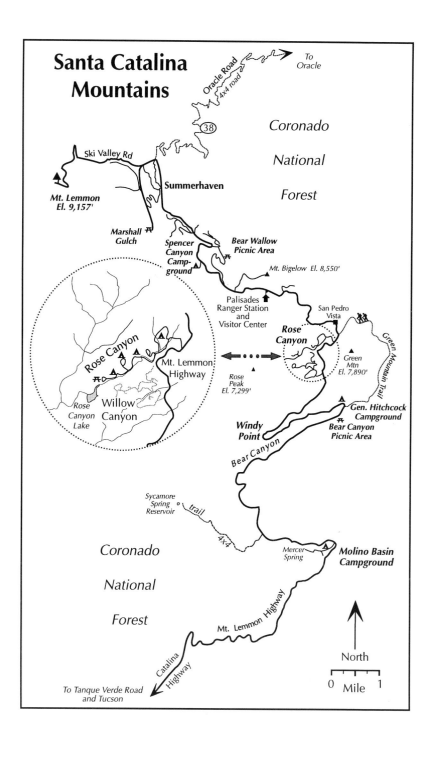

Santa Catalina Mountains

Oracle Road

4x4 road

To Oracle

38

Coronado

National

Forest

Ski Valley Rd

Summerhaven

Mt. Lemmon
El. 9,157'

Marshall
Gulch

Spencer
Canyon
Camp-
ground

Bear Wallow
Picnic Area

Mt. Bigelow El. 8,550'

Palisades
Ranger Station
and
Visitor Center

San Pedro
Vista

Rose
Canyon

Rose Canyon

Mt. Lemmon
Highway

Green Mountain Trail

Green
Mtn
El. 7,890'

Rose
Peak
El. 7,299'

Rose
Canyon
Lake

Willow
Canyon

Gen. Hitchcock
Campground

Bear Canyon
Picnic Area

Windy
Point

Bear Canyon

Sycamore
Spring
Reservoir

trail

4x4

Coronado

National

Forest

Mercer
Spring

Molino Basin
Campground

Mt. Lemmon Highway

Catalina
Highway

To Tanque Verde Road
and Tucson

North

0   Mile   1

CHAPTER 2

SANTA CATALINA MOUNTAINS

For most visitors and many residents, the Santa Catalina Mountains are part of Tucson itself. Rising nearly 7,000 feet above the desert floor, the blue crest of the Catalinas completely dominates the northern Tucson skyline. The Saguaro-studded canyons that drain into the Tucson basin are the city's emblem—embedded in the public imagination and depicted in untold postcard and magazine images.

Two full days are required to bird all three areas described in this chapter. In summer, the two lower areas—Sabino Canyon and Redington Pass—should each be visited as early in the day as possible, both to avoid the heat of the day and to see the birds before they are disturbed by an awakening Tucson. The starting point for all three trips is the intersection of Tanque Verde Road and Sabino Canyon Road in northeast Tucson.

Catalina Highway to Mount Lemmon
(72 miles/one day)

The road from Tucson (El. 2,200 feet) up the south flank of the Santa Catalina Mountains to the top of Mount Lemmon (El. 9,157 feet) is one of the most spectacular in the United States. Birders will be impressed not only by the magnificent scenery and the sweeping vistas, but also by the tremendous diversity of plants and animals. The road climbs through five radically different life zones. Changes in the flora and fauna over the 35-mile trip up the mountain are equivalent to those on a journey from Mexico to Canada.

Stretching about 25 miles east-west and encompassing over 200 square miles, the Santa Catalinas are mountains exceeded in size in Southeastern Arizona only by the Chiricahuas. Winter snowfall can be

33

heavy. From November through March the highway is occasionally closed after major storms, or tire-chains may be required above certain elevations. Even in summer, the heights are far cooler than Tucson, and likely to be cold if skies are overcast. Always take along a jacket for any trip to the top, and remember that summer monsoons may bring torrential cloudbursts and lightning. When in doubt call 520/741-4991 to check road conditions. Gasoline is not available on the Catalina Highway.

The starting point for this tour is the intersection of Tanque Verde Road and Sabino Canyon Road. Continue straight ahead (east) on Tanque Verde Road to the Catalina Highway (2.5 miles). Turn left here. Leave early and try to avoid weekends; the Coronado National Forest, which administers this area, estimates that the Santa Catalina Mountains receive no fewer than one million visitors per year.

You are in the Lower Sonoran Life Zone over the first stretch of the Catalina Highway as it crosses the desert to the base of the mountains (4.4 miles). Saguaro cactus on the hillsides symbolizes the Sonoran Desert in Arizona, as do other plants such as Foothills Palo Verde, Ocotillo, and Brittlebush. Mileage-markers erected by the U.S. Forest Service along the Catalina Highway are convenient indicators for the stops on this tour. Forest Service milepost 0 is set at 2,900-foot elevation at the base of the mountain.

Initially, the road climbs rapidly up the front range through gray-and-white-banded gneiss formed 17 to 30 million years ago. Scenic pull-outs over the next few miles offer a chance to see some of the typical birds that are more or less restricted to the Lower Sonoran Life Zone. Among these are Gambel's Quail, Gila Woodpecker, Verdin, Cactus Wren, Black-tailed Gnatcatcher, Curve-billed Thrasher, and Black-throated Sparrow.

Saguaros give way to Mexican Blue, Arizona White, and Emory Oaks as the road approaches **Molino Basin**, elevation 4,370 feet (5.5 miles). Mexican Blue Oak, with light bark and small, bluish leaves, is confined to Southeastern Arizona. Pale-barked Arizona White Oak has larger leaves than the Mexican Blue—fuzzy beneath and with prominent venation—and the leaf color is always green. Emory Oak has dark green, holly-shaped leaves and dark, comparatively smooth bark.

The campground here (open in winter; parking pull-outs and restrooms only during summer) is in the Upper Sonoran Life Zone, an area too cold for most cacti to colonize. Stop at the campground to look for oak-zone birds like Acorn Woodpecker, Ash-throated Flycatcher (summer), Western Scrub-Jay, Mexican Jay, Bridled Titmouse, Bushtit,

Oak-zone species, such as Crissal Thrasher and Black-chinned Sparrow, are possible at 4,370-foot-elevation Molino Basin Campground.

Bewick's and Rock Wrens, Black-throated Gray Warbler (summer), Canyon Towhee, Rufous-crowned Sparrow, and Scott's Oriole (summer).

Specialty birds at Molino Basin are Crissal Thrasher and Black-chinned Sparrow. Both of these species are particularly fond of the dense, low-growing thickets on the arid slopes which ecologists classify as Interior Chaparral. Pointleaf Manzanita, easily identified by its wine-red bark, is the dominant species in the chaparral belt. Alligator Juniper and Border Pinyon Pine are the small trees that polka-dot the brushy mountainsides.

Beyond the campground, the road winds across a dry hillside ornamented with Palmer Agaves, or "century plants," that blossom once during the life of the plant—usually in July and August—and then die. The plants are actually only 10 to 25 years old when they flower. The thorn-fringed leaves of agaves form a compact rosette, and their large, bell-shaped, yellow flowers are borne on stalks that may reach 15 feet in height. Hummingbirds, woodpeckers, and orioles are attracted by the flowers. Both the stalk and the artichoke-like heart at the base of the plant were used as food by the Apaches. In Mexico, agaves are cultivated to make a coarse thread called sisal, and for use in the manufacture of alcoholic beverages. Tequila is the most celebrated of the agave liquors.

As the road continues to ascend the main massif, a new oak becomes common. Silverleaf Oak is easily recognized by the white undersurface of its leaves. On breezy days whole hillsides shimmer like a forest of coins. Silverleaf Oak grows on rocky, south-facing slopes most of the remaining distance to the crest of the mountain range.

The Catalina Highway enters **Bear Canyon** at milepost 10 (4.5 miles). Once again the character of the vegetation changes. Both shady and cool, Bear Canyon is the home of the champion Arizona Cypress tree in the United States. It measures 20 feet in circumference at breast height and stands 93 feet tall. The north-facing slope of Bear Canyon hosts the most impressive stand of Arizona Cypress in the Santa Catalina Mountains. Aside from the beautifully symmetrical, blue-green foliage of the cypress trees, Bear Canyon also supports a stringer of Arizona Sycamore trees along the little stream, and a scattering of both Ponderosa and Chihuahua Pines. To explore the birding in Bear Canyon turn right, either just beyond milepost 11 for the Upper Bear Canyon Picnic Area (1.1 miles) or at milepost 12 at the entrance for General Hitchcock Campground (0.9 mile). Elevation here is 6,000 feet, approximately midway between the valley and the highest summit, as well as about halfway up the road to Mount Lemmon.

Warblers love Bear Canyon. In springtime, it is not uncommon to hear the combined voices of Virginia's, Yellow-rumped "Audubon's", Black-throated Gray, Grace's, Red-faced, and Olive Warblers, and Painted Redstart, all contributing to the morning chorus. These songs are likely to be augmented by assorted chips and calls of migrating Townsend's, Hermit, and Wilson's Warblers until mid-May. Other birds of the tall timber in Bear Canyon include Band-tailed Pigeon, Flammulated Owl, Whip-poor-will, Acorn and Strickland's Woodpeckers, Northern "Red-Shafted" Flicker, Dusky-capped Flycatcher, Western Wood-Pewee, Bewick's Wren, Solitary and Hutton's Vireos, Hepatic Tanager, Spotted Towhee, and Yellow-eyed Junco.

Farther up the road, 6,623-foot-elevation Windy Point (2.0 miles) offers a stupendous overlook of Bear Canyon in the foreground, backdropped by the Tucson basin. Nowhere are the geological forces that wrought the Santa Catalinas more apparent. A volcano erupted below here some 70 million years ago with a force estimated to be one thousand times greater than the explosions that shook Mount St. Helens in 1980. More recently, owing to plate tectonics, the old volcano slid west off the uplifting granitic mountain, and the Catalinas assumed much the shape we see today. Except in midwinter—and on occasional sunny days even then—White-throated Swifts are common at Windy Point. Listen for the cascading songs of Canyon Wrens on the strange rock formations called "hoodoos" by geologists.

A pass just before milepost 16 (1.8 miles) marks the abrupt division between oak woodland and the Ponderosa Pine forest that mantles the uplands above 7,000 feet. Ponderosa Pine, the tree indicator of the Transition Life Zone, signals the shift to a community of Rocky Mountain plant and animal species that is also reflected in the avifauna. Some of the resident birds of this zone are Wild Turkey, Band-tailed Pigeon, Mexican and Steller's Jays, Common Raven, Mountain Chickadee, White-breasted and Pygmy Nuthatches, Brown Creeper, Olive Warbler (more common in summer), Yellow-eyed Junco, Red Crossbill, and Pine Siskin. In summer, look for Zone-tailed Hawk, Peregrine Falcon, Magnificent and Broad-tailed Hummingbirds, Greater Pewee, Violet-green Swallow, Virginia's (in brush), Yellow-rumped, Grace's, and Red-faced Warblers, Black-headed Grosbeak, and Hepatic Tanager. Dark-eyed, especially "Oregon," Juncos are common in winter.

There are three summer (April to October) campgrounds that offer birders a springboard into this area. Turn left (west) just after milepost 17 (1.3 miles) for popular **Rose Canyon Lake**. Walking the lower, paved road that drops down through an open forest to the seven-acre impoundment (1.25 miles) can be very productive—except on summer weekends. On weekends and holidays, Tucson anglers take their recreation cheek by jowl as they whip the water into whitecaps in quest of elusive hatchery trout. But, on summer weekdays, Red-faced Warblers are common along the little creek, and—if you look hard enough—Olive Warblers can be found gleaning in the pine-tops, even in winter. In winter, watch also for Williamson's Sapsucker (rare) and Cassin's Finch (rare and irregular). The introduced Abert's Tassel-eared Squirrel, Cliff Chipmunk, and Rock Squirrel frequent the campground.

Although Black Bear and Mountain Lion both roam the highlands, the only large mammal truly common in the upper Catalinas is the Coues subspecies of the White-tailed Deer. In this race bucks seldom weigh over 90 pounds and does average under 70. In North America only the subspecies endemic to the Florida Keys is smaller than a Coues White-tailed Deer.

Reptiles, also, are well-represented in the high Santa Catalinas. Short-horned Lizards, called "Horny Toads" by Tucson children, are relatively commmonplace. Everything about Short-horned Lizards is designed to discourage predation. Their silver-dollar shape makes them difficult to swallow, as do their serrated lateral fringe, jagged dorsal scales, and the corona of "horns," which gives this species its name. Short-horned Lizards also have the capacity to shoot blood from the corners of their eyes into the face of a would-be predator. Most important, their cryptic coloration and habitat of freezing before they're noticed make them extremely difficult to detect.

The Western "Arizona Black" Rattlesnake is a subspecies that occurs in the Ponderosa Pine belt of the Catalina and nearby Rincon Mountains. These beautiful reptiles may be almost solid black. This heat-absorbing adaptation probably allows these cold-blooded animals to remain active at high elevations for a longer period of the year than otherwise.

Spencer Canyon Campground (4.3 miles) basically duplicates the birding opportunities of Rose Canyon Lake, but a short distance beyond, **Bear Wallow** Picnic Area (0.8 mile) is set among the mixed conifers of the Canadian Life Zone. The Catalina Highway crosses the crest of the range just before milepost 22. As it curves down a long, cool, north-facing slope into Bear Wallow Canyon, the Ponderosa Pine yields to a twilit forest of tall Douglas-fir and White Fir. A lush broadleaf association features Gambel's Oak, Bigtooth Maple, Box Elder, and Quaking Aspen, all competing for light along the tiny brook. Bracken Fern, Wild Raspberry, Red-osier Dogwood, and a host of wildflowers carpet the understory. While birders may experience no more than a cathedral-like hush in late October and November, it is hard not to recommend a pilgrimage to Bear Wallow in autumn. The fall colors in the soft light of late afternoon are simply superb.

Turn right to enter the picnic area. Many of the same birds that occur in the Transition Life Zone also use the boreal forest at Bear Wallow. Numerous from Rose Canyon to the summit of Mount Lemmon, Mountain Chickadee is a perfect example of these ubiquitous birds of the forest. The Mountain Chickadees that frequently lead mixed flocks of small birds in the high Catalinas represent the southernmost population of their species in all North America. Like chickadees anywhere, these animated little bundles of energy are quick to mob a birder who pishes or imitates an owl.

Other birds—Hermit Thrush and American Robin for example—are far more common in moist areas such as Bear Wallow. Some deep-timber specialists to watch for here include Northern Goshawk, Spotted Owl, Hairy Woodpecker, Cordilleran Flycatcher, Steller's Jay, Red-breasted Nuthatch, House Wren, Warbling Vireo, Western Tanager, and possibly Evening Grosbeak.

The Catalina Highway lies just below the crest after leaving Bear Wallow. *The old control road to Oracle that drops off the "back" (north) side of the mountain to the right is not recommended (2.5 miles). High-clearance is a requirement, the road is 28 miles long, it's rough and*

Red-faced Warbler
Narca Moore-Craig

dusty, and neither the scenery nor the birding can match the scenery or the birding along the paved Catalina Highway.

The major junction in the upper Santa Catalinas lies just beyond the Oracle Road intersection (0.1 mile). For a hot lunch at 7,680-foot-high Summerhaven (0.3 mile), curve left downhill. There are several cafes in the little village, as well as a snack bar, a bakery, and a post office. Only the Alpine Inn, however, has dinner service after 5pm. Continuing down the canyon below Summerhaven, the road ends at Marshall Gulch Picnic Area (1.1 miles). Habitat and birds here are approximately the same as those listed above for Bear Wallow, especially along the Lemmon Creek Trail that starts by the outhouse.

To complete this trip take the **Ski Valley Road** at the Summerhaven intersection. There is little opportunity for birding until the 8,320-foot-elevation lodge (1.2 miles). Sugar-water feeders on the veranda at the Iron Door Restaurant afford birders all the genteel comforts that one could wish for, as well as the possibility of a summering White-eared Hummingbird. By August, these feeders are pinwheels of color. Among the regular species competing for a sip are Magnificent, Calliope, Broadtailed, and Rufous Hummingbirds. Also, watch for Steller's Jay, Common Raven, and American Robin winging across the ski bowl, while Yellow-eyed Juncos hop tamely among cars in the parking lot.

Unless deep snows have closed it, the paved road continues on to the very top of 9,157-foot-high Mount Lemmon (1.7 miles). This last short, steep leg offers a unique opportunity to see breeding species typically confined to the deep forests of the Rocky Mountains farther north. On the penultimate curve below the summit is a stand of Corkbark Fir, probably marooned here since the last ice age, 11,000 years before the present. This cool, moist north-facing slope also hosts graceful sprays of Rocky Mountain Maple and deep groves of Quaking Aspen. Nesting species here are Cordilleran Flycatcher (summer), Golden-crowned Kinglet, and Pine Siskin.

Bracken-choked glades and meadows, often created artificially by early logging or construction activities, radiate from the summit of Mount Lemmon. Snowberry, Gooseberry, and Scouler Willow thickets fringing these clearings represent the last remnants of the relic habitat used by breeding Orange-crowned Warblers in the Santa Catalina Mountains. Since a damp, iris-trimmed patch near Summerhaven was bull-dozed by developers in the early 1950s, there are no other known nesting locations for Orange-crowned Warblers in the range.

Mount Lemmon has no view from the summit, but a short trail (0.6 mile) leads to Lemmon Rock Lookout at 8,800 feet. As the path descends through an open forest of Ponderosa Pine, Southwestern White Pine, and Douglas-fir en route to the stupendous monolith on which the lookout perches, watch for Mountain Chickadee, Pygmy Nuthatch, Grace's (summer), Red-faced (summer), and Olive Warblers, Chipping Sparrow, Yellow-eyed Junco, and Red Crossbill (irregular). The lookout itself seems to be balanced on a granite egg 1,500 feet above the 56,933-acre Pusch

Ridge Wilderness Area. Lemmon Rock makes a tremendous observation dome from which to watch for Zone-tailed and Red-tailed Hawks and Peregrine Falcons soaring by on the updrafts, while Tucson shimmers like a mirage in the desert heat over a vertical mile below.

Sabino Canyon

(9 miles/one-half day)

The starting point is the intersection of Sabino Canyon and Tanque Verde Roads. Turn left (north) onto Sabino (Sah-BEE-no) Canyon Road and continue to the Sabino Canyon Recreation Area (4.5 miles).

At the entrance to the recreation area, turn right into the large parking area at the visitor center. Birders are welcome to hike into either Sabino or Bear Canyon at any hour, any day of the week. Backpackers must camp at least one-quarter mile beyond paved roads.

The small visitor center is open from 8am to 4:30pm weekdays, and from 8:30am to 4:30pm on weekends. Birders will probably arrive before the Forest Service opens shop, but the facility provides an interesting and welcome rest stop when you return. Be sure to check the exhibits and inspect the book store.

Watch for Gambel's Quail, Greater Roadrunner, Cactus Wren, Northern Cardinal, and Pyrrhuloxia at the ticket booth by the tram stop. Tickets for the Sabino Canyon Shuttle cost $5 per adult, $2 for 3- to 12-year-olds. It departs hourly from 9:00am to 4:00pm July through November; every half- hour, 9:00am to 4:30pm, December through June. The 45-minute ride takes you to the end of the Sabino Canyon Road (3.8 miles) and back again. A separate shuttle into Bear Canyon goes 2.5 miles to the Lower Bear Picnic Area and the Seven Falls Trailhead: $2 per adult, $1.25 for 3- to12-year-olds, with hourly departures from 9am to 4pm year-round. Both shuttles allow you to disembark or board at any part of the route.

The trams are contracted to a private firm, and the Sabino Canyon trip includes a narrated program over loudspeakers which will interest first-time visitors. Sabino Canyon is a picturesque spot where Saguaros march down to meet sparkling green Fremont Cottonwoods and Arizona Sycamores along a beautiful little stream, all against a backdrop of stupendous cliffs. The knife-like ridge that divides Sabino from Bear Canyon towers over 2,500 feet above.

Given its dramatic scenery and its proximity to Tucson, you can expect to share Sabino Canyon with other nature-lovers. On a typical day, Sabino receives 2,700 visitors. The Coronado National Forest estimates that annual visitation exceeds one million people. *Hint: birders should try to avoid weekends.*

To dodge the crowds and partake of a slice of the solitude that used to characterize Sabino, arrive early and plan to hike. *Don't forget a canteen—the water in the streams is unsafe to drink.* Leave from the far right (southeast) corner of the visitor center parking area. A wide trail parallels the Forest Service boundary-fence 0.8 mile to Bear Canyon Road. Follow Bear Canyon Road east another 0.4 mile to a paved road junction next to Sabino Creek. Turn left (north) here. It is 0.3 mile to the end of this road at the Lower Sabino Picnic Area. Shuttle-users should ride the Bear Canyon tram to Stop Number Two, then follow the road to the picnic area. A small, one-acre pond lies just upstream behind a Civilian Conservation Corps rock-and-concrete dam. The large willows around the pond and elsewhere along the creek host many migrants, in season. Many Eastern warblers have been found here through the years, as well as oddities such as Winter Wren and Purple Gallinule.

Some of the resident birds to watch for are Cooper's and Red-tailed Hawks, Gambel's Quail, Mourning Dove, Greater Roadrunner, White-throated Swift, Gila and Ladder-backed Woodpeckers, Gilded Flicker, Northern Beardless-Tyrannulet, Black Phoebe, Common Raven, Verdin, Cactus, Canyon, and Rock Wrens, Black-tailed Gnatcatcher, Northern Mockingbird, Curve-billed Thrasher, Phainopepla, House Finch, Lesser Goldfinch, and Black-throated Sparrow.

In summer, check the entrance to Saguaro cavities for sleeping Elf Owls. Also summering are White-winged Dove, Lesser Nighthawk (dawn and dusk), Broad-billed and Black-chinned Hummingbirds, Ash-throated and Brown-crested Flycatchers, Purple Martin, Bell's Vireo, Lucy's Warbler, Varied Bunting, Bronzed Cowbird, and Hooded Oriole. In winter, towhees are numerous. It is possible to see Green-tailed, Spotted, Canyon, and Abert's Towhees all foraging practically simulta-neously beneath a single picnic table in Lower Sabino in a single morning. Black-chinned Sparrows are uncommon, but regular, in winter. Farther along the road, and during sporadic winters, American Dippers may take advantage of the numerous cascades and falls along the stream. Look, especially, below bridges created by the CCC when the Sabino Canyon Road was constructed in the 1930s.

Tanque Verde Road and Redington Pass

(54 miles/one day)

The first half of this trip visits a series of mesquite bosques and oases adjacent to Tanque Verde Road in northeast Tucson. Redington Pass, which divides the Santa Catalina from the Rincon Mountains, is the last half of the trip. Either part of the Tanque Verde Road/Redington Pass trip is perfect for a half-day birding outing. To begin the full tour or to do either half-day segment, turn east onto Tanque Verde Road at its inter-section with Sabino Canyon Road.

Vermilion Flycatchers link all of the areas along Tanque Verde Road. The first locale to check for these brilliant red birds is **Woodland Road**, the first turn-off on the right (south) after Tanque Verde Road crosses the long bridge over Tanque Verde Wash (0.3 mile past the wash; 1.6 miles east of the starting point).

Real estate prices are high along Woodland Road. These spacious properties are situated on the broad, level terrace just north of the stream, where silt deposition over the millennia has fostered deep, rich soils. A mesquite bosque—or woodland—formerly flourished along the banks of Tanque Verde Wash. Many grand old trees remain, some over 30 feet high. Homeowners have cleared others to create horse-pastures. This is wonderful habitat for Vermilion Flycatchers. Other species to look for in this area of shade and pasture include American Kestrel, Gambel's Quail, White-winged (a few overwinter) and Mourning Doves, Greater Road-runner, Lesser Nighthawk (summer), Gila Woodpecker, Gilded Flicker, Western Kingbird (summer), Barn Swallow (summer), Mountain Bluebird (irregular in winter), Northern Mockingbird, Cedar Waxwing (winter), Phainopepla, Orange-crowned Warbler (winter), Lucy's Warbler (sum-mer), Yellow-rumped "Audubon's" Warbler (winter), Northern Cardinal, White-crowned Sparrow (winter), Great-tailed Grackle, House Finch, and Lesser Goldfinch. A well-manicured pecan orchard (0.8 mile) halfway along Woodland Road is a convenient place to park to check for Red-naped Sapsuckers in winter.

Woodland Road is shaped like a horseshoe; it rejoins Tanque Verde Road just 100 yards east of the turn-off to the Catalina Highway (0.9 mile). Turn right (east) onto Tanque Verde Road. The left (north) turn-off onto Soldier Trail (3.4 miles) for Agua Caliente Park is well-signed. Continue north to Roger Road (2.0 miles) and turn right (east). Turn left at the entrance to Agua Caliente Park (0.5 mile) and pull into the parking area for **Agua Caliente Lake**.

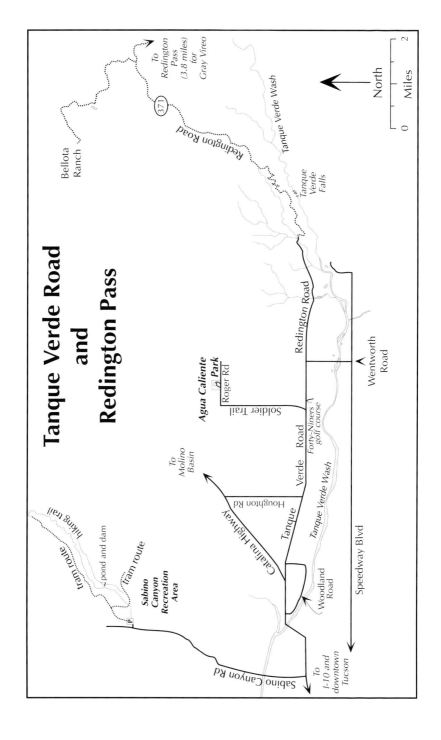

Tanque Verde Road and Redington Pass

Surrounded by palms, cottonwoods, and tamarisks, this lovely 2.5-acre pond is a magnet for both waterfowl and desert species alike. Ordinarily, a Great Blue Heron or a Green Heron is stalking the shallows, and a few dabblers and American Coots are plying the open water. Watch for Wood Duck here. This is the best place in the Tucson basin for Soras; look for them along the edge of the tules that line most of the far side of the pond. Sometimes hundreds of roosting Red-winged Black-birds blacken the cattails and the surrounding trees.

The tall trees at Agua Caliente provide excellent habitat for Great Horned Owls, as well as a variety of other birds. Both Broad-billed and Black-chinned Hummingbirds (summer) nest here, as do Northern Beard-less-Tyrannulet, Vermilion Flycatcher, Bell's Vireo (summer), Lucy's Warbler (summer), Northern Cardinal, and Hooded Oriole (summer). Agua Caliente, Spanish for "warm water", refers to the perennial spring that feeds the pond. A line of palm trees running east from the pond leads to the nearby spring.

Retracing your route, Soldier Trail rejoins Tanque Verde Road oppo-site the long, false-adobe fence of the Forty-Niners Golf Course. Turn left (east) to continue this trip. The entrance to the golf course (0.2 mile) is marked by enormous double pylons on both sides, but unless you arrive very early, golfers will have flushed all the birds. Anyway, birders are not permitted on the paths after 8am.

Agua Caliente Lake, a lovely oasis in northeast suburban Tucson, is a great place to bird while you enjoy a picnic brunch.

A better bet is to continue east to Wentworth Road (0.9 mile), and turn right (south) to access **Tanque Verde Wash** (0.7 mile). Park on the north bank for birding. *Do not attempt to cross Tanque Verde Wash after heavy storms, if there are barriers in place, or if you have any doubt about the depth of the water.* One of the Sonoran Desert's regrettable but oft-repeated initiation-rites for newcomers and the unwary is to drown their vehicles—and occasionally themselves—in these normally "dry" desert rivers. Tanque Verde Wash consumes cars every year.

Once again, the first bird which you see as you exit your car may be a Vermilion Flycatcher. Check for it in the pasture on the left (east) side of the road. A barbed-wire fence cuts off access upstream, but the broad, sandy wash provides an open route west down Tanque Verde Wash. Thick trees and brush along the banks may harbor year-round Gila and Ladder-backed Woodpeckers, Gilded Flicker, and Abert's Towhee, and summering Northern Beardless-Tyrannulet, Bell's Vireo, Lucy's Warbler, Yellow-breasted Chat, Summer Tanager, and Blue Grosbeak. In winter, search the same areas for Orange-crowned and Yellow-rumped Warblers, Green-tailed Towhee, Lawrence's Goldfinch, and a variety of sparrows. White-crowns are usually the most abundant, but other wintering sparrows that occur here include Chipping, Brewer's, Black-chinned (rare), Lark, Black-throated, Savannah, Fox (rare), Song, and White-throated (rare).

Tanque Verde Wash is also perfect habitat for migrant warblers. The most common are MacGillivray's and Wilson's. Surprise Eastern vagrants such as Nashville, Northern Parula, Chestnut-sided, Yellow-rumped "Myrtle", and Black-and-white Warblers, as well as American Redstart, have occurred. Years separate sighting-reports for some of these species.

Return up Wentworth to Tanque Verde Road—now officially known as Redington Road—and consider how much time you have budgeted for this tour. To the left (west) lies Tucson (8.3 miles to the starting point at the intersection with Sabino Canyon Road). To the right (east) the pavement ends at a major tributary that feeds Tanque Verde Wash (2.8 miles). Steep, rocky, dusty, and wash-boarded, Redington Road snakes its way up to the pinyon/juniper woodland and interior chaparral of the Upper Sonoran Life Zone. **Redington Pass** has proven a reliable location for Gray Vireo (11.2 miles beyond the end of the pavement, 3.8 miles beyond the Bellota Ranch Road junction), an otherwise difficult species to locate in Southeastern Arizona.

If winter storms have closed the Catalina Highway, Redington Pass offers an access point to a new community of birds in the immediate vicinity of Tucson. Some of these include Acorn Woodpecker, Western Scrub-Jay, Mexican Jay, Bridled and Plain Titmice, Bushtit, Blue-gray Gnatcatcher, Western and Mountain (irregular) Bluebirds, Crissal Thrasher, Spotted Towhee, and Black-chinned Sparrow. In summer additional species include Cassin's Kingbird, Solitary Vireo (more common than Gray Vireo), and Black-throated Gray Warbler.

Care is needed to distinguish Gray Vireo from the "Plumbeous" subspecies of Solitary Vireo that breeds in Redington Pass. Neither species has any tinge of yellow. The bold, white spectacles that join in a crisply-demarcated line above the Solitary's bill give the Solitary an acute, "scholastic" expression quite distinct from the vague, mild-looking face of the Gray Vireo. Note that the Gray has a thin eye-ring that does not fuse on the forehead. Gray Vireo also lacks the heavy, double, white wing-bars of a Solitary. If you can't decide whether the wing-bars are heavy or fine, it's a Solitary. At first glance, the brownish-gray wings of a Gray Vireo often do not seem to have wing-bars at all. Unless you really are an expert on the songs of *both* species, don't make your call based on vocalizations. Variations in the song of Solitary Vireo account for almost all reported sound identifications of Gray Vireo in southeastern Arizona. Don't fool yourself.

It is about 22 miles back to the starting point in Tucson on the Redington/Tanque Verde Road.

Campgrounds, Restaurants, and Accommodations:

The U.S. Forest Service maintains four campgrounds in the Santa Catalina Mountains. General Hitchcock, Rose Canyon, and Spencer Canyon are all-summer (April to October) campgrounds above 7,000 feet. Molino Basin (El. 4,500 feet) is open for camping from September through April. Motels and hotels are abundant in Tucson.

The Iron Door Restaurant in the Mount Lemmon Ski Valley has a full menu for lunch and offers breakfast on weekends. In Summerhaven there are several cafes, and Alpine Inn offers dinners after 5pm.

Local-guide referrals for the Tucson area, as well as for all of South-eastern Arizona, are available from Tucson Audubon Society, 300 E. University Boulevard #120, Tucson, AZ 85705; telephone 520/629-0510.

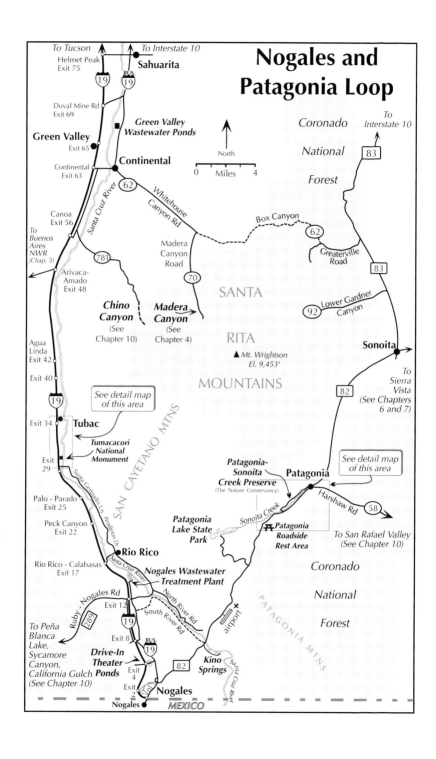

Nogales and Patagonia Loop

To Tucson
Helmet Peak
Exit 75

To Interstate 10

Sahuarita

19   BUS 19

Duval Mine Rd
Exit 69

Green Valley
Exit 65

*Green Valley
Wastewater Ponds*

Continental

Continental
Exit 63

62

Whitehouse
Canyon Rd

Canoa
Exit 56

To
Buenos
Aires
NWR
(Chap. 5)

781

Arivaca-
Amado
Exit 48

Madera
Canyon
Road

70

Coronado

National

Forest

To
Interstate 10

83

North

0   Miles   4

Box Canyon

62

Greaterville
Road

83

SANTA

*Chino
Canyon*
(See
Chapter 10)

*Madera
Canyon*
(See
Chapter 4)

RITA

92   Lower Gardner
Canyon

Sonoita

Agua
Linda
Exit 42

Exit 40

19

▲ Mt. Wrightson
El. 9,453'

MOUNTAINS

To
Sierra
Vista
(See Chapters
6 and 7)

82

*See detail map
of this area*

Exit 34

Tubac

SAN CAYETANO MTNS

*Tumacacori
National
Monument*

Exit
29

Santa Gertrudis Ln

Pendleton Dr

Santa Cruz River

Palo - Parado
Exit 25

Peck Canyon
Exit 22

Rio Rico

Rio Rico - Calabasas
Exit 17

*Nogales Wastewater
Treatment Plant*

Ruby - Nogales Rd

289

Exit 12

North River Rd

South River Rd

*Patagonia-
Sonoita
Creek Preserve*
(The Nature Conservancy)

Patagonia

*See detail map
of this area*

Harshaw Rd   58

Sonoita Creek

*Patagonia
Lake State
Park*

*Patagonia
Roadside
Rest Area*

To San Rafael Valley
(See Chapter 10)

Coronado

National

Forest

airport

PATAGONIA MTNS

To Peña
Blanca
Lake,
Sycamore
Canyon,
California Gulch
(See Chapter 10)

19

Exit 8

BUS 19

*Drive-In
Theater Ponds*

Exit
4

82

*Kino
Springs*

Santa Cruz River

Exit
2

Nogales

Nogales   MEXICO

CHAPTER 3

NOGALES AND
PATAGONIA LOOP

(181 miles/two days)

This tour follows the green cottonwoods of the Santa Cruz River upstream (south) to Nogales, then loops around the south end of the Santa Rita Mountains to Patagonia and the verdant waters of Sonoita (So-NOY-tah) Creek. From here, it passes through a lush grassland east of the mountains before dropping back to the desert at Tucson.

There are many good birding areas along the way, but the most outstanding is the Patagonia-Sonoita Creek Preserve at Patagonia. Probably, more rarities and vagrants are discovered annually in the vicinity of Patagonia than in any other area in Southeastern Arizona. To properly bird The Nature Conservancy Preserve and the Patagonia Roadside Rest Area, plan to spend a night in town. Patagonia is also the best place to begin a winter birding excursion out to the San Rafael Valley.

From the starting point at the intersection of Interstates 10 and 19 in Tucson, go south on I-19 toward Nogales. *Note: this is the only highway in the United States signed for distances in kilometers. Exit numbers are useful, but they will not agree with odometers on U.S. cars.*

Much of Arizona's history in the 17th and 18th centuries occurred in the Santa Cruz River Valley. Visible on the right near the river-crossing (6.0 miles) are the white domes and towers of San Xavier (sahn-ah-VEER) Mission, founded by Father Kino in 1700. (For details on birding the Mission, see Chapter 1.) Along the river on the left are irrigated pastures where once stood a forest of giant mesquite trees. Until 1945, the Santa Cruz flowed permanently above the ground through the San Xavier Reservation. This *bosque*—or woodland—was the home of thousands of

White-winged Doves and other birds (including Common Black-Hawks and Gray Hawks).

Steadily increasing demands on the upper watershed, as well as from Tucson, finally bled the river dry after World War II. There was a wholesale die-off of mesquite. With the trees went the wildlife. Members of the Tohono O'odham tribe chopped down the dead mesquite forest for firewood, and now only these blackened stumps remain. The death of the lower Santa Cruz River at Tucson is one of the saddest chapters in human/wildlife interaction in Southeastern Arizona in this century.

For a preview of future changes, look ahead on the right at the huge, barren piles of tailings from a copper pit-mine. Eventually, much of the West may look like this if the mining industry continues to gouge the earth in search of copper, coal, and other ores without proper environmental safeguards. Several wells in Green Valley (16.2 miles) have been abandoned in recent years as a consequence of ground-water pollution from the mines.

As you continue south down the interstate, you will pass the exits for three birding areas described later in the book. The first is Madera Canyon in the Santa Rita Mountains at exit 63 for Continental (1.3 miles). Madera Canyon is featured in the next chapter. Canoa Interchange, exit 56 (4.2 miles), is the departure point for a Chino Canyon side-trip, if you have the time or inclination (Chapter 10). Finally, exit 48 at Arivaca/Amado (5.3 miles) marks the beginning of the Arivaca Cienaga/Buenos Aires Wildlife Refuge Loop (Chapter 5).

The first stop on this tour is the renowned artists' community at **Tubac**, exit 34 (8.7 miles). Tubac began as a *visita,* or part-time mission, established by the Jesuit padres in 1691. The Pima Revolt in 1751 led the Spanish to construct Arizona's first *presidio*—walled fortress—here in 1752. In 1775, Captain Juan Bautista de Anza left Tubac on the California expedition that gave rise to present-day San Francisco. A frequent target of Apache raids, Tubac was deserted several times before it was finally sacked and burned to the ground in 1849.

Two intrepid prospectors, Charles Poston and Henry Ehrenberg, restored life to the little hamlet in 1854. Arizona's first newspaper was printed here in 1858, and, by 1859, the population was approximately 800. But, over the next few turbulent decades, the residents of Tubac fled to nearby Tucson again and again as Native Americans besieged their settlement. Continuous occupation of the site did not really begin until early in the 20th century. Now Tubac is an arts-and-crafts center, with a museum and a State Historic Park.

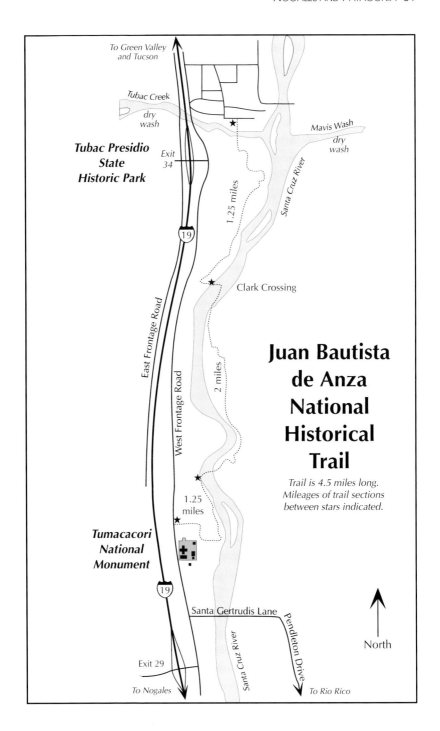

To Green Valley and Tucson

Tubac Creek
dry wash

Mavis Wash
dry wash

Tubac Presidio State Historic Park

Exit 34

Santa Cruz River

1.25 miles

19

Clark Crossing

East Frontage Road

West Frontage Road

2 miles

Juan Bautista de Anza National Historical Trail

Trail is 4.5 miles long. Mileages of trail sections between stars indicated.

1.25 miles

Tumacacori National Monument

19

Santa Gertrudis Lane

Pendleton Drive

Santa Cruz River

North

Exit 29

To Nogales

To Rio Rico

To bird Tubac leave Interstate 19 at exit 34, cross under the freeway, and turn left (north) onto the Frontage Road (0.6 mile). Follow the Frontage Road to the prominent entrance to the town (0.4 mile). Bear right around the boutiques and galleries that crowd the principal boulevard, and continue east until the pavement makes a right turn at Tubac State Historic Park (0.3 mile). Public restrooms are located just north of the parking area, and a small history museum (admission $2) is across the street inside the crook of the elbow.

Birders should arrive early to hike the Juan Bautista de Anza National Historical Trail. The elevation of the Santa Cruz River at Tubac is only 3,200 feet, and, during most of the year, the temperature climbs rapidly after sunrise. Except in winter, bird activity almost ceases after 10am.

Vermilion Flycatchers are permanent residents in the picnic area at the trailhead. The 1.25 miles to the first river-crossing offers a good cross-section of birding opportunities along the entire 4.5-mile-long path between Tubac Presidio and Tumacacori Mission. The trail threads in and out of a mesquite bosque, eventually reaching strands of Fremont Cottonwood on the riverbank. Melting adobe walls near the beginning of the broad, well-signed trail are almost all that remains of the first two centuries of the town's history.

In summer, watch for Gray Hawk, White-winged Dove, Yellow-billed Cuckoo, Broad-billed and Black-chinned Hummingbirds, Bell's Vireo, Lucy's Warbler, Yellow-breasted Chat, Summer Tanager, Blue Grosbeak, and Hooded and Bullock's Orioles. In winter, look for Sharp-shinned and Cooper's Hawks, Gray Flycatcher, Anna's and Costa's Hummingbirds, Red-naped Sapsucker, House Wren, Yellow-rumped Warbler, and a host of sparrows—especially Chipping, Savannah, and White-crowned. Year-round residents include Great Blue Heron, Mourning and Inca Doves, Gila Woodpecker, Gilded Flicker, Northern Beardless-Tyrannulet, Common Raven, Bewick's Wren, Phainopepla, Northern Cardinal, Pyrrhuloxia, Canyon and Abert's Towhees, and Lesser Goldfinch.

Birders hiking the de Anza Trail should *plan on carrying plenty of water*, especially in summer; the water in the river is not potable. En route to Tumacacori, the trail crosses the Santa Cruz several times, and walkers need to be prepared to wade. *Do not attempt to cross the river if the water is high.* This trail is located on an easement through private property; both camping and off-trail use are prohibited.

There is no need to re-enter the interstate to access Tumacacori. Simply stay on the Frontage Road south from the underpass road to the old church (2.4 miles). (If you elected not to visit Tubac, take Interstate

19 exit 29 for Tumacacori, 3.1 miles south of Tubac, cross under the freeway, and go north on the Frontage Road 0.7 mile.)

Tumacacori (Tooma-COCK-or-ee) National Monument preserves one of the missions founded by the Jesuits in northern Mexico and southern Arizona some 300 years ago. Father Eusebio Kino built the first structure here in 1701, but the present adobe church probably dates from the Franciscan era in the 1790s. By the mid-19th century, under continuous pressure from the Apaches, the mission was abandoned. It came under the protection of the National Park Service in 1908. The museum and church are well worth a visit.

To bird Tumacacori, park off the north (Tubac) end of the stuccoed adobe wall enclosing the ruins, and walk north up the Frontage Road (0.1 mile) to find the de Anza Trailhead at a gate in the fence. The first half-mile of the trail leads east to the Santa Cruz River; then the route turns left (north) following the west bank of the river. The first crossing is another 0.75 mile downstream (north) from the trailhead. It is a total of 4.5 miles to the end of the trail at Tubac. If you can budget a half-day for a hike, and if you can find someone who shares your interest in the area, the de Anza Trail makes a perfect place for a car-key swap at the midpoint. Or you can always ask a sympathetic partner to wait for you at the far end. Birds here are the same as those mentioned above for Tubac.

To continue the main tour, follow the Frontage Road south from Tumacacori to the turn-off that leads under the freeway (0.7 mile), turn right, go under it, and turn left to access I-19 (0.2 mile).

If the Santa Cruz is low, Santa Gertrudis Lane (0.4 mile south of Tumacacori) provides a pleasant alternative to the busy interstate. Turn left (east) and begin serious birding. Soon you will reach a river-ford that should not be crossed if the water is high (0.2 mile). *Do not ignore barriers or warning signs, and do not enter the river when in doubt.* After the river-crossing, Santa Gertrudis Lane ends at the base of the bluff on the east side of the valley (0.5 mile). This area is entirely privately-owned, and the irrigated fields and woodlands in the Santa Cruz River bottom are very birdy. *Do not cross fences or enter private property.*

Santa Gertrudis Lane is the nearest location to Tucson to look for Tropical Kingbird (rare, summer). Other species to watch for along the floodplain include Gray Hawk (summer), Ladder-backed Woodpecker, Northern Beardless-Tyrannulet, Black Phoebe, Vermilion Flycatcher, Ash-throated and Brown-crested Flycatchers (summer), Western Kingbird (summer), Northern Rough-winged, Cliff, and Barn Swallows (summer), Verdin, Phainopepla, American Pipit (winter), Bell's Vireo (summer),

Lucy's Warbler and Yellow-breasted Chat (summer), Summer Tanager (summer), Pyrrhuloxia, Blue Grosbeak (summer), Lazuli Bunting (primarily migration), Green-tailed (winter) and Abert's Towhees, Rufous-winged and Lark Sparrows, Bullock's Oriole (summer), and Lesser Goldfinch.

Turn right (south) onto Pendleton Drive to explore the east side of the Santa Cruz River. Turn right (west) again at Rio Rico (7.3 miles), the first paved intersection. There is a bridge across the river here, and it's just a short hop back to the interstate at the Rio Rico interchange, exit 17 (1.3 miles).

Continuing south, leave Interstate 19 at Ruby Road, exit 12 (10.6 miles from the Tumacacori exit; 3.1 miles from Rio Rico) and turn left to cross over to the Frontage Road (0.5 mile) on the east side. Turn left (north) and go to a group of warehouses on the right. Watch between the buildings (just north of the Ritz warehouse on the right) for a small road that crosses the railroad tracks (1.0 mile) and then jogs left to the sewage ponds (0.1 mile). The sign that formerly marked the turn-off was removed in 1993. You must register at the office for permission to bird around the ponds, and you must also sign out when you leave. This 90-acre facility is open from 7am to 4pm seven days per week.

The **Nogales Sewage Ponds** typically harbor one of the largest concentrations of wintering waterfowl in Southeastern Arizona. There are ordinarily no fewer than one thousand ducks on the 17 ponds from November through March; sometimes there are several times that number. While the smallest pond covers only a couple of acres, the weedy overflow-reservoir on the north end of the facility is a substantial 23 acres when full. A spotting scope is definitely an asset here. Nogales often produces 15 or more species of waterfowl in midwinter.

The most abundant ducks are Mallard, Northern Pintail, Northern Shoveler, American Wigeon, and Ruddy Duck, but there is always a smattering of other species, too. These include all the teals, Gadwall, Canvasback, Redhead, Ring-necked Duck, and Lesser Scaup. Also usually present are one or a few Common Goldeneye, Bufflehead, or Common Merganser—or some other duck seemingly wholly misplaced in the arid Santa Cruz Valley. A gorgeous drake Eurasian Wigeon appeared at Nogales in January 1993 and stayed until mid-April. It, or another, has wintered at Nogales ever since.

The Nogales Sewage Ponds also provide a convenient site where you may find Black-bellied Whistling-Ducks.

A good variety of other birds is also attracted to the 50-plus acres of water at Nogales. This is one of the best locations in the southeast corner for a flock of Black Vultures all year round, and often a lone Turkey

Vulture in winter. Also watch for Great Blue Heron, Northern Harrier (winter), Gray Hawk (summer), American Coot, Killdeer, Spotted Sandpiper (winter), Black Phoebe, six species of swallows (summer and migration), Common Raven, American Pipit (winter), Common Yellowthroat, Yellow-breasted Chat (summer), Bobolink (rare, migrant), Redwinged and Brewer's (winter) Blackbirds, and House Finch.

Fluctuating water-levels in the huge north reservoir create a series of mudflats, channels, and weedy vegetation perfect for waterbirds. Check the north pond for migrant egrets, White-faced Ibis, geese and ducks, plovers, sandpipers, gulls, and terns.

Return to Ruby Road and cross back to the west side of the interstate. Peña Blanca Lake, Sycamore Canyon, and California Gulch (all described in Chapter 10) are all located off Ruby Road to the west. To continue the Nogales/Patagonia tour, turn left (south) back onto I-19. Move into the left lane to take the first Nogales off-ramp, exit 8 (2.2 miles). You are now

Black-bellied Whistling-Duck
Gail Diane Yovanovich

driving south on Business 19. Be prepared for an abrupt right turn onto the first paved road on the right, Country Club Drive (1.0 mile).

This is an optional side-trip to the Drive-In Theater Ponds (0.2 mile), located on both sides of the road. Park at the wide pull-out on the south side of the road. *Be aware of traffic here.* The Drive-In Theater Ponds are excellent for Virginia Rail—they even breed here. The ponds are also a good location for Sora for virtually the entire year except June. Look also for Black-bellied Whistling-Duck, and Green Kingfisher is rare but possible. Throughout the winter, Vermilion Flycatchers and Yellow-rumped Warblers dart among the bare boughs of the willows.

The Drive-In Theater Ponds would be a wonderful birding site if it were not for the murderous onslaught of commuter traffic throughout the day. Given the narrow shoulder, it is all too easy to image yourself splattered across the landscape like a crate of ripe tomatoes. Country Club Pond is located just 100 yards inside the entrance to Meadow Hills Estates (0.4 mile farther west), but in some years it has been drained. If so, and without the promise of Black-bellied Whistling-Ducks or the possibility of Tropical Kingbirds at Country Club Pond at Meadow Hills, you may wish to omit this side-trip altogether and drive directly to Kino Springs.

To do so, turn right onto Business 19 to access Highway 82 in south Nogales (4.0 miles). Get into the right lane and cross the overpass above

If you're able to ignore the thundering traffic on Country Club Drive, the Drive-In Theater Ponds might yield breeding Virginia Rails or a Sora almost any time of the year.

Business 19. The entrance to **Kino Springs** is on the right (south) side of Highway 82, at an elaborately landscaped junction with a stucco wall, just west of the Santa Cruz River (4.3 miles).

It pays to watch for birds beginning just inside the entrance, but *remember to pull completely off Kino Springs Road.* Rock Wrens breed on the rocky hill on the right (west) side of the pavement, and, in spring, they occasionally sing from the stucco wall across the road. Varied Buntings (summer) also inhabit the rocky knoll. Sometimes male Varieds use the power-line on the left side of the road as a song perch. Watch for Black Vultures soaring overhead or perched on hillside boulders, awaiting updrafts. As the road swings away from the little hill, keep an eye peeled for Gray Hawks (summer) on the left near the river. They often use the short utility-poles for perches in this comparatively treeless stretch along the Santa Cruz. Other bird possibilities include Say's Phoebe, Western Kingbird (summer), and Blue Grosbeak (summer). A grove of tall cottonwoods on the left signals the first pond at Kino Springs (1.0 mile). There is ample room to park well off the pavement on either side of the road.

Traditionally, the first pond at Kino is the most reliable site for Common Moorhen in Southeastern Arizona (although they also began breeding at Kingfisher Pond on the San Pedro River in the summer of 1993). Other birds to look for in or near the water include Pied-billed Grebe, Great Blue and Green Herons, Virginia Rail, Sora (primarily winter), American Coot, Yellow-billed Cuckoo (summer), Belted King-fisher (winter), Black Phoebe, Tropical Kingbird, Vermilion Flycatcher, Marsh Wren (winter), Yellow Warbler (summer), Common Yellowthroat, and Song and Swamp Sparrows (winter). Usually during winter—and sometimes even in summer—there are a dozen or so ducks on the pond. The most common species are Northern Shoveler, Gadwall, American Wigeon, Ring-necked Duck, and Lesser Scaup, but almost any other duck can occur here and many have done so.

Over the years Kino Springs has also acquired a reputation as a potential location for two Southeastern Arizona specialties. Although they are more likely to be seen in winter than summer, there are now records for Green Kingfisher every month of the year. Scan for Green Kingfisher on low branches overhanging the water. In recent years, winter observations of Rufous-backed Robin at Kino have almost come to be expected. Rufous-backed Robins are far more likely to skulk than their much more common American cousins. Look for them within deep cover, but do not cross the cable without prior permission. (Inquire at the pro shop.)

There are three distinct habitats at the first Kino Springs pond. Each has its own subset of birds, but—as you can imagine—some species freely use more than one. This is especially true of the dry-land birds that are most common in the big Fremont Cottonwoods and Netleaf Hackberry trees that lie on the far (north) side of the pond. Don't neglect the mesquite thicket on the east side of the pond. Some of the resident and summering birds to watch for here include Common Ground-Dove, Costa's Hummingbird, Gila and Ladder-backed Woodpeckers, Gilded Flicker, Northern Beardless-Tyrannulet, Brown-crested Flycatcher, Cassin's, Thick-billed (rare), and Western Kingbirds, Verdin, Bushtit, White-breasted Nuthatch, Bewick's Wren, Curve-billed Thrasher, Phainopepla, Bell's Vireo, Lucy's Warbler, Summer Tanager, Northern Cardinal, Lazuli and Varied Buntings, Abert's Towhee, Hooded and Bullock's Orioles, and Lesser Goldfinch. In winter and migration, watch for Northern "Red-shafted" Flicker, Hammond's Flycatcher, Ruby-crowned Kinglet, Mountain Bluebird (irregular), Hermit Thrush, American Robin, Western Tanager, Yellow-rumped "Audubon's" Warbler, Chipping Sparrow, and American Goldfinch.

After birding the first pond, continue on the road through the Kino Springs Golf Course to access the second, larger pond. Passing through the greens you may see Greater Roadrunner, Say's Phoebe, and Western Kingbird (summer). On warm days in the winter, up to one thousand American Wigeon may be grazing on the golf course in a compact flock that's bound to grab your attention. Watch for a ridiculously self-important male Bronzed Cowbird patrolling the immaculately groomed lawn in front of the club house throughout the summer. Turn right (0.8 mile) at the club house and park here; do not park on the road. Drop by the pro shop to request permission to walk around the large golf-course pond across the road. *Do not distract the golfers and stay off the golf course itself.*

Less than three miles from the Mexican border, the 3,700-foot-high golf-course pond is known as the most reliable location for Tropical Kingbird in the United States. Frequently, however, it is necessary to walk down the dirt track on the right (north) side of the pond up to one-quarter mile to find one. You are likely to encounter Cassin's and Western Kingbirds here, as well, so do not assume that every kingbird is a Tropical. Note the Tropical Kingbird's distinctly greenish back, large bill, contrasty dark ear-patch, and lack of a dark gray breast. The notched tail may not be visible. Most important, listen for the Tropical's twittering, high-pitched song—quite distinct from the guttural *C'mere!* of a Cassin's or the querulous *What-a-deal-we've-got!* calls of Western Kingbirds.

First pond at Kino Springs has been reliable for Common Moorhen, but keep an eye open for Green Kingfisher perched on the low branches overhanging the water.

Duck-watchers will welcome the walk to the far end of the pond to the area by the caved-in old boat dock. Often, a flock of Black-bellied Whistling-Ducks is resting on the opposite bank. From late April to mid-May 1990, the Kino Springs golf-course pond hosted a Fulvous Whistling-Duck, strictly a vagrant to southeast Arizona. A hybrid Eurasian Wigeon wintered here at least three times in the early 1990s. This is also a good spot to see a beautiful male Cinnamon Teal in winter. Cormorants—usually Double-crested but occasionally Neotropic—are possible.

The swallow flocks here can be amazing. During the prolonged migration periods, it is not uncommon to detect five or six species in a single flock of 50 to 500 birds. Even two Cave Swallows were high-graded from one such mixed flock in August 1992. Remember to scan the banks for Green Heron and check the trees for Gray Hawk (summer), Zone-tailed Hawk (summer) or a sleeping Great Horned Owl. Sometimes a flock of Black-crowned Night-Herons roosts in one of the trees on the far end of the lake.

Red-winged Blackbirds, Yellow-headed Blackbirds (erratic, but especially likely in winter), and Great-tailed Grackles are far more common at the golf-course pond than at the first pond. Otherwise, the bird lists for both ponds at Kino Springs are much the same; nevertheless, they should both be checked on every trip.

To continue this tour, return to Highway 82 and prepare to turn right. *Look both ways.* The Kino Springs junction lies at the bottom a steep hill on the left and a bridge on the right. Traffic can be treacherous. Don't try to pull out onto Highway 82 unless traffic is clear for a long distance in both directions. After turning right (east) onto Highway 82, you will cross the Santa Cruz River. Here, again, you may see a Gray Hawk, but it is very unsafe to stop or even slow down on the bridge or on the curve beyond.

The next birding site is Nogales Airport (2.8 miles). This is an optional stop only, primarily for Botteri's and Cassin's Sparrows after the summer monsoons have begun. Turn right into the lush mesquite grassland at the airport entrance to find the sparrows.

The left (west) turn-off into **Patagonia Lake State Park** (3.8 miles) leads to a more important stop. This 265-acre lake on lower Sonoita Creek was constructed in 1968 primarily for fishing and water-skiing. Since then, however, it has become a reliable location for Neotropic Cormorant. To find the cormorants, follow the paved and winding road to the entrance station (3.9 miles), then bear right 100 yards later near the bottom of the hill. From here the road runs almost straight east through the campground until it ends at the trailhead (0.4 mile). The day-use fee is $5 per car. Day-use hours for non-campers are from 8:00am to 10:00pm.

Views of the "no wake area" in the upper lake (where larger boats and water-skiing are prohibited) can be had by hiking a short distance on the trail. The lake is 2.5 miles long and nearly 0.5 mile wide—a scope is essential. Both Double-crested and Neotropic Cormorants share the upper basin, and, without a scope, it's very difficult to distinguish between these species. In winter, scan the lake carefully for Common Loon, Pied-billed and Eared Grebes, and deep-water ducks such as Common Goldeneye, Bufflehead, and Common Merganser. Don't forget to check the trees—both Osprey and Merlin are recorded during winter.

The 0.6-mile-long trail winds down to the back side of the reeds on the near (south) shoreline. With careful perusal, in winter, you may find Virginia Rail, Sora, Common Snipe, Marsh Wren, Common Yellowthroat, and Swamp Sparrow slipping among the stems. Eventually, the trail dead-ends at Sonoita Creek.

For the intrepid, who don't mind wading, it is possible to cross Sonoita Creek and follow horse-hoofprints to an old road that stays on the north side of the canyon all the way to a ranch fence (about 1.0 mile). Thornscrub on the hillsides, in conjunction with foothill canyon groves, creates a subtropical habitat that is rare in Arizona. Irregular, but potential, species here are Ruddy Ground-Dove (winter), Violet-crowned

Hummingbird (summer), Thick-billed Kingbird (summer), Rose-throated Becard (summer), and Varied Bunting (summer). All of these species are more commonly found and more easily accessed upstream a few miles at the Patagonia Roadside Rest Area. An Elegant Trogon has twice wintered along lower Sonoita Creek in the past decade. Rock Wren and Green-tailed Towhee, however, are the regular winter fare.

The best bird ever recorded at Patagonia Lake was a male Black-vented Oriole in April 1991. Although a previous sighting was reported from Cave Creek Canyon in the Chiricahua Mountains 20 years earlier, a photograph of this individual provided indisputable documentation. The Black-vented Oriole was eating oranges supplied by a camper.

Return to Highway 82 and turn left (north) to continue this tour. The next stop at the **Patagonia Roadside Rest Area** (3.3 miles) on the right (east) side of the highway is one of the most famous roadside birding areas in the world. At least two first records of birds in the United States have come from here: Black-capped Gnatcatcher in May 1971 and Yellow Grosbeak in June 1971. The first Rose-throated Becard seen this century in Arizona was discovered along Sonoita Creek in September 1947. More "life-list" becards come from the little colony that presently lives along this section of Sonoita Creek than anywhere else in the United States.

The Patagonia Roadside Rest Area is no more than a 0.3-mile-long stretch of old pavement that parallels repositioned Highway 82 at the base of a steep ridge. There are several concrete picnic tables set in a long, narrow island of cottonwood, ash, and walnut trees that divide the Rest Area from the highway. Sonoita Creek lies on the opposite side of the highway. Birders should walk along the Rest Area road in search of summering Gray Hawk, White-winged Dove, Broad-billed and Black-chinned Hummingbirds, Cassin's and Thick-billed Kingbirds, Brown-crested Flycatcher, Northern Beardless-Tyrannulet, Phainopepla, Bell's Vireo, Hooded and Bullock's Orioles, Summer Tanager, Pyrrhuloxia, and Rufous-crowned Sparrow. Listen for the melodic, descending whistles of Canyon Wrens cascading down from the cliffs on the north end of the Rest Area, as well as for the excited chittering of White-throated Swifts, which nest in crevices in the same rocks.

The arid thornscrub on the hillside is excellent for Varied Buntings. Males typically sing from the highest-available exposed perches. In 1969, Five-striped Sparrows were discovered breeding in this area, and, by 1975, the population had reached 25 birds. The following summer, only 4 returned, and, ultimately, all the sparrows vanished. Nonetheless, the habitat seems perfect for Five-stripes, and, sooner or later, they will probably be back. Equally unpredictable, observations of Ferruginous Pygmy-Owl have been separated by calendar years since the first one was detected in June 1975. Here, too, a Buff-collared Nightjar was calling in July 1975. The Roadside Rest Area is still producing tropical rarities: a Yellow Grosbeak spent four days here in June 1994.

At a point directly opposite the north end of the Patagonia Roadside Rest Area, across the highway, a trail created by birders drops down under the big Arizona Sycamore trees that grow along Sonoita Creek. Within 10 yards, it encounters a tautly-strung barbed-wire fence marking the property-line of the Circle Z Guest Ranch. From there, the path turns upstream and parallels the fence for approximately 150 yards. *Do not trespass on Circle Z Guest Ranch property.*

This trail offers the best vantage points for seeing Rose-throated Becards. Almost any summer, one or two pairs are in residence in the streamside sycamores. They nest in huge, loosely-woven, globular structures, either hanging straight above the water or dangling directly over the trail. Finding the nests is easy, but finding the occupants can take luck and patience. Listen for the their thin, high, shrill little cries that suddenly die off like a ricocheting BB shot. Rose-throated Becards ordinarily arrive in early May. They fledge their young by mid-August, and then disperse before departing in September. After the young leave the nest, the becards are as likely to be seen in the trees in the median between the highway and the Rest Area as in the riparian grove along Sonoita Creek.

Even if it's a slow day for becards, the canyon grove may be teeming with birds. This is one of the best places to see Gray Hawk, as well as Thick-billed Kingbird. Other interesting species to look for include Zone-tailed Hawk, Violet-crowned Hummingbird, Northern Beardless-Tyrannulet, Phainopepla, Lucy's and Yellow Warblers, Yellow-breasted Chat, and Lesser Goldfinch. Watch the far hillside for Collared Peccary (locally known as Javelina) and Desert Mule Deer, especially at daybreak. Both bird and mammal activity subsides after 10am.

By now, it is late enough for either lunch or supper (unless you drove straight through from Tucson, 63 miles away). It may even be time to scout up lodging or a campground for the night. Drive into Patagonia (4.2 miles). Although the population of Patagonia is only approximately 1,200, there are four restaurants, a grocery store, one RV park, five bed-and-breakfasts, and one small hotel. The town park on the right side of Highway 82 offers a shady and tranquil area with restrooms and a water-fountain for those who bring their own picnics. *No camping or picnicking is permitted in the Patagonia-Sonoita Creek Preserve.*

Vermilion Flycatcher
Narca Moore-Craig

To continue this loop, turn left (west) off Highway 82 opposite the park restrooms onto 4th Avenue (there is a bar on the southwest corner of the intersection with the highway). Go two blocks and turn left (south) onto Pennsylvania Avenue. It soon becomes a dirt road that crosses Sonoita Creek on a concrete-lined ford (0.2 mile from Highway 82). *Do not attempt to cross Sonoita Creek if barriers are in place or if the stream is obviously flash-flooding.* (Even parking by a "dry" crossing is inadvisable; a flash flood might fill the creekbed with little warning.)

Your next stop depends on the time of the day, day of the week, season of the year, and—to a lesser extent—the birds that you wish see. A visit to the hummingbird feeders at **Wally and Marion Patons' home** on Pennsylvania Avenue is suggested—you will be welcome there any day or any time of day you're passing by. The hummingbirds tend to be present all day, even after activity dries up in the Patagonia-Sonoita Creek Preserve by mid-morning during the warmer months. The Patons' driveway is on the left side of the road 100 feet beyond the Sonoita Creek ford. A sign on their chain-link fence reads "Hummingbirders Welcome." If the small parking area by the gate is full, continue another 75 yards and *pull completely off the road* under the shade of some big Arizona Cypress trees that border the road. *Please do not block the Patons' driveway!*

The Paton home is the most dependable site for Violet-crowned Hummingbirds in the United States. Aside from Violet-crowns coming in at 10- to 20-minute intervals from March through September (and sometimes throughout the winter, too), other regular clients at their sugar-water feeders include Broad-billed, Black-chinned, and Anna's Hummingbirds. Costa's is outnumbered, but present, in spring, rare in summer and fall; Rufous Hummingbirds are uncommon in spring, but common in July and August. Allen's are undoubtedly here in late summer, but only adult males can be safely separated in the field from Rufous, and adult male Allen's Hummingbirds are rare here.

Plain-capped Starthroat is always a summer possibility anywhere in the Patagonia area, primarily from late June through late August. Starthroats exhibit a complex of characters that should render them inconfusable, but every year birders turn in erroneous reports from Patagonia. The distinct, elongated white oval on the lower back is duplicated by no other U.S. hummingbird. Only a female Magnificent (unlikely here) can match the tremendously long bill of a starthroat, and she will never show a blackish throat (the lower, diamond-shaped gorget of a starthroat has a dull, orange-red iridescence that is seldom visible). Size alone should eliminate all other Patagonia hummingbirds, for neither

Blue-throats nor Magnificents are likely to stray down to this 4,000-foot-elevation locale.

To date, there is only one acceptable record of Cinnamon Hummingbird in the United States. That bird was photographed at the Patons' home in July 1992. The Cinnamon is just another proof that this place is a magnet for hummingbirds; frequently it seems that there are more hummers at the Patons' feeding stations than at any other place in the state of Arizona.

But not only hummingbirds frequent the Patons' property. Selected other summer visitors include Great Blue Heron, Black Vulture, Gray and Zone-tailed Hawks, Gambel's Quail, Inca Dove, Yellow-billed Cuckoo, Gila and Ladder-backed Woodpeckers, Northern Beardless-Tyrannulet, Vermilion Flycatcher, Bewick's Wren, Bell's Vireo, Lucy's Warbler, Yellow-breasted Chat, Northern Cardinal, Abert's Towhee, Song Sparrow, Bronzed Cowbird, Hooded and Bullock's Orioles, and Lesser Goldfinch. In winter, watch for House Wren, Hermit Thrush, Cedar Waxwing, Green-tailed Towhee, Lincoln's, White-throated (uncommon), and White-crowned Sparrows, and Pine Siskin. Wally and Marion have even gone so far as to put up a canvas awning to shelter neat rows of chairs for visiting birders. In the summer of 1995, the Patons constructed a recirculating waterfall in order to attract even more birds. This is a very special place, and the owners are truly special people to share it so unselfishly.

It is best to visit nearby **Patagonia-Sonoita Creek Preserve** as early as possible in the morning. In 1995, the hours were 7:30am to 4:00pm, Wednesday through Sunday.

Partially to comply with visitation hours, but—more important—because the birding there can be superb, many local birders first work the upper (north) section of the Preserve from the road that bounds its west edge. Beyond the Patons' home, Sonoita Creek swings close to a bluff at the north boundary of the Preserve (0.2 mile), juxtaposing a mature Fremont Cottonwood gallery forest on the left side of the road with desertscrub dominated by Velvet Mesquite on the right. This is the area where Arizona's third Crescent-chested Warbler was discovered in September 1992. After spending the whole winter of 1992-1993 essentially between the Preserve and the Patons', what was in all probability the same bird returned to the same area for an encore performance over the winter of 1993-1994. The Crescent-chested Warbler was almost always seen in mixed flocks with Bridled Titmice and Yellow-rumped Warblers. *Park completely off the road if you bird this area and do not enter the Preserve here. Future plans call for a short trail to parallel the west side*

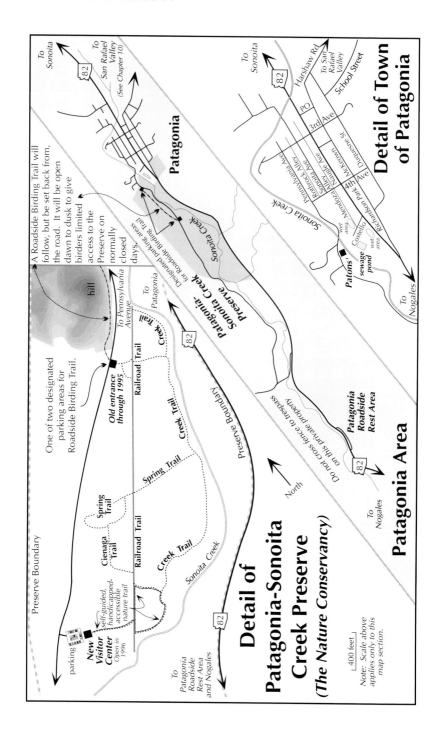

To Sonoita

To San Rafael Valley (See Chapter 10)

82

Patagonia

A Roadside Birding Trail will follow, but be set back from, the road. It will be open from dawn to dusk to give birders limited access to the Preserve on normally closed days.

hill

One of two designated parking areas for Roadside Birding Trail.

Designated parking areas for Roadside Birding Trail

Sonoita Creek

Patagonia-Sonoita Creek Preserve

Old entrance through 1995.

To Pennsylvania Avenue

To Patagonia

Preserve Boundary

Railroad Trail

Creek Trail

82

North

Spring Trail

Spring Trail

Cienaga Trail

Railroad Trail

Creek Trail

Sonoita Creek

Preserve Boundary

Self-guided, handicapped-accessible nature trail

New Visitor Center
Open in 1996

parking

Detail of Patagonia-Sonoita Creek Preserve
(The Nature Conservancy)

To Patagonia Roadside Rest Area and Nogales

82

400 feet

Note: Scale above applies only to this map section.

To Nogales

Patagonia Roadside Rest Area

82

Do not cross fence to trespass on this private property

Patagonia Area

To Sonoita

82

Harshaw Rd

To San Rafael Valley

School Street

PO

3rd Ave

Duquesne St

McKeown

4th Ave

Naugle Ave

Pennsylvania Ave

Roadside Alley

Middle Ave

Richardson Park Rd

Costello

Sonoita Creek

wet area

wet area

Patons'

sewage pond

Detail of Town of Patagonia

To Nogales

of the road along this stretch, with designated parking areas at both ends. Birders will thus be able to access this productive part of the Preserve on days when public entry is otherwise prohibited.

It's worth the effort to walk all the way through this ecological bottleneck to the former main entrance to the Preserve (0.4 mile). (This gate will be phased out in early 1996.) In summer, there is almost invariably a pair of Gray Hawks nesting in the closed area across the stream. This is also a favorite haunt for Gilded Flicker, Northern Beardless-Tyrannulet, Olive-sided (migration), Dusky-capped (summer), and Brown-crested (summer) Flycatchers, Bridled Titmouse, Rufous-backed Robin (rare, winter), Yellow (summer) and Yellow-rumped (winter) Warblers, and Yellow-breasted Chat (summer).

Cactus Wren, Verdin, Curve-billed Thrasher, and Rufous-crowned Sparrow, as well as other desert species, are likely on the thornscrub hillside to the right.

A new visitor center is scheduled for dedication in February 1996, the 30th anniversary of the Preserve's acquisition. It will be located on the south end of the Patagonia-Sonoita Creek Preserve (0.5 mile; see map). At that time the old main entrance one-half mile north will be phased out. When the Arizona Chapter of The Nature Conservancy purchased this Preserve in 1966 it contained only 312 acres; today, some 750 acres are permanently protected from development. Visitors are requested to obey a set of rules designed to perpetuate the unique wildlife and plant resource at Patagonia. *Birders must stay on established trails.*

Other environmental safeguards include bans against smoking, picnicking and camping, swimming and wading, hunting and fishing, and bicycling and horse-back riding. Additionally *no tape-players or radios are permitted* and no pets are allowed inside the Preserve. There is a $5-per-person suggested donation.

This lush oasis attracts an abundance of birds at all seasons, including many rare and exotic species. One of the flashiest has to be the Vermilion Flycatcher, which is common in summer and fairly common in winter. Other birds to look for include Gambel's Quail, Common Ground-Dove, Greater Roadrunner, Western Screech-Owl, Great Horned Owl, Acorn, Gila, and Ladder-backed Woodpeckers, Gilded and Northern "Red-shafted" Flickers, Black and Say's Phoebes, Mexican Jay, Bridled Titmouse, Verdin, Bushtit, White-breasted Nuthatch, Bewick's Wren, Eastern Bluebird, Phainopepla, Northern Cardinal, Canyon and Abert's Towhees, Song Sparrow, and Lesser Goldfinch.

In summer, watch for White-winged Dove, Yellow-billed Cuckoo, Elf Owl, Lesser Nighthawk, Common Poorwill, Broad-billed and Black-chinned Hummingbirds, Northern Beardless-Tyrannulet, Cassin's, Thick-billed, and Western Kingbirds, Dusky-capped and Brown-crested Fly-catchers, Bell's Vireo, Lucy's (especially in mesquite) and Yellow (especially in cottonwoods) Warblers, Yellow-breasted Chat, Summer Tanager, Blue Grosbeak, Lazuli and Indigo Buntings (rare), Bronzed Cowbird, and Hooded and Bullock's Orioles. Most years, there are at least three pairs of Gray Hawks raising young on the Preserve. Although Rose-throated Becards have nested in the big cottonwoods on the north end, your chances of finding one of these tropical specialties are best in the sycamores near the Patagonia Roadside Rest Area.

In winter, look for Red-naped Sapsucker, Ruby-crowned Kinglet, American Pipit, Solitary Vireo (uncommon), Orange-crowned and Yel-low-rumped "Audubon's" Warblers, Green-tailed Towhee, Dark-eyed "Oregon" and "Gray-headed" Juncos, and White-crowned and Lincoln's Sparrows, and—during irruption years—Lawrence's Goldfinch (rare). Green Kingfisher sightings usually come from the north Railroad Trail bridge abutment, and are more common in winter than in summer.

The Creek Trail is the best Preserve path for passage *Empidonax* flycatchers. Willow and Pacific-slope are strictly migrants, but a few Hammond's, Dusky, and Gray Flycatchers may pass the entire winter in the thickets that border Sonoita Creek. In December 1992, a Yellow-bel-lied Flycatcher was detected on the annual Christmas Count. Only the second accepted record of this Eastern species in Arizona, the bird lingered until the spring of 1993.

Probably the most frequently seen mammal on the Preserve is the beautiful, silvery-tailed Arizona Gray Squirrel. Other wildlife species found at Patagonia include Sonoran Opossum, Raccoon, Coati, Ring-tail, Western Spotted, Striped, Hooded, and Hog-nosed Skunks, Gray Fox, Coyote, Bobcat, Rock Squirrel, Harris's Antelope Ground-Squirrel, Ante-lope and Black-tailed Jackrabbits, Desert Cottontail, and White-tailed Deer. Many of the mammals are nocturnal and difficult to observe.

Several species of birds are more common farther south along the road than on the Preserve. As you approach the rocky, normally dry stream-crossing at Temporal Gulch (0.3 mile), be especially alert for Common Ground-Doves. The wash itself may harbor Rock Wrens. *Do not attempt to cross Temporal Wash if it is flooded.*

Soon, a series of low, scenic rocky outcrops flank the right (west) side of the road. Aside from both Rock and Canyon Wrens, this is the best area for Zone-tailed Hawk and Thick-billed Kingbird. The area on the left (east) side of the road is private property and is posted "No Trespass-

Drive slowly across this Salero Road ford of Sonoita Creek, but don't stop to bird here—it's all private property.

ing". *Do not cross the fence line. Do not stop and block this narrow, winding road. Park completely off the road.*

Make a left turn at the major intersection with Salero Road (1.3 mile). In 200 yards Salero Road crosses Sonoita Creek at a sandy ford unsuited for low-slung cars. This is the area where the first Blue Mockingbird recorded in the United States was found in December 1991. As a consequence of the actions of a few thoughtless birders who trespassed, the Circle Z Guest Ranch now asks birders *not* to stop at the ford area. A couple of hundred yards later, Salero Road ends at Highway 82 on the east side of Sonoita Creek.

Turn right (south) if you care to make a second pass at the nearby Patagonia Roadside Rest Area (0.9 mile). But to continue to the final birding area at Patagonia, turn left (north) and drive to the first street on the left (unsigned, dirt Costello Road) as you enter town on Highway 82 (2.5 miles). Go 25 yards to the junction with Mendoza Alley on the right, and park here where service vehicles will have no trouble avoiding your car. The Patagonia Sewage Ponds are in front of you.

There is usually only one species of waterfowl on the pond: Black-bellied Whistling-Duck. You can see them on the far (south) half of the pond by standing at the gate and looking to the left. *Visitors are not allowed inside.* The tall cottonwoods between Highway 82 and the far end of the pond support Patagonia's only Great Blue Heron rookery. A dozen or so nests are visible in the upper third of the trees. Wet, reedy patches on either side of the entrance drive are good for wintering Virginia Rail, Sora, and Swamp Sparrows. The area just north of the Patagonia Sewage Ponds was a favorite of the Crescent-chested Warbler for the two winters when it was present.

Exit the Patagonia Sewage Ponds up Mendoza Alley, keeping an eye peeled for any small doves. A small flock of Ruddy Ground-Doves spent the winter of 1992-1993 in downtown Patagonia, primarily in the vacant lot north of the Big Steer Bar off Main Street, but also here in Mendoza Alley. Patagonia must be the only town in the United States that can boast of Ruddy Ground-Doves—not gangs—hanging out in its alleys. Turn right onto 4th Avenue (0.2 mile), go 50 yards to return to Highway 82, and turn left (north).

Leaving Patagonia on Highway 82, you soon climb into the Sonoita Grassland, which turns lawn green after the monsoons drench the landscape in July and August. A sign on the left (west) is all that remains to mark the site of old Camp Crittenden (9.3 miles), established in 1867 and deactivated in 1873. Camp Crittenden was abandoned because the soldiers living there contracted malaria. Its desertion tells something about how marshy this area was before the drought of 1892. By the time the rains finally returned, cattle had grazed the grasses to mineral soil, and subsequent erosion cut the channel in which Sonoita Creek still runs today. Working near Camp Crittenden, the indefatigable Army surgeon Elliot Coues collected the type specimen for the small subspecies of White-tailed Deer that bears his name. "Coues Flycatcher", the old name for Greater Pewee, formerly honored this pioneer ornithologist of the American Southwest.

The little settlement of **Sonoita** (2.9 miles) is in the heart of the grassland. Here, Golden Eagle, Loggerhead Shrike, Say's Phoebe, Horned Lark, Grasshopper Sparrow, and Eastern Meadowlark are common throughout the year. Swainson's Hawks are summer residents, and Northern Harriers and Prairie Falcons course over the sweeping prairie in winter.

To sample the birds of the Sonoita Grassland, simply continue straight ahead (east) on Highway 82 at the only intersection in downtown Sonoita. A substantial gravel pile on the left (north) side of the road (0.9 mile) just beyond the last buildings offers a convenient place to park. When they are singing in late summer, this is usually a sure-fire stake-out for Cassin's Sparrows. Scan the fence-lines on both sides of the highway for Grasshopper Sparrows. If none is evident, wait until the highway is entirely clear of traffic, then watch for any small bird on the lower three strands

Prairie Falcon
Narca Moore-Craig

of barbed-wire as you continue driving east. The trick is to find a bird near a safe pull-out. East of Sonoita, until the road climbs out of the grassy headwaters of Cienaga Creek (6.5 miles), most of Highway 82 has no shoulder whatsoever. This is a truck route—*if you stop here, park completely off the pavement.* Other summer residents include Common Nighthawk (very local in Southeastern Arizona) and Western Kingbird.

Vast flocks of ground-birds move onto the Sonoita Grassland in winter. Most are Brewer's, Vesper, Savannah, and Lark Sparrows, but there may be longspurs, too. Chestnut-collared is far and away the most common longspur in the Sonoita Grassland, but McCown's is possible, also. (Specific locations for longspurs in the nearby San Rafael Valley are discussed in Chapter 10.)

A herd of Pronghorns has been introduced into the Empire-Cienaga Resource Conservation Area on the left (north) side of Highway 82. Watch for these speedsters in the tall grasses at the bottom of the swales. Sometimes, a small group of Pronghorns rests or browses, oblivious of curious human onlookers, within 100 yards of the highway. A quarter-mile off, however, is more typical.

To visit the Huachuca Mountains (Chapter 6) or the San Pedro Valley (Chapter 7), continue on Highway 82 to the Highway 90 intersection, then turn right (south) toward Sierra Vista (32.5 miles from Sonoita).

To complete this loop though, return to Sonoita and turn right (north) onto Highway 83. Lower Gardner Canyon, to the left of Highway 83, can be a good birding spot. The road to Gardner turns off west at the bottom of the first steep hill (4.1 miles). Cassin's and Botteri's Sparrows can be heard singing in July and August in the Sacaton grassland just off the highway. The next four miles of broad, grassy canyon, where the road stays in the bottom, is a good place to find Montezuma Quail. University of Arizona researchers, working with trained dogs, estimated that there were 40 adult quail per square mile in this area in the early 1960s—and that figure is probably still accurate today.

The road continues up to pine/oak woodland, but beyond the ranch (7.5 miles) it becomes very rough and rocky. The left fork (9.0 miles) continues another five miles to a basin in upper Gardner Canyon. The right fork continues a comparable distance before dead-ending in upper Cave Canyon. *You should not attempt to drive to the road ends in either Gardner or Cave Canyon without high clearance and 4-wheel-drive.* Elegant Trogons summer high up in both of these seldom visited drainages, and an Eared Trogon was found using upper Gardner Canyon in August 1991.

Back on Highway 83, continue northward. At the Greaterville Road (3.8 miles), you can choose how to end this tour. To return to the starting point in Tucson, go straight ahead (north) on Highway 83 to Interstate 10 (17.2 miles), then west on Interstate 10 (21.3 miles). If you plan to visit Madera Canyon, the Greaterville Road cuts off about 60 miles of travel. You should be aware, however, that after the pavement ends (3.1 miles), the Greaterville Road turns into a rough, rocky, steep, narrow, and wash-boarded track in Box Canyon before it rejoins the pavement leading up to Madera from Continental (10.8 miles). *Do not attempt to pull a trailer over the Greaterville Road.*

Campgrounds, Restaurants, and Accommodations:

A fee campground is available at Patagonia Lake State Park (P.O. Box 274, Patagonia, AZ 85624; telephone 520/287-6965): non-hook-up sites are $10 per night, hook-up sites are $15, and the gate is locked at 10pm and opened at 5am. Patagonia RV Park (P.O. Box 768, Patagonia, AZ 85624; telephone 520/394-2491) is located on the outskirts of Patagonia.

Gasoline, groceries, four restaurants, and other services are available in the little town of Patagonia. In Patagonia the Western-flavor Stage Stop Inn (P.O. Box 777, Patagonia, AZ 85624; telephone 520/394-2211) has a good restaurant and is only a half-mile from the Patagonia-Sonoita Creek Preserve. There are also no fewer than five bed-and-breakfast establishments to choose among: Rothrock Cottage (P.O. Box 526, Patagonia, AZ 85624; telephone 520/394-2952); The Little House B & B (P.O. Box 461, Patagonia, AZ 85624; telephone 520/394-2493); Patio B & B (P.O. Box 271, Patagonia, AZ 85624; telephone 520/394-2571); Duquesne House B & B (P.O. Box 772, Patagonia, AZ 85624; telephone 520/394-2732); and The Black Dove B & B (P.O. Box 462, Patagonia, AZ 85624; telephone 520/394-2080). Two guest ranches are also available: Circle Z Guest Ranch (P.O. Box 194, Patagonia, AZ 85624; telephone 520/287-2091) and the Crown C Ranch (P.O. Box 507, Sonoita, AZ 85637; telephone 520/455-5739).

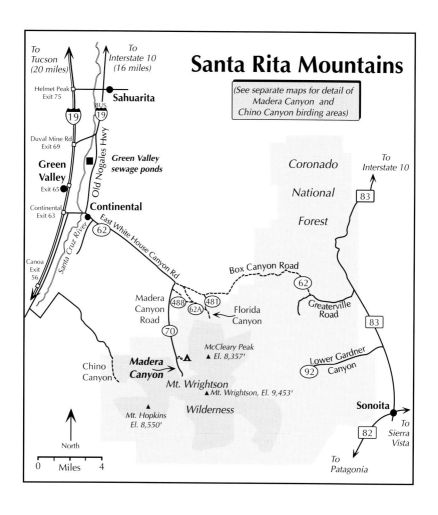

Santa Rita Mountains

(See separate maps for detail of
Madera Canyon and
Chino Canyon birding areas)

To
Tucson
(20 miles)

To
Interstate 10
(16 miles)

Helmet Peak
Exit 75

Sahuarita

BUS.
19   **19**

Old Nogales Hwy

Duval Mine Rd.
Exit 69

**Green
Valley**

*Green Valley
sewage ponds*

Exit 65

Continental
Exit 63

Continental

Santa Cruz River

62

East White House Canyon Rd

Canoa
Exit
56

Box Canyon Road

62

Madera
Canyon
Road

488

62A

481

Florida
Canyon

Greaterville
Road

83

70

McCleary Peak
▲ El. 8,357'

Chino
Canyon

**Madera
Canyon**

▲

Lower Gardner
Canyon

92

Mt. Wrightson
▲ Mt. Wrightson, El. 9,453'

Sonoita

▲
Mt. Hopkins
El. 8,550'

Wilderness

82

To
Sierra
Vista

To
Patagonia

Coronado

National

Forest

To
Interstate 10

83

North

0   Miles   4

CHAPTER 4

SANTA RITA
MOUNTAINS

(From Green Valley: 29 miles/one day)

(From Tucson: 76 miles/one day)

Madera Canyon in the Santa Rita Mountains is, perhaps, the best-known and most-often-visited birding spot in Arizona, with good reason. You can find most of the species of Southeastern Arizona within 15 linear miles. Only an hour south of Tucson, Madera Canyon is the nearest and easiest place to see the full panoply of Sierra Madrean hummingbirds, Elegant Trogon, Sulphur-bellied Flycatcher, and other pine/oak woodland specialties confined to the border ranges. If you have time to bird only a single location in spring or summer, visit Madera Canyon.

The starting point for this tour is at the Continental exit on Interstate 19. Coming south on I-19 from its junction with Interstate 10 in Tucson, it is 23.5 miles to exit 63. Turn left (east) under the freeway and continue to East White House Canyon Road (1.4 miles), located halfway through a bend in the midst of a pecan grove. To follow the main tour, turn right (south) here.

In winter, or with adequate time, an interesting side-trip is to continue straight ahead on what soon becomes the Old Nogales Highway. This little-traveled road runs north along an enormous pecan grove to a Pima County Department of Transportation maintenance yard on the left (west) side of the highway (2.1 miles). Unless it is busy, which is unusual, this provides a good place to park. A young Red-headed Woodpecker took up residency in the workyard in November 1991. By the time it disappeared in May 1992, it had molted into full adult plumage.

The perimeter trees at the maintenance area include the pecan grove and a hedgerow of mesquite. When the trees are bare in winter, you may find Orange-crowned (uncommon) and Yellow-rumped Warblers, Chipping, Brewer's, Vesper, Lark, Savannah, and White-crowned Sparrows, and Lesser, Lawrence's (rare and erratic), and American (uncommon) Goldfinches. A migrating Gray Vireo (rare) was detected here in late March 1992. *Do not enter the pecan grove.*

Continuing north on the Old Nogales Highway, the pavement now parallels an enormous artificial clearing. Keep an eye out for White-tailed Kites, which are occasionally seen along this stretch. Regularly occurring winter raptors include Northern Harrier, Red-tailed Hawk, and American Kestrel. Gambel's Quail is common in this large grassland, as are Greater Roadrunner, wintering sparrows, Lark Bunting, and wintering Western Meadowlark. The Green Valley Wastewater Ponds (0.9 mile) are on the left (west) side of the road. Officially open from 7am to 2pm weekdays (and sometimes—mysteriously—*not* open), this is a quick stop for waterfowl and shorebirds in winter and migration. Park by the maintenance building (0.3 mile) and request permission to bird the small ponds. A spotting scope will be useful here.

The shorebirds and ducks at Green Valley are neither as diverse nor as numerous as in Tucson or Nogales, but they are far more convenient for birders based in Madera Canyon. Occasionally, surprises turn up, such as a Red Phalarope in October 1993. The little ponds are, oddly, good for raptors—a Crested Caracara was recorded in December 1993. Every year produces Zone-tailed Hawk, Peregrine Falcon, and Merlin (winter) sightings. After birding the ponds, return to East White House Canyon Road (3.0 miles) to continue the Santa Rita Mountains route.

An interesting community of birds can be found in the immediate vicinity of Continental (0.3 mile). These include Gambel's Quail, Phainopepla, Bell's Vireo, Lucy's Warbler, Northern Cardinal, Pyrrhuloxia, and Hooded Oriole. In summer, look for Ash-throated Flycatcher, Western Kingbird, and Blue Grosbeak, and, in winter, Sage Thrasher (irregular), Green-tailed Towhee, and Lincoln's Sparrow. Usually, all of these can be found in Florida Wash as well—much closer to Madera. Unless you have more than one day to devote to this tour, you would be wise to go straight to Madera Canyon.

Once the road leaves the Santa Cruz bottomlands at Continental, it swings left up onto a *bajada,* or alluvial apron of material washed down from the Santa Rita Mountains since they were formed over 75 million years ago. This broad, grassy steppe is managed by the University of Arizona as the Santa Rita Experimental Range. The purple cactus with

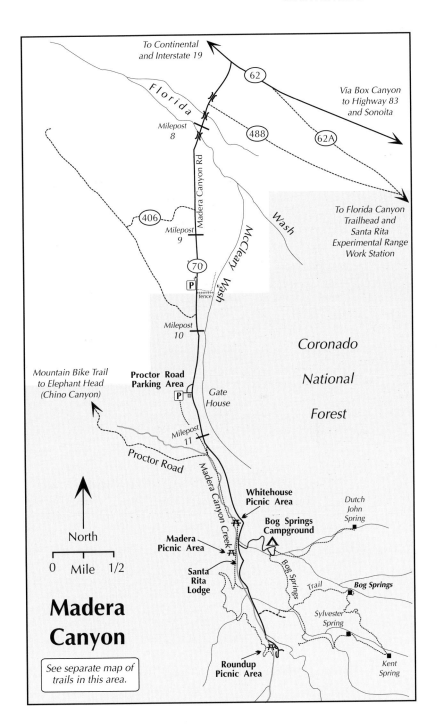

To Continental
and Interstate 19

62

Florida

Via Box Canyon
to Highway 83
and Sonoita

Milepost
8

488

62A

Madera Canyon Rd

Wash

To Florida Canyon
Trailhead and
Santa Rita
Experimental Range
Work Station

406

Milepost
9

70

P

Fence

McCleary Wash

Milepost
10

Coronado

National

Forest

Mountain Bike Trail
to Elephant Head
(Chino Canyon)

Proctor Road
Parking Area

P

Gate
House

Milepost
11

North

Proctor Road

Madera Canyon Creek

Whitehouse
Picnic Area

Bog Springs
Campground

Dutch
John
Spring

0   Mile   1/2

Madera
Picnic Area

Santa
Rita
Lodge

Bog Springs Trail

Bog Springs

Madera

Canyon

Sylvester
Spring

See separate map of
trails in this area.

Roundup
Picnic Area

Kent
Spring

In summer, look for Cassin's and Botteri's Sparrows in the desert grassland between Madera Canyon Road and Elephant Head.

the large, flat pads is Santa Rita Prickly Pear, a much sought-after ornamental in Southwest landscaping. The purple one with the small, round stems is Staghorn Cholla (CHO-yah). The abundant, large, green cholla with the chains of green fruit is called Chain Fruit Cholla.

It is rumored that joints of the Chain Fruit Cholla can actually lunge out and stick themselves to you as you pass by. This is, of course, not true, but it is hard to convince people who have had an unfortunate encounter with this species. The segments of this cholla are loosely attached because the plant's primary method of propagation is vegetative. When people or other mammals brush against the spines—even very lightly—the joint pins itself aboard. Potential new plants are thereby transported away from the parent, and that leads to an alternative name for the species—"Jumping Cholla". Use a comb or a stick to remove the piece of cactus, should you find yourself the unwitting host of a future Chain Fruit Cholla.

Some of the birds to watch for in this desert grassland are Turkey Vulture, Red-tailed Hawk, Gambel's Quail, Greater Roadrunner, Say's Phoebe, Common Raven, Verdin, Cactus Wren, Curve-billed Thrasher, and House Finch. In winter, Chipping and White-crowned Sparrows are abundant.

The rare Antelope Jackrabbit, whose range barely extends into the United States, can sometimes be found here. It is larger and paler than the more-common Black-tailed Jackrabbit, and has a habit of showing the white on its flanks as it bounds away. In addition to the hares, you should see Harris's Antelope Ground-Squirrel. Like a chipmunk it has stripes on its sides, but unlike any chipmunk, it lacks facial stripes. Chipmunks do not occur in the Santa Rita Mountains.

To continue the main tour route from the junction of Box Canyon Road (7.0), follow the pavement and turn right (south) toward the soaring blue pinnacles of the Santa Ritas. Box Canyon Road, leading east from this intersection, is the short-cut to Sonoita, Sierra Vista, and Patagonia, lopping off over 60 miles from the alternative route through Tucson. Be aware, however, that the stretch to the pavement at the Greaterville Road (10.8 miles), is steep, narrow, and badly wash-boarded. The final link to Highway 83 (3.1 miles) is paved. Vehicles pulling trailers should not use Box Canyon Road.

As a side-trip from this intersection, if you would like to visit the upper part of Florida Canyon, take unpaved Box Canyon Road (Road 62) to Road 62A (0.3 mile) which angles off to the right (east) through an area of tall grass, mesquite, and Ocotillo (Oh-co-TEE-yo). The bright red Ocotillo flowers attract Black-chinned and Costa's Hummingbirds from April to mid-May. This road passes Road 488 on the right in 1.4 miles, Road 481 on the left in 1.1 miles, and continues up Florida Canyon to the Santa Rita Experimental Range Work Center (0.4 miles). Here, by the parking lot, you will find the trailhead for the trail up Florida Canyon, which links up with other trails at Baldy Saddle (7.0 miles). Wintering Black-chinned Sparrows can often be found near the start of the trail, and the very rare Lucifer Hummingbird was found here one summer. Ordinarily, however, the birding is far better in Madera Canyon.

To continue the main tour, soon after you have turned right (south) onto Madera Canyon Road, it passes over three one-lane bridges. Scan the road on the opposite side for fast-approaching traffic before committing yourself to crossing any of these bridges. *Don't even dream of slowing down or stopping on a bridge!* The third, and final, bridge (0.8 mile) crosses **Florida Wash**. There are convenient pull-outs on both sides of the road just before the bridge, and a stile for crossing the barbed-wire fence on the left (east) side. Florida is pronounced Flow-REE-dah, and means "full of flowers" in Spanish. A walk up or down this broad, perennially dry watercourse seldom produces many flowers, but you may encounter Gambel's Quail, Ladder-backed Woodpecker, Verdin, Cactus Wren, Curve-billed or Crissal Thrashers, Phainopepla, Northern Cardinal, Pyrrhuloxia, Canyon Towhee, and Black-throated Sparrow. In summer, look for Black-chinned and Costa's (primarily spring)

Hummingbirds, Northern Beardless-Tyrannulet, Ash-throated Flycatcher, Bell's Vireo, Lucy's Warbler, and Varied Bunting.

Florida Wash is also good for the highly local Rufous-winged Sparrow. The chestnut wing patch is hard to see on most birds, but the bright, clear song is very distinctive. Luckily, Rufous-winged Sparrows sing a lot. Listen for two or three opening chips followed by a trill.

The only other summer sparrows here are Black-throated and Rufous-crowned, which also occur higher up where canyons enter the foothills. Rufous-crowned is superficially similar to Rufous-winged, but Rufous-crowned Sparrow is a much huskier bird with a solid rusty crown, and a bold, black moustachial stripe. In winter, there are a number of other sparrows. Immature White-crowned could possibly be confused with Rufous-winged, but White-crowns of any age always show an orange or pink bill.

Dense patches of mesquite and thornscrub along the streambed constitute prime Crissal Thrasher habitat. The bright rufous undertail coverts and strong malar stripe are good field marks, but be sure to note the bill shape and eye color. Curve-billed Thrasher, also common in Florida Wash, lacks the scythe-like bill of a Crissal, and has a bright golden eye, not the dull eye of a Crissal Thrasher.

After crossing Florida Wash, Madera Canyon Road runs south arrow-straight over the next several miles of desert grassland, as if aimed directly at the Smithsonian Astrophysical Observatory on top of 8,585-foot-high Mt. Hopkins. The giant, multiple mirror telescope, positioned on the summit of Mt. Hopkins in 1979, is one of the most advanced telescopes in the world. Use this opportunity to familiarize yourself with the topography of Madera. The 7,100-foot-high pass left (east) of the observatory is called Josephine Saddle. The massive volcanic dome all the way to the left (east) is Mt. Wrightson, at an elevation of 9,453 feet the highest point in the Santa Rita Mountains. With the highest and most expansive drainage-area in the range, it is not surprising that Madera is the best-watered canyon in the Santa Ritas.

Continuing up Madera Canyon Road above Florida Wash, you will come to Forest Road 406 (0.6 mile) on the right (west). Both Botteri's and Cassin's Sparrows nest along this dirt track during the rainy season in July and August. With some practice, you may notice that Botteri's tends to look browner, but unless you manage a prolonged, full-frame scope view, it is best to separate the two by song. Botteri's sings a "rock-and-roll" jumble of short, hard notes; Cassin's song is composed of clear, long-drawn notes, infinitely poignant.

Farther up the canyon, you will come to a cattle-guard (0.7 mile; 1.3 miles above the Florida Wash Bridge). This is the famous **Buff-collared Nightjar site in McCleary Wash** (which is often erroneously referred to as Florida Wash). There is an ample dirt pull-out on the right (west) side

Whiskered Screech-Owl
Georges Dremeaux

of the Madera Canyon Road on the down-slope (north) side of the cattle-guard. A cobbly trail created by birders begins across the road from the parking area, passes through a wire gate (please shut it behind you), and parallels the fence-line for 150 yards east to the edge of McCleary Wash. A viewpoint between two large Ocotillos here overlooks the quarter-mile-wide floodplain of the big, dry drainage.

To hear the Buff-collared Nightjar, plan to arrive soon after sundown to take a position. Don't forget a sweater—the cold air sinking from 8,357-foot-high McCleary Peak off the north end of the Santa Rita crest can plunge temperatures more than 20 degrees within a half-hour after sunset.

The nightjar is most likely to vocalize at late dusk between mid-April and June. In spite of a well-publicized protocol that asks birders to *refrain from playing tapes to attract the Buff-collareds*, the pair of nightjars in McCleary Wash is probably exposed to more taped playbacks of their ascending, piano-like song than any other pair of birds in all Southeastern Arizona. The miracle is that they returned to nest every year through 1994, since they were originally discovered at this site in 1985. Like other over-taped species, however, they were soon "taped-out", and seldom responded to recordings of their song after the middle of May. *Do not use tapes here.*

To see the Buff-collared Nightjar, therefore, you will need a powerful light. Like Whip-poor-wills, the Buff-collared hunts moths and other nocturnal insects from tree-perches. Pan your light across the dead branches that project above the mesquites that fill the wash. *Don't go thrashing about down among the rattlesnakes in the wash, but stay on top* and look for the nightjars' glowing orange eyeshine. Buff-collareds tend to use the same perch for multiple sallies, and they rest only briefly between each foray. Common Poorwills, by contrast, most often use ground-perches and, generally, do not return repeatedly to the same place.

There are more Common Poorwills at McCleary Wash than Buff-collared Nightjars. Skepticism is in order. When possible, use voice to separate the two species; but if the bird in question is silent, note the Buff-collared Nightjar's Whip-poor-will-like proportions, especially its long tail. Poorwills have comparatively short tails and a bull-headed jizz. The buffy hindcollar of this rare nightjar is difficult to discern at night without a spotting scope and a bright light.

There are many other reasons for an evening visit to McCleary Wash. Listen for the songs of both Botteri's and Cassin's Sparrows in the nearby desert grassland, and watch for Rufous-crowned Sparrows on the rocky brink of the ravine. Given the superb acoustics, you may even hear a herd of Desert Mule Deer walking along the far side of the wash before you pick out their soft gray shapes in the gathering dusk. As evening descends, the monotonous, tri-noted mimicry of Northern Mockingbird is the most typical bird song emanating from the dark thickets below. Check behind you for the fluttery flight of a Lesser Nighthawk (summer) over the grassland. The western sunsets over Baboquivari Peak, 40 miles away—the sacred peak of the Tohono O'odham Nation—are invariably spectacular. Twenty-five miles due north, the lights of Tucson gradually appear at the base of the solid-black silhouette of the Santa Catalina Mountains. The quavering, high-pitched wails and yips in the distance come from the original song-dog, the Coyote. Once the sky is fully dark, a Western Screech-Owl or a Great Horned Owl may join the evening chorus. With or without the Buff-collared Nightjar, this is one of Southeastern Arizona's most enjoyable birding spots.

Flocks of Mountain Bluebirds (irregular) are partial to the grassland between the McCleary Wash parking area and **Proctor Road Parking Area** (1.2 miles) during some winters. In spring, look for a Common Raven nest on a telephone pole on the right (west) side of the road in the same area. On weekends and holidays, all traffic is funneled through an entrance station staffed by volunteers. A $2-per-vehicle donation to the Friends of Madera Canyon is suggested. On extremely busy weekends, visitors may be turned back if the canyon is "full."

The Proctor Road Parking Area is the trailhead for a paved and bridged Forest Service trail that follows lower Madera Creek upstream all the way to the Madera Picnic Area (1.3 miles) and beyond. Walking at least part of this trail is suggested. In summer, try to arrive before sunrise for the most activity. Birds at the Proctor Road Parking Area include Ash-throated Flycatcher, Verdin, Phainopepla, Northern Cardinal, and Blue Grosbeak. Look for Varied Bunting in the mesquite and Ocotillo thickets that edge the lot.

The best birding is along the stream. As the trail descends through dense oak and hackberry watch for Ladder-backed Woodpecker, Northern Beardless-Tyrannulet, Bell's Vireo, and Lucy's Warbler. The trail strikes the streambottom in 200 yards near the old Proctor Road. In this area look for Black Phoebe, Cedar Waxwing (winter), Summer Tanager (summer), Lazuli Bunting (migration), Lincoln's Sparrow (winter), Hooded Oriole (summer), and Lesser Goldfinch. The first U.S. record of Five-striped Sparrow came from the mouth of Madera Canyon in June 1957. It has not been seen in this area since. Other vagrants of note include breeding Thick-billed Kingbirds from 1963 through 1965 and a Rose-throated Becard in May 1979.

Madera Creek above the Proctor Road crossing is one of the best rarity-traps in the Santa Rita Mountains. Some years, a Greater Pewee winters between the ford and the Madera Picnic Area on the upper end of the trail. Also, in winter, a Louisiana Waterthrush has been annual along Madera Creek above Proctor Road since at least 1990.

Proctor Road proper (0.2 mile beyond the paved parking area) is a rocky, rough, steep dirt track that crosses the stream (0.1 mile), and continues on as a 4-wheel-drive route through a habitat of stunted oak and mesquite. It is a favorite with Tucson mountain-bikers. Because the birds are the same as those found in Florida Wash and at the Proctor Road Parking Area, it is suggested that you *not* wreck your car on this hot and dusty detour to nowhere.

The Madera Picnic Area (1.0 mile), on the right (west) side opposite the Bog Springs Campground junction, presents a lush, new habitat to explore. From here to the end of the road, you will be in the Sierra Madrean pine/oak woodlands of the Upper Sonoran Life Zone. In a serendipitous and unusual overlap of geopolitical and ecological boundaries, Madera Canyon Road leaves Pima County and enters Santa Cruz County just 100 feet up the road from the picnic area. Elegant Trogon, Sulphur-bellied Flycatcher, and Painted Redstart are the typical summer birds of upper Madera Canyon.

The Madera Picnic Grounds can be a delightful place to bird, although on weekends you may have to share the place with 50 or more noisy non-birders. In summer, you should see Western Wood-Pewee, Painted Redstart, Hepatic Tanager, and Black-headed Grosbeak. The huge syca-mores over the lower tables usually host a pair of nesting Sulphur-bellied Flycatchers, which can easily be located by their high-pitched, squeaky calls. At night, narcissistic Whip-poor-wills repeat their names from the shadows of the live oaks, and Common Poorwills do the same from positions on the oak hillside across the stream. In July 1993, a Yellow-throated Vireo spent most of the month grooming the picnic-area trees.

A hike downstream from the picnic grounds can be productive in the early morning. The stillness is broken by the loud cries of Cassin's Kingbirds in the sycamores and by the trilling of Canyon Tree Frogs from the water. A pair of Black Phoebes calls *p-seee* from near their nest under the bridge. Listen for the harsh whinny of a Strickland's Woodpecker nesting in a big cottonwood. The west bank of the stream is worth inspection, also. Look for Canyon Wren on rocky ledges, and for Bewick's Wren and Bushtit among the Emory Oaks.

Three very similar *Myiarchus* flycatchers summer here—Dusky-capped, Ash-throated, and Brown-crested. Separating these three bushy-crested flycatchers seems difficult at first, but with sufficient practice one can attain mastery. The smallest is the Dusky-capped. This species has a dark crest and a long, thin bill. Adults lack rufous in the tail, and its trailing, *peeur* whistle is one of the characteristic sounds of Sierra Madrean pine/oak woodland. The medium-sized Ash-throated Fly-catcher has a comparatively short bill and a medium-sized brown crest, gives a soft-voiced, burry *ka-brick* call, and its cinnamon tail is tipped with dark corners. The weak-sulfur color of its belly is softer and less noticeable than the pale-yellow bellies of both Dusky-capped and Brown-crested Flycatchers. Distinctly larger, the kingbird-size Brown-crested has a long, thick bill and narrow rufous inner webs extending to

Elf Owl with
  Black-headed Snake
Narca Moore-Craig

the tail tip, and its loud, clear *whilp* and *whit-or-bew* notes ring out exclusively from the tall trees along Madera Creek.

Opposite the picnic ground is the paved road to the Bog Springs Campground (0.5 mile). Situated on an arid slope well above the canyon floor, the camp is not particularly good for birding. Bog Springs itself can be reached from a small, dirt road that takes off from the third campsite on the right (south) as you enter the camp. Walk this narrow, sandy road to the top of a little rise (0.7 mile). A steel sign on the left indicates the well-used trail that climbs to Bog Springs (0.8 mile). A pair of truly stupendous Silverleaf Oaks among the tall Arizona Sycamores marks the site of the spring.

Birds to look for here are Northern Pygmy-Owl, Elegant Trogon (summer), Sulphur-bellied Flycatcher (summer), House Wren, Grace's Warbler (summer), and Painted Redstart (summer). In the open woodland on the dry hillsides look for Strickland's Woodpecker, Ash-throated Flycatcher (summer), Bushtit, Hutton's Vireo, and Black-throated Gray Warbler (summer). A Flame-colored Tanager was discovered at Bog Springs in May 1994, and three of these tropical tanagers were using the area in May 1995.

Santa Rita Lodge (0.15 mile), elevation 5,000 feet, is situated smack in the heart of this great birding area. The gift shop has a good selection of gifts, books, and bird checklists. Visitors are welcome to watch the feeders from a parking lot on the right side of the road. *Please respect the privacy of the guests. No snacks or public restrooms are available. Picnicking is prohibited.* With advance reservations, visitors are also welcome to participate in a series of nature programs and bird walks offered periodically in spring and summer. There is a small charge. Contact the lodge for the schedule of events. To stay at the Santa Rita Lodge during the prime spring and summer months, birders should make reservations a year in advance. Call 520/625-8746 or write: HC 70 Box 5444, Sahuarita, AZ 85629.

Some of the regularly occurring birds at this point in Madera Canyon are Turkey Vulture, Zone-tailed Hawk (summer), Golden Eagle (rare), Montezuma Quail (rare), White-winged Dove (summer), Whip-poor-will (summer), White-throated Swift (summer), Northern "Red-Shafted" Flicker, Acorn and Strickland's Woodpeckers, Western Wood-Pewee (summer), Dusky-capped, Brown-crested, and Sulphur-bellied Flycatchers (summer), Mexican Jay, Common Raven, Bridled Titmouse, Bushtit, White-breasted Nuthatch, Brown Creeper, Bewick's and Canyon Wrens, Eastern Bluebird (rare), Hermit Thrush, Solitary (summer) and Hutton's Vireos, Black-throated Gray Warbler (summer), Painted Redstart, Hepatic Tanager (summer), Black-headed Grosbeak (summer), Rufous-sided Towhee, Yellow-eyed Junco, Bronzed and Brown-headed Cowbirds (summer), Scott's Oriole (summer), and House Finch. Migration brings Red-naped Sapsucker, Olive-sided Flycatcher (uncommon), Warbling Vireo, Townsend's and Hermit Warblers, and Western Tanager. In winter, look for Ruby-crowned Kinglet, Townsend's Solitaire, American Robin, Dark-eyed Junco, and Cassin's Finch (irregular).

Beginning in the last decade, a Painted Redstart or two has overwintered at the Lodge and at private upcanyon residences, adding a new dimension to the annual Christmas Count. Joining them at the sugar-water feeders sometimes are one or two Blue-throated (one in the winter of 1994-1995) and Magnificent Hummingbirds.

The Santa Rita Lodge is justifiably famous for its hummingbirds. In summer, Broad-billed, Blue-throated, Magnificent, Black-chinned, Anna's, and Broad-tailed are the common species. Costa's is an uncommon wanderer upslope from Florida Wash. Rufous Hummingbirds, uncommon in spring, pass through in droves in late summer and fall, accompanied by an occasional Allen's. (Only adult male Allen's is field separable.) Calliope is rare in spring and uncommon in fall. The sought-after and seldom-seen Sierra Madrean specialties include White-eared, Berylline, Violet-crowned, and Lucifer Hummingbirds. In a feat that brings new insight into this unique family's powers of flight, a Berylline Hummingbird banded in Ramsey Canyon one July afternoon in 1987, appeared at the feeders at the Santa Rita Lodge the following morning. The straight-line distance between Ramsey and Madera Canyons is 40 miles. An immature Blue-throated Hummingbird navigated the same route overnight the following month.

Santa Rita Lodge is also renowned for two species of owls. At dusk, every evening from April through June, guests and visitors gather to watch for the tiny visage of an Elf Owl framed in its utility-pole nest-hole. At last, almost to an audible gasp from the gallery, the one-ounce parent shoots out into the night to begin foraging for its offspring. Whiskered Screech-Owl is the other specialty species. Like Elf Owl, the Whiskered Screech-Owl has been known to use Acorn Woodpecker holes in power-line poles for nest cavities at the Santa Rita Lodge. More frequently, one is sighted behind the lodge or below the Madera Picnic Area on a day-roost in a sycamore cavity overlooking Madera Creek.

Birders will have to find these owls and the canyon's other species without using tapes—*the Forest Service has forbidden the use of all bird tapes in Madera Canyon*. With patience, it may be possible to view an owl calling from a fixed position.

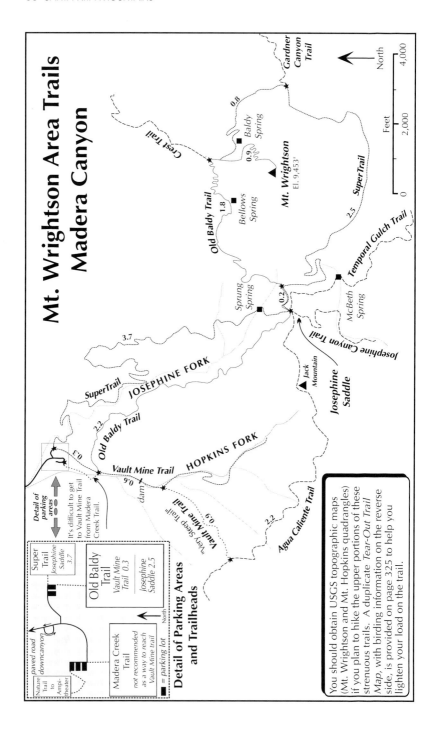

Mt. Wrightson Area Trails
Madera Canyon

Gardner Canyon Trail

North

Feet

4,000

2,000

0

Crest Trail

0.8

Baldy Spring

0.9

Mt. Wrightson
El. 9,453'

1.8

Bellows Spring

Old Baldy Trail

SuperTrail

2.5

Temporal Gulch Trail

McBeth Spring

Sprung Spring

0.2

3.7

SuperTrail

JOSEPHINE FORK

Josephine Canyon Trail

Jack Mountain

Josephine Saddle

2.2

Old Baldy Trail

0.3

HOPKINS FORK

Vault Mine Trail

0.6

dam

Very Steep Trail

Vault Mine Trail

0.9

2.2

Agua Caliente Trail

Detail of parking areas

It's difficult to get to Vault Mine Trail from Madera Creek Trail.

Super Trail
Josephine Saddle
3.7

Old Baldy Trail
Vault Mine Trail 0.3
Josephine Saddle 2.5

Madera Creek Trail
not recommended as a way to reach Vault Mine trail

Nature Trail to Ampi-theater

paved road downcanyon

North

■ = parking lot

Detail of Parking Areas and Trailheads

You should obtain USGS topographic maps (Mt. Wrightson and Mt. Hopkins quadrangles) if you plan to hike the upper portions of these strenuous trails. A duplicate *Tear-Out Trail Map*, with birding information on the reverse side, is provided on page 325 to help you lighten your load on the trail.

The Madera Amphitheater is located on the right (west) side of the road—an easy quarter-mile walk above the lodge. A nature trail, with labeled plants along the first 200 yards, begins at the Amphitheater. Beyond the stream, the trail climbs the dry west hillside before it rejoins the road in the lowest parking area in the Hopkins Fork of Madera Canyon (1.7 miles). From there you can walk back down the road to your vehicle, or you can arrange a car shuttle with another birder. The birding is not particularly good along the trail, but there are repeated views of Madera Canyon backdropped by Mt. Wrightson 4,000 feet above.

Palisport Gift Shop (0.6 mile above the Amphitheater; 0.85 mile above Santa Rita Lodge), is located just beyond the second of two one-lane bridges. Parking is limited to two or three vehicles here; *do not park on the road.* Sometimes there are more hummingbirds at the concentration of feeders here than are visible from any one spot at Santa Rita Lodge. A female Lucifer was using the feeders at Palisport in July and August 1990. A pair of Flame-colored Tanagers nested, albeit unsuccessfully, uphill from Palisport in the summer of 1992.

Just beyond the gift shop, the road divides around an oval planted with introduced Arizona Cypress trees (0.1 mile). The lanes rejoin in 50 yards, just short of a "T" junction. The road on the left leads to a two-tier parking area on the west side of the Josephine Fork of Madera Creek (0.1 mile). Most birders will want to use this road. The fork on the right passes the Roundup Picnic Area and ends at a tri-level parking area on the east side of the Hopkins Fork of Madera Creek (0.1 mile). The lower lot in the Hopkins Fork is the well-signed upper end of the Madera Nature Trail. Both lots fill up with hikers on weekends and holidays; no overnight camping is allowed.

The **Hopkins Fork** of Madera Canyon is both the best and the most popular destination for birders who care to hike. To reach the trailhead, it is recommended that you turn left just beyond the oval to reach the uppermost Josephine Fork parking area. A cable on the right, uphill end of the lot marks the easiest point of access for Hopkins Fork.

An abandoned dirt road contours 0.3 mile across the ridge that divides Josephine Fork from the Hopkins Fork of upper Madera Canyon. It joins the Hopkins Fork near the beginning of the Old Baldy (an alternative, unofficial name for Mt. Wrightson) Trail in 0.3 mile. This steep short-cut to Josephine Saddle is 2.2 miles long (instead of the 3.7-mile alternative). Birders should ignore the Old Baldy Trail and take the route continuing straight up the bottom of Hopkins Fork.

Probably the first bird that you encounter here will be a House Wren. The upper branches of Madera Canyon have the largest concentration of

House Wrens in Southeastern Arizona. A few minutes of quiet observation, on a given spring morning, should be enough to see one enter a nest-cavity in a sycamore. One of a handful of Aztec Thrushes discovered in Madera Canyon was found using the stretch of Hopkins Fork immediately above the Old Baldy Trail junction in August 1989. Elegant Trogons have tried to nest just below the trail junction, but photographers invariably cause these nests to fail.

The most reliable area for Elegant Trogons in the Hopkins Fork has traditionally been in the basin one-quarter mile farther upcanyon. The trail follows the left side of the stream for a couple hundred yards, then climbs a steep and rocky hill. Links of an old pipeline are frequent up to a concrete spring-box on the right side of the path. This marks the lower end of the trogon-nesting zone, although pairs patrol the whole length of Hopkins Fork. Other summering species that share the big Silverleaf Oaks and Alligator Junipers in the shady basin include Cooper's Hawk, Flammulated Owl, Magnificent Hummingbird, Greater Pewee, Cordilleran, Dusky-capped, and Sulphur-bellied Flycatchers, Solitary and Hutton's Vireos, Grace's Warbler, Painted Redstart, and Hepatic Tanager. Warbling Vireo, and Western Tanager are common in migration. One or two Red-faced Warblers are often here in April and May. Look for a nesting pair of Painted Redstarts near a permanent spring that cascades between a pair of slab-like boulders just 100 yards above the spring-box. This little falls is trimmed with flowering Golden Columbine in May. Two Aztec Thrushes were discovered using the stretch of Hopkins Fork above the spring-box in August 1994.

The trail crosses the stream in a quarter-mile, then divides 200 yards beyond. The Vault Mine Trail to the Agua Caliente Trail is the "very steep trail" mentioned on the sign at the trailhead. *(It leads one-half mile to the abandoned Vault Mine, over 600 feet above. The Vault Mine Trail above this junction is not recommended.)* Birders who still have not seen the trogon should veer left another 200 yards up the bottom of Hopkins Fork to where the trail disappears into the rocks of the stream channel itself. The quarter-mile stretch above the stream-crossing to where the trail ends in the streambed is just as good for trogons as the quarter-mile stretch below the stream-crossing. If the trogons are nesting you may have to wait patiently all morning for a nest-exchange before a bird passes by. *Under no circumstances should you disturb or knowingly approach an active nest tree.* From here back to the Josephine Fork parking area is 0.9 mile.

At the left (northeast) end of the **Josephine Fork** parking area, you will find the start of the eight-mile-long Super Trail to Mount Wrightson. If you have plenty of stamina, this scenic path is great for birding. *Don't forget to carry plenty of water.* At first, you will be in the oak belt, and the birds will be about the same as those which occupy the middle canyon near the Santa Rita Lodge. Elegant Trogons occasionally nest in sycamores along the stream, approximately one mile up Josephine. A male Tropical Parula was using this area of Josephine from mid-July to mid-September 1984; a possible female Tropical Parula was seen with the male, for one day only, in late July.

After one mile, the trail makes a sharp switchback to the left to climb a dry hillside. Hutton's Vireo, Black-throated Gray Warbler, and Scott's Oriole are the typical birds. Approximately three miles above the Josephine parking area, the trail enters a Ponderosa Pine forest, the home of Greater Pewee, Grace's Warbler, and Yellow-eyed Junco. Watch for Red-faced Warbler at Sprung Spring (3.8 miles above the parking area). This is about as low as the Red-faced Warbler is found in the nesting season. The first Eared Trogon recorded in the Santa Rita Mountains was sighted here in July 1991. There were two more sightings from nearby areas during the following month, but none subsequently. Josephine Saddle is only 0.2 mile beyond. The elevation-change between the 5,400-foot-high parking area and 7,100-foot-high Josephine Saddle is approximately 1,700 feet.

In the forested glades of the remaining four miles on the Super Trail to the 9,453-foot-high summit of Mt. Wrightson, you should find a community of Transition and Canadian Life Zone birds which includes Broad-tailed Hummingbird, Hairy Woodpecker, Steller's Jay, Red-breasted and Pygmy Nuthatches, Brown Creeper, House Wren, Yellow-rumped, Grace's, Red-faced, and Olive Warblers, Hepatic and Western Tanagers, Yellow-eyed Junco, Red Crossbill (irregular), and Pine Siskin. The Baldy Saddle area (elevation 8,800 feet; 0.9 mile below Mt. Wrightson) is a particularly good location for most of these species. In May 1993, a Buff-breasted Flycatcher was reported from the saddle. All of these birds occur at road-accessible locations in the high Santa Catalina, Huachuca, or Chiricahua Mountains. But there is nothing quite like the satisfaction of seeing them in the 25,260-acre Mt. Wrightson Wilderness Area.

Campgrounds, Restaurants, and Accommodations:

Bog Springs Campground, Madera Picnic Area, and Roundup Picnic Area in Madera Canyon have water, tables, fire pits, and toilets, but no showers. Camping overnight is permitted only at Bog Springs Campground.

Continental Feedlot Cafe in downtown Continental serves hearty breakfasts after 7am. Other restaurants are located at interstate exits in Green Valley.

The Santa Rita Lodge (HC 70 Box 5444, Sahuarita, AZ 85629; telephone 520/625-8746) is a popular spot. Each room and cabin has a picture-window that looks out on bird-feeders. Make reservations for spring and summer visits one year in advance. 'Cute' and 'cozy' are probably the best words to describe the gingerbread-style cabins at the Madera Kubo, just above the amphitheater in Madera Canyon (HC 70, Box 5449, Sahuarita, AZ 85629; telephone 520/625-2908). The Quality Inn (111 S. La Cañada, Green Valley 85614; telephone 800-344-1441) also caters to birders.

Northern Pygmy-Owl spies Katydid
Narca Moore-Craig

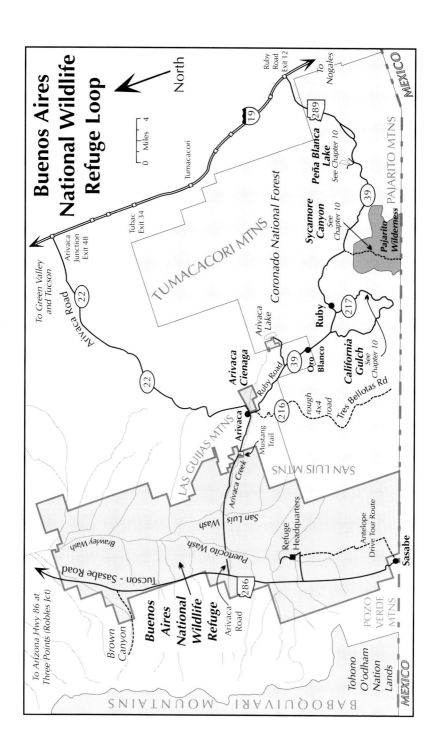

Buenos Aires
National Wildlife
Refuge Loop

North

0 Miles 4

Ruby Road
Exit 12

To
Nogales

19

289

Tumacacori

PAJARITO MTNS

Peña Blanca
Lake
See Chapter 10

Tubac
Exit 34

Sycamore
Canyon
See
Chapter 10

39

Arivaca
Junction
Exit 48

TUMACACORI MTNS

Coronado National Forest

Pajarito
Wilderness

To Green Valley
and Tucson

22

Arivaca
Lake

Ruby

217

22

Arivaca
Cienaga

39

Oro
Blanco

California
Gulch
See Chapter 10

Arivaca Road

Arivaca

Ruby Road

216

Tres Bellotas Rd

LAS GUIJAS MTNS

Mustang
Trail

rough
4x4
road

Arivaca Creek Rd

SAN LUIS MTNS

San Luis
Wash

Brawley Wash

Puertocito Wash

Refuge
Headquarters

Tucson - Sasabe Road

Buenos Aires
National
Wildlife
Refuge

Antelope
Drive Tour Route

To Arizona Hwy 86 at
Three Points (Robles Jct)

286

Arivaca Road

Brown
Canyon

Sasabe

POZO
VERDE
MTNS

MEXICO

Tohono
O'odham
Nation
Lands

MEXICO

BABOQUIVARI MOUNTAINS

CHAPTER 5

BUENOS AIRES WILDLIFE REFUGE LOOP

(153 miles/one or two days)

Purchased at a cost of nine million dollars in 1985, the 115,000-acre Buenos Aires National Wildlife Refuge boasts the largest ungrazed tract of grassland in Arizona. Broad, grassy swales in the bottom of the Altar Valley provide the only habitat for "Masked Bobwhite," a subspecies of Northern Bobwhite, in the United States. Arivaca Cienaga, a disjunct unit of the refuge acquired in 1990, preserves the headwaters of the only perennial stream in the Altar Valley. Recently, in 1995, the U.S. Fish and Wildlife Service added a four-mile-long stretch of Brown Canyon in the Baboquivari Mountains to the Refuge holdings. Set in Madrean pine/oak woodland, the beautiful sycamores of Brown Canyon lend a new dimension to both the Buenos Aires and our national refuge system. This loop-trip describes all three of these rare and vanishing habitats.

Plan on a full day to visit Arivaca Cienaga and the Refuge Headquarters area in the upper Altar Valley. If you can schedule a visit to Brown Canyon, a second morning is advised. Although Arivaca and the Refuge Headquarters offer exciting birding throughout the year, Brown Canyon is best in spring and summer. (Brown Canyon should open sometime in late 1996.)

The starting point is the junction of Interstate 10 and Interstate 19 in southwest Tucson. Take I-19 south to exit 48 for Arivaca and Amado (33 miles). Turn right (west) away from the underpass (0.3 mile), then right again (0.1 mile) to find the beginning of Arivaca Road opposite the giant steer horns (0.1 mile). Turn left (west) onto Arivaca Road.

Elevations from the beginning of Arivaca Road in the Santa Cruz Valley to the Buenos Aires Headquarters in the Altar Valley range between 3,000-4,000 feet, and the route traverses a belt formerly covered by a deep carpet of desert grasses. Wholesale changes in the savanna occurred in the late 1880s and early 1890s, when ranchers stocked this corner of Arizona with 1.5 million cattle. A seven-year-drought began in 1885. By the time the rains returned in 1893, over half of the herd had starved to death, and the native grasses had been gnawed down to mineral ground. Without sod to check the run-off from the heavy thunderstorms of summer, flash floods ensued. Most of the water funneled uselessly into newly-cut erosion-channels, pouring off the sun-baked soil. Lacking a continuous stand of grass to carry fire, the land developed a shrub community dominated by mesquite, replacing the grassland. Even today, mesquite remains the most conspicuous plant in this arid landscape.

From late February through April, though, vast swards of Mexican Gold Poppy transform the rolling hills into fields of gold. In spring, there are more photographers than birders along the winding Arivaca Road.

Ash-throated Flycatchers are common from spring through late summer; during the cooler months they are as common here as in any location in the state. Other species that occur here, such as Gambel's Quail, Ladder-backed Woodpecker, Verdin, Cactus Wren, and Curve-billed Thrasher, are typical residents of the Sonoran Desert. This is also a good area for Desert Mule Deer. A large sign on the left (south) side of the pavement marks the parking area for **Arivaca Cienaga** (22.3 miles), just a short distance east of the small village of Arivaca (0.6 mile).

The Spanish root-words for "cienaga" (see-EN-ah-gah) literally translate to "100 waters," denoting a marsh. There are actually seven springs in this 1,000-acre unit of the refuge. The U.S. Fish and Wildlife Service has constructed a two-mile-long loop trail—in part a boardwalk—that keeps your shoes dry while exploring the far reaches of this unique Southwest habitat.

Vermilion Flycatcher is likely to be the first species that you see upon arriving at Arivaca. In winter, probably more Vermilion Flycatchers are concentrated in the boggy grassland here than at any other location in Southeastern Arizona. Other resident species include Great Blue and Green Herons, Killdeer, Common Ground-Dove, Gila Woodpecker, Northern "Red-shafted" Flicker, Black Phoebe, Bewick's Wren, Common Yellowthroat, Song Sparrow, Eastern Meadowlark, and Lesser Goldfinch. Joining these in summer are Gray Hawk, White-winged Dove, Yellow-billed Cuckoo, Cassin's and Tropical Kingbird, Barn Swallow, and Yellow

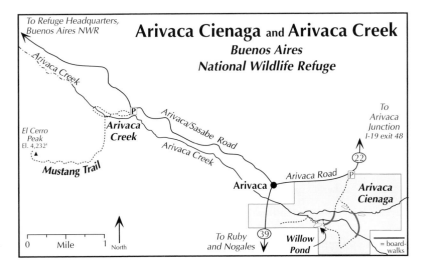

Arivaca Cienaga and Arivaca Creek
Buenos Aires
National Wildlife Refuge

Warbler. In winter, watch for Green-winged Teal, Northern Pintail, Northern Shoveler, Gadwall, American Wigeon, Northern Harrier, Prairie Falcon (rare), Virginia Rail, Sora, Common Snipe, Marsh Wren, Yellow-rumped Warbler, Savannah, Lincoln's, and Swamp Sparrows, and Western Meadowlark. A Streak-backed Oriole stole the show at the December 1991 Christmas Bird Count.

Probably the most sought-after bird at the Arivaca Cienaga is Green Kingfisher (rare), usually found at the largest impoundment, Willow Pond. Look for it perched low over the water, and, occasionally, on the barbed-wire fence at the back side of the tank (a local name for 'pond'). Black-bellied Whistling-Ducks may also be present.

News of exciting recent sightings, a bird checklist, and general information about Buenos Aires National Wildlife Refuge can be obtained on winter weekends at a small office next to the grocery in Arivaca (0.5 mile west of the Refuge parking area). The office is located on the right side of the road just before the main intersection. It is staffed by part-time volunteers, though future plans call for year-round hours. Bear right onto the Arivaca/Sasabe Road at the only major intersection in Arivaca (0.1 mile) to continue on to the main Buenos Aires National Wildlife Refuge Headquarters.

A few minutes away, a parking area on the left (south) signed "Wildlife Viewing Area" (2.5 miles) provides the only public access to **Arivaca Creek** at a point where the stream is permanent. Trimmed with large Fremont Cottonwoods, this foothills stream is reminiscent of parts of Sonoita Creek near Patagonia—but without the crowds of birders. Many of the birds, too, are the same as those found at the Patagonia-Sonoita Creek Preserve. A well-marked quarter-mile-long trail loops down to the creek. More-ambitious birders can continue downstream another half-mile, wade across, and return along the far bank. This longer route passes by the family homestead of author Eva Wilbur-Cruce, who wrote *A Beautiful, Cruel Country* about her experiences growing up and living here in the early 1900s. *This is private property—please respect No Trespassing signs.*

The summering birdlife along Arivaca Creek includes seven pairs of Gray Hawk, Broad-billed Hummingbird, Northern Beardless-Tyrannulet, Brown-crested Flycatcher, Thick-billed Kingbird (rare), Yellow-billed Cuckoo, Bell's Vireo, Lucy's Warbler, Yellow-breasted Chat, Summer Tanager, and Hooded and Bullock's Orioles. All of these species depart before winter. Some of the cold-weather birds that replace them are Gray Flycatcher (uncommon), Ruby-crowned Kinglet, Hermit Thrush, Yellow-rumped Warbler, Green-tailed Towhee, and Chipping, Savannah, Fox (rare), White-throated (uncommon), and White-crowned Sparrows. There are records of Buff-collared Nightjar here from 1991 and 1993. (*Please do not use tapes.*) Up to four pairs of Rose-throated Becards nested here in the early 1980s. They have since disappeared but may return again; the habitat is excellent.

The hiking route with the best scenery and the fewest birds ascends 4,232-foot-high El Cerro Peak. Called the Mustang Trail, this path leaves

Baboquivari Peak, at an elevation of 7,730 feet, dominates the western horizon as you drive west from Arivaca toward Buenos Aires National Wildlife Refuge.

the creekside path at the ford one-quarter mile downstream, and gains 750 feet of elevation in 2.5 miles. Mustang Trail is very steep and rocky in sections. Watch for Rock Wren, Rufous-crowned Sparrow, and Scott's Oriole (summer) in the oak grassland on El Cerro's slopes.

After birding Arivaca Creek, continue west into the Altar Valley on the Arivaca/Sasabe Road to Highway 286 (9.4 miles). Turn left (south) here. Turn left (east) again onto the entrance road (4.4 miles) signed for the Buenos Aires National Wildlife Refuge headquarters. The well-graded thoroughfare swings southeast across the floor of the Altar Valley to an intersection with Antelope Drive (2.0 miles). For much of the year, Pronghorns are as common along the entrance road as they are farther south along the road that bears their name (although Pronghorns are not members of the Old World family of true antelopes). The herd of Pronghorns presently on the Refuge—62 adults in 1995—stems from a 1987 transplant of the Chihuahuan subspecies.

To find the **Buenos Aires National Wildlife Refuge Headquarters**, continue straight ahead at the Antelope Drive junction (0.3 mile). The office is open 7:30am through 4:00pm, Monday through Friday, except on holidays. Stop here for a bird checklist and road-condition informa-tion, or to use the picnic tables and restrooms. Bird-seed feeders on the north side of the building occasionally attract the Masked Bobwhite subspecies of Northern Bobwhite—the bird for which the national wild-life refuge was created. Prior to the Refuge's establishment, the last time wild Masked Bobwhite was recorded in Arizona was in 1897.

The Buenos Aires Ranch actually predates the 1884 discovery of Masked Bobwhite, a race in which the male has a black throat and chestnut plumage. Pedro Aguirre had established a stage-stop on the site in 1864. One hundred years later, Jim and Seymour Levy of Tucson discovered a remnant population of Masked Bobwhite near Benjamin Hill in Sonora, 100 miles due south of Buenos Aires Ranch. Birds captured at Benjamin Hill in the 1960s formed the nucleus of the breeding-stock used by the U.S. Fish and Wildlife Service for their captive-breeding program.

By 1974, Masked Bobwhites were being returned to their former range on the Buenos Aires Ranch. After good reproduction in 1979, a double-whammy of drought and grazing had virtually exterminated the wild population again by 1982. It was obvious that the only hope for Masked Bobwhite lay in a cattle-free range. After several years of political bickering, Buenos Aires National Wildlife Refuge came into existence in 1985. Using sterilized Northern Bobwhites from Texas as foster parents, the Buenos Aires population grew to approximately 500 Masked Bobwhites in 1995. The birds are still perilously closed to the brink of extinction as a wild subspecies, and the goal at the Refuge is a population of 500 breeding pairs.

The Headquarters area is good for a variety of other birds, also. Some of the resident and summering species here include Greater Roadrunner, Gambel's Quail, Costa's Hummingbird, Ladder-backed Woodpecker, Say's Phoebe, Western Kingbird, Chihuahuan Raven, Cactus Wren, Curve-billed Thrasher, Lucy's Warbler, Blue Grosbeak, Canyon Towhee, and both Hooded and Bullock's Orioles. Eastern Meadowlarks are common in the grassland. During the winter months, Western Meadowlarks join the Easterns. Western Meadowlarks have nested on the Refuge, especially after winters with exceptionally high rainfall. Watch for an occasional Crested Caracara coasting by the Headquarters in search of an easy meal.

From the Headquarters area, the road descends into the bottom of the Altar Valley and continues north to Grebe Pond and Aguirre Lake (cheek by jowl at 1.2 miles). Originally constructed in the 1870s to provide water for irrigation of alfalfa, Aguirre Lake varies in size from a small mud-puddle to a 100-acre reservoir. It is most likely to hold significant water after the summer rains. The best bird seen here was Arizona's first record of Garganey in April of 1988. This was also the spot for the state's fourth record of White-rumped Sandpiper in mid-May 1993 and Southeastern Arizona's second record of Upland Sandpiper in May 1989. When at least some water is present during migration periods, other species likely to be encountered include Eared Grebe, Great Blue Heron, White-faced Ibis, Willet, Solitary Sandpiper, Spotted, Western, and Least Sandpipers, Long-billed Dowitcher, and Wilson's Phalarope. Occasionally, up to one thousand ducks use the lake—assuming that it's wet! Bring a spotting scope, just in case.

Antelope Drive begins a short distance south of Headquarters (0.25 mile). Part of a complex of approximately 200 miles of dirt tracks, Antelope Drive follows the Altar Valley nearly to the Mexico border, before swinging west to Sasabe (10.4 miles). The rich Velvet Mesquite grassland on both sides of the road hosts a world of sparrows. A sample of the species that occur here includes Botteri's (summer), Cassin's (summer), Rufous-winged, Rufous-crowned, Chipping (winter), Brewer's (winter), Black-chinned (winter), Vesper (winter), Lark, Black-throated, Savannah (winter), Baird's (rare, winter), Grasshopper, Lincoln's (winter), White-throated (uncommon, winter), and White-crowned (winter) Sparrows. The Refuge's major claim to fame, of course, is quail, with four species present. There are more here than at any other single location in the United States. Both Scaled and Gambel's Quail are common along this road; Montezuma Quail and Masked Bobwhite are uncommon. Antelope Drive is also excellent for Pronghorn. *Birders should be aware that this and other Refuge roads are impassable after heavy rains. Some roads should not be attempted without 4-wheel-drive; off-road travel is not permitted.*

From the Refuge, the shortest way back to Tucson is north straight up Highway 286 to Three Points (also known as Robles Junction) (37.5 miles from the entrance). The Altar Valley is a hawk-alley throughout the year, but especially during migration and winter. The most abundant species are Northern Harrier (winter), Cooper's (winter), Swainson's (summer), and Red-tailed Hawks, and American Kestrel. Less common, but present, are White-tailed Kite (4 to 6 pairs on the Refuge), Sharp-shinned Hawk (winter), Golden Eagle, Merlin (rare, winter), Prairie Falcon (winter), and Peregrine Falcon (winter). Altogether, 20 species of raptors have been recorded in the Altar Valley. On a good winter day, it is possible to see 100 individual birds of prey between the Refuge entrance and Three Points.

Masked Bobwhite
Narca Moore-Craig

In 1995 the U.S. Fish and Wildlife Service completed negotiations to add 2,000 acres of **Brown Canyon** in the Baboquivari Mountains to the Buenos Aires National Wildlife Refuge. The Brown Canyon drainage extends to the ridgeline north of the 7,730-foot-high summit of Baboquivari Peak. Interpretations vary, but the word Baboquivari is probably derived from Tohono O'odham roots meaning "Water-on-the-mountains." Some canyons, such as Brown, hold year-round springs that make them magnets for wildlife. It is easy to see how this stupendous granitic dome, looming some 3,000 feet above the canyon floor, came to be revered by the people of the Tohono O'odham Nation.

Brown Canyon is on the left (west) side of Highway 286 between mileposts 20 and 21 (13 miles north of the Buenos Aires entrance). *There is no access for the general birding public at this time.* A visitor center located at a former dwelling is proposed about 4.5 miles up the canyon. Even with a possible opening of Brown Canyon in late 1996, access to the upper canyon may be limited by permit. Currently, however, tours for groups of 12-25 may be arranged if Refuge staffing is available.

Sycamores dominate the canyon floor throughout the entire four-mile-long section of canyon managed by the Refuge, forming an especially lush grove in the area two miles above the proposed visitor center. Resident and summer birds using the sycamores and surrounding oak hillsides are Zone-tailed Hawk, Montezuma Quail, Acorn and Strickland's Woodpeckers, Western Wood-Pewee, Sulphur-bellied and Dusky-capped Flycatchers, Mexican Jay, Bewick's Wren, Black-throated Gray Warbler, and Painted Redstart. Golden Eagles soaring overhead are a fairly common sight. Eight species of hummingbirds have been recorded in the canyon, and Elegant Trogons were sighted a few times by the former owners. The dense hackberry and mesquite thickets in the foothill area harbor Buff-collared Nightjar and Varied Bunting. In many respects, the bird community in Brown Canyon resembles that found at the lower elevations of Madera Canyon to the east. When opened, this location should become a real attraction for birders.

To conclude this trip, return to Highway 286 (4.0 miles) and turn left (north). Continue to Three Points (25 miles) and turn right (east) onto Highway 86 (Ajo Highway), which arrows its way—almost without curves—straight into Tucson at Interstate 19 (19.2 miles). To find the starting point at the junction of Interstates 19 and 10, turn left (1.0 mile).

Campgrounds, Restaurants, and Accommodations:

There are 90 primitive campsites located throughout Buenos Aires National Wildlife Refuge (P.O. Box 109, Sasabe, AZ 85633; telephone 520/823-4251). Camping is permitted only at these designated sites. Lodging, trailer-sites, and camping are all available at Universal Ranch (P.O. Box 1, Arivaca, AZ 85601; telephone 520/398-9815) two miles southeast of Arivaca, which also provides a restaurant, mini-mart, and laundry facilities for its guests. Rancho de la Osa (P.O. Box 1, Sasabe, AZ 85633; telephone 520/823-4257) is an authentic Western guest ranch located six miles south of the Buenos Aires National Wildlife Refuge headquarters. From September through May, non-guests with advance reservations may partake of their noon-time lunch buffet.

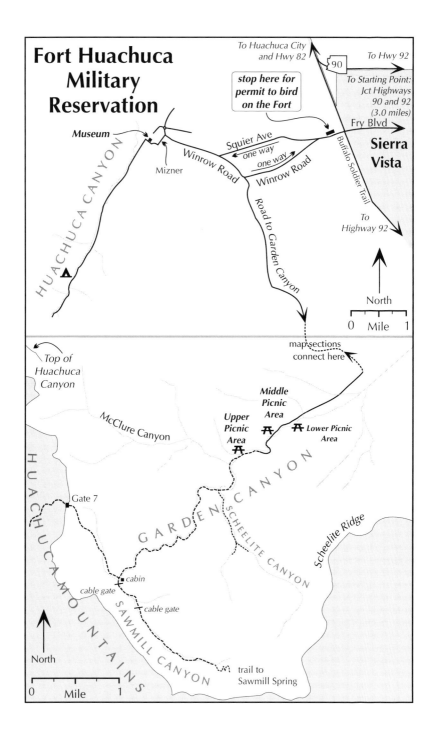

Fort Huachuca Military Reservation

To Huachuca City and Hwy 82

To Hwy 92

90

To Starting Point: Jct Highways 90 and 92 (3.0 miles)

Fry Blvd

Sierra Vista

stop here for permit to bird on the Fort

Museum

Mizner

Squier Ave
one way
one way

Winrow Road

Winrow Road

Buffalo Soldier Trail

Road to Garden Canyon

HUACHUCA CANYON

To Highway 92

North

0   Mile   1

map sections connect here

Top of Huachuca Canyon

McClure Canyon

Middle Picnic Area

Upper Picnic Area

Lower Picnic Area

Gate 7

GARDEN CANYON

SCHEELITE CANYON

Scheelite Ridge

cabin

cable gate

cable gate

HUACHUCA MOUNTAINS

SAWMILL CANYON

trail to Sawmill Spring

North

0   Mile   1

CHAPTER 6

HUACHUCA
MOUNTAINS

The blue, alp-like peaks of the Huachuca Mountains actually straddle
the international border at Coronado National Memorial and provide
a home for a community of birds and wildlife which has its roots in the
Sierra Madre of Mexico. Viewed from Sierra Vista, four major summits
dominate the 20-mile-long skyline of the Huachuca Mountains. Highest
and easternmost is Miller Peak (El. 9,466 feet). Jutting up to the west, in
order of their appearance, are Carr Peak (El. 9,220 feet), Ramsey Peak (El.
8,725 feet), and Huachuca Peak (El. 8,410 feet). The word "Huachuca",
pronounced wa-CHOO-ka, comes from Apache roots meaning "Thunder
Mountain".

Two full days are required to bird the wet canyons and forested
highlands of the Huachuca front range. Most birders will also want to
visit the adjacent San Pedro River to look for Gray Hawks and Green
Kingfishers (see Chapter 7), adding a third or fourth day to their stay in
the Sierra Vista area. With over 400 species of birds having been
recorded within 15 miles of city limits, your time here will seem all too
brief.

Access:

The starting point for this tour is the intersection of Highways 90 and
92 in east Sierra Vista, 75 miles southeast of Tucson. From Tucson take
Interstate 10 east 42 miles to the well-signed junction with Highway 90
at exit 302. Turn right onto Highway 90 and proceed south. (While on
Highway 90, just before milepost 300, you will pass a signed gate on the
right for French Joe Canyon. A few miles up this rough road in
spring/summer of 1995 up to three Rufous-capped Warblers entertained
many observers.) At Huachuca City (23 miles) continue to the traffic
signal at the Highway 90 Bypass on the north side of Sierra Vista (5.5

miles). Turn left (east) here. Follow the bypass several miles until it turns right (south) to intersect Highway 92 at a traffic signal (4.7 miles).

Birders starting in Willcox—or points farther east—should follow Interstate 10 for 38 miles west of Willcox to exit 302 for Highway 90. Then, use the directions above to follow Highway 90 south to its intersection with Highway 92.

If you are birding east from Patagonia (Chapter 3), it makes sense to access the Huachuca Mountains via Highway 82. Drive north from Patagonia to Sonoita (12 miles), and continue directly east through town on Highway 82 across the grassland to the intersection with Highway 90 (19 miles). Turn right (south) here. Follow Highway 90 south through Huachuca City (4.0 miles) to the bypass (5.5 miles), turn left, and continue to its junction with Highway 92 (4.7 miles), as described above. The grassland east of Sonoita is excellent for Grasshopper and Cassin's Sparrows on the fence-lines, Common Nighthawks early in the morning and at dusk, and a herd of Pronghorns that usually stays on the left (north) side of Highway 82. Pronghorns, the fastest land mammals in North America, are usually sighted in the grassy swales between the rolling hills in the first eight miles east of Sonoita.

From Douglas take U.S. Highway 80 west to Bisbee (23 miles), turn right at the traffic circle (on your left), pass the Lavender Pit, and continue through the Mule Mountain Tunnel to a well-signed turn-off to Sierra Vista and Highway 90 (9 miles). From here, Highway 90 crosses the broad San Pedro River Valley before it reaches Sierra Vista and the junction with Highway 92 (20 miles). *Note:* When approaching Bisbee from Douglas, the signs for Sierra Vista are via Highway 92, not Highway 90. That road winds up in the same place as the intended route, but is ten miles longer.

SIERRA MADREAN CANYONS

Garden Canyon/Ramsey Canyon Tour

(49 miles/one day)

Unlike most other places in the southeast corner of Arizona, Sierra Vista is relatively new. It was founded after Fort Huachuca was reactivated in 1954. In the past four decades the population has gone from approximately 100 to over 40,000. Until the U.S. government abolished it in 1876, these lands were part of the Chiricahua Indian Reservation. The military post was established in the spring of 1877 to control marauding Apache warriors, who resented being forcibly removed from their ancestral homelands, and it remained active until Geronimo surrendered for the fourth, and final, time in the fall of 1886. Today, Fort Huachuca serves as a communications center and an electronics proving-ground for the U.S. Army.

Begin this tour early in the morning. The miles are not many, but the trail up Scheelite Canyon is steep, and you will want to move slowly there to maximize your chance of seeing Spotted Owl, as well as the other species that share this beautiful wilderness defile. Don't forget to bring a canteen.

To begin this tour drive west on Fry Boulevard from the starting point to the East Gate of Fort Huachuca (3.0 miles). The Fort is normally open to entry by the public during daylight hours (roughly 5:30am to 5:30pm in the summer), but officials may close portions of the Fort, either for gunnery practice or as a fire-prevention measure. *You must stop at the guard station on the right for a permit.* You will be required to show your driver's license, proof of insurance, and vehicle registration if you are the car owner; rental-car drivers must present their driver's license and a rental contract. Display your permit on your dashboard, get into the left lane, and proceed past the water tower on your right (1.8 miles), to a well-marked hard-left (south) turn for Garden Canyon (0.3 mile). There is a sign for **Garden Canyon** straight ahead (0.4 mile) at the intersection at the bottom of the hill.

Resist the temptation to hurry to Garden Canyon. *Speed limits are strictly enforced on the post, and MPs are less inclined to leniency than civilian police.* Furthermore, every dry ravine on the road is lined with concrete. These constitute speed dips. Unless you slow down to *no more than 10 miles per hour* at each and every one, they can bend a car's chassis and sprain your neck. Seriously.

For the next several miles you will be traveling across a lush mesquite grassland populated by Botteri's, Cassin's, and Rufous-crowned Sparrows. Botteri's and Cassin's are almost impossible to locate unless they are singing. Your best chance of finding these birds is in July and August, after the summer rains have begun. *Remember to park completely off the pavement, and do not walk in the grass*—you might stumble upon live ammunition. Red-tailed Hawk and American Kestrel are both resident, but during migration in September, multitudes of both species invade from the north, capping nearly every power-pole with a raptor. It's an amazing spectacle. Other birds that share this grassland include Northern Harrier (winter), Greater Roadrunner, Black-chinned Hummingbird (summer), Rufous Hummingbird (on the flowering agaves, midsummer), Western and Cassin's Kingbirds (summer), Cactus Wren,

Scheelite Canyon, Fort Huachuca

Duplicate Tear-Out Trail Map of Scheelite Canyon is provided on page 321.

● = Spotted Owl sighting locations since 1978

······ = foot trail

Contour Interval: 100 feet

From data recorded by Robert T. Smith

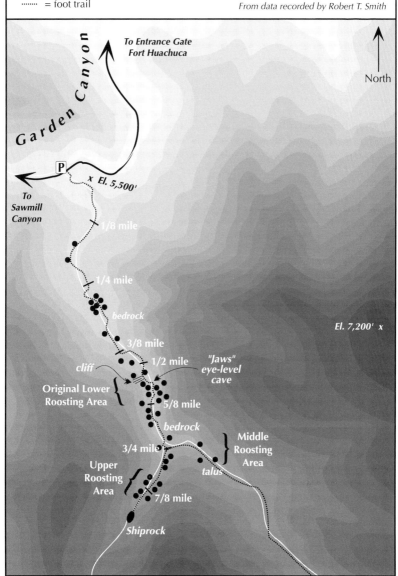

Loggerhead Shrike, Blue Grosbeak, Canyon Towhee, Lark Sparrow, Eastern Meadowlark, and both Hooded and Scott's Orioles (on the flowering agaves, summer). Pronghorns are occasionally sighted early in the morning.

As the road approaches the canyon mouth, there are three picnic areas. Montezuma Quail is possible along the edge of the road anywhere above the Lower Picnic Area (mile 4.0). Birders should continue on to the **Upper Picnic Area** (2.7 miles) without delay, especially on a weekend. After 9am on weekends, it is likely that crowds of boom-box-toting post employees will utterly demolish the birding acoustics. Remember, it's their duty station.

Well-watered and with tall, shady trees, the Upper Picnic Area is a terrific place for Strickland's and Acorn Woodpeckers, Sulphur-bellied Flycatcher (summer), Eastern Bluebird, Hutton's Vireo, Black-throated Gray Warbler (summer), Painted Redstart (summer), Lesser Goldfinch (especially summer), and many other species. From May through September, Elegant Trogons are almost always present in the groves of sycamores just upstream or immediately downstream from the picnic ground. Arizona's first record of Crescent-chested Warbler came from this area in September 1983.

Option: You may want to bypass Scheelite Canyon now in order to bird first at Sawmill Canyon, which catches the morning sun earlier than Scheelite Canyon does.

The pavement ends here, but Garden Canyon Road is both broad and well-graded up to **Scheelite Canyon** (0.7 mile). Park at a wide pull-out on the right side of the road. Ordinarily, a pair of Painted Redstarts is fluttering in and around the grove of Bigtooth Maples that shades the creek by the parking area. The entrance to the trail is across the road behind enormous boulders meant to discourage off-road vehicles. The trail up Scheelite Canyon is steep and mined with rolling rocks. *There is no drinking water in the canyon.* Nonetheless, owing to the work of a single man, Scheelite is one of the most-visited areas in the Huachuca Mountains.

Robert T. Smith, "Smitty" to over 6,000 birders whom he has led up the canyon since 1978, should be credited as the protector of the Spotted Owls of Scheelite Canyon. Even the trail to the owls is due, in a large part, to his planning, and accomplished with the labor and cooperation of Fort Huachuca staff. After showing birders what is undoubtedly the most-often-seen pair of Spotted Owls in the U.S., Smitty has then made sure that his guests did not unwittingly disturb these precious birds. In 1994, local bird guide Stuart Healy began to assume part of Smitty's responsibilities as custodian of both the owls and the unique canyon in which they live.

Scheelite is most famous for its Spotted Owls, but it is also a good location for an impressive array of other pine/oak woodland birds. Watch for Strickland's Woodpecker, Red-naped Sapsucker (winter), Bridled Titmouse, Virginia's Warbler (summer), and Rufous-crowned Sparrow in the lower drainage. This is also the best stretch for Montezuma Quail, Hammond's and Dusky Flycatchers (migration), Dusky-capped Flycatcher (summer), Western Scrub-Jay (screeching from the brushy slopes above), Hutton's Vireo, Black-throated Gray Warbler (summer), Black-headed Grosbeak, and Spotted Towhee. After ½ mile (indefatigable Smitty painted these useful mileage-markers), the trail approaches an area with a towering cliff on the right side. This is the start of the "Lower Area" commonly used by the owls for roosting (although they can occur as low as ¼ mile). Canyon Wrens generally sound the alarm as you approach. In summer, Painted Redstarts are invariably here, as well as a pair of Red-faced Warblers. Summering Cordilleran Flycatchers, too, nest in this cool, shady zone.

A rock formation on the left side of the trail, baptized "Jaws" by Smitty, is set amidst tall timber. Near Jaws, listen for the distinctive vocalizations of Northern Pygmy-Owl, Whip-poor-will (occasionally even in the day-time during summer), Red-breasted Nuthatch, House Wren, and Hepatic Tanager (summer).

Ordinarily, the Spotted Owls take perches under 20 feet in height, preferably on a major limb in the lower half of a tree. In large oaks, they may park well out on a bough, but look for them to sit near the trunk in small trees and conifers. The pair is often side by side, and usually within 300 feet of one another if both are present, but they may be in different roosting areas. The code of self-restraint which Smitty asks birders to exercise is simple:

Do not approach within 50 feet of the birds;

Do not talk loudly;

Do not point at the birds or wave your arms;

Photographers should not use flash or make noise to get the birds' attention;

Do not use tape recordings or try to imitate the calls of Spotted Owls. (Spotted Owl calls are specifically prohibited on Fort Huachuca.)

Approximately 100 yards beyond the 5/8-mile marker, Scheelite narrows to a rocky chute with a small spring, except in extremely dry years. The platter-sized pools attract up to three species of warblers bathing in a single puddle. You may spot Montezuma Quail on the slopes

Spotted Owl
Gail Diane Yovanovich

above the pools. White-throated Swifts and Violet-green Swallows (summer) zoom overhead, and an occasional Golden Eagle floats across the narrow slit of sky. Check here for Greater Pewee (summer) and the "Plumbeous" form of Solitary Vireo. Mexican Jays occur throughout Scheelite, but above the chute Steller's Jays are common, also. At mile-marker ¾, approximately 150 paces beyond the seep, Scheelite splits into two major canyons. Elevation here is 6,350 feet, some 850 feet above the parking area.

The main trail continues up the left fork another 2.8 miles, climbing steeply 2,000 feet before it joins the Crest Trail. The Spotted Owls sometimes roost near the junction—and, infrequently, in the first 200 yards up the left fork, but usually the birds are up the unmaintained track ascending the right-hand fork. Look for them in dense stands of maple or oak, especially between 200 and 650 yards upcanyon from the junction. The trail peters out 200 yards or so beyond "Shiprock", a prow-shaped boulder in the center of the dry creek-bed. Smitty, who was born in 1918 and still climbs the Scheelite Trail several times a week, calls this stretch the "Upper Area." If you go this far to find the owls, I'm sure you'll agree that the name is well chosen.

Beyond the Scheelite Canyon parking area, Garden Canyon Road narrows, requiring either high-clearance or skill and determination to negotiate the steep, concrete-lined stream-crossings. An abundance of purple Rothrock's Star-Thistle and magenta Wheeler's Thistle, which trims the road after the summer rains, transforms upper Garden Canyon into a butterfly-lover's paradise. Over 130 species have been recorded so far. The huge, black-and-yellow beauty is a Two-tailed Swallowtail—a show-stopper in anyone's book. Most of the rare plants which occur in the Huachuca Mountains can be found here, some *very* close to the established trails, where they could be trampled by careless hikers or birders. *Please stay on the trails.*

For a five-minute cultural detour, park on the right side of the road by a bridge (1.5 miles). From here, a 100-foot-long path leads through a grove of Bigtooth Maples to a cliff with petroglyphs that probably date back to at least A.D 1200. Depicted among the two dozen or so figures are some plainly discernible raptors. This artwork should remind birders to scan the skies. Red-tailed Hawks, Zone-tailed Hawks, and Golden Eagles are all regular in Garden Canyon.

Continue up the canyon to an old log cabin at the entrance to **Sawmill Canyon** (0.6 mile). A seldom-used campground for military personnel lies 200 yards beyond a cable-gate on the left. Buff-breasted Flycatchers (summer) are likely anywhere from the cable gate to the far end of the campground. A loose colony of, perhaps, as many as ten pairs nests in the ¾-mile-long open stand of Chihuahua and Apache Pines.

Also using the area in summer are Greater Pewee, Western Wood-Pewee, Dusky-capped Flycatcher, Cassin's Kingbird, Solitary "Plum-beous" Vireo, Painted Redstart, Grace's Warbler, Hepatic Tanager, Black-headed Grosbeak, and Scott's Oriole. Year-round residents include Cooper's Hawk, Northern Pygmy-Owl, Pygmy Nuthatch, Brown Creeper, Steller's Jay, Eastern Bluebird, Hutton's Vireo, Olive Warbler, Yellow-eyed Junco, and in winter only, Dark-eyed Junco. Occasionally, Sawmill Canyon hosts Northern Goshawk, Elegant Trogon (summer), and Evening Grosbeak (which nested in 1994 and 1995). Strickland's and Hairy Woodpeckers are regular, and several pairs of Williamson's Sapsuckers usually overwinter. Beyond the campground, above the second cable-gate, Red-faced Warbler (summer) becomes common. In migration, look for Hermit and Townsend's Warblers.

It will be hard to leave Garden Canyon and its tributaries, but unless you've had exceptional luck, the day is half gone and bird activity has practically dried up. The sensible way to pass the slow afternoon is to drowse in the shade at Ramsey Canyon Preserve, watching the eye-candy at the hummingbird feeders with eyelids at half-mast, perhaps sauntering out on the trail as the afternoon cools. On the other hand, white-knuckle listers may wish to hike all the way to Hamburg Meadow in upper Ramsey Canyon to sample the high-Huachuca avifauna.

Either way, to find Ramsey Canyon return to the East (Main) Gate and leave the Fort. Continue straight ahead (east) onto Fry Boulevard through Sierra Vista to the starting point at Highway 92 (3.0 miles). Turn right (south). The road into Ramsey Canyon turns right (west) off Highway 92 after exactly 6.0 miles. *An alternative route* is to turn right onto Buffalo Soldier Trail as you leave the Fort. This road joins Highway 92 south of town, bypassing busy Fry Boulevard.

Along Ramsey Canyon Road, look for Swainson's (summer) and Red-tailed Hawks perched on the utility-poles, and Scaled Quail pecking in the yards along the right (north) side of the pavement over the first stretch of mesquite savanna (2.2 miles). The desert grassland leading into the canyon entrance is also prime habitat for Greater Roadrunner, Ladder-backed Woodpecker, Ash-throated Flycatcher (summer), Cassin's and Western Kingbirds (summer), Cactus Wren, Curve-billed Thrasher, Pyrrhuloxia, Blue Grosbeak (summer), and Lark Sparrow.

Parking is prohibited along the shoulder of Ramsey Canyon Road after it enters the oak woodland and the canyon proper. Approximately 100 yards after the Ramsey Creek crossing (1.3 miles; 3.5 miles from Highway

92), the road passes the right-hand turn-off and parking area (guests only) for the Ramsey Canyon Inn. Not surprisingly, the same hummingbirds use the feeders at this bed-and-breakfast establishment as at the Preserve just 50 yards beyond. The kitchen-window feeder on the east side of the main building is sometimes the best stake-out in the whole canyon for White-eared Hummingbird. *Non-guests are asked to birdwatch from Ramsey Canyon Road, and may not park here.*

   With 30,000 visitors annually, The Nature Conservancy's 300-acre **Ramsey Canyon Preserve** is indisputably the most popular birding site in the Huachuca Mountains. Parking space is extremely limited (to 13 vehicles), and parking reservations are *required* for weekend and holiday visits (520/378-2785), as well as for all groups. Six parking slots are

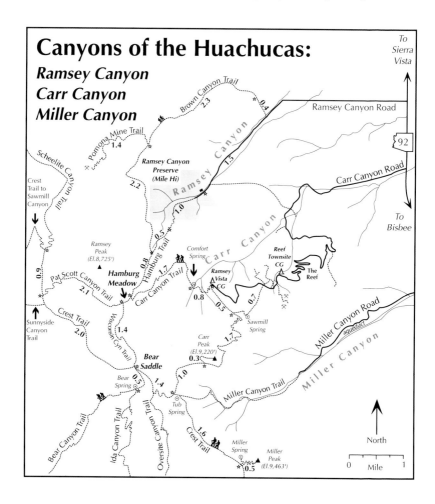

Canyons of the Huachucas:
Ramsey Canyon
Carr Canyon
Miller Canyon

available for weekday reservations. Please do not attempt to bring your RV or any vehicle over 20 feet long up this steep, narrow, winding mountain road. The Preserve is open daily from 8am to 5pm, except for Christmas and New Year's Day. *Pets are not permitted and no picnicking is allowed. The use of tape players is forbidden at Ramsey Canyon Preserve.*

Much of Ramsey's reputation comes from the diversity and numbers of hummingbirds that patronize the Preserve's sugar-water feeders. Up to 12 species have been recorded on a single August day, although six to ten is more typical. The regular species which you can expect to see from April through August are Broad-billed (uncommon), Blue-throated, Magnificent, Black-chinned, Anna's (absent some springs), and Broad-tailed. Recently, Ramsey has been the most reliable location in Arizona for White-eared Hummingbird.

An afternoon spent watching the feeders usually produces at least a few bonus hummers. During fall migration—July through September for this family—the core group of species is joined by Calliope, Rufous, and Allen's (uncommon). Additionally, the Sierra Madrean species, which breed after the rainy season, are most likely to appear in late summer. These include such sought-after living-jewels as Berylline, Violet-crowned, and Lucifer Hummingbirds.

Costa's is the only member of the clan most likely to visit Ramsey in the spring. To date, Plain-capped Starthroat has yet to put in an appearance at the Ramsey Preserve, although there are hearsay accounts, and the starthroat has been recorded elsewhere in the Huachuca Mountains. Ramsey Canyon has the distinction of being the only place in the U.S. where Bumblebee Hummingbird has, possibly, occurred. Two females were collected in July 1896. There has never been a subsequent observation, and many speculate that the locality for the specimens was mislabeled. With or without the Bumblebee, in this century 14 species of hummingbirds have been found at the Ramsey Canyon Preserve.

The combination Ramsey Canyon visitor center/book store/gift shop is set at an elevation of 5,550 feet among cool sycamore, maple, oak, and conifer trees next to the perennial waters of Ramsey Creek. Because all wildlife is protected, birdlife of all kinds is common. Some of the many species that occur here are Wild Turkey, Mexican Jay, Bridled Titmouse, White-breasted Nuthatch, Bewick's Wren, Solitary "Plumbeous" Vireo (summer), Black-throated Gray Warbler (summer), Hepatic Tanager (summer), Black-headed Grosbeak (summer), Yellow-eyed Junco, and Scott's Oriole (summer). Occasionally, a Whiskered Screech-Owl chooses a day-roost visible from the parking area, or Golden Eagles occupy a ledge directly above the book store, but these sightings are never guaranteed. During most summers, a lone Coati—a tropical relative of the Raccoon—can be seen foraging for insects and lizards among the six rental cabins. (To rent a cabin in Ramsey make your reservation early—a year in advance is suggested.)

The best way to see the most birds in Ramsey is from the 0.7-mile-long trail. *You must check in at the office to obtain a trail permit,* because the number of hikers is limited to protect both the wildlife and the quality of your experience. The same birds occur here as are found in the lower canyon. Also, watch for Zone-tailed Hawk (summer), Montezuma Quail, Acorn and Strickland's Woodpeckers, Greater Pewee (especially near the staff residence just beyond the "frog pond" in summer), Western Wood-Pewee (summer), Hammond's Flycatcher (migration), Dusky-capped and Sulphur-bellied Flycatchers (summer), Hutton's Vireo, Grace's Warbler (summer), Painted Redstart (mainly summer, although one occasionally overwinters), and Western Tanager (summer). In 1994, Elegant Trogons nested successfully in the Preserve for the first time since it was established in 1974; they repeated the feat in 1995. In the past few years both Aztec Thrush and Flame-colored Tanager have been sighted nearly annually in Ramsey. However, your chances of sighting either the thrush or the tanager are remote.

The steep, rocky, switchbacking Hamburg Trail that leads to **Hamburg Meadow** has seen a substantial increase in birder traffic since 1991, the year that Eared Trogons were discovered nesting in upper Ramsey Canyon. Although months may elapse between sightings, even the remote chance of seeing one of these 13-inch-long birds flashing brilliant red, green, and white colors as it launches across a wilderness canyon is enough to quicken nearly anyone's pulse. (Listen for the distinctive *squee-chuck!* calls of the Eared Trogons.

But a warning is in order: this is emphatically *not* a walk for the faint-hearted or for those who are out-of-shape. It may be especially difficult for people coming from sea-level. Allow at least four hours to complete the 4.6-mile-long round trip to Hamburg Meadow, and remember that the Preserve closes at 5pm. If the purpose of your hike is truly birding, you will want to spend the whole day and pack a lunch. *Remember there is no picnicking at Ramsey Canyon Preserve, so you must be off the property for lunch.* Although there may be water in Ramsey Creek, it's always best to carry a canteen.

The Hamburg Trail begins as a service-road that follows the south side of the canyonbottom to the staff residence (0.4 mile). One hundred yards beyond, the road swings left and begins to climb through a Madrean

Eared Trogan
Narca Moore-Craig

pine/oak woodland. A pair of Crescent-chested Warblers appeared and
sang near here in April and May 1984, but failed to nest. This is also the
area of the canyon used by a nesting pair of Flame-colored Tanagers from
April to July 1993. In winter, watch for Red-naped Sapsucker and
Hammond's Flycatcher (very rare) in the vicinity of the staff residence.
   The trail switchbacks up 700 feet to an elevation of 6,390 feet at
Ramsey Vista (0.6 mile). Downstream lies a wide expanse of the grassy
San Pedro River Valley; upcanyon Ramsey is heavily forested. Common
summer birds at the viewpoint are White-throated Swift, Violet-green
Swallow, Canyon Wren, and Spotted Towhee. Pause here to listen for
the calls of the magnificent Eared Trogons. This is the lower end of the

zone in Ramsey that they most often use, and the acoustics at the viewpoint are superb.

After a gradual descent to the stream (0.3 mile), the trail crosses the water and continues to a junction with Brown Canyon Trail (0.2 mile), 1.5 miles from the Preserve book store. In no other place in the Huachuca Mountains are Red-faced Warblers (summer) so common as they are here.

Other birds to watch for in this moist area of Bigtooth Maple and White Fir include Cooper's Hawk, Northern Goshawk (rare), Band-tailed Pigeon, Spotted Owl (rare), Hairy Woodpecker, Greater Pewee (summer), Cordilleran Flycatcher (summer), Steller's Jay, Common Raven, White-breasted and Red-breasted Nuthatches, Brown Creeper, American Robin, Hermit Thrush, Warbling Vireo (summer), Yellow-rumped and Grace's Warbler (summer), Western Tanager (summer), and Yellow-eyed Junco. Williamson's Sapsucker is regular here in winter. After the Brown Canyon junction, the trail climbs steadily but, generally, stays on the bottom of Ramsey Canyon, winding through tall conifers broken by glades of maple, until it connects with the Carr Canyon Trail (0.8 mile; elevation El. 6,850 feet), just 50 yards below Hamburg Meadow. (Carr Canyon Trail is described in the next tour.) Your return from Hamburg Meadow to the Ramsey Canyon Preserve parking area is 2.3 miles—a drop of 1,300 feet in elevation.

From the Ramsey Canyon Preserve parking area back to the starting point at the intersection of Highways 90 and 92 is 9.5 miles. To reach the starting point turn left (north) at the Ramsey Canyon Road junction with Highway 92.

For the ambitious who have planned ahead and have a spouse, relative, or friend waiting with transportation, it is possible to continue up the Carr Canyon Trail to Ramsey Vista Campground (2.3 miles; about 600 feet elevation-change). The trail from the Ramsey Canyon Preserve up to Ramsey Vista Campground (4.6 miles total; 1,850 feet elevation-change) is probably the most rewarding hike for finding high-elevation birds in the Huachuca Mountains.

HUACHUCA HIGHLANDS

Carr Canyon/Miller Canyon Tour
(39 miles/one day)

Both Carr and Miller Canyons provide birders with an alternative to the heavily-visited Ramsey Canyon Preserve, especially on weekends and holidays, since no reservation is required. Upper Carr Canyon Road offers the only vehicular access to the Ponderosa Pine of the high Huachuca Mountains. Upper Miller Canyon plumbs the highest peaks of the range, and offers reasonable foot access to a cool, streamside forest of Douglas-fir and White Fir.

To find **Carr Canyon** from the starting point at the intersection of Highways 90 and 92, follow Highway 92 due south exactly one mile past the Ramsey turn-off to the well-marked junction (7.0 miles; signed Forest Road 368). A housing development in the lower drainage precludes serious birding until after the pavement ends (1.1 miles; the last house is actually mile 1.4). National Forest property above here presents the birder with an opportunity to see most of the species found in Ramsey Canyon, without the crowds. There are several pull-outs with unimproved picnicking and camping sites in this short stretch.

Birds in lower Carr are representative of the Madrean pine/oak woodland—Cooper's Hawk, Montezuma Quail, Western and Whiskered Screech-Owls (night), Blue-throated, Magnificent, and Black-chinned Hummingbirds (summer), Acorn and Strickland's Woodpeckers, Northern "Red-shafted" Flicker, Western Wood-Pewee (summer), Dusky-capped, Ash-throated, and Brown-crested Flycatchers (summer), Cassin's Kingbird (summer), Mexican Jay, Bridled Titmouse, Bushtit, White-breasted Nuthatch, Bewick's Wren, Solitary "Plumbeous" Vireo (primarily summer), Virginia's and Black-throated Gray Warblers (summer), Painted Redstart (summer), Black-headed Grosbeak (summer), Canyon and Spotted Towhees, and Rufous-crowned Sparrow. In the summer of 1994, a pair of Buff-breasted Flycatchers was using the area near the stream crossing (0.8 miles).

This is the same part of the canyon where Jim Lane lived in the early 1960s. Jim launched the *Lane Guides* in 1965, with the first edition of this book for Southeastern Arizona. If you bird in Carr at daybreak, and witness the red rocks of the high Huachucas catching the first butterscotch light of dawn, the source of Jim's inspiration will be obvious.

Painted Redstart
Narca Moore-Craig

   The next section of the road climbs 1,750 feet up the stupendous band of Cambrian-age cliffs known as The Reef (3.9 miles). Vehicles over 20 feet long and trailers over 12 feet long are not permitted on the hair-pin turns above. If you are bothered by driving near the edge of cliffs, you might *not* want to attempt this road. Carr Canyon attracts 4x4s on weekend jaunts, however, so you might prefer a weekday birding trip up this challenging road when there is less traffic.

The one-lane track zigzags nine times up the towering east wall of Carr Canyon to a vista that sweeps all the way from the Santa Catalina Mountains north of Tucson to the Sierra Madre Mountains in northern Mexico. Sierra Vista and the Upper San Pedro River Valley lie directly below. Beyond the viewpoint atop **The Reef**, the road passes Reef Townsite Campground (0.4 mile), and then wanders through an open stand of primarily Ponderosa Pine before it ends at the Ramsey Vista Campground (1.25 mile; elevation 7,400 feet). The U.S. Forest Service charges fees at both campgrounds according to the following schedule: Parking area—$2, Day use—$3, Overnight camping—$5. Drinking water was *not* available at either area in 1995.

Most of the high-elevation species of the border ranges can be found by birding along this beautiful stretch of forest. Watch the tops of dead trees for Band-tailed Pigeon and Greater Pewee, and scan the living pines for Grace's and Olive Warblers. A human-caused fire in June 1977 consumed 10,000 acres before the onset of the summer rainy season extinguished the blaze. Time has healed the worst scars and several species—notably Buff-breasted Flycatcher—have actually benefited from the burn. Other highland birds underscore the strong Rocky Mountain influence on the avifauna in the upper elevations of the Huachucas. Some of these are Whip-poor-will (after dusk, summer), Broad-tailed Hummingbird (summer), Hairy Woodpecker, Cordilleran Flycatcher (summer), Steller's Jay, Pygmy Nuthatch, House Wren, Yellow-rumped Warbler (summer), and Western Tanager (summer). In migration, watch for Olive-sided Flycatcher in dead tree-tops, and for mixed flocks containing dozens of Townsend's and Hermit Warblers.

The well-marked trail to **Comfort Spring** begins off the west end of the Ramsey Vista Campground, drops 200 feet in elevation, and loops through the burn around the headwater ravines of Carr Canyon. There are Red-faced Warblers in the Gambel's Oak in the first draw just a quarter-mile below the trailhead, and the past decade has seen records of Berylline Hummingbird (1986), Eared Trogon (1990), and Aztec Thrush (1991-1992)—all between the parking area and Comfort Spring (0.6 mile). Comfort Spring is a permanent seep that seems always to harbor a pair of Buff-breasted Flycatchers. Sharing this open area are Eastern Bluebirds, which also enjoy the lush undergrowth amid the skeleton forest left behind by the fire. This is also a fine spot for Northern Pygmy-Owl.

If you have the time and can make suitable arrangements, continue beyond the spring to Hamburg Meadow (1.7 miles) in upper Ramsey Canyon, then down Ramsey to the Preserve's visitor center (2.3 miles; see description of that trail in the previous Garden Canyon/Ramsey Canyon tour). *Please note, however, that both a hiking permit and a parking permit for your friend are required by Ramsey Canyon Preserve before you begin this 4.6-mile-long hike.*

Assuming you do not have a ride waiting for you in Ramsey, a rewarding plan is to relax among the whispering pines at the end of the Carr Canyon Road. Probably any species that you missed in the morning will come wafting by on an updraft generated by The Reef itself. During summer there is no cooler place reached by road for a picnic lunch anywhere in the Huachucas.

To continue this tour, however, you must return to Highway 92 (7.7 miles). Turn right (south) onto Highway 92. A large sign marks the entrance to **Miller Canyon** (2.0 miles; 9.0 miles south of the junction of Highways 90 and 92). Of all the canyons in the front range, Miller has the highest headwaters. Draining the 9,466-foot-high summit of Miller Peak itself, this canyon contains nearly all of the habitats and nearly all of the birds of the border ranges; most of these special species can be found somewhere in or along the tall riparian forest that follows Miller Creek down the mountain to the 5,000-foot-elevation canyon outlet. The two major reasons why birders visit Miller, however, are nightjars and owls along the road and rarities such as Eared Trogon along the trail in the upper canyon.

Miller Road begins in a housing area set in a grassland punctuated by Soaptree Yucca, Honey Mesquite, and an occasional Arizona Sycamore. The large white flowers of the Arizona Prickly Poppy and the magenta flowers of the Wheeler's Thistle add color to the roadside in summer. This is the home of Greater Roadrunner, Acorn and Ladder-backed Woodpeckers, Say's Phoebe, Mexican Jay, Chihuahuan Raven, Verdin, Cactus Wren, Northern Mockingbird, Curve-billed Thrasher, and Pyrrhuloxia. In summer, Western Kingbirds sit on the fence-lines, utility-wires, and other conspicuous perches. After the rains start in early July, listen for the songs of both Botteri's and Cassin's Sparrows. The desert grassland and the housing both end with the pavement (0.85 mile).

As the graded road enters the mountain, the birds are approximately the same as those found in nearby Garden, Ramsey, and Carr Canyons. At night (primarily in the spring and summer) listen for the calls of Flammulated Owl, Western and Whiskered Screech-Owls, Great Horned Owl, Common Poorwill, and Whip-poor-will. During the day, look for

Cooper's, Zone-tailed, and Red-tailed Hawks, Northern "Red-shafted" Flicker, Acorn and Strickland's Woodpeckers, Mexican Jay, Bushtit, White-breasted Nuthatch, Bewick's Wren, Blue-gray Gnatcatcher, Hutton's Vireo, Spotted and Canyon Towhees, and Lark and Rufous-crowned Sparrows. In summer, expect Ash-throated, Dusky-capped, and Brown-crested Flycatchers, Western Wood-Pewee, Solitary "Plumbeous" Vireo, Black-throated Gray Warbler, and Black-headed Grosbeak. Montezuma Quail is most common at the canyon-mouth, particularly in grassy woodland.

Miller Canyon Road terminates at an oval parking lot cut into a dense grove of oaks at an elevation of 5,750 feet (1.7 miles; 2.5 miles from Highway 92). Blue-throated, Magnificent, and Black-chinned Hummingbirds, White-breasted Nuthatch, Solitary "Plumbeous" Vireo, and Painted Redstart enliven the road-end during the day, and, at night, the same grove makes a good starting point for an owl-prowl.

Ambitious, well-conditioned hikers may elect to continue up the canyon in search of some of the most prized birds in the Huachucas. To do this area, and yourself, full justice, arrive at daybreak. *Do not forget to bring water.* The best birding is along an abandoned road in the canyon-bed between mile 0.5 and mile 2.2.

Beatty's Orchard and Apiary (no trespassing) lies just upstream from the parking lot. The first half-mile of the **Miller Canyon Trail**, marked by a Forest Service sign across from the parking lot, circles north around the Beatty property through a stand of manzanita, oak, and juniper. Then it rejoins the old road to the City of Tombstone's water-supply in a moist, steep-walled section of the canyon. Ignore Hunter Canyon Trail at the junction and stay right (0.1 mile). A road branching left toward the stream a short distance beyond leads 100 yards to the fenced intake of the spring that provides 20 percent of Tombstone's water supply. Colorful birds summering among the large sycamores include Sulphur-bellied Flycatcher, Painted Redstart, Hepatic Tanager, Scott's Oriole, and—sometimes—an Elegant Trogon. In winter, check for Red-naped and Williamson's (uncommon) Sapsuckers, and listen for the halting carols of Townsend's Solitaires on still, sunny mornings.

The main trail continues straight ahead as the canyon walls loom progressively higher. After 0.5 mile (1.5 miles above the parking area), the pathway crosses the stream and climbs through a coniferous forest on the shady, north-facing side of the canyon. Watch closely for Spotted Owls on a day-roost in the section up to the next stream-crossing (0.7 mile). The Miller Peak tributary cascades down to the main canyon just above here, and creates an especially propitious situation for highland birds.

In the summer of 1994, an Eared Trogon was roaming this zone of Miller Canyon. Here, too, in mid-April 1980, Slate-throated Redstart was recorded for the first time in the United States. The only summer report of Townsend's Solitaire in the Huachuca Mountains came from Miller Canyon in July 1983. Regular occupants of the upper canyon, however, include Northern Pygmy-Owl, Broad-tailed Hummingbird (summer), Hairy Woodpecker, Greater Pewee (summer), Cordilleran Flycatcher (summer), Steller's Jay, Common Raven, Red-breasted Nuthatch, Brown Creeper, House Wren, Hermit Thrush, Grace's and Red-faced Warbler (both summer), Western Tanager (summer), Chipping Sparrow, and Yellow-eyed Junco. Birds in the upper canyon reflect the Huachuca Mountain's position midway between the Rockies to the north and the Sierra Madre of Mexico to the south.

Do not attempt to follow Miller Canyon into the 20,190-acre Miller Peak Wilderness unless you have budgeted a full day for the outing, have plenty of food and water, and have made appropriate transportation arrangements. Do not forget to bring a map showing the hiking trails of the Huachuca Mountains. There are no regularly occurring birds in the Wilderness Area that warrant this expenditure of time and energy. There are, however, breath-taking panoramas that encompass vast tracts of southern Arizona and northern Mexico.

Over the next 1.3 miles, the Miller Canyon Trail climbs 1,700 feet up to the Crest Trail at Bathtub Spring, elevation 8,540 feet. Most of the route lies within the blackened, picket-post remains of the 1977 Carr Fire. To the southeast, the Crest Trail continues another 2.1 miles to the aspen-clad summit of 9,466-foot-high Miller Peak, then descends to Montezuma Pass, elevation 6,575 feet, in Coronado National Memorial (5.0 miles). To the west, the Crest Trail joins feeder-routes leading to the end of the Carr Canyon Road (3.2 miles) and Ramsey Canyon Preserve (5.2 miles).

The vegetation along much of the Crest Trail is Ponderosa Pine and Gambel's Oak. Aside from Quaking Aspen, the north face of Miller Peak is a verdant admixture of White Pine, Douglas-fir, and a few Rocky Mountain Maples. The birds are the same as those listed for upper Miller Canyon. Northern Goshawk, Red-tailed and Zone-tailed Hawks, American Kestrel, and Golden Eagle are often seen soaring over the mountain-tops.

To return to the starting point from the Miller Canyon parking area, follow the road back to Highway 92, and turn left (north). The total distance from the Miller Road end to the junction of Highways 90 and 92 is 11.5 miles.

Campgrounds, Restaurants, and Accommodations:

Reef Townsite and Ramsey Vista at the end of the Carr Canyon Road are the only improved campgrounds (vehicles over 20 feet long not permitted; no trailers over 12 feet long). *Drinking water is not available at either campground.*

The Tombstone KOA (PO Box 99, Tombstone, AZ 85638; telephone 520/457-3829) is recommended for RVers and trailer-campers.

Ramsey Canyon has two facilities: Ramsey Canyon Preserve has six housekeeping cabins available to birders; reservations should be made a year in advance for the prime birding season between April and September (Ramsey Canyon Preserve, 27 Ramsey Canyon Road, Hereford, AZ 85615; telephone 520/378-2785). The Ramsey Canyon Inn (31 Ramsey Canyon Road, Hereford, AZ 85615; telephone 520/378-3010), just 50 yards downcanyon, is an attractive bed-and-breakfast with the same hummingbirds as the neighboring Preserve.

There are numerous restaurants and motels in Sierra Vista. Owing to their proximity to Ramsey Canyon, most birders gravitate to either Thunder Mountain Inn (1631 S. Highway 92, Sierra Vista 85635; telephone 520/458-7900 or 800/222-5811), which has a wonderful salad bar in its restaurant, or the Ramada Inn (2047 S. Highway 92, Sierra Vista, AZ 85635; telephone 520/459-5900 or 800/825-4856), which includes breakfast in its room rate. A new B & B catering to nature enthusiasts is located on ten acres adjoining the San Pedro River. The Casa de San Pedro B & B has feeders, a pond, and nature trails that link up with those in the Riparian National Conservation Area (8933 S. Yell Lane, Hereford, AZ 85615; telephone 520/366-1300). On the west side of the river, midway between the Hereford Bridge and Highway 92, is the new San Pedro River Inn (8326 S. Hereford Road, Hereford, AZ 85615; telephone 520/366-5532).

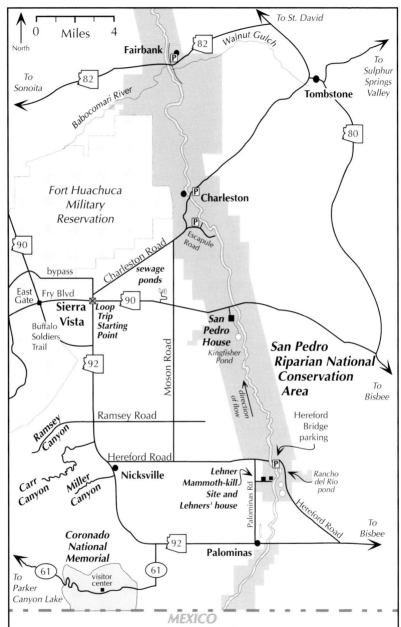

San Pedro Riparian National Conservation Area:
Upper and Lower San Pedro Valley Loops

CHAPTER 7

SAN PEDRO
VALLEY LOOPS

D raining all the way from Sonora, the long, shady pools of the upper San Pedro River constitute the most important valley/riparian system in all Southeastern Arizona. More Gray Hawks live here than anywhere else in the United States. The San Pedro also hosts the largest concentration of Yellow-billed Cuckoos in the western United States, as well as Arizona's largest population of Green Kingfishers. This continuous, 40-mile-long grove of cottonwood and willow trees provides migratory birds with a conduit of food and cover unmatched elsewhere in the American Southwest.

The Bureau of Land Management acquired this mile-wide, 50,000-acre tract of river-bottom only in 1986. After that government bureau designated the upper San Pedro a Riparian National Conservation Area the following year, all grazing and farming were halted. The ensuing surge of new plant growth in the riverine forest has astonished even seasoned ecologists. And bird populations simply exploded. Song Sparrows, for example, have increased fifty-fold. All told, at least 350 species of birds have been recorded along the San Pedro River in just the past decade. Today, the San Pedro Riparian National Conservation Area represents what is probably the most miraculous conservation achievement in the recent history of Arizona.

That does not mean that the future of the NCA is secure. With constant population growth and groundwater pumping in the area, there is the potential to reverse this accomplishment. Moreover, the grazing and farming along the San Pedro that were eliminated in 1988 will be up for public review in 2003.

The starting point for both loops in this chapter is the intersection of Highways 90 and 92 on the east side of Sierra Vista. (Access to this junction is described in detail in Chapter 6 for the Huachuca Mountains.)

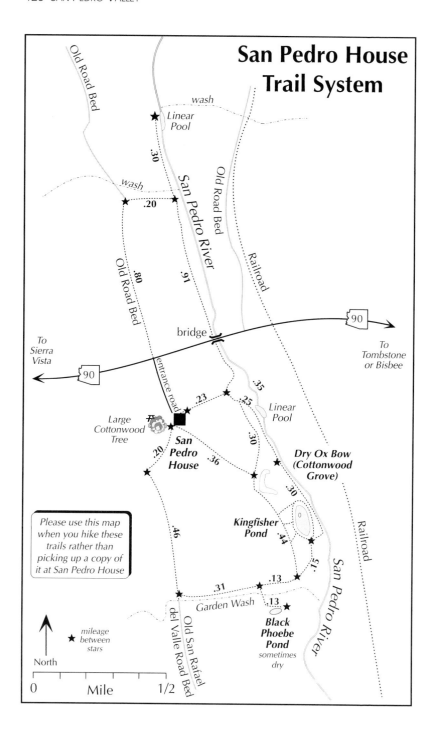

San Pedro House
Trail System

Old Road Bed

wash

★ Linear
Pool

.30

San Pedro River

Old Road Bed

wash

.20

Railroad

.80

Old Road Bed

.91

90

To
Tombstone
or Bisbee

bridge

To
Sierra
Vista

90

entrance road

.35

.23

.25

Linear
Pool

Large
Cottonwood
Tree

San
Pedro
House

.20

.36

.30

Dry Ox Bow
(Cottonwood
Grove)

.30

Please use this map
when you hike these
trails rather than
picking up a copy of
it at San Pedro House

.46

Kingfisher
Pond

.44

.51

Railroad

San Pedro River

.31

.13

★

North

mileage
between
stars

Garden Wash

.13

Black
Phoebe
Pond
sometimes
dry

Old San Rafael
del Valle Road Bed

0   Mile   1/2

In summer it is important to bird the gallery forest along the river early, since most bird activity subsides by 10am.

Upper San Pedro Valley Loop

(56 miles/one day)

This loop begins with a sunrise trip to the river, by-passing the Sierra Vista Wastewater Ponds (3.0 miles), where the waterfowl and shorebirds tend to be present throughout the day.

Take Highway 90 due east from the starting point. The pavement descends gradually through a parched Chihuahuan Desert landscape characterized by thorny shrubs until, abruptly, the lush green ribbon of the San Pedro appears directly ahead. Turn right (south) at the base of the terrace at the well-signed entrance drive to the **San Pedro House** (3.9 miles). A combination book store/gift shop/information center, San Pedro House (0.2 mile) is run entirely by a non-profit conservation group called Friends of the San Pedro River. The House is open daily from 9:30am to 4:30pm.

Nearly every bird known from the San Pedro corridor has occurred in the general neighborhood of the San Pedro House and the nearby Highway 90 Bridge. A typical summer list of species seen along the entrance drive and around the parking area will include Swainson's Hawk, American Kestrel, Gambel's Quail, Black-chinned Hummingbird, Gila Woodpecker, Gilded Flicker, Vermilion Flycatcher, Say's Phoebe, Cassin's and Western Kingbirds, Cactus Wren, Lucy's Warbler, Summer Tanager, Blue Grosbeak, Canyon and Abert's Towhees, Eastern Meadowlark, and Bullock's Oriole. In late July and August, listen for the characteristic songs of Botteri's and Cassin's Sparrows on the perimeter of the parking area. In winter, watch for Northern Harrier, Northern "Red-shafted" Flicker, Mountain Bluebird (rare), Green-tailed Towhee, Vesper and Brewer's Sparrows, and Western Meadowlark. Lark Buntings are usually present, except in midsummer.

A loop trail leads to the appropriately named **Kingfisher Pond**, an abandoned gravel quarry that has filled with groundwater, on the south end of the circuit. The trail begins off the south side of San Pedro House. *A note of caution:* if there has been a significant rain within 24 hours, deep mud can render the trail almost impassable and the banks of the river treacherous. If you decide to venture down to the pond anyway, there's a hose in front of the house. As one who's trudged back from the river on two-inch-thick mud suction-cups weighing at least 10 pounds each, I give you my solemn word that you'll be ridiculously grateful to hose off the adobe gunk caked to the soles of your boots.

Rainfall only averages 12 inches per year, so heat is usually the most serious problem here. Open-country birds—doves, kingbirds (summer), shrikes, and meadowlarks—are the common species as the route crosses an abandoned alfalfa field to a line of cottonwood trees (0.3 mile). Turning right (south), the trail continues along the edge of an old river-terrace through tall Sacaton Grass and mesquite to the west edge of the approximately one-acre pond (0.3). Along the way, look for Vermilion Flycatcher (primarily summer), Summer Tanager (April-September), and the abundant Abert's Towhees. There are more Abert's Towhees here than any other area of Arizona or the U.S.

Gaps in the pond shoreline's cottonwoods and willows allow glimpses of the far bank. Take time to check low branches overhanging the water for the pond's Green Kingfishers. Since 1993 a pair of Tropical Kingbirds (summer) has also frequently used a dead cottonwood tree halfway along the far edge. Early in the morning, watch for possible Snowy Egrets (uncommon, late summer) or Black-crowned Night-Herons on this same conspicuous perch. Other birds present include Green Heron, Common Moorhen, Lesser Nighthawk (skimming the pond surface on summer mornings), Cliff Swallow (summer), Common Yellowthroat, and Red-winged Blackbird.

Green Kingfisher is often found at Black Phoebe Pond (when it has water). The pond should be checked if you have been unable to locate this bird elsewhere. Garden Wash is good for Green-tailed Towhee (common here in winter), Pyrrhuloxia, Crissal Thrasher, and Common Ground-Dove (uncommon). Many of the desert birds of the area can be found along the old San Rafael del Valle Road that loops back to San Pedro House—Cactus Wren, Black-tailed Gnatcatcher, Black-throated Sparrow, and Verdin, for example.

Probably the two most-abundant species along the San Pedro in the summer are Yellow Warbler and Common Yellowthroat, but Yellow-breasted Chat and Summer Tanager are also commonplace. To find the river, circle the far (south) end of Kingfisher Pond about halfway, nearly to the dead cottonwood tree, then veer right (east) onto the trail-of-use for about 50 yards to the bank of the river. Turn left (north or downstream) to continue the loop. Unless there have been recent heavy rains, the San Pedro River will be a series of long, quiet pools linked by a stream 10 to 20 feet wide. These pools are inhabited by the subspecies of Mallard formerly known as "Mexican Duck." Drakes have yellow-olive bills, but, otherwise, look like dark-plumaged hen Mallards. Also watch for Great

Blue Heron, Gray Hawk, Yellow-billed Cuckoo, Great Horned Owl, Belted Kingfisher (primarily migration periods), Black Phoebe, Brown-crested Flycatcher (summer), White-breasted Nuthatch, Bewick's Wren, and Song Sparrow.

The path that parallels the river is narrow but generally well-defined. During migration, Lazuli Buntings dodge in and out of the rank growth along the water. Possible passage *Empidonax* flycatchers—Willow, Hammond's, Dusky, Gray, and Pacific-slope, sprinkled among the young of both Western Wood-Pewees and Vermilion Flycatchers—create enough identification challenges for even the most masochistic of birders. The trail leaves the cottonwoods almost due east of the parking lot (0.4 mile). Check the river in both directions for Green Kingfisher before hiking the last leg. Since first confirmed as an Arizona nesting species in

Green Kingfisher
Narca Moore-Craig

1988, the San Pedro population has steadily increased. A 1993 census found 15 kingfishers using the upper river.

It is approximately 300 yards across an open field to the comfortable chairs on the front porch of the San Pedro House. Picnickers will find a couple of tables under one of the most enormous cottonwoods in the Southwest. Don't forget to record your observations at the visitor center, and remember that any profits from the books, T-shirts, and sodas sold here go to support the critical conservation efforts of the Friends of the San Pedro.

North of Highway 90, the area between the old road bed and the river harbors many Botteri's and Cassin's Sparrows in summer. Brown-crested Flycatcher is more common north of the highway, especially near the wash. Ruddy Ground-Doves were present one winter.

To visit the **Sierra Vista Wastewater Ponds** turn left (west) onto Highway 90, and retrace your route back toward the city. Watch for the large green fields on the right (north) that signal your approach to the entrance into the facility (3.9 miles). Just 10 feet inside the chain-link fence (gate open from 7am to 3:30pm Monday through Friday, occasionally on weekends) turn right (east) at the sign that reads "Wetlands." The pavement follows the edge of an alfalfa field—first east, then north—until it arrives at a corner overlooking a rectangular sewage pond with barren banks (0.3 mile). Birds are everywhere.

As you roll to a stop it's possible that you will flush up a White-faced Ibis or a flock of Mallards, Northern Pintails, or Northern Shovelers, but the other shorebirds and ducks usually stay put. A scope will come in handy as you work the waterfowl paddling to the rear of the 300-yard-long pond. Nearly all of Arizona's duck species have appeared here, including a Garganey in May 1991. Don't overlook the sandpipers on the bare banks. In migration, an occasional Franklin's Gull, crowds of Western, Least, and Baird's Sandpipers (primarily in fall), Long-billed Dowitcher, and either Wilson's or Red-necked Phalaropes, may be joined by smaller numbers of White-faced Ibis, Black-necked Stilt, American Avocet, both species of yellowlegs, Solitary and Spotted Sandpipers, and a few Short-billed Dowitchers. Semipalmated Sandpipers are rare, but annual, here between mid-July and mid-September. With patience, skill, and an element of luck, they can be finessed out of the flocks of peeps by noting the combination of dark legs, short, blunt-tipped tubular bill, flaring eyebrow, clean white underparts, and lack of any rust color in the scapulars. Even more rare, Red Phalaropes were recorded at the Waste-water Ponds in June and December of 1992. Snow, Ross's, and Greater White-fronted Geese are occasional in winter.

Scan the field behind you. Among the plethora of species which you may see are Red-tailed and Swainson's Hawks (summer, especially on the center-pivot irrigation rig), Greater Roadrunner, Lesser Nighthawk (at dawn and dusk in summer), Say's Phoebe, Western and Cassin's Kingbirds (summer), Horned Lark (winter), Chihuahuan Raven, American Pipit (winter), Lark, Vesper, and other mixed sparrows (primarily winter), Lark Bunting (fall through spring), Eastern and Western (winter) Meadowlarks, Brewer's Blackbird (winter), Great-tailed Grackle, and Brown-headed Cowbird.

In 1992, volunteers from Sierra Vista planted an artificial marsh in the next pond west, as well as constructing a viewing platform at the end of the dirt road (0.2 mile). Check the open leads between the rushes for species such as Eared Grebe (winter), Snowy Egret (primarily migration periods), and American Coot. Ruddy Ducks usually stick to the open water, but an impressive row of sleeping ducks may queue up on the levee that runs due east from the platform. Watch for Lazuli Buntings, which are abundant in August—sometimes numbering in the dozens—and Yellow-headed Blackbirds, occasionally scarce but sometimes several thousand strong, depending on the day. In mid-August, one to two dozen migrating Black Terns may work either the pond or the marsh, and literally hundreds of swallows—frequently of five or six different species—skim the fields and the water. The Wastewater Ponds are the most reliable location in the Sierra Vista area for passage Bank Swallows. Look for Purple Martins in April and July.

Depending on your luck with the birds, chances are that by now the sun is high. If your lunch plans involve an air-conditioned restaurant, now is the time to return to Sierra Vista (3.0 miles to the starting point). If it's a particularly warm day, I suggest an afternoon in the shady confines of nearby Ramsey, Carr, or Miller Canyons in the cool Huachucas (see Chapter 6). But during migration periods and winter a visit to the upper San Pedro River Valley warrants the effort required.

To continue with the loop, turn left (east) onto Highway 90. At the far end of the Sierra Vista Wastewater fields, angle right (south) at the sign for Moson Road (0.9 mile; 3.9 miles east of the starting point). Throughout its length, Moson Road cuts through Chihuahuan desertscrub dominated by mesquite and acacia. Watch the power-poles, utility-wires, and fence-lines for an occasional Golden Eagle, Prairie Falcon (winter), Great Horned Owl (night), Scaled Quail, Ladder-backed Woodpecker, Ash-throated Flycatcher (summer), Western Kingbird (summer), Chihuahuan Raven, Cactus Wren, Northern Mockingbird, Curve-billed Thrasher,

Loggerhead Shrike, and Pyrrhuloxia. Turn left (east) where Moson ends at a "T" intersection with Hereford Road (7.9 miles).

Hereford Road drops like a plumb bob through mesquite grassland that hosts Swainson's (summer) and Ferruginous (uncommon, winter) Hawks, Scaled Quail, Greater Roadrunner, Verdin, Bendire's Thrasher, and Black-throated Sparrow. Botteri's and Cassin's Sparrows sing in tracts of tall grasses during the summer monsoon months. A Scissor-tailed Flycatcher added interest to the drive to the river in August of both 1992 and 1993. The one-lane **Hereford Bridge** (5.1 miles) provides another access-point to the San Pedro. *It is unsafe to stop on the bridge.* Birders should continue east to the BLM parking area on the right (south) side of the road (0.2 mile). From here, it is possible to hike along unmaintained trails on the east side of the river, both north and south of the Hereford Bridge.

Today the Upper San Pedro averages 10 to 20 feet in width, but in former times it had numerous marshes and beaver ponds. John Spring, who served at Fort Huachuca in the late 1800s, wrote that it was necessary to detour well into Mexico to cross the river during the rainy season. He also recalled seeing huge flocks of ducks and geese, which were shot for the mess. By his estimate, fur trappers took over one million Beavers from this area at the turn of the century.

Although the strand of cottonwoods is narrow along this stretch of the San Pedro, an impressive list of regional rarities has been observed here. These include Little Blue Heron, Black Swift (still hypothetical in Arizona), Elegant Trogon, Thick-billed Kingbird, Gray Catbird, Rufous-backed Robin, Brown Thrasher, Prothonotary Warbler, and Orchard Oriole. Wild Turkeys are suspected of breeding somewhere between San Pedro House and the Hereford Bridge. More expected near the Hereford Bridge parking area are Gambel's Quail, Common Ground-Dove, Great Horned Owl, Gila and Ladder-backed Woodpeckers, Gilded Flicker, Verdin, Curve-billed and Crissal Thrashers, Phainopepla, Northern Cardinal, Pyrrhuloxia, and Abert's Towhee. In summer, watch for White-winged Dove, Yellow-billed Cuckoo, Lesser Nighthawk, Black-chinned Hummingbird, Ash-throated Flycatcher, Bell's Vireo, Yellow-breasted Chat, Summer Tanager, Blue Grosbeak, and Bullock's Oriole. In winter, Green-tailed Towhee, Western and Mountain Bluebirds (some years), and White-crowned Sparrow are typically common. Rare or uncommon sparrows of interest that have appeared here include Baird's, Black-chinned, Fox, and Sage.

Turn right (east) from the BLM Hereford Bridge parking area to continue the tour. Hereford Road soon swings south to the Rancho del

Rio Pond (1.0 mile), a pretty little cottonwood-lined pond which has proved to be a good spot year-round for Black Phoebe and Vermilion Flycatcher. Occasionally, Black-bellied Whistling-Ducks settle here, and, in summer, Tropical Kingbirds are possible. Visitors are asked to view the pond from the edge of the highway without disturbing the owners.

After Rancho del Rio, two more ponds are visible from Hereford Road; although distant (scope recommended), neither is screened from view by trees (0.6 and 0.3 miles). Belonging to the San Pedro River Inn, both of these ponds are more likely to attract migrating waterfowl than Rancho del Rio's. Yellow-headed Blackbirds use the huge fields beyond the ponds throughout the year, but on late winter afternoons the cottonwood trees near these ponds may fill up with thousands of Yellowheads in a spectacle not soon forgotten.

After passing the last pond, Hereford Road swerves away from the river and enters an area of limestone soil with low, thorny brush. Vegetation is Chihuahuan desertscrub in which the dominant plants are Littleleaf Sumac, Tarbush, Sandpaper Bush, Creosote Bush, and White-thorn Acacia. This is good habitat for Cactus Wren, Crissal Thrasher, and Black-throated Sparrow. Turn right (west) onto Highway 92 (3.6 miles).

Before you lies a panorama of the San Pedro Valley that spans two nations and embraces a written history of more than four and one-half centuries. This is the valley through which Francisco Vásquez de Coronado first rode into the present-day United States in 1540, accompanied by 225 other bold explorers, four priests, and nearly a thousand Native Americans for support. They passed through the San Pedro Valley in search of the fabulous Seven Cities of Cíbola. Although no golden cities were ever discovered, the Coronado Expedition opened the American Southwest to European colonization.

Coronado National Memorial, at the east end of the Huachuca Mountains, interprets the history of early Spanish exploration. The visitor center features exhibits and a small book store. To take this side-trip to the Memorial, drive due west to the well-signed junction (9.1 miles) and turn left (south). The visitor center is situated in an oak woodland at the mouth of Montezuma Canyon (4.8 miles). Be sure to check the small wildlife watering pool outside the rear windows. Plain-capped Starthroat has been sighted out these windows on several occasions in the past decade. Beyond the visitor center, the road narrows and zigzags up the steep canyon walls to Montezuma Pass (3.5 miles). A vast expanse of Sonora and Southeastern Arizona is visible from the summit (6,575 feet in elevation). Hikers can connect to the Huachuca Crest Trail from the west side of Montezuma Pass (see the trail description under Miller Canyon in Chapter 6).

If you have decided to skip Coronado National Memorial and/or wish to continue the main tour, follow Highway 92 west, from its intersection with Hereford Road, back over the San Pedro River to the small community of Palominas (3.0 miles). (The river here is only five miles north of the border with Sonora.) After crossing the San Pedro River, turn right (north) just beyond and across from the post office onto Palominas Road (0.5 mile).

Watch for **Palominas Pond**, a quarter-mile-long farm pond (0.3 mile) about 300 yards east of the road (scope recommended). Green Heron, American Coot, Vermilion Flycatcher (almost guaranteed in winter), and Yellow-headed Blackbird are all regular here, and, occasionally, Cattle Egret and Black-bellied Whistling-Duck put in an appearance. Possible rarities in winter include Greater White-fronted Goose, Bald Eagle, and Sandhill Crane. In late August 1988 a Tricolored Heron stayed at Palominas Pond for a full week. *Motorists are reminded to pull completely off the pavement.*

The most extensive grassland in the upper San Pedro Valley is on the west side of Palominas Road. Birds using this grassland include White-tailed Kite, Northern Harrier (winter), Scaled Quail, Greater Roadrunner, Lesser Nighthawk (summer evenings), Western Kingbird (summer), Scissor-tailed Flycatcher (sporadic in summer), Chihuahuan Raven, and Loggerhead Shrike. Winter birding is especially rewarding. Both Ferruginous and Rough-legged Hawks (rare) are possible, as are Short-eared Owl (January 1986) and Northern Shrike (winter 1988-1989). This is also excellent winter habitat for Sprague's Pipit (rare), Mountain Bluebird (numbers fluctuate), and both McCown's (casual) and Chestnut-collared (regular) Longspurs.

Continue north up Palominas Road to the signed junction with Lehner Road on the right (east) side (2.4 miles). The dirt road drops due east down toward the San Pedro River. A parking area on the left (north) with a National Historic Landmark plaque (0.5 mile) commemorates the site where Ed Lehner discovered an enormous bone in 1952. Excavations conducted by the Arizona State Museum in 1955-1956 and 1974-1975 revealed the fossil remains of 12 immature Woolly Mammoths, as well other members of the Pleistocene megafauna including tapir, bison, camel, and horse. Clovis Culture projectile points, stone tools, fire hearths, and other artifacts, dated through both radiocarbon and stratigraphy, place these prehistoric hunters here 11-13,000 years before the present. The Lehners have generously donated this important site to the Bureau of Land Management.

With a phone call in advance (520/366-5554), birdwatchers are welcome to continue beyond the National Historic Landmark to the ranch owned by Ed and Lynne Lehner (0.3 mile). Ponds and fields here have hosted Black-bellied Whistling-Duck, Purple Gallinule (June and July 1981), and Sandhill Crane. Barn Owls frequent the cottonwoods along the San Pedro River, and Pyrrhuloxias use the mesquite thickets along the edge of the terrace where the mammoths once roamed.

To complete this loop, continue north on Palominas Road to the "T" intersection with Hereford Road (1.3 mile). Turn left (west) here and follow Hereford Road up to its junction with Highway 92 (7.4 miles). Turn right (north) onto Highway 92 to return to the starting point (8.25 miles).

Lower San Pedro River Loop

(50 miles/one day)

History buffs will appreciate that this tour actually connects three dots on the map which were made famous as outlaw hide-outs. Charleston and Fairbank are ghost towns today, but Tombstone is a thriving community with a population of 2,000 people. For birders, the Lower River Loop offers three more access points to the San Pedro, downstream from the popular San Pedro House and the Highway 90 Bridge. While the birds are much the same as those found upriver, some of the more wary species such as Gray Hawk may be easier to see at these less-visited areas.

The first birding site is **Escapule** (Es-cah-POO-lee) **Wash**. It behooves birders to start early, for activity on the river usually dies after 10am. From the starting point, drive north on Highway 90 to the next traffic signal and turn right onto Charleston Road (0.25 mile). The right-hand (south) turn-off onto Escapule Wash Road (6.0 miles) is well away from Sierra Vista, halfway through the first major curve on Charleston Road. A short link of gravel secondary-road leads to a BLM pull-out on the left (east) side (0.3 mile), where a stile over a fence marks the start of a trail that parallels the wash.

Escapule Wash proper cuts across the road beyond the pull-out (0.1 mile). Birders are advised to park their vehicles at the designated pull-out, and then hike down the wash bed itself. Scattered cottonwood trees shade the wide, sandy wash as it gradually descends approximately 0.5

mile to the San Pedro River. Halfway down, a 3-foot-high stone ledge forces a permanent spring to the surface. Some of the best birding is near this short stretch of permanent water.

A pair of Gray Hawks (summer) nests annually along Escapule Wash, and this tendril of tall cottonwoods is an excellent migrant-trap for passerines. Among the birds of passage are Willow, Hammond's, Dusky, Gray, and Pacific-slope Flycatchers, as well as Orange-crowned, Nashville, Chestnut-sided (casual), Townsend's (rare), Black-and-white (rare), American Redstart (rare), Northern Waterthrush (rare), MacGillivray's, Hooded (rare), and Wilson's Warblers. Summer breeders include Northern Beardless-Tyrannulet (locally rare along the upper San Pedro), Bell's Vireo, Yellow-breasted Chat, Summer Tanager, and Abert's Towhee.

Once down to the river, it is possible to turn left (north) downstream and bushwhack all the way to the Charleston Bridge (about 1.5 miles). Birders should be aware that no trail exists and that knee-deep pockets of quicksand create tough slogging. The old railroad line on the east—opposite—side of the San Pedro offers reasonably easy going for the final mile or so, *but hikers need to watch and listen for trains.* Originally laid in the early 1880s, these tracks are still in use today.

Return to Charleston Road and turn right to continue the loop. Although the highway is winding, **Charleston Bridge** is almost due north of the junction with Escapule Wash Road (1.5 miles). A BLM parking area lies off the southeast corner of the bridge (0.1 mile).

Lacking adequate water in Tombstone, a stamp mill for the silver mines was located on the San Pedro just north of here in 1879. The mill site was given the prosaic name of Millville, and the village across the river, where the workers and merchants lived, was called Charleston. According to legend, banditos like Curley Bill Brocius used Charleston as a bedroom community for commuting to work in nearby Tombstone. In spite of its low reputation in the East, no shipment of bullion nor monies for payroll were ever lost to outlaws in the one short decade the town thrived. The end was in sight after the mines flooded in 1886, when the water pumps were shut down by striking miners.

The best birding is from an abandoned bridge adjacent to the parking area. Western Screech-Owl is reliable all year on the northeast side of the bridge, about 500 yards from the parking area. Lazuli, Indigo, and even Varied and Painted Buntings are all possible from the old Charleston Bridge in August and September. Search for Gray Hawk (summer) and Green Kingfisher. Varied Bunting, Black-throated Sparrow, and Rufous-crowned Sparrow are all more likely in the arid mesquite thickets along the railroad tracks which serve as a de facto trail north and south of the

Charleston Road. *Please note, however, the railroad line is still in operation: birders must use caution if they walk the railroad right-of-way.*

Charleston Road climbs through Chihuahuan desertscrub and slices through a low group of hills before arriving in Tombstone (8.8 miles). The roads that lead to Highway 80 a couple of hundred yards to the east are fairly obvious. Charleston Road changes into Sumner Street; at the stop-sign, turn right (south) onto Allen Street. Go one block, then turn left (east) onto the continuation of Sumner Street. Highway 80 is straight ahead. To continue the tour without even a backward glance at history turn left (north) onto Highway 80.

There are few birds in the immediate precincts of Tombstone, although the nearby Tombstone Hills have historically served as winter quarters for a roost of Long-eared Owls. Today, souvenir and antique shops line the business district. But the lineaments of "the town too tough to die" are still visible on a stroll up Allen Street.

Founded on top a fabulous silver lode discovered by prospector Ed Schieffelin in 1878, Tombstone only a few years later boasted a population of 20,000, and was the largest city between St. Louis and San Francisco. The wealthy citizenry supported the arts, and the Bird Cage Theatre hosted some of the most famous performers of the era. Tombstone is probably best known for the gunfight at the OK Corral. In 1881, Wyatt Earp, his brothers Virgil and Morgan, and their friend Doc Holliday

The old Charleston Bridge offers birders an excellent vantage point for checking the San Pedro River for Green Kingfishers and many other species.

faced six cowboy gunslingers led by Ike Clanton. When the smoke cleared, three of the gunslingers had run and the other three lay dead.

But their feud was not over. Virgil and Morgan were both ambushed in the next few months, crippling Virgil for life and killing Morgan. Morgan's assailants were identified by eyewitnesses, but Sheriff Johnny Behan, bitter over losing the affections of a woman named Josephine Marcus to Wyatt, decided that all four men had credible alibis, and released them. Wyatt executed his own revenge. Within a week he had gunned down three of the perpetrators, including the notorious Curley Bill Brocius. Then he left town with Josephine Marcus. She was still with him when he died peacefully in California in 1929.

In 1886 the mines under Tombstone flooded, and the town never recovered. The Tombstone County Courthouse Building, the Bird Cage Theatre, and other buildings date back to the first turbulent decade of the town's existence, and a sandwich hour spent on Allen Street can't help but evoke a sense of this chapter of America's past.

Drive north on Highway 80 to continue the tour. Boothill Graveyard (0.2 mile from the intersection of Sumner Street) on the right (east) side marks the outskirts of old Tombstone. A few minutes later turn left (west) onto Highway 82 (2.6 miles). The highway follows the north edge of Walnut Gulch almost down to the river bank at **Fairbank**, established in 1883 (5.9 miles). The entrance on the right (north) side of the highway is easy to overshoot—get ready to turn right when you see red corrals on the left.

Fairbank is a natural vagrant trap situated at the axis of Walnut Gulch from the east and the Babocomari River from the west. Aside from the summer-green of cottonwoods along the San Pedro, the site supports a large mesquite bosque, or woodland. Today, all that remains of the town of Fairbank is the historic Adobe Commercial Building. Several modern house-trailers, one staffed by a BLM host, are nearby. A pair of easily-seen Vermilion Flycatchers haunts the grassy park between these structures. Until 1994 the Bureau of Land Management administered the entire San Pedro National Conservation Area from Fairbank. As a consequence the list of vagrants recorded at Fairbank is long. Included are species from the high Huachucas, such as Red-breasted Nuthatch, and from Mexico, such as a Yellow Grosbeak recorded here in May 1992.

Birders have a choice of two trails at Fairbank. A narrow path wanders from the parking area to a railroad overpass (300 yards), then tunnels through shady mesquites to the San Pedro River (400 yards). In summer, this woodland is alive with the voices of Gambel's Quail, Gila Woodpecker, Northern Beardless-Tyrannulet, Ash-throated Flycatcher, Bewick's Wren, Bell's Vireo, Summer Tanager, and Abert's Towhee. Watch for a Gray Hawk fly-by as you approach the river. Gray Flycatcher and Green-tailed Towhee occupy the same bosque in winter. The Highway 82 Bridge is only 100 yards south, just below the confluence of the Babocomari River with the San Pedro. Although the Babocomari is no more than a small stream, it nonetheless represents the single largest tributary entering the upper San Pedro River north of Mexico and south of Interstate 10.

Continuing south upstream another 300 yards, it is possible to make a loop by turning left and hiking east up the dry bed of Walnut Gulch. Bell's Vireo, Yellow-breasted Chat, and Varied Bunting are common in the brush in the lower wash during summer. From the confluence of Walnut Creek with the San Pedro to Boquillas Ranch Road is only 300 yards farther. Fairbank is approximately 100 yards north across Highway 82. The round trip hike is one-mile-long.

The other trail begins straight across Highway 82 from the parking area at Fairbank. This is the dirt road that leads south to Boquillas Ranch (2.0 miles), currently used to house research staff for the BLM. Private vehicles are not permitted on the road, but walking it in summer should produce Ladder-backed Woodpecker, Ash-throated Flycatcher, Cactus Wren, Curve-billed Thrasher, and Varied Bunting. Chances of seeing these and other desert species are improved with an early start. There is no reason this loop, which features a possible hike either at Fairbank or Escapule Wash, cannot be run beginning with Fairbank.

To return to the starting point in Sierra Vista, turn right (east) and cross the San Pedro River (0.3 mile). Continue east to the intersection of Highways 82 and 90 (9.6 miles). Turn left (south) to follow Highway 90 to its intersection with Highway 92 (13.5 miles).

Campgrounds, Restaurants, and Accommodations:

Facilities for the San Pedro Valley are identical to those for the Huachuca Mountains described in the preceding chapter.

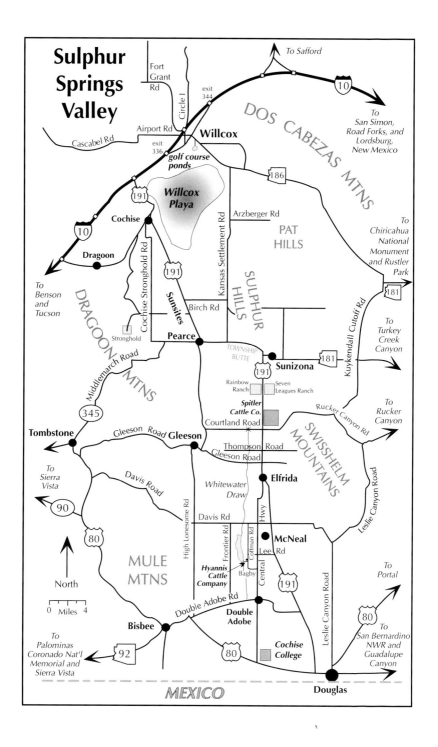

Sulphur Springs Valley

To Safford

10

To San Simon, Road Forks, and Lordsburg, New Mexico

Fort Grant Rd

exit 344

Circle I

Airport Rd

Willcox

exit 336

Cascabel Rd

golf course ponds

191

Willcox Playa

186

DOS CABEZAS MTNS

Cochise

10

Dragoon

Arzberger Rd

Kansas Settlement Rd

PAT HILLS

To Chiricahua National Monument and Rustler Park

To Benson and Tucson

DRAGOON MTNS

Cochise Stronghold Rd

191

Sunsites

Birch Rd

SULPHUR HILLS

181

To Turkey Creek Canyon

Stronghold

Pearce

TOWNSHIP BUTTE

191

Sunizona

181

Kuykendall Cutoff Rd

Middlemarch Road

345

Rainbow Ranch

Seven Leagues Ranch

Spitler Cattle Co.

Courtland Road

Rucker Canyon Rd

To Rucker Canyon

Tombstone

Gleeson Road

Gleeson

Thompson Road

Gleeson Road

SWISSHELM MOUNTAINS

Leslie Canyon Road

To Sierra Vista

Davis Road

Whitewater Draw

Elfrida

90

80

High Lonesome Rd

Davis Rd

Frontier Rd

Coffman Rd

Central Hwy

McNeal

Lee Rd

To Portal

MULE MTNS

North

Hyannis Cattle Company

Bagby

191

Leslie Canyon Road

0   Miles   4

Double Adobe Rd

Double Adobe

80

To San Bernardino NWR and Guadalupe Canyon

Bisbee

92

80

Cochise College

To Palominas Coronado Nat'l Memorial and Sierra Vista

Douglas

MEXICO

CHAPTER 8

SULPHUR SPRINGS VALLEY TOUR

(88 miles to Douglas/one day)

(129 miles to Sierra Vista/one day)

(160 miles round-trip from Willcox/one day)

Stretching 100 miles on a north-south axis and ranging from 15 to 25 miles in width, the 4,000-foot-high Sulphur Springs Valley has earned a reputation as the best winter raptor location in Southeastern Arizona. Up to 14 species of birds of prey find a cold-season niche in the broad grasslands and extensive farms in what has come to be known as Arizona's "hawk alley". Additionally, approximately 10,000 Sandhill Cranes make these fields their winter headquarters. With shorebird migrations ending in June and beginning again in July, this important migratory bird corridor is actually a prime destination throughout the year.

The starting point for this tour is the town of Willcox. Willcox is located on Interstate 10 approximately 80 miles east of Tucson. Take exit 336 and follow Haskell Street directly into downtown Willcox to the one and only traffic signal (mile 4.0). —If you are connecting to this tour from Portal, drive north on the San Simon Road to Interstate 10 (23 miles), then follow the interstate west to Willcox exit 344 (38 miles). The distance from the exit overpass down Haskell Street to the stoplight is 4.2 miles. —Coming from Chiricahua National Monument (see Chapter 9), take Highway 181 to a "T" intersection with Highway 186 (3.0 miles from the entry station), then follow Highway 186 northwest to Willcox (28 miles).

Willcox hosts one of the largest concentrations of Chihuahuan Ravens in Southeastern Arizona. Harris's Hawk, Golden Eagle, Scaled Quail, and Burrowing Owl are occasionally spotted on any approach to Willcox.

Birders starting from Douglas or Sierra Vista may well choose to run this tour in reverse sequence, and then deadhead back to their point of origin, or continue from Willcox to another loop. There is no major birding advantage to beginning this tour either from the north end at Willcox or from the south end near Douglas. If you are looking for thrashers, however, they are more common in the south end of the valley and are easier to find early in the morning.

The most renowned single location in the Sulphur Springs Valley is the area known as the **Willcox Playa**. Technically speaking, the Willcox Playa itself is the large dry lake-bed, inaccessible to birders except at a few points. But the area also includes perennially-green Willcox Munici-pal Golf Course and two permanent holding ponds for treated wastewa-ter—an important oasis in the otherwise arid and barren northern valley. (Locals call these ponds "Twin Lakes" and most birders refer to the larger of the two as "Willcox Lake.") To find these ponds from the traffic signal, turn east onto Highway 186 toward Chiricahua National Monument (a right turn off Haskell if you are coming from Tucson; a left if coming from Portal). One block east of the signal the road crosses the railroad tracks that gave rise to this western town. Founded in 1882, Willcox was an important cattle-shipping point on the Southern Pacific line. The live-stock industry remains an integral part of the town's economy, but today agriculture is the biggest employer for the 4,000 people who call Willcox home. Corn, sorghum, lettuce, and cotton are the most important crops, followed by watermelon, chile peppers, apples, and pecans. Birders should also note that there is a thriving Ostrich industry north of town!

Continue east to Rex Allen Jr. Drive on the right side of the highway at a sign for the municipal golf course (0.5 mile). Turn south here. Birds along the road to the club house (1.0 mile) are typical of the grasslands the entire length of the Sulphur Springs Valley. Watch for Red-tailed Hawk, Greater Roadrunner, Burrowing Owl (uncommon), Cactus Wren, Northern Mockingbird, Bendire's (uncommon) and Curve-billed Thrashers, Loggerhead Shrike, Eastern Meadowlark, and House Finch. In summer there are almost always Swainson's Hawks and Western King-birds present. In winter, Northern Harrier, American Kestrel, and Lark Bunting are common.

Look for Scaled Quail from the cattle-guard that marks the beginning of the golf course. The golf course, and the area adjacent to the ponds, is probably the most reliable location in Arizona for "Cottontop Quail", as the locals call them. A particularly good spot to check is the workyard on the right, just south of the club-house. Gambel's Quail are also present in smaller numbers.

The road divides 100 feet beyond the workyard; both forks lead 100 yards to ponds, and each pond is likely to have different species. Straight ahead is the earthen embankment of the principal sewage lagoon. To both sides are seasonal puddles that may harbor a migrating Solitary Sandpiper or a wintering Common Snipe. A third, practically permanent puddle across the road has a solid bottom, but after heavy rains the rim of the big pond may be a muddy quagmire. Do not attempt to drive up on it after a recent storm. The road follows the rim around the pond.

The ducks usually are concentrated on the back end of the quarter-mile-long pond. The raised elbow, halfway along the western edge, offers the best vantage-point for scanning. A scope is highly recommended. The sandy spit directly in front of the remnants of an old pier and the comparatively barren near-shoreline usually harbor the most shorebirds. Although they are irregular, Willcox represents the only breeding-location for Eared Grebe and Snowy Plover in southern Arizona. In season, cormorants, White-faced Ibis, Greater White-fronted Goose (rare), Black-necked Stilt (uncommon), American Avocet (summer), Long-billed Curlew, and other long-legged waders seem to favor the western arm of the big sewage lagoon. Depending on water levels, tussocks of grass and tall weeds may conceal them. Other birds to watch

Willcox Lake, easily accessible from the interstate, is well worth a visit any time of year.

for in, around, and over the water include Great Blue Heron, Horned Lark, American Pipit (winter), Lark Sparrow (summer) and Savannah Sparrow (winter), as well as up to six species of swallows in migration.

The big pond at Willcox Playa (the one called "Willcox Lake") is often blanketed with birds early in the morning. These may include ten or more species of ducks: Green-winged Teal, Mallard (usually the "Mexican Duck" subspecies is the predominant form), Northern Pintail, Blue-winged and Cinnamon Teals, Northern Shoveler, Gadwall, American Wigeon, Canvasback, Redhead, Ring-necked Duck, Lesser Scaup, Bufflehead, and Ruddy Duck. Thousands of Wilson's and lesser numbers of Red-necked Phalaropes gyroscope on the surface, and hundreds of Long-billed Dowitchers jab in the shallows like miniature oil-rigs. Check the early-arriving fall dowitchers for Short-bills. The red-breasted immatures are the easiest targets, for their Long-billed counterparts are ordinarily pale-breasted by August. Other migratory shorebirds occurring regularly at Willcox include Greater and Lesser Yellowlegs, and Spotted, Western, Least, and Baird's Sandpipers. Less common, but annual, are Willet, Marbled Godwit, Semipalmated Sandpiper, Pectoral Sandpiper, Dunlin, and Stilt Sandpiper. Ring-billed Gull is the typical larid, but Black Terns pass through from May to September, and Franklin's and Bonaparte's Gulls are annual. Least Terns have shown up for at least one day every May for the past few years, but Forster's Terns are more likely than Least Terns. Cassin's Sparrows are found here (primarily in summer), and Dickcissel has been recorded in fall.

The big pond at Willcox has hosted too many rarities to recount in any complete way. A sampling would include Pacific Loon, Horned Grebe, Oldsquaw, American Golden-Plover, White-rumped Sandpiper, Red Phalarope, Sabine's Gull, and Black Skimmer—mostly one-day wonders. A checklist of the birds recorded here is available at Tucson Audubon's Nature Shop (see Chapter 1).

After working the big pond return to the junction near the workyard and turn left (west) for the smaller, cattail-ringed golf-course pond (100 yards). There is a convenient parking area on the east (or near) side of the water. Early in the morning during winter, watch for Common Snipes to wander across the nearby greens, for all the world as blasé as a group of starlings. It is always worthwhile to scan the golf course and its trees for raptors, Scaled Quail, Say's Phoebe, other flycatchers, thrashers, Loggerhead Shrike, migrant warblers, Lark Bunting (winter), and Brewer's Blackbird (winter). Once again, a scope will be useful here.

Approach the pond quietly. The eastern end is rimmed with a narrow mudflat that may harbor shorebirds nearly any month of the year.

Scaled Quail
Narca Moore-Craig

Resident are Ruddy Duck, American Coot, Killdeer, Black Phoebe, Common Yellowthroat, and Red-winged and Yellow-headed (uncommon) Blackbird. During winter, these are joined by other ducks and, occasionally, a Snow Goose (with a Ross's Goose for comparison during the winter of 1992-1993), Marsh Wren, and both Song (common) and Swamp (rare) Sparrows. Hundreds of Lazuli Buntings pass through during August in migration, along with a few Willow Flycatchers. While Bank Swallows may use either of the two principal ponds at the Willcox Playa during migration, they seem to prefer the one at the golf course. Watch for Sora in migration.

A short, abandoned road parallels the left (south) edge of the golf course pond. This may yield some additional species, especially if there is water in the weedy swale on the left side of the dead-end track. A handful of Hudsonian Godwits has used this patch of water sporadically during May, although none has been recorded since 1988. More reliably, most years a flock of up to 100 Long-billed Curlews rests here in late summer. During winter the weeds along the road are usually good for a few extra sparrows.

An earthen bank on the right side at the west end of the road offers a good vantage point—with the serious disadvantages of tricky footing and spooking the birds—overlooking the far (west) end of the golf-course pond, as well as a temporary pond to the southwest that may harbor the same ducks as the big pond. If you haven't yet spotted your Scaled Quail, scan the surrounding area carefully, especially the golf course. This end of the golf couse pond is also a favorite hang-out for a Vermilion Flycatcher.

Allow at least one hour—preferably two—to do a proper job of birding at Willcox Playa area. Return to Highway 186 and turn right. The road traverses an area of dunes that date back at least 8,000 years to when the whole Willcox Playa was a 50-square-mile lake. Fossil evidence discovered on the shores of ancient Lake Cochise discloses that thousands of years earlier Native Americans were killing the young of Woolly Mammoths with a uniquely fluted spearhead known as the Clovis point. Scientists today speculate that the people of the Clovis culture, by concentrating on killing immature animals, hunted mammoths to extinction throughout North America in just 500 years. Fossil pollen analysis from Willcox Playa shows that no abrupt climatic changes occurred that would otherwise account for the sudden extinction of these grand elephants.

Watch for White-tailed Kite as you approach the "Y" junction with **Kansas Settlement Road** (7.0 miles; 5.4 miles from the Highway 186/Rex

Allen Jr. Drive intersection). Turn right (south) here. The first fields of this agricultural development begin about three miles down the road. Farming gets the credit for attracting the Sandhill Cranes that use the area today. Midwesterners migrated to the east side of Willcox Playa during the dust-bowl years of the 1930s, and over the next few decades, they converted over 26,000 acres of desert grassland to irrigated cropland. Cranes were first noted using the fields in the 1960s, and in 1970 the first Arizona Game & Fish Department census tallied approximately 850 Sandhills. Recent winter surveys in the 1990s show that the present Sulphur Springs Valley population fluctuates between 9,500 and 12,500 birds—approximately the same number that winters at the well-known Bosque del Apache National Wildlife Refuge in New Mexico.

The daily regimen of valley Sandhills includes several shuttles between roosts and feeding areas that may be up to 10 miles apart. Cranes prefer open cornfields where the stalks have been cultivated, disked under, or trampled by cattle. Look for cranes in any patch of corn-stubble from mile 3 to mile 15 along the Kansas Settlement Road. If you do not locate any birds, wait, listen, and watch the skies to see where the flocks are settling down. Lateral farm lanes provide access to outlying fields.

Cranes are not the only attractions along the Kansas Settlement Road. Ferruginous Hawks are fairly common in winter, Red-tails are abundant, and roadside corrals may harbor huge flocks of Yellow-headed Blackbirds. Golden Eagles are possible, especially near the crane flocks, but are resident year-round.

Follow Kansas Settlement Road south to its terminus at Highway 191 (20.2 miles). Turn left (east) at the "T" intersection. Watch for Golden Eagles where the highway swings across the north side of a rocky foothill known as Township Butte. A pair has nested near here for many years. Wintering Ferruginous Hawks perched on utility poles become fairly common south of Sunizona (4.9 miles). The route which follows can also be good for wintering Rough-legged Hawk.

Bare fields at Seven Leagues Ranch on the left (east) side of the highway (4.8 miles) literally swarm with wintering Horned Larks. With a good scope and enough patience, it is usually possible to finesse one or more McCown's Longspurs out of the flock. Horned Larks are also found in the lush, green alfalfa fields across Highway 191 at the Rainbow Ranch. During winter, check these flocks for Chestnut-collared Longspurs.

Several prominent grain silos on the left (east) side of the road mark the headquarters of the **Spitler Land and Cattle Company** (3.3 miles). *Stop at the office to obtain permission to drive along the farm lanes that* *divide their half-mile-wide fields.* If pressed for time, another strategy is simply to continue down Highway 191 to the east-side junction with well-graded Rucker Canyon Road (0.5 mile). Most of the best birds can usually be found by scoping from the edges of this public thoroughfare. Spitler Cattle Company is a raptor-lover's paradise throughout the year, but it is especially wonderful in winter. Among the wintering species which one could tally in a couple of hours are Bald Eagle, Northern Harrier, Sharp-shinned Hawk, Cooper's Hawk, Red-tailed Hawk, Ferruginous Hawk, Golden Eagle, American Kestrel, Merlin, Peregrine Falcon, and Prairie Falcon. Check any conspicuous perch; aside from fenceposts, power-line poles, and a few scattered cottonwoods, all of the eagles, hawks, and falcons are fond of the costly center-pivot irrigation rigs used to irrigate the fields. Two of these hunters are comfortable even sitting complacently in the grass—female Northern Harriers are hard to spot on the ground, but the white chest of Ferruginous Hawks will probably attract your attention in a flash.

A raptor identification guide will come in handy at Spitler, both for birds in flight and for those in variant plumages. Aside from immatures,

Mountain Plover
David A. Sibley

Spitler is famous for its red- and dark-morph Redtails, as well as dark-form Ferruginous Hawks.

If you can tear yourself away from this feast of raptors, there is a nice assortment of other birds that winter at Spitler. These include Killdeer, Barn Owl in the outbuildings, Say's Phoebe, Horned Lark, Chihuahuan Raven, Mountain Bluebird (irregular, but present most winters), Bendire's Thrasher in mesquite hedge-rows, American Pipit, Loggerhead Shrike, Brewer's, Vesper, Lark, and White-crowned Sparrows, Lark Bunting, McCown's (rare) and Chestnut-collared Longspurs, Red-winged Blackbird, Eastern and Western Meadowlarks, and Brewer's Blackbird. Mountain Plovers prefer short-grass fields—particularly those with recent irrigation—and, less often, bare dirt. Although the plovers are sizable, they can require lots of patience to locate.

Summer offers its own rewards to the birder. A half-dozen or more Swainson's Hawks may come together to perform graceful, aerial ballets in the wake of the mowing-machines, feeding on the insects and mice left without cover. Like Ferruginous Hawks, the Swainson's perch on the ground between forays. During August, the alfalfa fields load up with Mallard, Blue Grosbeak, Lazuli Bunting, Red-winged Blackbird, and Eastern Meadowlark. Don't forget to scan the skies for Golden Eagle, which are year-round guests at the Spitler Cattle Company.

During winter, raptor enthusiasts will enjoy a side trip on Courtland Road, which leads west from the Highway 191/Rucker Canyon Road intersection. Follow the pavement to a large field on the right (north) side of the road (1.7). Perhaps owing to its strategic location at the head of Whitewater Draw, this single field ordinarily hosts several Ferruginous Hawks throughout the winter. Frequently, there are more, and concentrations of up to a dozen are occasionally recorded. At least one of these birds is almost guaranteed to be a dark-morph Ferruginous. This one field is probably the best single location for Ferruginous Hawks in Southeastern Arizona. The best place to observe the hawks is from the driveway entrance on the far (west) corner of the field. *Remember, however, not to block the farmer's driveway or to trespass on his private property.*

During wet winters Sandhill Cranes also use this area. Track their loud, trumpeting calls to locate the birds if they are not conspicuous in the field itself. An area of shallow standing water north of the small Whitewater Draw Bridge is a frequent day roost. Once again, wherever there are cranes watch for eagles. Don't be surprised if you also see Coyotes. These handsome canines are probably the chief predator on cranes (aside from man) in the Sulphur Springs Valley.

Return to Highway 191 and turn right (south). Watch for a small group of Harris's Hawks in the desert on the left (east) side of the highway for the next few miles. You may even find them sharing a cottonwood roost with a Great Horned Owl. Thompson Road (3.0 miles) to the east, at the landfill, is good for Crissal Thrasher, which is also regular west of the highway opposite a large cottonwood.

To continue the tour, return to Highway 191, and turn south. Elfrida, Arizona, population approximately 500, begins at the junction with Gleeson Road (1.0 mile). The town features a church, a gas station, a post office, and a small cafe called A Family Restaurant whose food is highly recommended. There is a major "Y" junction on the south end of Elfrida (1.3 miles). Highway 191 veers left and ends at U.S. 80 just west of Douglas (23 miles). To continue the tour, drive south on what is now Central Highway to a major four-point intersection with Davis Road at McNeal (6.1 miles).

Corn-stubble fields here are another excellent area for viewing Sandhill Cranes. There are two major flocks wintering in the Sulphur Springs Valley, and the Whitewater Draw area represents the southern roost. To find their usual mid-day resting place, turn right onto Davis Road. Go west on Davis to a signed intersection with dirt Coffman Road (1.0 mile). Unless there have been unusually heavy winter rains, turn left (south) onto Coffman. (Ruts left behind by farm machinery and trucks will tell you whether or not Coffman is passable.) En route to the cranes, don't ignore the barren desert or any newly plowed fields on the left (east) side of the road. Both Mountain Plover and McCown's Longspur are possible, and Horned Lark is probable in these seemingly sterile areas. Watch for Scaled Quail, Greater Roadrunner, Cactus Wren, and Bendire's, Curve-billed, and Crissal Thrashers in the road-edge thickets, as well as Pyrrhuloxia and a host of sparrows.

The Hyannis Cattle Company has created a shallow pond on the right (west) side of the road that may extend over two miles in length during wet periods. In dry years the **Hyannis Pond** shrinks to little more than a mud-puddle. The Sulphur Springs Valley is so level that it may be difficult to determine whether the water level is high or low, but—if present—the cranes should be eminently visible about a quarter-mile off Coffman. Midwinter Arizona Game & Fish Department surveys have recorded up to 5,000 Sandhills on the shores of Hyannis Pond. A scope is necessary. *Bird only from the road.*

Two or three Bald Eagles—always a rarity in Southeastern Arizona—regularly winter at Hyannis, and Golden Eagles are likely to soar over several times each day, every day of the year. During some winters, a

Rough-legged Hawk frequents the same area. And, just for a sweetener, White-tailed Kites have nested in the scrawny little cypress trees at the lone house on the right that marks the entrance road to Hyannis Pond (2.6 miles). For the record, however, in some summers the kites are absent altogether from the lower Sulphur Springs Valley.

The Hyannis Pond was open to birders in the 1980s and it may again open its gates. If so, it will definitely be worth a stop. *You must inquire with the Tucson Audubon Society or local birders, however, in order to learn the current status of access to this private property.* The owner pastures cattle next to the dirt drive that leads down to the dam (0.4 mile), and he closed the access as a consequence of thoughtless visitor behavior.

During the few years when it was open, an astonishing number of water birds were recorded. A short sampling includes Common Loon, Western and Clark's Grebes, Double-crested and Neotropic Cormorants, Great, Snowy, and Cattle Egrets, Black-crowned Night-Herons, Black-bellied Whistling-Duck, Tundra Swan, Greater White-fronted, Snow, Ross's, and Canada Geese, and virtually every duck, rail, shorebird, gull, and tern known to have occurred in the southeastern corner of Arizona. When Hyannis Pond is high, it can be stated without exaggeration that overwintering waterfowl number in excess of 10,000 birds.

Scan the fields on both sides as you round the broad curve where Coffman turns east and becomes Bagby Road (0.5 mile). Long-billed Curlews have been sighted along Bagby nearly every month of the year, and they are actually fairly common during spring and fall migration periods. Bagby rejoins the pavement at Central Highway (1.0 mile). If you are looking for Sage Sparrow in winter, turn left (north) for one mile to Lee Road, where they are common.

To continue the route, turn right (south) onto Central Highway. The remaining distance to Double Adobe Road (6.0 miles) passes through a major chile pepper growing region. Once again, the hedgerows are excellent habitat for Bendire's Thrasher.

One of the great unsolved avian mysteries of the Sulphur Springs Valley involves the disappearance of the Harris's Hawks of Double Adobe. Readily seen throughout the 1980s, this communally nesting species abruptly abandoned the area in July 1991. At this writing in 1995, they still had not re-pioneered Double Adobe, but any dark raptor in the vicinity deserves a second look. Platform nests in every Soaptree Yucca within a half-mile radius of the Double Adobe/Central Highway intersection are all that remain today.

Continuing straight ahead, Central Highway turns into a well-graded gravel road. Chihuahuan desertscrub characterizes the terrain on both sides. Appropriately, Chihuahuan Ravens are probably the most conspicuous bird along this stretch. Where the grass has been overgrazed, there are patches of mesquite. You will notice that nearly every shrub has a mound under it. Sometimes erroneously attributed to prairie-dogs, they are actually the work of Banner-tailed and Merriam's Kangaroo-Rats.

The last prairie-dogs in Southeastern Arizona were poison-baited into oblivion by the Federal government in 1938 in a misguided effort to improve the range for livestock use. Without the thousands of Black-tailed Prairie-Dogs burrows to capture rainwater, sheet flooding and erosion ensued, and aquifers were not recharged. Grasses have disappeared, the range sustains fewer cattle than ever, and Coyotes have learned to augment their diet with occasional entrées of veal. The demise of the grassland in the southern Sulphur Springs Valley probably accounts for the absence of Aplomado Falcons. The last individual in the lower valley was recorded in this vicinity in November 1939.

Desertscrub is still good for Crissal Thrashers and Sage Sparrows (winter). During summer, Swainson's Hawks are common on the telephone pole crossarms. Golden Eagles tend to sit on top the pole itself. Early in the morning it is sometimes possible to count a half-dozen of these magnificent birds of prey between Double Adobe and U.S. 80 (6.2 miles).

Unless time is short, a good way to conclude the Sulphur Springs Valley tour is with a quick visit to the main campus of **Cochise College**. To find the school, turn left (east) onto Highway 80. Turn left again (north) at the well-signed entrance (0.6 mile). Like Willcox Playa, Kansas Settlement, Spitler Cattle Company, and Hyannis Pond, Cochise College is an oasis surrounded by desert, affording birds both greenery and water. The entrance road divides just 100 yards inside the gate and describes a one-mile-long loop around this attractive and modern campus.

In winter, unless there's a car right behind you, pause to scan the evergreen lawn in front of the first tier of buildings. American Pipits strut around the well-groomed grass like so many chickens from November through March. The mammal sharing the turf is the Spotted Ground-Squirrel, otherwise uncommon in Southeastern Arizona. Turn right to park in the visitors lot (100 yards). Flycatchers gravitate to the basketball and tennis-court area just east of the parking area. Say's Phoebe is resident, and Ash-throated Flycatcher passes the summer here. The half-dozen Arizona Cypress trees rimming the basketball courts are, occasionally, the day-roost for Barn or Great Horned Owls.

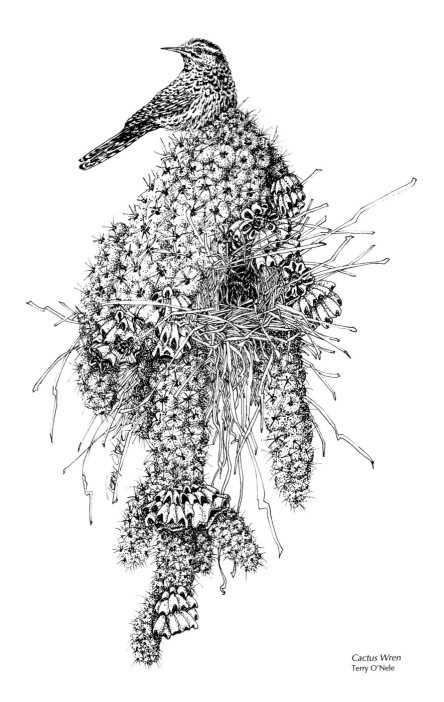

Cactus Wren
Terry O'Nele

Lake Irma, though not as beautiful as the rest of the Cochise College campus, can produce some surprises.

Return to your car and continue to the next parking lot on the right (0.2 mile). Due east lies the running-track, enclosing another oval of well-irrigated green. Horned Larks and Killdeer are habitués of the grass here throughout the winter. The baseball diamond is obvious to the southeast. In early spring a Bendire's Thrasher occasionally uses the backstop for an elevated song perch. Watch for Mountain Bluebirds catching flies in the outfield.

A 100-yard-long line of Tamarisk trees runs due east from the baseball field to the Cochise College Sewage Lagoon, otherwise known as Lake Irma (for one of the college's first receptionists). Check the trees and the patch of nearby desert for Gambel's Quail, Verdin, Cactus Wren, House Wren (winter), Ruby-crowned Kinglet (winter), Northern Mockingbird, Curve-billed Thrasher, Loggerhead Shrike, Orange-crowned and Yellow-rumped Warblers (winter), Western Tanager (migration), Northern Cardinal, Blue Grosbeak (summer), White-crowned Sparrow (winter), and Bullock's Oriole (summer).

Lake Irma is about 300 yards long, so a scope is helpful. Resident birds include Great Blue Heron, the olive-billed "Mexican Duck" form of Mallard, Killdeer, Black Phoebe, and Red-winged Blackbird. Migration periods bring the most interesting birds. A Sabine's Gull arrived here in mid-September 1986, and an early Yellow-billed Cuckoo showed up in late May 1988. White-tailed Kites (summer) are fairly regular off the far (east) end of the pond.

During summer, the buildings on campus provide a perfect nest substrate for hundreds of Cliff and Barn Swallows. Eastern Meadowlarks and Great-tailed Grackles use the expansive green between the dorms and the classroom areas. Ornamental plantings attract significant numbers of female and immature Calliope Hummingbirds every fall. During summer, the trees pull in both Cassin's and Western Kingbirds. Nearby tracts of desert grassland are used by Scaled Quail, Burrowing Owl, Ladder-backed Woodpecker, and Pyrrhuloxia. Finally, at night, the well-lit parking areas are a magnet for Lesser Nighthawks from May through September.

To reach Douglas turn left (east) onto U.S. 80 (8 miles). Turn right (west) to find Sierra Vista (49 miles).

Campgrounds, Restaurants, and Accommodations:

There are basic campgrounds available at Chiricahua National Monument (33 miles east of Willcox), Cochise Stronghold (15 miles west of the junction of Kansas Settlement Road with Highway 191), and Rucker Canyon (21 miles east of Spitler Cattle Company). Willcox has a modern KOA with full hook-ups and amenities (telephone 520/586-3977) off Interstate 10 just west of exit 340.

A number of fast-food chains are represented in both Willcox and Douglas at each end of the tour. A Family Restaurant in Elfrida (telephone 520/642-3348) is probably the best place to eat along the route. The historic Gadsden Hotel restaurant (telephone 520/364-4481) in Douglas has a wide selection of entrées, including Mexican food that I can personally endorse. The restaurant opens at 6am. Among the accommodations in Willcox are a Motel 6 (telephone 520/384-2201) and a Best Western (telephone 520/384-3556). The Best Western has a good restaurant which opens at 6am. In Douglas, the Gadsden Hotel (telephone 520/364-4481) has an authentic, turn-of-the-century flavor with refurbished rooms at reasonable rates. Comparably priced and strictly institutional, is the Motel 6 (telephone 520/364-2457).

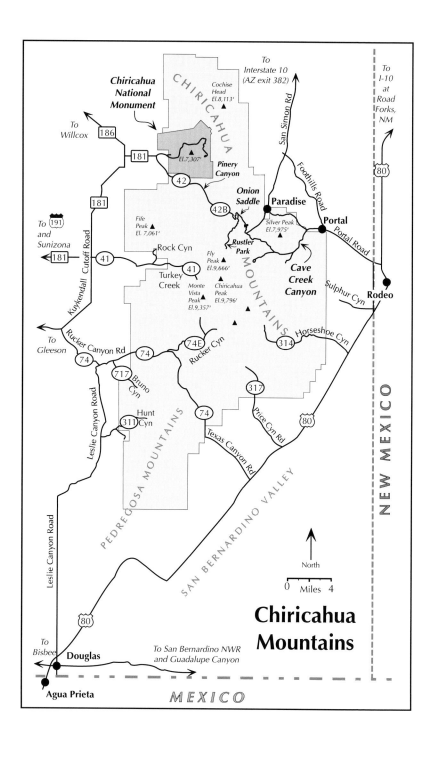

Chiricahua Mountains

Chiricahua National Monument

To Willcox

CHIRICAHUA

Cochise Head El.8,113'

To Interstate 10 (AZ exit 382)

To I-10 at Road Forks, NM

San Simon Rd

186

181

El.7,307'

42

Pinery Canyon

Onion Saddle

Paradise

Foothills Road

80

181

42B

Portal

To (191) and Sunizona

Fife Peak ▲ El. 7,061'

Silver Peak El.7,975'

Portal Road

Rock Cyn

Rustler Park

Cave Creek Canyon

Rodeo

41

Fly Peak ▲ El.9,666'

181

Turkey Creek

41

Monte Vista Peak ▲ El.9,357'

Chiricahua Peak ▲ El.9,796'

MOUNTAINS

Sulphur Cyn

Kuykendall Cutoff Road

74E

314

To Gleeson

Rucker Canyon Rd

74

Rucker Cyn

Horseshoe Cyn

74

717

Bruno Cyn

317

Hunt Cyn

311

74

80

Leslie Canyon Road

Price Cyn Rd

Texas Canyon Rd

PEDREGOSA MOUNTAINS

SAN BERNARDINO VALLEY

North

0 Miles 4

NEW MEXICO

80

To Bisbee

Douglas

To San Bernardino NWR and Guadalupe Canyon

Agua Prieta

MEXICO

CHIRICAHUA
MOUNTAINS

Even in scenic Arizona, the Chiricahua Mountains are spectacular. Homeland of the Chiricahua Apaches, these mountains boast airy panoramas, a unique geology, and the single most diversified land-bounded plant and animal community in the United States. Many birders consider the Chiricahuas the premier birding location in all North America.

The name "Chiricahua," according to Native Americans, comes from Opata words meaning "Big Mountain." Stretching over 40 miles in length, and measuring 25 miles in width, the Chiricahuas encompass an area of approximately 1,000 square miles. Rising from Chihuahuan desertscrub at an elevation of about 3,800 feet in the San Simon Valley to Hudsonian spruce forest on the 9,796-foot-high summit, the Chiricahuas are the single largest mountain-mass south of the Gila River in Arizona. In order to do the Chiricahua region justice, you should plan on birding here no fewer than two full days—excluding travel days—and three or more are preferable.

Access:

The starting point is the hamlet of Portal at the outlet of Cave Creek Canyon on the eastern flank of the range. There are no fewer than four possible approaches to Portal, and depending on recent weather events, your departure point, and your time-limitations, each has its own advantages. From Tucson, the fastest way to reach Portal is to follow Interstate 10 past Willcox (about 80 miles; last inexpensive gas and groceries) to exit 382, San Simon/Portal Road (42 miles), on the east side of San Simon. Follow the frontage road east past the truck weigh station to the signed turn-off on the right (south at 1.1 miles) for Portal. The first 7.4 miles are paved, but the remaining 17.8 to the beginning of the pavement at Portal

Road are a well-graded gravel route—unless there have been heavy rains. Turn right toward the mountain to find Portal (0.7 mile).

After recent storms this route is *not* recommended because of flash-flood danger. Instead of exiting at San Simon, then, continue east on I-10 to Road Forks, New Mexico (15.0 miles), and turn south onto U.S. 80.

Road Forks (17 miles west of Lordsburg, last cheap gas) is also the best exit if you are approaching Arizona on Interstate 10 from the east. It is 28 miles south on U.S. 80 to the well-signed right-hand turn-off to Portal. A lumberyard—starkly evident in the sparsely vegetated desert—marks the beginning of the 7.0-mile drive to the village. Although this route adds an additional 27 miles to the total distance from Tucson, it has the advantage of being entirely paved and is open in any weather.

From May through October, during most years, and if time is not a major consideration, the most scenic route from Tucson to Portal is via the Trans-mountain Road over Onion Saddle, elevation 7,600 feet. To reach the Trans-mountain Road follow signs along State Highway 186 from Willcox to Chiricahua National Monument (31 miles), then turn right (south) onto the unpaved road into Pinery Canyon just 100 yards before the entry station into the Monument. It is 26 miles over Onion Saddle (described later in this chapter) to Portal. Snow frequently closes this pass between November and April. It is not recommended for vehicles over 20 feet in length or for anyone towing a long trailer.

If you are approaching from the lower Sulphur Springs Valley or the Sierra Vista area, take U.S. 80 northeast from Douglas. Watch for Golden Eagle, Scaled Quail, and Grasshopper Sparrow in the mile-high grassland between milepost 390 (mile 22.0) and milepost 400 at the Price Canyon turn-off (mile 32.0). Pronghorns are frequently sighted east of the highway in this area. The Rodeo Store (last gas) is on the right side of the highway, 2 miles into New Mexico (mile 47.0). A lumberyard, the only building in the barren desert, marks the turn-off to Portal 2.5 miles beyond Rodeo (49.5 miles from Douglas). From the junction with Highway 80 turn left (west) for Portal (7.0 miles).

There are three ecologically different birding areas within easy reach of Portal: desert valley, canyons, and mountain highlands. Ideally, each deserves an early-morning visit for the most productive birding, but realistically, it is possible to combine any two in a single day, using Portal as a base.

Desert Valley Loop

(30 miles/one morning)

This route should be birded in the morning. Not only are desert birds far more likely to sing and be active early in the day, but also from May through September, temperatures in the valley can easily reach 90 degrees by 10am. Once the heat comes up, the day frequently becomes windy in the San Simon Valley.

Downtown **Portal** is comprised of about a dozen homes, a library, the post office, and a combination store, cafe, and lodge (highly recommended). Many of the residents are birders, and the town fully warrants a walk up the only paved street for a taste of their yardbirds. If you arrive before daylight in the spring, listen for Western Screech-Owl, Great Horned Owl, and Elf Owl. All three species nest in the sycamores that line the 0.2-mile length of pavement. The complete list of birds that join

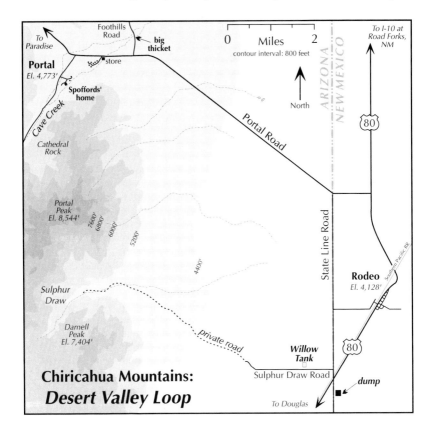

Chiricahua Mountains:
Desert Valley Loop

the Portal dawn chorus from April through September contains about 60 species. Some of the more noteworthy are Cooper's Hawk, Gambel's Quail, White-winged Dove, Acorn and Ladder-backed Woodpeckers, Northern Beardless-Tyrannulet (uncommon), Western Wood-Pewee, Black Phoebe, Dusky-capped, Ash-throated, and Brown-crested Flycatchers, Cassin's and Western Kingbirds, Violet-green Swallow, Western Scrub-Jay, Mexican Jay, Bridled and Plain Titmice, Verdin, White-breasted Nuthatch, Cactus and Bewick's Wrens, American Robin, Northern Mockingbird, Curve-billed and Crissal Thrashers, Bell's and Solitary Vireos, Lucy's and Black-throated Gray Warblers, Summer Tanager, Northern Cardinal, Black-headed and Blue Grosbeaks, Lazuli Bunting, Canyon Towhee (frequently under your car if you park by the store), Bronzed Cowbird (vastly outnumbered by Brown-headeds), Hooded, Bullock's, and Scott's Orioles, House Finch, and Lesser Goldfinch. Unfortunately, there are also plenty of European Starlings and House Sparrows.

The greater Portal area (including the Spoffords' home) is probably the best place in Southeastern Arizona to see Calliope Hummingbirds during fall migration—from late July through September. Most of the other hummers for which the Chiricahuas are famous visit the feeders at the Portal Store, and a Plain-capped Starthroat put in a appearance at a feeder hung across the street from the post office for much of August 1992. You may even be fortunate enough to catch the Thick-billed Kingbird that generally shows up in metropolitan Portal for one day each summer. If you are a newcomer to Arizona birds, or even if you just like to see lots of birds, you'll certainly enjoy early morning in this sleepy little hamlet.

Tear yourself away. The Portal Road parallels Cave Creek for the first 0.7 mile east of Portal to a "T" junction immediately beyond a cattle-guard with the San Simon Road. After the summer monsoons arrive in July, it is worth the time to stop at this intersection to look for Cassin's Sparrows in the grasses opposite the intersection. During winter, the mesquite scrub here is good habitat for Sage Thrasher.

Turn left (north) onto San Simon Road and proceed 0.5 mile to the big thicket that flanks lower Cave Creek on both sides of the road. *This is private property, but it is permissible to bird from the road edges.* Specialties of the **Big Thicket** include Crissal Thrasher, Abert's Towhee (quite local in the Chiricahua region), and Varied Bunting. Most of the desert birds mentioned for Portal are more common here, including Gambel's Quail, Ladder-backed Woodpecker, Cactus Wren, Verdin, Bell's Vireo, and Lucy's Warbler. Gila Woodpecker, usually restricted to the cottonwood groves and Saguaro cactus forests farther west, is occasional here, as are Scaled Quail and Black-tailed Gnatcatcher. One of the most abundant residents is Black-throated Sparrow. Aggregations of Lesser Nighthawks at dusk may number up to a hundred or more during the summer. Just after dark, and an hour or two before first light, this is a favored area to hear Common Poorwills giving their poignant, two-note calls.

Usually a half-hour to one hour is enough time to bird the big thicket. Return south to the paved Portal Road and turn left (east) to descend to the floor of the San Simon Valley. Burrowing Owls formerly occupied the Chihuahuan desertscrub along Portal Road, but they disappeared, mysteriously, in the early 1980s and have not been seen since. Swainson's Hawk, Golden Eagle, Scaled Quail, Greater Roadrunner, Western Kingbird, Loggerhead Shrike, Black-throated Sparrow, and Scott's Oriole still remain. At the cattle-guard delineating the boundary between Arizona and New Mexico (5.6 miles), turn right (south) onto Stateline Road—unless there have been recent heavy rains.

Dust is usually a worse problem than mud on Stateline Road, but give the road at least 24 hours to dry out before attempting it if you see fresh ruts left by farm trucks. Stateline Road is surveyor-straight and 4.0 miles long. The agricultural area beyond the back road into Rodeo, New Mexico (2.5), offers the most intriguing birding. Bendire's Thrashers occur along the entire route, but are most likely to be seen at thickets, especially near the derelict buildings south of the Rodeo Cut-off. In August scores of Blue Grosbeaks gather in the hedge-rows along the irrigated fields of cotton and chile peppers, mixed with flocks of Lazuli Buntings, and early-arriving Lark Buntings. When present, but still not found every year, White-tailed Kites hunt the same fields. From mid-October through February a small flock of Sandhill Cranes is usually on the far side of the fields in the stubble.

Turn right (west) onto Sulphur Draw Road (3.8 miles) just before Stateline Road intersects with U.S. 80. It is only 0.6 mile to **Willow Tank**, arguably the most important pond on the eastern flank of the Chiricahuas. A single Weeping Willow on the raised bank near the road gives its name to this one-acre rectangular impoundment. During winter, this tree is frequently the perch of a Merlin or some other raptor; be sure to check it closely before leaving your car. *There is no parking area, so please pull as far off the road as possible; be careful, however, not to mire your car in deep mud if the road is wet.* Loose barbed-wire strands about 25 yards before the pond allow access to the water. Try to approach quietly, because there is very little cover for any birds present, and they flush easily.

While birds are not usually abundant here, the quality of birds is high. One group surprised a Tricolored Heron here in August 1994, and what was probably a Trumpeter Swan was found at Willow Tank during the Christmas Count of the same year. Tundra Swans are very rare but regular winter visitors. The "Mexican Duck" form of the Mallard is a year-round resident, as are Great Blue Heron, American Coot, a variety of shorebirds, Common Yellowthroat, and Red-winged Blackbird—all otherwise scarce in this waterless valley. During winter, Willow Tank hosts Marsh Wren, Song Sparrow, Swamp Sparrow, Chestnut-collared Longspur (in the swale behind the pond), and an occasional Yellow-headed Blackbird.

Upper Sulphur Draw Road is ordinarily not particularly productive for birds; the best plan is to return to Stateline Road (2.0 miles), and turn right to U.S. 80 (0.2 mile). If you still haven't seen a Bendire's Thrasher, there are several locations on the return route through New Mexico that are worth checking. The first is directly across the Stateline Road at the Rodeo Town Dump. Turn left into the dump after 0.15 mile. The raised dumping-ramp offers an ideal viewing-platform from which to check for the bird in piles of debris.

Return to U.S. 80 and follow it north 2.0 miles to the Rodeo Store on the right (east) side of the highway. (Gasoline is expensive here, but unavailable in Portal.) The vacant lots surrounding the church just a block behind (east of) the store provide another good site for Bendire's. While in Rodeo, watch for Scaled Quail, Inca Dove, Gila Woodpecker, and Great-tailed Grackle.

To return to Portal take the dirt road opposite the Rodeo Store back to Stateline Road (1.1 miles). Initially this farm lane parallels the highway, then swings due west in front of a house (0.2 mile). Bendire's Thrasher is almost always found in the mesquite and soaptrees on the west side of the house. A short distance beyond, a cotton-gin on the right (0.3 mile) usually harbors a Barn Owl. The field on the right side of the road after the cotton-gin is good for Cassin's Sparrows.

At the "T" junction with Stateline Road, turn right (north). It is 2.5 miles back to the pavement at Portal Road. Turn left (west) here and continue back to Portal (6.3 miles). By now, bird activity has subsided in the lowlands, so perhaps the best way to cap off the morning is with a visit to the **Spoffords' home**. To find their private sanctuary stay on the pavement up Cave Creek Canyon 1.2 miles beyond the Portal Store to a left-hand turn-off opposite a driveway with a tall entry gate constructed from telephone poles. Turn downhill onto a cobbly dirt lane through a mesquite scrub community punctuated by hundreds of agave (century plant) stalks. Turn right at the "T" intersection (0.2 mile), and go another

Blue-throated Hummingbird
Georges Dremeaux

100 yards. The Spoffords' home is the first driveway on the left, framed by a tall crossbar signed Aguila Rancho, "Eagle Ranch."

There is parking space for only four standard-sized passenger vehicles at the gate. Please do not try to visit the Spoffords in large rigs such as mobile-homes, busses, or cars with trailers. There is simply no room to turn around. Park off the main road and walk. Signs direct visitors to the feeders behind the house. Visitors are requested to refrain from smoking and to sign the guest register. (Visiting hours are 7:30am to 5:30pm. *Please respect their privacy hours.*)

For many, Spoffords' home is the highlight of their birding trip to Southeast Arizona. During late April and early May and again throughout August, the iridescent colors of a dozen different species of hummingbirds paint a picture not soon forgotten. At present, the Spoffords' home is the best single location in Arizona for Lucifer Hummingbird. All three species of regularly occurring orioles—Hooded, Bullock's, and Scott's—along with crimson Summer Tanagers lend sound and color to the summertime show.

Winter birding in Sally and Walter's yard is nearly as exciting. Usually a few Blue-throated and one or two Magnificent Hummingbirds spend the coldest months alternating bouts of amazing aerial gnat-catching proficiency with visits to the feeders. These are the two largest members of their family in the United States, and their large body-sizes enable them to withstand snow and temperatures down to zero. Typically, a black, white, and crimson Painted Redstart vies with the hummingbirds for

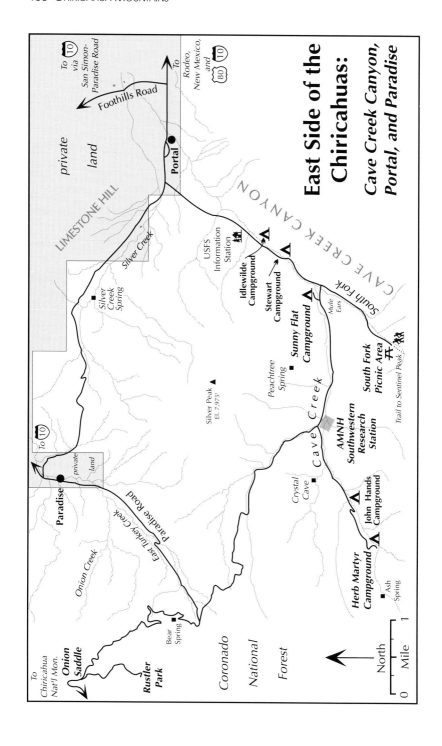

East Side of the Chiricahuas:
Cave Creek Canyon, Portal, and Paradise

attention all winter long. In some years, Cassin's Finches and Evening Grosbeaks lead the onslaught of House Finches and Pine Siskins at the seed-trays, while Acorn Woodpeckers, Bridled Titmice, and White-breasted Nuthatches patronize the suet sticks. The first winter-record of an Aztec Thrush (January 1991) and what was probably the second U.S. record of a Blue Mockingbird (January through mid-April 1995) both came from next door on the grounds of the Cave Creek Ranch Motel. Altogether, Sally and Walter have recorded nearly 200 species of birds on their yardlist. No wonder approximately 15,000 birders visit the Spoffords' home every year!

Canyons Loop

(25 miles/one day)

This loop begins at Portal and circles 7,975-foot-high Silver Peak, exploring five ecologically different canyon areas. The view up Cave Creek Canyon from Portal is one of the most spectacular vistas in the American Southwest.

A half-mile west of Portal a dirt road on the right, at a conspicuous "Y" intersection, leads up Silver Creek to the old mining town of Paradise. This road will be treated as the last link in the Canyons Loop; for now, continue upcanyon on the pavement. You are traversing an alluvial flat covered by shrubby mesquite, which harbors a surprising variety of birds. Early in the morning, you may find Montezuma Quail on the road edges, and during summer you'll pass several male Blue Grosbeaks singing from mesquite-tops. In July and August watch the flowering agave stalks for hummingbirds (Rufous is the most common), as well as for all three species of breeding orioles—Hooded, Bullock's, and Scott's. In winter, it's usually possible to high-grade a few Black-chinned and Rufous-crowned Sparrows out of the big flocks of White-crowns and Chippies. Dark-eyed Juncos traveling with them are an assortment of "Oregon", "Pink-sided", and "Gray-headed", with a few Yellow-eyed Juncos mixed in for good measure. Adding a touch of winter cheer, almost every flock contains Northern Cardinal and Pyrrhuloxia.

The road soon passes between twin rock pylons at a cattle-guard marking the boundary of the Coronado National Forest, and then drops through a long curve to the parking area in a large field on the right for the U.S. Forest Service Portal Information Station (1.3 miles). This is a good place to get a status report on road conditions; the small book store offers a nice selection of natural history materials. Several rattlesnake species and lizards are on display in glass terrariums. Feeders on the porch attract an occasional rarity, such as a White-eared Hummingbird in May 1994. The large grassy field, adjacent to the parking area north of the station, is a good place to see and hear Common Poorwills on summer evenings.

Beyond the Information Station the road tunnels through a beautiful gallery-forest of broadleaf trees dominated by graceful, white-barked Arizona Sycamore. The multi-tiered, strawberry-colored rhyolite walls of Cave Creek Canyon stair-step over 3,000 feet above. You have entered the premier habitat for Elegant Trogons in the U.S. With them comes a community of birds commonly associated with the pine/oak woodlands of the Sierra Madre of Western Mexico. Some of the birds to watch for as you drive—or better, walk—up Cave Creek Canyon include Montezuma Quail, Band-tailed Pigeon, White-throated Swift, Blue-throated and Magnificent Hummingbirds, Acorn and Strickland's Woodpeckers, Western Wood-Pewee, Dusky-capped, Brown-crested, and Sulphur-bellied Flycatchers, Mexican Jay, Bridled Titmouse, White-breasted Nuthatch, Brown Creeper, Canyon and Bewick's Wrens, Solitary ("Plumbeous" is the breeding race) and Hutton's Vireos, Virginia's, Black-throated Gray, and Grace's Warblers, Painted Redstart, Hepatic Tanager, Black-headed Grosbeak, Spotted Towhee, Rufous-crowned Sparrow, and Lesser Goldfinch.

Diurnal raptors that hunt Cave Creek Canyon are Cooper's, Zonetailed, and Red-tailed Hawks, with an occasional sweep-through by a Peregrine Falcon. On the night shift, Cave Creek Canyon is famous for its owls. Flammulated Owl and Whiskered Screech-Owl replace the Western Screech-Owls found lower in the canyon, joined by Northern Pygmy-Owls and Spotted Owls. Elf Owls, while concentrated near Portal, span Cave Creek up to the Southwestern Research Station.

A gentle ¾-mile-long trail hugs the base of Silver Peak between the bridge just before Stewart Campground (park in Stewart, 0.7 mile, and cross the bridge on foot back to the trailhead) and Sunny Flat Campground (1.8 miles), threading through a magnificent stand of streamside sycamores.

For most birders, however, the walk up **South Fork Cave Creek** is the most desirable hike in the Chiricahua Mountains. To find South Fork Road drive upcanyon beyond the entrance to Stewart Campground an additional 0.9 mile (2.9 miles above the Portal Store). The pavement veers right at the junction; South Fork Road continues straight ahead as a dirt road. Many knowledgeable birders with previous experience in South Fork elect to hike the entire length of South Fork Road (1.3 miles).

Elegant Trogon
David A. Sibley

Lower South Fork is wider; thus, viewing opportunities are enhanced. The first Elegant Trogons to arrive in April are often found in this scenic lower stretch of the canyon. *To protect the trogons the use of tape players for any birds, including owls, is prohibited in South Fork Cave Creek.*

Since the 27,500-acre Rattlesnake Fire in 1994, the South Fork ford (mile 0.9) has become treacherous. *Do not attempt to drive across the stream with your car if the Forest Service has set up barriers.* South Fork Road ends at a turn-around oval and a picnic area 0.4 mile beyond. (Camping here is no longer allowed.) Do not rush hastily up the trail. Elegant Trogons patrol through the picnic area several times a day throughout the summer, and generally there is a Strickland's Woodpecker present until the onset of the summer monsoons in July. Other regulars in the picnic area include Blue-throated Hummingbird, Sulphur-bellied Flycatcher, Mexican Jay, Bridled Titmouse, Brown Creeper, Hutton's Vireo, Black-throated Gray and Grace's Warblers, Painted Redstart, and Hepatic Tanager. In some years Yellow-eyed Juncos hop tamely under the picnic tables, but in other years they are absent.

Much of South Fork's reputation is owing to the spectacular scenery. Towering rose-colored cliffs, pocked with grottoes and stained lime-green or citrus-orange on protected facades, shelter the ribbon of forest that follows the sparkling-clear little stream. However, up to 10 pairs of Elegant Trogons nest in South Fork Cave Creek. It was here, in October 1977, that the first Eared Trogon known to enter the U.S. was discovered, and the first Flame-colored Tanager north of the international boundary arrived in South Fork in April 1985. Even if there were no scenery, South Fork would be important in the annals of North American ornithology.

The trail up South Fork continues 7.25 miles to the Chiricahua Crest Trail. The best birding occurs in the first 2.25 miles below The Nose, a gargantuan rock formation on the right (north) side of the canyon as you ascend. Peregrine Falcons have maintained an eyrie here in recent years. Groves of Bigtooth Maple along the stream at the base of The Nose also harbor the lowest-elevation breeding Mexican Chickadees and Red-faced Warblers in the canyon, although post-breeding-season wandering in August may bring both species all the way down to the picnic area. After the maples change color in early November, Winter Wrens and American Dippers are occasional in upper South Fork.

South Fork Trail leaves the canyon bed after 2.5 miles, growing progressively steeper as the canyon narrows. At mile 4.0, it deserts the main canyon and continues up the dry Sentinel Fork tributary, switch-backing over 2,500 feet up the remaining several miles to the Crest Trail. Since the big fire in 1994, in places the uppermost portion of the trail is no longer discernable.

To rejoin the Canyons Loop return down the South Fork Road to paved Cave Creek Road and turn left.

The main canyon of Cave Creek is peppered with numerous caverns along the base of the cliffs, formed when vast quantities of volcanic ash were expelled from a nearby caldera in a series of violent eruptions approximately 15-25 million years ago. Gas pockets, trapped in the falling ash, created the plethora of pot holes and small caves that visitors see as they drive up the canyon today. These caverns formerly sheltered prehistoric peoples who were part of the Mogollon cultural tradition. Artifacts, bits of broken pottery, and corn cobs—some dating back 1,000 or more years—have been discovered in grottoes within the main canyon near its confluence with South Fork. *Remember, it is unlawful to remove any relic of our prehistoric past from public lands.*

In the late 1500s a new wave of immigrants entered the area from the northeast—the Chiricahua Apaches. The Chiricahuas apparently used caverns like these for concealed burial-chambers, interring their deceased behind a wall constructed of native rock and adobe. Their natural mausoleums are so well-camouflaged that only three such traditional Apache burial-sites have ever been discovered in the Southwest, and just one from the Chiricahua Mountains.

The artificial clearing on the right side of the road dates back to a homestead founded approximately 1900; a few apple trees still survived in 1995. It was across the road from the old Maloney Orchard that Arizona's first recorded Rufous-capped Warbler attempted to nest in July 1977, and then reappeared in April 1978. Zone-tailed Hawk and Elegant Trogon are frequently observed above and below the Maloney Orchard during summer.

Turn left onto Herb Martyr Road (1.8 miles above South Fork Road), cross the creek, and go another 50 yards to reach the entrance to the Southwestern Research Station. The American Museum of Natural History maintains the facility as a field station and laboratory for scientists, but cabins, with meals, are available to birders and naturalists from March through May, and, again, from September through November. From June through August researchers are given preference, and no advance reservations are accepted from birders. Most of the projects at the Southwestern Research Station focus on biological and ecological questions, and more dissertations in the natural sciences have been based on research conducted in the Chiricahua Mountain region than in any other area in the United States.

Please remember that this is a study area, not a public museum. Although the staff is friendly, they do not have time to give you a guided tour. A small gift shop in the office is open to everyone. Next door, the log cabin incorporated into the director's residence was built in 1879 by pioneer Stephen B. Reed, the first settler on the east side of the Chiricahuas. Birders are welcome to watch the hummingbird feeders in the central clearing.

Situated in a shady cottonwood grove at the confluence of the main branch of Cave Creek with North Fork Cave Creek, the Research Station has been the site of the discovery of numerous rarities. Records include a Pine Warbler in March 1991 and a Yellow Grosbeak in June 1974. Buff-breasted Flycatchers often spend all of May on the grounds; they possibly breed nearby. Some of the pine/oak birds that occur on a regular basis are Zone-tailed Hawk, Montezuma Quail (in the grasses just across the Herb Martyr Road from the entrance), Flammulated Owl (especially in dense junipers), Whiskered Screech-Owl, Common Poorwill, Whip-poor-will, Magnificent Hummingbird, Elegant Trogon, Strickland's Woodpecker, Sulphur-bellied Flycatcher, Painted Redstart, and Yellow-eyed Junco. Black Phoebes hang out by the swimming pool, and Say's Phoebes nest under the porch roofs of the cabins. Protected here from hunters, the Coues form of the White-tailed Deer is a regular evening visitor to the central meadow between the cabins and the dining hall.

Exiting the Southwestern Research Station, turn left onto the dirt road to **Herb Martyr Campground**. For the first 1.1 miles the road parallels Main Fork Cave Creek. Wild Turkey, Hepatic and Western Tanagers, and Red Crossbill use this wet stretch of the main canyon. Above the John Hands Dam the road climbs up into arid pine/oak woodland frequented by Montezuma Quail, Strickland's Woodpecker, Mexican Jay, Bridled Titmouse, Bushtit, Bewick's Wren, Hutton's Vireo, Black-throated Gray and Virginia's Warblers, Spotted Towhee, and Scott's Oriole. There is an almost continuous view of 396-foot-high Winn Falls, almost straight ahead, all the way to the parking area at Herb Martyr Campground (1.1 mile).

Tall, dead snags near the parking lot provide perches for Greater Pewee, whose melodic *José Maria* calls are one of the characteristic calls of the dawn chorus in spring. At the crack of daylight, a dozen or more

Strickland's Woodpecker
Narca Moore-Craig

species may be working the perimeter of the parking area, including Grace's Warbler and Painted Redstart. If the birds seem to be concentrating on one tree alone, check it carefully for a possible Northern Pygmy-Owl.

A short but potentially rewarding trail from Herb Martyr leads to Ash Spring and the Cima Creek Cienaga. Birds here include Steller's Jay, Mexican Chickadee, Red-breasted Nuthatch, Warbling Vireo, and Western Tanager. Take the trail that begins off the southwest corner of the parking lot, cross Cima Creek, and continue to a trail junction 150 yards beyond. Turn right (north) here and take the Basin Trail 0.7 mile to a stream-crossing in a grove of very tall Douglas-fir and White Fir, interwoven with the white limbs of exceptionally tall Arizona Sycamores. A series of small springs emerge in the cool shade of the conifers below the trail, creating an isolated pocket of habitat similar to that found along the Chiricahua Crest, three thousand feet above. This area is excellent for Flammulated Owl. Ash Spring is only 200 yards beyond the stream-crossing. Red-faced Warbler occasionally nests in the wet ravine below the spring. A steep, rocky, abandoned road drops from Ash Spring 0.7 mile down to the Herb Martyr parking area. There are superb views of Winn Falls en route. The whole loop is only 1.5 miles long, and the elevation change is from 5,750 feet at Herb Martyr to 6,200 feet at Ash Spring.

Return to the Cave Creek Road (2.2 miles), and turn left. The pavement ends 100 yards beyond the Southwestern Research Station, but the gravel road which continues is suitable for standard passenger vehicles—except after heavy winter storms. The road follows the canyonbottom of North Fork Cave Creek at the base of Silver Peak through a grassy area of scattered sycamores, walnuts, and junipers. Eastern Bluebirds prefer these open glades over other riparian habitats in the Chiricahuas. Ordinarily, one or two pairs of Elegant Trogons occupy this stretch of North Fork, too. After the upper stream-crossing (1.7 miles), the road enters the same short-stature Sierra Madrean pine/oak woodland as along the upper Herb Martyr Road, and the birds are identical. Once the summer rains commence, this is a good area in which to watch for Montezuma Quail and Strickland's Woodpecker.

The next birding stop is at the Paradise Road junction (2.3 miles). The grove of Douglas-fir and Gambel's Oak on the shady slope above East Turkey Creek usually contains the lowest road-accessible Mexican Chickadees on the east side of the Chiricahuas. Other breeding birds here include Northern Goshawk (occasionally soaring over), Steller's Jay, Red-breasted Nuthatch, Brown Creeper, Hutton's Vireo, Virginia's,

Grace's, and Red-faced Warblers, Western Tanager, and Yellow-eyed Junco. All of the these birds are more common in the high Chiricahuas, but if time is at a premium the East Turkey Creek crossing is a good place to try for them.

Make a sharp right turn onto Paradise Road to continue the Canyons Loop. The road crosses East Turkey Creek three times in the next few miles, as it drops out of the pines into the oaks and junipers at Paradise (2.6 miles). Founded in 1901, and once boasting a population of 1,500, Paradise was a classic boom-and-bust silver-mining camp. By 1910, the population had dwindled to fewer than 50, and in 1970, there were only three families in the settlement. But, the past decade has seen a resurgence of new residents, here to take advantage of the cool summer temperatures that the early miners likened to Paradise itself. A few of the old buildings still remain, including the home of the original postmaster, George Walker. Refurbished in 1993 by owners Dale and Michael Julian, the George Walker House opened as a guest house the following year. A Berylline Hummingbird was among their first visitors, in June 1994, and a family of Plain Titmice are year-round habitués at the seed-trays. Birders are welcome to watch the feeders. To find the George Walker House, look for the small sign on the left (west) side of the road in mid-town Paradise (0.4 mile).

To continue the loop, follow the road north to a "T" junction (0.3 mile), and turn right (east) across the concrete bridge over East Turkey Creek. A pair of Western Screech-Owls ordinarily holds a territory centering on the bridge. Across the stream the road winds through an open, grassy juniper woodland that attracts wintering Western Bluebirds, Townsend's Solitaires, and Cedar Waxwings. The habitat changes abruptly at Silver Creek Pass (1.5 miles).

Silver Creek's pinyon/juniper woodlands and interior chaparral are a consequence of the drainage's geographic position in the rainshadow of Silver Peak and of the crest of the Chiricahuas to the south and west. This arid habitat attracts a triplet of species more typical of Central Arizona: Western Scrub-Jay, Plain Titmouse, and Black-chinned Sparrow. Cactus, acacia, and Ocotillo on the hot, south-facing slopes support an enclave of desert birds that include Greater Roadrunner, Ash-throated Flycatcher, Rock Wren, Crissal Thrasher, Canyon Towhee, and Scott's Oriole. Sporadically present as migrants in April-May and August-September are Gray Flycatcher and Gray Vireo (very rare). In July and August watch the flowering agave stalks for hummingbirds. Rufous is the most abundant species, but Calliopes are not uncommon, and a Plain-capped Starthroat was here in August 1987. The best place to try for these birds is between

Silver Creek Spring and the right-hand roadside pull-outs over the next 0.7 mile. Walking the road from the spring to the pull-outs is recommended.

To find Silver Creek Spring watch for an abrupt right-hand lane that leads a few yards to an oval parking area with one big oak (1.3 miles). Here, too, a 200-yard-long path follows the stream down to a collapsed corral and water-trough under some huge old sycamores. If Cave Creek is running too strongly in Portal to hear the Elf Owls and Western Screech-Owls, this sycamore grove is a handy, nearby location with flood-proof acoustics.

Exercise caution as you continue down the Silver Creek Road; the road is narrow and has several blind curves. An inconspicuous lane on the right side near the lower end of the canyon (2.0 miles) leads to a small parking area near a stock-tank. The area near the pond can be dynamite—or dead. Both Indigo and Varied Buntings have attempted to colonize this area, but in some years neither is present. White-throated Swifts and Violet-green Swallows both drink from the small pool behind the earthworks. Both Curve-billed and Crissal Thrashers nest in the nearby ravines. Black-throated Sparrow is regular here throughout the year. Black-chinned Sparrows are fairly common by the pond in winter.

It is one more mile down Silver Creek Road to paved Cave Creek Road. Portal is 0.5 mile downcanyon to the left.

Mountain Highlands Transect

(24 miles/one-half day to Rustler Park)

(80 miles/one day to Chiricahua National Monument)

The first 8.7 miles of this trip—from Portal to the Paradise Road junction at East Turkey Creek—are described above in the Canyons Loop section. Assuming that you do not detour on either the South Fork or Herb Martyr Road en route to East Turkey Creek, it will take you approximately 30 minutes to reach East Turkey Creek from Portal.

The Trans-mountain Road above the crossing is a narrow, steep, and winding mountain route. *It is important for drivers to keep to the right on blind curves. We strongly recommend sounding the horn before entering them.* This road is not safe for vehicles over 20 feet in length or for vehicles pulling trailers. During winter, and after major summer thunderstorms, the road may be closed. Nonetheless a visit to Rustler Park and, time permitting, Chiricahua National Monument is one of the

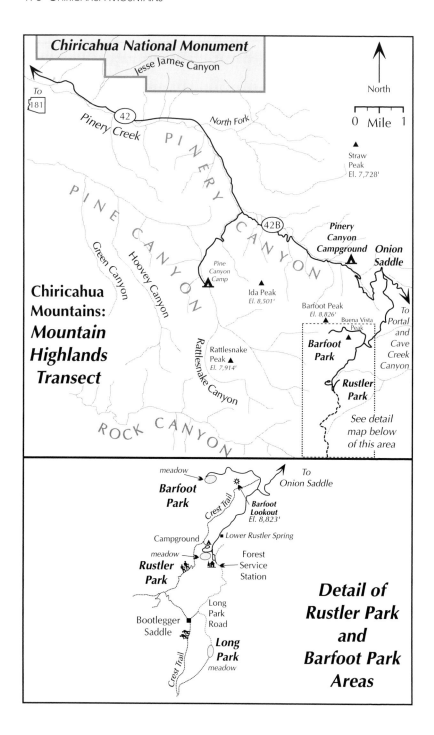

Chiricahua National Monument

Jesse James Canyon

To 181

Pinery Creek

42

North Fork

PINERY

PINE CANYON

Green Canyon

Hoovey Canyon

CANYON

42B

North

0 Mile 1

Straw Peak
El. 7,728'

Pinery Canyon Campground

Onion Saddle

Pine Canyon Camp

Ida Peak
El. 8,501'

Barfoot Peak
El. 8,826'

Buena Vista Peak

To Portal and Cave Creek Canyon

Barfoot Park

Rustler Park

Chiricahua Mountains:
Mountain Highlands Transect

Rattlesnake Peak
El. 7,914'

Rattlesnake Canyon

ROCK CANYON

See detail map below of this area

meadow

Barfoot Park

Crest Trail

To Onion Saddle

Barfoot Lookout
El. 8,823'

Lower Rustler Spring

Campground

meadow

Rustler Park

Forest Service Station

Long Park Road

Bootlegger Saddle

Long Park
meadow

Crest Trail

Detail of Rustler Park and Barfoot Park Areas

highlights of any birder's pilgrimage to Southeastern Arizona. Nothing gladdens a birder's day like the sight, sound, and smell of a highland meadow surrounded by fir and aspen, filled with bird voices, and aromatic with the fragrance of Ponderosa Pine.

Among birders who maintain a North American list, Mexican Chickadee is perhaps the bird most-wished-for when they visit the Chiricahua Mountains. Unlike Elegant or even Eared Trogons, Mexican Chickadees simply do not occur elsewhere on public lands north of Mexico. In fact, the small population on the privately owned Gray Ranch in the adjacent New Mexico panhandle cannot be reached without a strenuous hike. Fortunately, Mexican Chickadees are common in the upper Chiricahuas. This does not mean that they are always easy to find. While chickadees are attending nests in April and May, it is often easier to see them at the East Turkey Creek crossing on the Trans-mountain Road, or in the forested ravines en route to Onion Saddle (3.3 miles), than at the end of the road in Rustler Park. Depending on the year, dead pine-snags along this stretch may also be the best place to search for Northern Pygmy-Owls during spring.

At Onion Saddle (El. 7,600 feet), turn left (south) toward Rustler Park. For the next two miles, the route follows the crest of the Chiricahuas, threading in and out of Ponderosa Pine stands, alternating with dense thickets of oak. These dry, brushy hillsides are good for Virginia's Warblers.

The vista at the oak grove between mile 1.3 to 1.6 is especially magnificent. Cave Creek Canyon—with 7,975-foot Silver Peak on the left and 8,544-foot Portal Peak on the right—cuts a chasm practically at your feet, and the rugged peaks of southwestern New Mexico unfurl for a hundred miles to the horizon. Do not forget to watch for birds. Aside from chickadees, the pines along the lower Rustler Road are also good for Hairy Woodpecker, Olive Warbler, Western Tanager (summer), Chipping Sparrow, Yellow-eyed Junco, and Red Crossbill (irregular).

After a big switchback, the road levels out and then "T's" at **Barfoot Junction** (2.0 miles). The left spur continues to Rustler Park (1.0 mile), while the right fork goes to Barfoot Park (1.0 mile). Bird here. *Vale la pena,* as they say in Mexico—it's definitely worth the trouble. Some of the birds present throughout the summer at Barfoot Junction include Hairy Woodpecker, Greater Pewee, Violet-green Swallow, Steller's Jay, Common Raven, Mexican Chickadee, Pygmy Nuthatch, Brown Creeper, House Wren (about half of them are the "Brown-throated" subspecies of the Sierra Madre), Eastern and Western Bluebirds, Yellow-rumped "Audubon's", Grace's, and Olive Warblers, Hepatic Tanager, Black-

Olive Warbler
Narca Moore-Craig

headed Grosbeak, and Yellow-eyed Junco. Other birds to watch for among the Ponderosa Pines are Northern Goshawk, Band-tailed Pigeon, and Northern Pygmy-Owl. Northern Saw-whet Owls have nested near the parking area on the right (north) side of Barfoot Junction. A little spring arises from the bed of Rocky Mountain Iris on the left (south) side of the road at the intersection. If bird activity seems light, a hundred-yard walk down to the spring is sometimes worth the time. Hammond's and Dusky Flycatchers are fairly common in this swale during spring and fall migration.

Barfoot Park, elevation 8,200 feet (1.0 mile), is a small, grassy meadow with a trickling spring, set directly beneath the talus-strewn slope of 8,826-foot-high Barfoot Peak. The last half of the road to Barfoot Park can be rough for cars with low clearance. You may want to walk after reaching the cattle-guard. Lacking improved campsites, Barfoot is ordinarily less crowded than Rustler Park. It is also one of the most reliable sites in the Chiricahuas for Zone-tailed Hawk. Watch for them to waft up over the half-dome of rhyolite on the south side of the meadow. Meanwhile, Broad-tailed Hummingbirds will be working the flowers by the spring near the pump-house. Be careful not to confuse the common Northern "Red-shafted" Flicker with female Williamson's Sapsuckers, which migrate through in May and September. Barfoot is excellent also for Greater Pewee, Red-breasted and Pygmy Nuthatches, and both Red-faced and Olive Warblers. The Red-faces prefer the aspen grove where the road drops into the meadow. Olives can be anywhere, but seem particularly fond of the pines near the Boy Scout buildings on the west side of the clearing.

Retrace your route back to Barfoot Junction (1.0 mile), and continue straight ahead to reach Rustler Park (1.0 mile).

As you follow the delightful road to **Rustler Park**, keep an eye out for Wild Turkeys (uncommon), particularly on the downhill side. The fingers of burnt timber are part of the enormous 1994 Rattlesnake Fire. Check the woodpeckers using the burn; Hairy is common, but Southeastern Arizona is overdue for its first record of Three-toed. A pull-out and restroom on the left marks the entrance to the Rustler Park Recreation Site, where a fee is required for camping or picnicking. Just beyond the pull-out there is a spring on the left enclosed by a rail fence. The short-needled, deep-green conifer inside is an Engelmann Spruce. A timberline species growing north to British Columbia, Engelmann Spruce stands in the Chiricahuas are the southernmost in North America.

Birds likely to be present in summer near the spring include Band-tailed Pigeon, Northern Pygmy-Owl, Steller's Jay, Mexican Chickadee,

Red-breasted and Pygmy Nuthatches, House Wren, Western Bluebird, Hermit Thrush, American Robin, Yellow-rumped, Grace's, and Olive Warblers, Hepatic and Western Tanagers, Black-headed Grosbeak, Chipping Sparrow, Yellow-eyed Junco, Pine Siskin, and Evening Grosbeak (irregular). Beyond the spring the road forks. The left branch goes to the ranger station (0.15 mile) while the right fork leads to campsites along the north edge of the meadow.

Rustler Park is an enchanting spot. In June, when it turns blue with Rocky Mountain Iris, the shrill trill emitted by the wings of airborne male Broad-tailed Hummingbirds competes for your ear with the flute-like notes of Hermit Thrushes. In August and early September hundreds of migrating Rufous Hummingbirds join the Broadtails in pitched battle over feeding rights to blossoming Bluebells and Delphiniums throughout the Chiricahua meadows, as well as in patches of Lemmon's Salvia on the rocky south-facing slopes.

The largest concentration of migrating hummingbirds occurs up the old Long Park logging road, south of the Rustler ranger station. Watch for them after the road levels off and makes an abrupt right turn (0.4 mile), and again in 9,000-foot-high Long Park itself (1.5 miles). This steep road is badly eroded and is better walked than driven.

Before hiking up the old logging road that leads from the ranger station to Long Park, spend a few moments birding around the small log cabins used by seasonal fire-fighters. Every summer, Cordilleran Flycatchers nest at the Forest Service horse corral and barn. Here, too, are the most-accessible breeding Golden-crowned Kinglets in Southeastern Arizona. If you are still searching for Red-faced Warbler, try the short fire-break trail behind the cabins that circles back to upper Rustler Park. Buff-breasted Flycatcher is occasionally found in the grassy burn 200 yards east of the Rustler cabins.

On the west end of the upper campground loop, an access trail climbs nearly straight up the slope for 250 feet and then divides. The left branch leads through the Chiricahua Wilderness to the top of 9,796-foot-elevation Chiricahua Peak (5.25 miles), the highest point in the range. This is an all-day hike, but rewarding. Along the way, the trail passes through a series of small meadows, swings across openings with vistas that encompass the entirety of Southeastern Arizona, and tunnels through beautiful stands of Engelmann Spruce. Since the 1994 Rattlesnake Fire, there are also long stretches of trail that cross blistered landscapes where not a single tree survived the holocaust. Birds in the unburned parts of the wilderness area are the same as those found at Rustler and Barfoot Parks.

The right fork of the trail above the campground follows the crest 1.25 miles north to Barfoot Lookout on 8,823-foot-high Buena Vista Peak. The first mile of the trail stays just under the east side of the ridge. This is great for seeing Yellow-rumped and Grace's Warblers and Western and Hepatic Tanagers right at eye-level. When you pause to rest, watch for a small brown lizard darting after insects amid the shocks of Muhly Grass. This is the Bunch Grass Lizard, a Sierra Madrean species confined, in the U.S., to the archipelago of high mountains along the Mexican border.

Birds are sparse in the final few hundred yards below the summit, but a Red-faced Warbler usually pops up where the trail zigzags through a grove of Gambel's Oak just under the top. Yellow-eyed Juncos hop around on the rocky crown itself. The view from Barfoot Lookout is superb. Beyond the billiard-green bowl of Barfoot Park the Sulphur Springs Valley (see Chapter 8) unrolls to the west, the Chiricahua Wilderness Area rises to the south, a vast tract of New Mexico stretches to the east, and to the north lies the jagged stone garden of Chiricahua National Monument with Cochise Head as a backdrop. White-throated Swifts zoom by almost continuously on a typical summer visit to Barfoot Lookout.

When you can finally force yourself to leave the Rustler Park area, return to Onion Saddle (3.0 miles). It is probably best to turn sharply right and return to Portal (11.7 miles) now if you have budgeted only half a day for your visit to the high country. If you have a full day for exploring, or if you intend to continue on to Willcox, Douglas, or Tucson, bear left to descend the west side of the mountain.

Heading west for the first mile or so, the road is narrow, winding, and a bit of a cliff-hanger, but it soon improves. Pinery Canyon Campground (2.0 miles below the saddle) is a good place to find Mexican Chickadee, the "Brown-throated" form of the House Wren, and Red-faced Warbler. Continue past the main campground entrance, and stop at a right-side pull-out 100 yards beyond, next to a huge Gambel's Oak. The clearing opposite this tremendous oak is often productive. A few squeaks or a Northern Pygmy-Owl imitation will usually bring out a swarm of birds.

Pinery Canyon Campground has earned a reputation for great owling. If Flammulated Owls are not calling in Cave Creek Canyon, they are usually vocalizing in Pinery. Watch for Flammies to sit close to the trunk of a fairly dense conifer or juniper. Whiskered Screech-Owls are common in Pinery; Northern Saw-whet Owl is occasional.

From here on, the birds are about the same as those observed on the Cave Creek side, but as a rule they are not so abundant here. Dead snags, the first few miles below Pinery Campground, are often used for perches by migrating Olive-sided Flycatchers. After the Trans-mountain Road crosses Pinery Creek (3.0 miles), check the road edges carefully for Montezuma Quail. Eastern Bluebirds like the open woodlands near the mouth of the canyon; American Kestrel, Horned Lark, Lark Sparrow, and Eastern Meadowlark are typical species of the final two miles of valley grassland leading to the pavement at the junction with of State Highway 181 (9.0 miles). Turn right (east) to enter **Chiricahua National Monument**.

Approximately 27 million years ago, volcanic magma eruptions nine miles south in the West Turkey Creek area buried this area under a 2,000-foot-deep mantle of white-hot ash and pumice, which solidified into a fine-grained rock called rhyolite. As the rock rapidly cooled, it cracked into hexagonal columns some hundreds of feet high. Eons of wind, rain, and frost widened the cracks, leaving the columns free-standing. One spire, called the Totem Pole, is over 300 feet tall and only 3 feet wide at the base. Big Balanced Rock has an estimated weight of over 1,000 tons, yet it sits on a pedestal only a few feet thick. Other columns have eroded into grotesque stone caricatures of people or animals. As you drive up Monument Road through this "wonderland of rock," as it is popularly known, with thousands of monoliths poised overhead, you will be impressed by the magnitude of the geological cataclysms that wrought the surrounding stone forest.

Stop at the Monument visitor center (fee) (2.0 miles) for a bird checklist and information about trails, campgrounds, and the history of this unique area. The book store here has a broad selection of books, maps, cards, and videos. An easy way to learn the trees is to take the short nature trail up Rhyolite Canyon from the parking lot. Birds along this level, quarter-mile-long route are typical of the Sierra Madrean pine/oak woodlands. If the National Monument marks your initial entry into the Chiricahuas, this is an excellent place to watch for your "life bird" Strickland's Woodpecker, Dusky-capped Flycatcher, Mexican Jay, Bridled Titmouse, Painted Redstart, and Scott's Oriole. Also, look for Apache Squirrels, endemic to this range alone.

As you drive into Bonita Canyon, check the Organ Pipe Formation (1.0 mile) for Prairie Falcons. A pair has nested in these towering rock columns in recent years. Also, scrutinize every Turkey Vulture—Zone-tailed Hawks frequent the same rhyolite spires as the falcons. A Berylline Hummingbird fledged two young near the Natural Bridge Trail pull-out in mid-September 1984, only the second known successful nesting in the U.S. Watch for Anna's Hummingbird in the roadside thistle-patches here.

At the end of the road to Massai Point (6.0 miles), there is another nature trail and a spectacular overlook of the Monument. Every year, a pair of Mexican Chickadees flits through the stunted Douglas-fir, Arizona Cypress, Pinyon Pine, and small oaks that crowd the 6,870-foot summit. Other summer birds at Massai include Red-tailed Hawk, White-throated Swift, Violet-green Swallow, Common Raven, Bridled Titmouse, Canyon Wren, Black-throated Gray Warbler, Painted Redstart, Spotted Towhee, and Black-headed Grosbeak. The best way to find these birds is take the half-mile-long interpretive trail that circles the western side of Massai Point.

As you begin the drive down, a mile-long stone profile of a man's face known as Cochise Head dominates the northern horizon and commemorates the great leader of the Chiricahua Apaches who strove so hard to protect his homeland. This is a fitting end to any visit to the Chiricahua Mountains.

From the Chiricahua National Monument entry station it is 25.7 miles east on the Trans-mountain Road over Onion Saddle to Portal. Willcox and Interstate 10 are 31 miles to the west on State Highways 181 and 186.

Campgrounds, Restaurants, and Accommodations:

There are basic campgrounds in Cave Creek Canyon, Rustler Park, Pinery Canyon, and in Chiricahua National Monument.

Good cooking and large portions of it can be had at the Portal Store Cafe adjacent to the Portal Peak Lodge (telephone 520/558-2223). Established in 1994, the lodge is modern and comfortable. The Southwestern Research Station has dormitory-style rooms, which include family-style meals (telephone 520/558-2396). Cave Creek Ranch has older housekeeping cabins and very birdy grounds (telephone 520/558-2334). The George Walker House in Paradise is an historic home that has been renovated recently for guests (telephone 520/558-2287). All of these facilities share the same address; only the owners are different. Write to the ones you are interested in at Portal, AZ 85632.

CHAPTER 10

OTHER LOCATIONS

A. PICACHO RESERVOIR

(61 miles north of Tucson/one-half day)

Picacho (Pea-CAH-cho, Spanish for "Peak") Reservoir is the best location in Southeastern Arizona for Least Bittern. Located at an elevation of just 1,500 feet in a desert basin near the confluence of the Santa Cruz and Gila Rivers, Picacho marks the usual eastern range-limit for a phalanx of species which are more common on the Lower Colorado River. Some of these in-clude American White and Brown Pelicans, Double-crested Cormorant, Amer-ican Bittern, and Clapper Rail. Picacho is also a magnet for lost birds. Some of the vagrants recorded recently are Least Grebe in January 1995, Yellow-crowned Night-Heron in late May 1992, White Ibis from late June through mid-September 1986, Roseate Spoonbill from June through October 1973, and Purple Gallinule in August 1993. Migrating terns also favor this area.

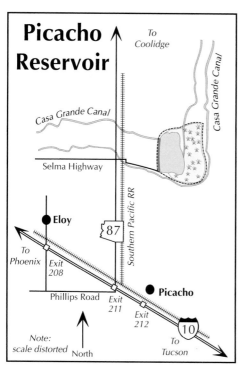

To find Picacho Reser-voir, take Interstate 10 north of Tucson to exit 211, just north of Picacho (50 miles north of Tucson at the junction of Interstates 10 and 19). Turn right (north) onto Highway 87 toward Coolidge. Follow this road to its intersection with Selma Highway (9.3 miles), on the right (east) side. In spite of the fancy name, this is only a dirt road and easy to miss. Watch for a big, water-filled canal, which passes under Highway 87 at this point. After turning right onto Selma Highway, you soon cross the canal (0.1 mile), and then cross railroad tracks (0.2 mile). Turn right (south) onto a dirt road (0.1 mile) along the tracks, and then turn left (east) onto the road on the top of the canal levee (0.1 mile). This dirt road will lead you to the embankment around Picacho Reservoir (0.8 mile). Turn left onto a small dirt road along the base of the earthen dam, and follow it until you can drive up onto its top. From here you can scope the water.

The cattails, drowned trees, and open water at Picacho Reservoir attract regularly occurring ducks and shorebirds, as well as Great Blue and Green Herons, Great and Snowy Egrets, White-faced Ibis, and other waders. The southwestern portion of the reservoir is generally best for birding. Check the mesquite trees near the irrigation canal off the southeast corner of the dam for passerines.

The water-level varies greatly, depending on seasonal differences and rainfall. *In dry years it may be nearly empty during summer. The temperatures from late spring through early fall are simply torrid. Carry water!* Picacho Reservoir is open to hunters. The area can be full of off-road vehicles on weekends. Also consider that rains can make the access roads very muddy.

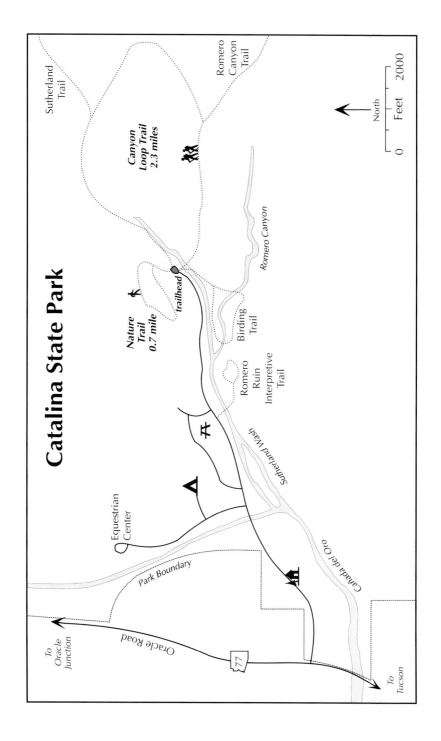

B. CATALINA STATE PARK

(16 miles north of Tucson/one-half day)

This 5,500-acre tract set aside by the State of Arizona in 1983, preserves a beautiful parcel of Saguaro-studded Sonoran Desert just a few miles north of Tucson. Three intermittent streams—Cañada del Oro, Sutherland Wash, and Romero Canyon—connect in a lush mesquite bosque at the foot of the Santa Catalina Mountains. A loop Nature Trail (0.7 mile long) and the Canyon Loop Trail (2.3 miles long) provide access to the full spectrum of Park habitats. *After heavy rains in the Santa Catalina Mountains, it is necessary to wade the streams to walk the Canyon Loop Trail. Do not cross if the streams are flash-flooding.* The common birds at the Park include Cooper's Hawk, Gambel's Quail, White-winged Dove (summer), Costa's Hummingbird (primarily spring), Gila Woodpecker, Gray Flycatcher (winter), Black Phoebe, Vermilion Flycatcher, Verdin, Cactus Wren, Western Bluebird (winter), and Northern Cardinal. Northern Beardless-Tyrannulet occurs throughout the year in the mesquites along Cañada del Oro, although it is rare in winter.

Night birding is a real treat at Catalina. Arrive early to watch the butterscotch-colored light fade on the west slope of the mountains, which loom more than 6,000 feet above. As dusk deepens in the valley, listen for the distinctive calls of Western Screech-Owl, Great Horned Owl, and Elf Owl (summer). The voice of Common Poorwill is also part of the summer evening chorus. May 1978 saw the first report of Buff-collared Nightjar in Sutherland Wash. This rarity has been reported near the road end at Catalina at widely-spaced intervals ever since. A Long-eared Owl roosted in the Tamarisks behind the group site during winter in the mid-1980s.

To find Catalina State Park drive north on Interstate 10 from the junction of Interstates 10 and 19 to exit 256, Grant Road (3.8 miles), and turn right (east). Continue to Oracle Road, Highway 77. Turn left (north) onto Oracle (0.7 mile) and stay on this highway as it crosses northwest Tucson and enters the foothills of the Santa Catalina Mountains. The well-signed entrance to Catalina State Park lies on the right (east) side of Highway 77 (12.0 miles). The entry station is staffed from 7am to 5pm; a map and a bird checklist are included in the entry fee ($3 per vehicle for day-use in 1995. Primitive campsites cost $8/night; full hook-ups for trailers were $13/night in 1995). For more information contact Catalina State Park, P.O. Box 36986, Tucson, AZ 85740; telephone 520/628-5798.

C. ARAVAIPA CANYON WEST and DUDLEYVILLE

(84 miles north to Aravaipa and Dudleyville/one day)

See the map for Section M of this chapter—page 220

This trip is designed primarily to see three species of raptors. The only road-accessible Common Black-Hawks in Southeastern Arizona occur in Aravaipa Canyon. Since their discovery in Arizona in 1970, Mississippi Kites have nested in the cottonwoods along a 40-mile-long stretch of the San Pedro River centering on Dudleyville. They share the cottonwood gallery-forest here with a healthy population of Gray Hawks. Both the Common Black-Hawks and Gray Hawks arrive in mid-March and depart in October.

To reach the west entrance to **Aravaipa Canyon**, drive north on Interstate 10 from the junction of Interstates 10 and 19 to exit 256, Grant Road (3.8 miles), and turn right (east). Continue east to Oracle Road (0.7 mile) and turn left (north). Follow Oracle Road, which becomes Highway 77, to Oracle Junction (21.0 miles). Continue on Highway 77 through Mammoth and across the San Pedro River (22.5 miles). Just beyond the milepost 124 marker turn right (east) onto Aravapia Road (7.9 miles). The first four miles of the Aravaipa Road are paved. Upper Aravaipa Road becomes a well-graded gravel route that ends at a house trailer that serves as the Bureau of Land Management entry station (12.1 miles). Buff-collared Nightjar was seen under the floodlight outside the ranger's home in the summer of 1980, and has reappeared sporadically. *Note: A flash-flood in January 1993 damaged the last three miles of the Aravaipa Road. A locked gate 0.8 mile before the stream-crossing prevents the public from driving upcanyon farther than 8.7 miles from Highway 77. Until the road is repaired (completion is scheduled for late 1995), a temporary parking area has been established several hundred feet above the stream at Brandenburg Camp.*

Fortunately for raptor enthusiasts, both Common Black-Hawks and Zone-tailed Hawks occur along the lower section of Aravaipa Road *before* it reaches the Wilderness Area.

Intrepid birders with permits may wish to explore the Aravaipa Canyon Wilderness Area. *You must walk on the road to the BLM entry station. The land on both sides of the road is privately owned.* Besides the calls of Canyon Wrens spiraling down from the thousand-foot-high walls that flank the stream, and occasional Peregrine Falcons dodging between the cliffs, Desert Bighorn Sheep are frequently sighted. Arizona

Game and Fish biologists estimated there were between 85 and 125 wild sheep roaming Aravaipa in 1995. With seven species of native fish, Aravaipa Canyon supports the most diversified sample of endemic pisci- fauna in all of Arizona. Two species, Spike Dace and Loach Minnow, are on the federal list of threatened wildlife.

Only 50 people per day are permitted in the 11-mile-long Aravaipa Canyon Wilderness Area. To obtain a permit contact the Bureau of Land Management, Safford District Office, 711 14th Avenue, Safford, AZ 85546; telephone 520/428-4040. Because of limited availability, the BLM strongly recommends making reservations by phone 13 weeks in advance. There is a charge of $1.50 per person per day. Plan on wearing stout, high-top shoes or boots to wade the stream: you will have to cross it dozens of times. High top footgear will eliminate some of the gravel sluicing into your socks.

The way to **Dudleyville** is the same as the way to Aravaipa Canyon Road. Instead of turning off at the canyon, however, continue north to just before the milepost 129 marker on Highway 77 (3.4 miles). Turn left (west) toward the San Pedro River. Within moments you enter "down-town" Dudleyville. At the stop sign turn right (north) onto Dudleyville Road, then left (west) onto the first paved side street, San Pedro Road. The pavement plays out just before the river (0.5 mile). *Park well off the road here; do not continue driving on the private, unpaved road leading to the river. Do not attempt to cross the river if the San Pedro is high.*

Watch for the Mississippi Kites and Gray Hawks all the way in from

Highway 77. Scan the cotton-woods along the river for perched birds. Other species recorded here include Tropical and Thick-billed Kingbirds. Streak-backed Orioles successfully nested at Dudleyville in the summers of both 1993 and 1994. *The land here is privately owned; bird from the road.*

Mississippi Kite
Gail Diane Yovanovich

D. SELLS, TOHONO O'ODHAM NATION

(54 miles west of Tucson/one-half day)

The only reliable Crested Caracaras in Southeastern Arizona occur west of the Baboquivari Mountains on the vast 2,800,000-acre Tohono O'odham Nation lands (formerly known as the Papago Indian Reservation). Approximately the size of Connecticut, this is the second-largest area owned by Native Americans in the United States. Some 8,000 Tohono O'odham (Piman words for "Desert People") call it home. Because most of this sprawling, Saguaro-spiked area lies in the Sonoran Desert at an elevation of 2,500 feet or lower, the best time to visit it is in winter. The caracaras can usually be spotted along Highway 86 between the turn-off to Kitt Peak and the tribal capital at Sells.

To look for the Crested Caracaras, start at the junction of Interstates 10 and 19, and follow I-19 south to the first freeway interchange, exit 99,

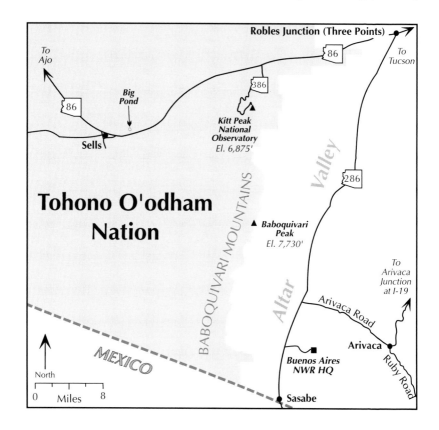

Ajo Way (1.0 mile). Turn right (west) onto Ajo Way. Continue west on Ajo Way, which becomes Highway 86, past Three Points (21.5 miles) onto Tohono O'odham Nation lands.

The well-signed road to Kitt Peak Observatory, operated by the National Science Foundation since its inception in 1958, is located on the left (south) side of Highway 86 (16.0 miles). This 13-mile-long paved road (open 9am to 3:45pm) climbs over 3,500 feet to the 6,875-foot summit of Kitt Peak, site of some 21 telescopes, including several that are among the world's largest. A picnic area at mile 11.5 offers the best birding spot. The common birds here include Acorn Woodpecker, Mexican Jay, Common Raven, Bewick's Wren, and Spotted Towhee.

Back on Highway 86, early morning is best for the Crested Caracaras. Watch for them to perch inside and below the tops of the mesquite and paloverde trees that line the Ajo Highway. Occasionally the birds can be seen soaring low over the desert. The pull-out for Big Pond, a quarter-mile-diameter stock tank, is located on the right (north) side of the highway just beyond the milepost 116 marker (15.5 miles). Walk the little road that goes 150 yards north to a corral. *Close any gate you have to open to get through.* Veer left around the corral and walk quietly for the last 100 yards through the mesquites to the impoundment. During winter and migration there are frequently herons, ducks, and shorebirds on Big Pond. A Solitary Sandpiper was found here on the late date of December 29, 1993. A scope will be useful. Black and Say's Phoebes, Vermilion Flycatcher, Verdin, and Black-tailed Gnatcatcher are the winter passerines. Occasionally a Crested Caracara is perched in the mesquites on the west edge. Watch for both Black and Turkey Vultures—fairly common here but rare elsewhere in Southeastern Arizona during the winter.

Gambel's Quail, Gilded Flicker, Curve-billed and Crissal Thrashers, Northern Cardinal, and Rufous-winged Sparrow are the common birds along the road back to your car. There are no facilities for tourists west of Big Pond in Sells (1.2 miles). *Directions to the Sells Dump reprinted in older guides are no longer usable, and a permit from tribal authorities is required to visit this site and other areas off Highway 86 belonging to the Tohono O'odham.* Contact them at PO Box 300, Sells, AZ 85634; telephone 520/282-2366.

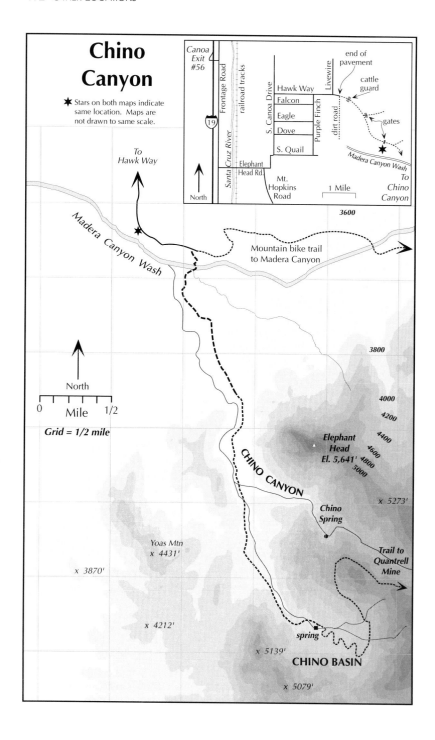

E. CHINO CANYON

(40 miles south of Tucson/one-half day)

In the 1980s Black-capped Gnatcatchers and Five-striped Sparrows were found nesting in Chino Canyon on the west slope of the Santa Rita Mountains. The last record of the gnatcatcher came in August 1991, and the sparrows disappeared even earlier. Birders with time and curiosity should consider visiting this location during spring and summer for other interesting birds of the Foothill Thornscrub, such as Northern Beardless-Tyrannulet, Bell's Vireo, Lucy's Warbler, Varied Bunting, and Rufous-crowned Sparrow. Go early in the morning and bring plenty of water. *The end of the road to Chino Canyon is very primitive and only suitable for vehicles with high clearance, preferably with four-wheel-drive.*

Take exit 56 (Canoa) off of Interstate 19, 27.7 miles south of the junction of Interstates 10 and 19 in Tucson. Go under I-19 to the frontage road on the east side. Turn right (south) to Elephant Head Road (3.1 miles). Follow Elephant Head Road across the Santa Cruz River (0.5 mile), across the railroad tracks, and past Mt. Hopkins Road (0.8) to a big curve where the pavement sweeps left (north) and the road name changes to S. Canoa Drive (0.2 mile). Immediately after crossing a cattle-guard (0.4 mile), take the left fork, Canoa Road. Traveling northward, the fourth road you encounter will be Hawk Way (1.8 miles) where you turn right (east). Stay on Hawk Way to the end of the pavement (2.0 miles). The road soon turns right (south). You are now traveling across State Trust Land. *No stopping, picnicking, or camping is permitted without a special permit.* Ignore the gated road to the left (0.8 mile) and continue south along a fence-line to a gate across the road on which you are traveling (0.7 mile). Just beyond here (0.4 mile), the road divides and turns south across Madera Wash. *Here it may be best to leave your vehicle, and walk the additional 1.4 miles into the canyon.* There will be two gates (0.2 mile and 0.9 mile) before you arrive at the traditional parking spot (0.3 mile) under an oak tree, at the base of Elephant Head. The mountain-bike trail up the valley, which follows an old road, provides a convenient route toward the head of the basin.

The Black-capped Gnatcatchers were found in and near hackberry trees close to the rock slope on the south side of Elephant Head, a large granite outcrop which is visible for miles. (Be aware that two other species of gnatcatcher are regularly seen here: Black-tailed and Blue-gray.) The Five-striped Sparrows were usually found on higher and drier slopes. There have also been some other surprises at Chino Canyon, such as Buff-collared Nightjar and Lucifer Hummingbird. There is a strongly-held belief among local birders that the Black-capped Gnat-catchers and Five-striped Sparrows are no longer found here because they were "taped-out" by visiting birders. *Do not use tapes here.*

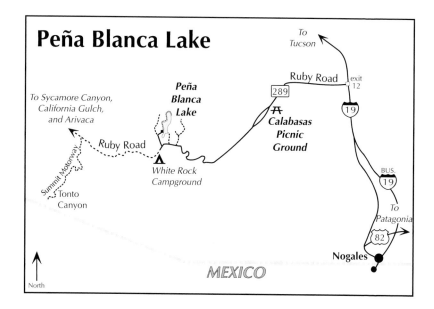

F. Peña Blanca Lake

(65 miles from Tucson/one day)

This trip is more for exploration than for birding. With the possible exception of Montezuma Quail, there are no birds to be regularly found in this area that cannot be seen more easily elsewhere. What makes this trip so enticing is its proximity to the border. Who knows what may wander up from Mexico?

The starting point is off Interstate 19, 55.5 miles south of the junction of Interstates 10 and 19 in Tucson or 7.2 miles north of Nogales. Take exit 12, Ruby Road (Highway 289). Going west on Ruby Road, you will pass through rolling grassland interspersed with mesquite and live oak—prime habitat for Montezuma Quail. They can often be seen feeding right along the road, particularly early in the morning.

At the Calabasas (Spanish for "squashes") Picnic Ground, elevation 4,000 feet (6.4 miles), look for Ash-throated Flycatcher, Mexican Jay, Bridled Titmouse, Bushtit, and Black-throated Gray Warbler in the Emory Oaks, and for Canyon Towhee and Rufous-crowned Sparrow in the brush.

The best birding on this trip is usually around Peña Blanca Lake Recreation Area (2.8 miles). The name is pronounced PAIN-yah BLAHN-cah and means "White Rock" in Spanish. In winter, there are normally a few Eared Grebes and ducks, as well as Marsh Wrens and Swamp Sparrows in the cattails. Great Blue Heron and American Coot are resident. Both Double-crested (uncommon) and Neotropic Cormorants (rare) also turn up at Peña Blanca. Numerous landbirds are attracted to the cover along the edge of this cerulean-blue, 50-acre impoundment. By hiking at least part-way around the lake on a fisherman's path that originates at the small store, you may see Black and Say's Phoebes, Vermilion Flycatcher, Bewick's and Rock Wrens, Phainopepla, Northern Cardinal, Pyrrhuloxia, House Finch, and Lesser Goldfinch. In summer, watch for White-winged Dove, Ash-throated Flycatcher, Cassin's and Western Kingbirds, Bell's Vireo, Black-headed and Blue Grosbeaks, and Scott's Oriole. In winter, look for Anna's Hummingbird, Red-naped Sapsucker, Hermit Thrush, Orange-crowned and Yellow-rumped Warblers, and Green-tailed Towhee.

Near Peña Blanca Lake is a primitive campground with tables, water, and pit toilets which is open year-round.

Sycamore Canyon

The darker the shading, the higher the elevation.

The darkest areas have elevations above 4,800 feet.

The lightest areas have elevations between 3,400 and 3,600 feet. Contour interval is 200 feet.

Duplicate Tear-Out Trail Map is provided on page 323.

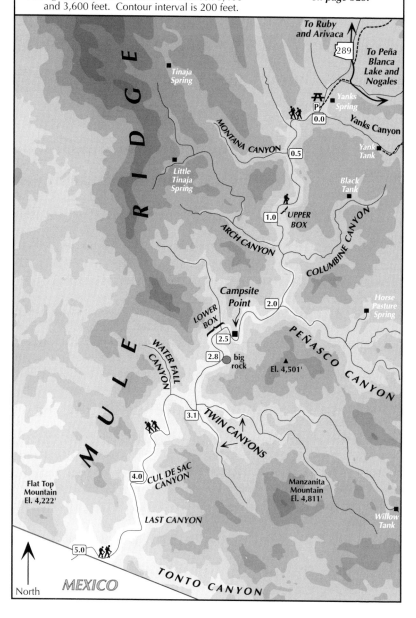

G. SYCAMORE CANYON

(75 miles south of Tucson/one day)
(26 miles west of Nogales/one day)

The signed turn-off for Sycamore Canyon is on the left (south) side of Ruby Road, a one-half to one-hour drive (9.4 miles) beyond the end of the pavement at Peña Blanca Lake (see access information for Peña Blanca Lake in the previous section, Section F; 74.1 miles from Tucson). Ruby Road is narrow, rocky, winding, and wash-boarded. Watch for oncoming traffic on blind curves. Park at the Hank and Yank Spring parking area south of the Ruby Road (0.5 mile). If you can hike over broken terrain, the drive in is worth it.

Sycamore Canyon, which originates in the Atascosa Mountains, is a rock-walled canyon set between elevations of 4,000 feet at the Forest Service parking area and 3,500 feet five miles downstream at the barbed-wire fence that marks the international boundary. The hillsides flanking the defile support the lowest pine/oak woodland in Arizona. Velvet Ash and Arizona Sycamore line a permanent, but intermittent, stream. Its waters empty into a tributary of the Río de la Concepción in Mexico, providing a natural gateway for tropical species from the south. Such novelties as the Tarahumara Frog (probably extinct since 1980) and a fish called the Sonoran Chub occur(red) nowhere else in the United States.

Sycamore's reputation for harboring southern rarities began in 1974 when Rose-throated Becards were first recorded in the canyon. The following year saw the arrival of Elegant Trogons. In 1977 Five-striped Sparrows appeared. Today there are more Five-striped Sparrows in Sycamore Canyon than any other location in Arizona. In the mid-1980s Black-capped Gnatcatchers nested. Other recent visitors include a Fan-tailed Warbler in June and early July 1987 and a Rufous-capped Warbler from mid-March through June 1994.

No one should attempt to hike down Sycamore Canyon without water. From April through October, plan on hauling three or four quarts per person. Unless you depart in the spooky gray light well before sunrise—which is recommended—carry lunch, too. Because there is no trail for most of the way, a spill is entirely possible, so add a first-aid kit to your knapsack. This is not a well-traveled area, and help may not appear for several days. If at all possible, bird Sycamore with a companion who could go for assistance in the event of a severe sprain or a broken leg. Flash-floods along this route are also possible. If you are prepared to accept the risks, however, a day birding in Sycamore can be one of the most enjoyable experiences in Southeastern Arizona.

The route begins at the melting adobe ruins of Hank Bartlett's and Yank Hewitt's 1880s homestead. After wet winters, huge patches of Parry Penstemon along a trail-of-use that leads to the stream are frequented by Costa's Hummingbird in April and May. Broad-billed and Black-chinned Hummingbirds (summer) are the common species beyond where the trail drops into the streambed. Ferruginous Pygmy-Owls have used an area just above Montana Canyon in the spring and summers of 1979, 1981, and 1986. The big ash trees at the confluence of Montana Canyon (0.5 mile) on the right (west) side of Sycamore ordinarily mark the upper limits patrolled by Elegant Trogons.

One mile downstream from the Hank and Yank parking area, the canyon twists around a small waterfall—best negotiated by climbing over a small spur on the left (east) side—and the first scrawny sycamores appear. A pair of Sulphur-bellied Flycatchers often nests here. The waterfall signals the beginning of the Upper Box area of Sycamore. For the next 0.25 mile, the water threads its way through a tortuous stone vise. At the bottom end of the Upper Box, the stream plunges across polished granite through a gap only 10 feet wide. Unless you are *very sure* of your footing, plan on getting wet. Acrobatic birders may be able to pass this pool by spidering along the right (west) wall of the stream.

A series of plunge pools carved out of solid rock—locally called *tinajas*—on the right (west) side immediately below the Upper Box indicate the confluence of Arch Canyon. A short distance beyond, a little brook trimmed with Golden Columbine trickles into Sycamore from the left (east) side. This is Columbine Canyon. Stay on the right side of Sycamore Canyon to negotiate the next few canyon bends and boulder fields. The canyon will suddenly widen, and sycamore trees will spread their delicious shade across the canyon floor for the remaining 0.25 mile down to the Peñasco Canyon tributary, which joins Sycamore from the left (east) side. Peñasco (pain-YAHS-coh) means a "large rock" or "crag" in Spanish. By now, you will be wondering why all the feeder canyons aren't named Peñasco.

It's worth the time to pause here to bird. All of the Madrean pine/oak woodland species of the border ranges occur in this area of Sycamore Canyon, many a full thousand feet below their usual altitudinal limits in the Chiricahua, Huachuca, and Santa Rita Mountains. Some of the summering species to watch for at the Peñasco confluence are Zone-tailed Hawk, Montezuma Quail, Band-tailed Pigeon, Elegant Trogon, Strickland's Woodpecker, Northern "Red-shafted" Flicker, Western

Wood-Pewee, Dusky-capped, Brown-crested, and Sulphur-bellied Fly-catchers, Cassin's Kingbird, Violet-green Swallow, Mexican Jay, Bridled Titmouse, Bushtit, White-breasted Nuthatch, Bewick's Wren, Hermit Thrush, Solitary "Plumbeous" Vireo, Painted Redstart, Hepatic and Sum-mer Tanagers, Black-headed Grosbeak, Spotted and Canyon Towhees, Rufous-crowned Sparrow, Hooded, Bullock's, and Scott's Orioles, House Finch, and Lesser Goldfinch. In migration, these are joined by Warbling Vireo and Western Tanager, and in winter by Red-naped Sapsuckers and Yellow-rumped Warblers (predominantly "Audubon's", but mixed with the "Myrtle" form as well). Watch for Louisiana Waterthrush (very rare) from mid-July through mid-March.

A trail-of-use generally hugs the base of the left (east) wall of Sycamore Canyon all the way down to Campsite Point, a spur with a natural flat top about 15 feet above the stream level that projects into the canyon from the right (west) side at about mile 2.5. I spent a sleepless night here on a trogon survey in the early 1980s, listening to the hoots, yips, and wails of a pair of Spotted Owls that may have been courting—or having a nasty domestic spat. Just beyond Campsite Point, the canyon takes a sudden jog to the north, then to the west, as it negotiates the Lower Box. Once again, depending on the topography of the streambed in the wake of the most recent flash-floods, wading may be unavoidable.

Tillandsia recurvata, or Ball Moss, is most common in the stretch of canyon below the Lower Box. Resembling nothing so much as a sea urchin, this air plant is a tropical relative of the bromeliad family. One-seed Juniper seems to be the preferred substrate for this Medusa-headed, pale gray epiphyte. It underscores the subtropical character of the lower half of Sycamore Canyon. It was just behind "Big Rock", a huge boulder on the left (east) side of the canyon at mile 2.8, that the Fan-tailed Warbler set up housekeeping in 1987. The mile or so of Sycamore Canyon below Big Rock is probably more likely to shelter an overwintering trogon (or two) than any other area in Arizona. During summer Varied Buntings are common below Big Rock.

Two canyon outlets coming in from the left (east) only a few yards apart at mile 3.1 identify the upper end of the Rose-throated Becard, Thick-billed Kingbird, and Five-striped Sparrow zone of Sycamore. Re-searchers call this double confluence "Twin Canyons". One or two football-shaped becard nests typically overhang the creek in the next 200 yards below a sharp elbow in the stream—when they are in residency. In some summers no Rose-throated Becards are found in Sycamore Canyon.

The Five-stripes, however, are probably present every year. While the population fluctuates, in an average summer there are about 50 adults. Listen for their songs coming from the steep hillsides above the stream from mid-April through August. The slopes of lower Sycamore Canyon used by the sparrows are those matted with impenetrable thickets of thornscrub. The males usually sing from exposed perches.

Unless you are conducting a census, ordinarily there is no reason to continue down the canyon beyond the "Cul de Sac Canyon" at mile 4.0 below Hank and Yank parking area. Saguaros now dominate both walls of Sycamore, and the birds are similar to those on the outskirts of Tucson. The trip back to your car will take at least as long as the hike down, even without birding. Watch your footing!

Five-striped Sparrow
Narca Moore-Craig

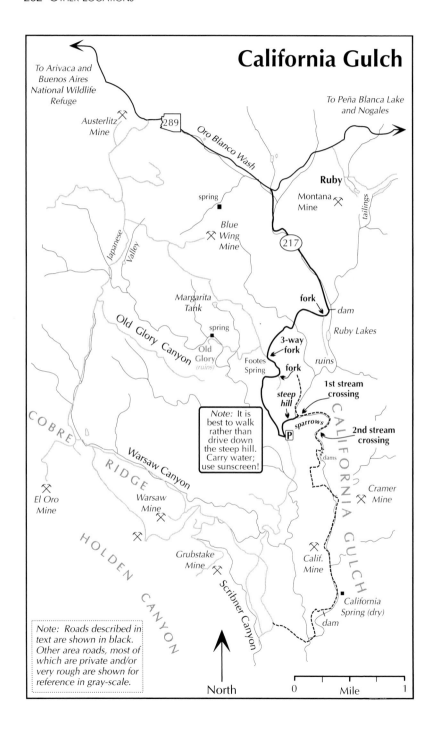

California Gulch

To Arivaca and
Buenos Aires
National Wildlife
Refuge

To Peña Blanca Lake
and Nogales

*Austerlitz
Mine*

289

Oro Blanco Wash

Ruby

spring

*Montana
Mine*

tailings

*Japanese
Valley*

*Blue
Wing
Mine*

217

*Margarita
Tank*

fork

dam

Ruby Lakes

Old Glory Canyon

spring

*Old
Glory
(ruins)*

**3-way
fork**

*Footes
Spring*

fork

ruins

**1st stream
crossing**

**steep
hill**

Note: It is
best to walk
rather than
drive down
the steep hill.
Carry water;
use sunscreen!

P

sparrows

**2nd stream
crossing**

dams

*El Oro
Mine*

*COBRE
RIDGE*

Warsaw Canyon

*Warsaw
Mine*

CALIFORNIA GULCH

*Cramer
Mine*

*Calif.
Mine*

*Grubstake
Mine*

HOLDEN CANYON

Scribner Canyon

*California
Spring (dry)*

dam

*Note: Roads described in
text are shown in black.
Other area roads, most of
which are private and/or
very rough are shown for
reference in gray-scale.*

North

0   Mile   1

H. CALIFORNIA GULCH

84 miles south of Tucson/one day

California Gulch has the only Five-striped Sparrows presently adjacent to a "road" in the United States. You will need a high-clearance four-wheel-drive vehicle here, although those willing to do some serious hiking might also attempt this trip. The sparrows can be found only when they are singing between mid-April and late August.

To find the steep, rocky, frequently washed-out track that leads into California Gulch continue west on the Ruby Road several turns beyond the old Ruby townsite (0.7 mile; 5.6 miles west of the turn-off to Hank and Yank Spring; see directions to Peña Blanca Lake and Sycamore Canyon in the two preceding sections). Watch for the turn-off for Forest Road 217 on the left (south) side of the Ruby Road at a sign that reads "Arizona Western Mine". (This sign may not be readily visible when you approach from the east.)

After an initial steep drop-off into a grassy canyon, you should be able to reach a dam (1.3) on the left (east) without much problem. This is the best area for Montezuma Quail. Bear right at the fork (0.1 mile) past the dam, turn left at the 3-way junction (0.8 mile), and then right soon thereafter (0.1 mile). Avoid the private roads on the left. *Although this is mostly Coronado National Forest land, be aware that there are private inholdings.* Watch for the conspicuous mining site and sign "Keep left for California and Warsaw Canyon" (1.2 miles). Here you proceed left uphill to a rocky new road on the ridge top (0.4 mile). Turn left and park in a small, flat area used by other vehicles.

To find the Five-striped Sparrows hike down a steep hill on the "old road" into California Gulch. This abandoned track crosses the streambed twice in a 0.25-mile-long stretch. Five-striped Sparrows have been found regularly between these two stream-crossings. Listen and look for males singing from exposed perches above the Foothill Thornscrub high on the steep slopes. Check also for Varied Buntings. Buff-collared Nightjars have also been found here.

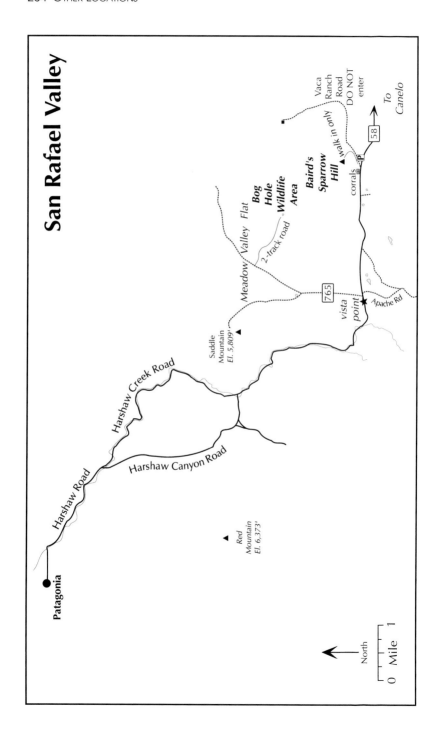

San Rafael Valley

Harshaw Road

Harshaw Creek Road

Harshaw Canyon Road

Patagonia

Red Mountain
El. 6,373'

Saddle Mountain
El. 5,809'

Meadow Valley Flat

Bog Hole Wildlife Area

2-track road

Baird's Sparrow Hill

walk in only

Vaca Ranch Road
DO NOT enter

To Canelo

58

corrals

765

Apache Rd

vista point

North

0   Mile   1

I. SAN RAFAEL VALLEY

(31 miles round-trip from Patagonia/one-half day)

The best grassland in Southeastern Arizona and one of the premier grasslands in the United States lies east of the Patagonia and west of the Huachuca Mountains. Cradled in gentle, rolling hills at an elevation of approximately 5,000 feet, the headwaters of the Santa Cruz River rise on a Mexican land grant dating back to 1825. Most of the San Rafael Valley is still in private ownership today. Visitors are asked to either bird from the public roads or to walk to their destination. *Off-road vehicular travel is prohibited.*

During summer all of the birds of prey and sparrows found in the San Rafael are easy to see at other more accessible locations. In winter, however, the San Rafael Grassland offers some of the best birding in Southeastern Arizona. To find this area start in Patagonia and take the street parallel to and one block east of Highway 82 (McKeown). Go north past the Post Office on the left (west) a short distance to a broad curve to the right (east). This is Harshaw Road.

Watch the pavement edges for enormous mixed flocks of sparrows (winter) as the road traverses the broad, flat agricultural area where Harshaw Creek meets upper Sonoita Creek. Soon after entering the foothills of the Patagonia Mountains, a well-graded road sheers off to the left at a "Y" intersection (3.1 miles from the Post Office). This is the Harshaw *Creek* Road, a fine alternate route that ties back into the main Harshaw *Canyon* Road if time is not an important consideration. During spring and summer Harshaw Creek hosts a pair of Zone-tailed Hawks, and in some winters a Rufous-backed Robin adopts the little orchard on the right side of the road (1.9 miles). The Harshaw Creek Road rejoins the Harshaw Canyon Road at a major confluence of two canyons (2.4 miles). Watch for Eastern Bluebirds here.

The easiest access to the San Rafael Valley is to stay right (south) on paved **Harshaw Canyon Road**. Golden Eagle and Montezuma Quail are relatively common over the entire length of Harshaw. A Spotted Owl has occasionally been found in the rocky grottoes high up the slope on the right directly above where the pavement ends (0.7 mile). This is a tough scramble up approximately 500 feet on a treacherous slope without any certainty that the owl will be waiting. It is not recommended for non-fanatics. *(See page 110 for Spotted Owl-watching etiquette.)*

There are two more major roads between the end of the pavement and the San Rafael Grassland. Ignore both the right fork (2.3 miles) and the left turn onto Harshaw Creek Road (0.5 mile; this route, however, offers a nice change of scenery upon your return). Stay on the widest, most well-used thoroughfare. Quite suddenly, just as the Harshaw Canyon Road tops out on a low ridge (3.9 miles), a breathtaking panorama of golden savanna unrolls across the valley to a blue horizon created by the Canelo Hills and the Huachuca Mountains. This sweeping vista of the San Rafael Grassland is one of the most satisfying visual experiences available to birders in all Southeastern Arizona.

There is a four-way intersection at the de facto vista point. The left (north) road follows the edge of the grasslands into Meadow Valley Flat. Turn right at a little track (2.0 miles) to find **Bog Hole Wildlife Area** (0.5 mile). If wet, this track may be impassable to regular cars, though you may wish to walk it. A concrete dam at the Wildlife Area backs up a few acres of water and an equal amount of cattail marsh. In winter the regular ducks are Green-winged Teal, Mallard (including the "Mexican Duck" race), Northern Pintail, Blue-winged and Cinnamon Teals, Northern Shoveler, Gadwall, and American Wigeon. American Coots are common, and both Marsh Wren and Swamp Sparrow lurk in the cattails. The dry uplands along the Meadow Valley Road are good for Sprague's Pipit and Chestnut-collared Longspur. Meadow Valley Flat is one of the few areas where Ferruginous Hawk occurs away from agricultural fields in the Southeast corner of Arizona. Also noteworthy is a herd of Pronghorns that tends to browse on the gentle, grassy hills downstream from Bog Hole.

Probably the single most important reason birders visit the San Rafael Grassland in winter, however, is to find Baird's Sparrow. Continue straight east into the valley from the vista point at the junction with the Meadow Valley Road. Stop just beyond the **Vaca Ranch Headquarters Road corrals** on the left (north) side of the road (2.4 miles). Inside and behind the corrals there is ordinarily a flock of several hundred Horned Larks. Mixed in with the Horned Larks there are almost invariably a few McCown's Longspurs. Until the end of January both sexes of the McCown's resemble nothing so much as female House Sparrows with pinkish bills. It is not until February that the males begin to develop the black cap, bill, moustache, and breast-band that distinguish them from all other finches and sparrows.

"Baird's Sparrow Hill," as it is called by the local birders, is the rocky-topped knoll with a single oak on the left (west) side located approximately one-half mile north of the road. The Vaca Ranch Headquarters Road swings around the east end of the hill. *This is a walk-in only proposition and is so signed by the owners. Park your car com-*

pletely off the main road where it will not block the Vaca Ranch Headquarters Road.

En route to the knoll the little road crosses a swale with tall, dense grasses. Watch the road edges for Sprague's Pipit. Other birds that frequent the area are American Kestrel, Say's Phoebe, Savannah Sparrow, and Eastern Meadowlark. Be careful not to confuse the Savannah with the Baird's. They are superficially similar, but Baird's has a buff median stripe on the crown and an overall rich-buff face and nape. In a quick glimpse the Baird's shows bolder contrast on the back-stripes. The Savannahs are more likely than Baird's to occur in the swale. Scope down the valley to the right (east) for Bald and Golden Eagles perched in the big cottonwoods. Prairie Falcons are also fond of this section of the San Rafael Grassland.

To find the Baird's Sparrows plan on climbing at least part way up the knoll. The birds will probably flush uphill from the deep grass on the alluvial apron. After a short, fast trajectory they drop back into the grasses. And then they run like the dickens, often more than 100 feet. A couple of sharp-eyed friends in a line on a contour are welcome here. Try to walk a potential Baird's into a rocky ravine between you and your friends. If all goes well it will appear farther up the ravine than you expected. A few seconds glance is all that you will get. If you continue climbing the hill the sparrow may eventually pause briefly on a rocky outcrop on the skyline, affording you one last fleeting look. No need to pursue it farther. You will never see it again. If you do scale the little knoll there's a fine vantage overlooking miles of appropriate Baird's Sparrow habitat. Watch for a nearby Rock Wren, scolding you as it bounces up and down in indignation at your trespass.

Farther east a confusing complex of roads connects the San Rafael Grassland to Sonoita, Fort Huachuca, and Coronado National Memorial. These roads are dusty and badly wash-boarded in dry weather, and are likely to mire you in deep clay during rains or snowstorms. The fastest and most straight-forward way to access these locations is to return the way you came from Patagonia (12.9 miles to the Post Office; add 0.4 mile if you detour down Harshaw Creek).

J. SOUTH AND WEST OF THE HUACHUCAS

(72 miles round-trip from Sierra Vista/one day)

This trip begins at an elevation of 6,575 feet in Montezuma Pass, the highest point reached by road in Coronado National Memorial. To find Montezuma Pass from the intersection of Highways 90 and 92 in Sierra Vista, follow Highway 92 south for approximately 10 miles through a huge curve east to the well-signed, right-hand turn-off for Coronado National Memorial (13.6 miles). Take the Monument Road to the visitor center (4.8 miles). (A brief history of Coronado's passage up the San Pedro River Valley is contained in the "Upper San Pedro Valley Loop" in

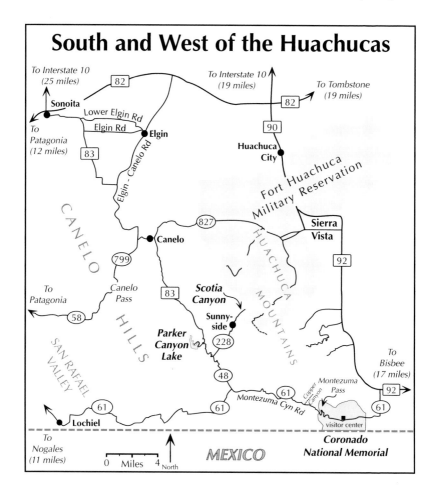

South and West of the Huachucas

Chapter 7). The road up to Montezuma Pass turns into dirt (1.2 mile) at a stream-crossing, but the final miles up to the top—although narrow, steep, and twisty—are well-graded and suitable for most passenger cars (2.1 miles; 21.7 miles from Sierra Vista). Montezuma Pass marks the southern end of the Crest Trail, which climbs nearly 3,000 feet in 5.5 miles to the 9,466-foot summit of Miller Peak.

Beyond Montezuma Pass, Forest Road 61 is a steep, rocky, dusty wash-boarded route that is definitely *not* suitable for sight-seeing. However, it does offer access to some scenic destinations with interesting birds. The first canyon on the right side is upper Copper Canyon (0.9 mile). Canyon Wrens nest just inside the rocky gates that flank the little stream. Occasionally an Elegant Trogon uses the basin by a small spring a few hundred yards inside Copper Canyon; Lucifer Hummingbirds have been observed in the same area. The next drainage to the west, Cave Canyon (2.7 miles), is more reliable for Elegant Trogons. A Canada Warbler was discovered here in early September 1993. Soon after the road swings right (north), FR 61 divides at a major junction (5.4 miles).

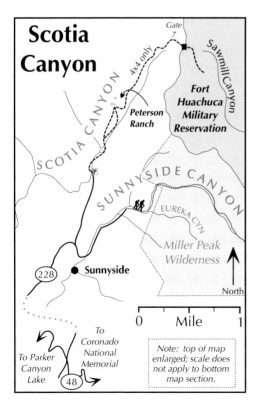

Birders should continue straight ahead onto FR 48, signed for Parker Canyon Lake, ignoring the abrupt left turn for FR 61.

One of the least birded yet most deserving sites in Southeastern Arizona is the **Sunnyside/Scotia complex** (3.1 miles) along FR 228. Located on the southwest corner of the Huachuca Mountains, both of these canyons host Elegant Trogons as well as Buff-breasted Flycatchers. The road that follows the grassy ridge most of the way to the junction between the drainages (2.6 miles) is one of the best places in Southeastern

Arizona to watch for Common Nighthawk (dawn and dusk, summer). Owling here is simply terrific. Flammulated Owl (uncommon) and Whiskered Screech-Owl are the two species most often heard, but Great Horned Owl and Northern Pygmy-Owl are also present. An imitation of the Whiskered Screech-Owl toot may attract up to five different birds at once.

The division between Scotia and Sunnyside lies in a basin inside Sunnyside Canyon just below the first real curve in the road. Go left to find a flat place to park on the brink of Scotia Canyon (0.2 mile). Both Elegant Trogons and Buff-breasted Flycatchers usually occur in the Chihuahua Pines in the first half-mile upstream. Turn right (downcanyon) at the "T" junction to enter Sunnyside. It is possible to drive slightly farther into Sunnyside (0.8 mile), but many of the best birds occur in this stretch of lower Sunnyside. Some of the other species to watch for include Northern Goshawk, Zone-tailed Hawk, Montezuma Quail, Band-tailed Pigeon, Strickland's Woodpecker, Greater Pewee, Sulphur-bellied Flycatcher, Eastern Bluebird, Hutton's Vireo, Grace's Warbler, Painted Redstart, and Hepatic Tanager. In surveys conducted in the early 1980s, I always found more Elegant Trogons in the Sunnyside/Scotia complex than in any other area of the Huachuca Mountains. Altogether there were usually six to eight pairs using the two canyons, occasionally interacting across the low-lying intervening ridge.

Return to Forest Road 48, turn right, and continue for 2.3 miles to join Highway 83 (paved at the junction for access to the lake and the campground). **Parker Canyon Lake**, one mile to the left, is mobbed by anglers on summer weekends and holidays. In winter, however, this is probably the best location in Southeastern Arizona for a visiting Common Loon. Eared Grebe and a variety of ducks, including Common Gold-eneye, Bufflehead, and Common Merganser, also use this 130-acre trout-fishery. Bald Eagles have stayed at the lake until early summer. Eastern Bluebird is typically common near the junction. This road has also been good for Montezuma Quail.

From Parker Canyon Lake it is almost exactly equidistant to return to Sierra Vista via Fort Huachuca (17.0 miles; 35.7 miles to the junction of Highways 90 and 92) or to retrace your route back to Montezuma Pass (14.4 miles; 36.2 miles to the junction of Highways 90 and 92). To completely circle the Huachuca Mountains, however, continue northeast on Highway 83.

The Canelo townsite junction (11.5 miles) is the only major intersection between the lake and the West Gate at Fort Huachuca. Highway 83 turns left (west) here and wanders through low hills with scattered oaks and spreading grasslands all the way to Sonoita (17.0 miles). To continue this tour, stay right onto Forest Road 827. Watch for Golden Eagle, Prairie Falcon, and Montezuma Quail.

Be prepared to show your driver's license and either your registration or rental agreement to enter the West Gate of Fort Huachuca (5.5 miles).

The Apaches called Southeastern Arizona "the land of two springs." Nowhere is the reason for this name more apparent than here on the south side of the Huachuca Mountains. For most of the year, a sea of coarse, dry grasses covers the crooked, yellow horizon. Neither the cold rains of winter nor the infrequent sprinkles of spring are sufficient to stir new growth. But, soon after the summer rains begin in July, new shoots transform the southern facade of the Huachucas into a verdant carpet dotted with blue and red wildflowers. Old-timers and birders heave a sigh of contentment. Once again, it's springtime in July!

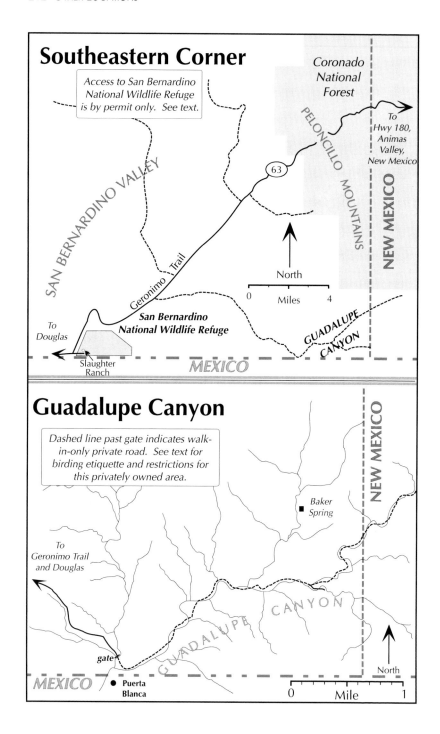

Southeastern Corner

Access to San Bernardino National Wildlife Refuge is by permit only. See text.

Coronado National Forest

PELONCILLO MOUNTAINS

To Hwy 180, Animas Valley, New Mexico

NEW MEXICO

SAN BERNARDINO VALLEY

63

North

0   Miles   4

Geronimo Trail

To Douglas

San Bernardino National Wildlife Refuge

GUADALUPE CANYON

MEXICO

Slaughter Ranch

Guadalupe Canyon

Dashed line past gate indicates walk-in-only private road. See text for birding etiquette and restrictions for this privately owned area.

NEW MEXICO

Baker Spring

To Geronimo Trail and Douglas

GUADALUPE CANYON

North

gate

MEXICO

Puerta Blanca

0   Mile   1

K. GUADALUPE CANYON
(31 miles east of Douglas/one-half day)

This trip follows the Mexican border east from Douglas to Guadalupe Canyon. Though there are no regularly occurring birds here that cannot be found closer to Tucson, Guadalupe Canyon remains a fascinating birding spot. The canyon is located in the Peloncillo Mountains in the extreme southeastern corner of Arizona on the headwaters of the Río Yaqui, which, in turn, serves as a natural conduit for Mexican species entering the United States. Buff-collared Nightjar in 1960 and Thick-billed Kingbird in 1958 were both first records for the United States. The first Fan-tailed Warbler in the U.S. came from a tributary drainage, Baker Canyon, in 1961. Another Fan-tailed Warbler was photographed in Guadalupe in September 1990.

Guadalupe Canyon is privately owned. Birders are allowed to enter Guadalupe only on foot. Moreover, groups of over four persons are not permitted. Overnight camping within the canyon is prohibited. The road leading to the canyon is often dusty and sometimes rough. It can also be difficult driving during the rainy season; after heavy storms the road may be impassable because of mud. The canyon is about 4,000 feet in elevation and summers there are hot. It is wise to arrive as early as possible in the morning. Do not forget to carry plenty of water.

The starting point is the intersection of Highway 80 (A Avenue) and 15th Street in Douglas. Go east on 15th Street toward the big "D" on the mountain. You are now on the Geronimo Trail. The pavement plays out a few miles east of Douglas near the summit of a low range of hills. All the way to the Guadalupe Canyon turn-off, the road passes through a section of the Chihuahuan Desert characterized by Creosote, Ocotillo, and White-thorn Acacia growing on limestone soil. Birds using this spare habitat include Golden Eagle, Swainson's Hawk (summer), Scaled Quail, Greater Roadrunner, Pyrrhuloxia, and Black-throated Sparrow.

The major "Y" junction for the **San Bernardino Ranch** is the first significant side road (17.0 miles). Turn right (south) if you wish to visit the old ranch and adjacent ponds (fee). The Refuge is now property of the Fish and Wildlife Service and *open by permit only;* it was once owned by Texas John Slaughter, the famous sheriff who cleaned up Tombstone after Wyatt Earp departed for California. Some of the birds that have nested here include Gray Hawk, Virginia Rail, and Tropical Kingbird. For permission to enter, contact the San Bernardino National Wildlife Refuge by calling or writing their office at 1408 10th Street, Douglas, AZ 85607;

telephone 520/364-2104. Arrange for your special use permit two to four weeks in advance of your visit.

Continue east on Geronimo Trail to find the turn-off to Guadalupe Canyon on the right (south) side (5.2 miles). Watch for Burrowing Owl, Lesser Nighthawk, and Bendire's Thrasher along the first several miles of the road. A stock tank on the right (south) side of the road (4.0 miles) usually holds a few "Mexican Duck" race Mallards. A short distance beyond, a swale filled by a deep stand of Sacaton Grass is excellent for Botteri's Sparrows after the summer rains have begun. From the Geronimo Trail to the canyon proper is 9.0 miles.

Guadalupe Canyon comes as a welcome relief from the dry, dusty desert. The view overlooking the bright green ribbon of trees winding between hills covered with low-growing Foothill Thornscrub will gladden any birder's heart. Large Arizona Sycamores and Fremont Cottonwoods grow along the valley floor, interspersed with patches of willow following an intermittent stream. A gate with parking spaces for two or three cars just as the road reaches the canyon floor marks the end of the drive. *Park outside the gate, even when the gate is unlocked; do not park on the road. By parking outside the gate, you will assist the landowner's very successful efforts to restore the riparian habitat in the canyon.* A white monument and a barbed-wire fence approximately 200 yards downcanyon to the right (south) marks the Mexican border. *Much of*

Park by the gate and walk thru the first mile of Guadalupe Canyon in early morning to enjoy the dawn chorus.

Guadalupe Canyon is private property and may be closed at some future date. Birding here is a privilege, not a right. Please behave in such a manner as to insure that birders will always be welcome.

Arrive early. Many birds quit singing by 10am. After mid-May the first bird you encounter at the gate may well be a purple-and-blue male Varied Bunting. Savor its colors until the querulous calls of Bell's Vireo or the brilliant hues of Northern Cardinal draw your attention elsewhere. Some of the other summer birds that share the lower end of Guadalupe are Cooper's and Zone-tailed Hawks, Montezuma and Gambel's Quail, White-winged Dove, Common Ground-Dove, Western Screech-Owl, Great Horned and Elf Owls, Common Poorwill, Black-chinned, Broad-billed, and Violet-crowned Hummingbirds, Northern "Red-shafted" Flicker, Acorn, Gila, and Ladder-backed Woodpeckers, Northern Beardless-Tyrannulet, Western Wood-Pewee, Black and Say's Phoebes, Vermilion, Dusky-capped, Ash-throated, and Brown-crested Flycatchers, Cassin's and Thick-billed Kingbirds, Western Scrub-Jay, Mexican Jay, Bridled Titmouse, Verdin, Bushtit, Cactus, Rock, Canyon, and Bewick's Wrens, Black-tailed Gnatcatcher, Curve-billed and Crissal Thrashers, Phainopepla, Solitary Vireo, Lucy's Warbler, Summer Tanager, Black-headed and Blue Grosbeaks, Spotted and Canyon Towhees, Rufous-crowned Sparrow, Bronzed Cowbird, Hooded and Bullock's Orioles, House Finch, and Lesser Goldfinch.

All of these birds can be seen in the first mile of Guadalupe Canyon. Only Sonoita Creek at Patagonia can match the density of Violet-crowned Hummingbirds found in Guadalupe, and it remains on a par with Patagonia for Thick-billed Kingbirds. The canyon is still a traditional site to try for Buff-collared Nightjar.

The nearest motels are in Douglas and Portal.

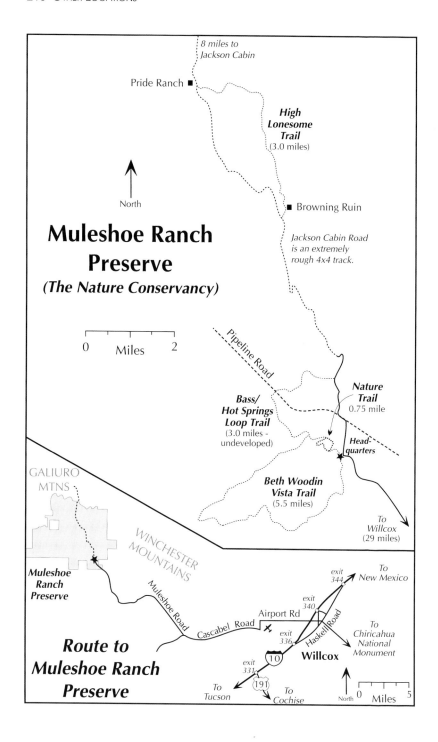

8 miles to
Jackson Cabin

Pride Ranch ■

**High
Lonesome
Trail**
(3.0 miles)

North

■ Browning Ruin

Muleshoe Ranch
Preserve
(The Nature Conservancy)

*Jackson Cabin Road
is an extremely
rough 4x4 track.*

0   Miles   2

Pipeline Road

**Nature
Trail**
0.75 mile

**Bass/
Hot Springs
Loop Trail**
(3.0 miles -
undeveloped)

**Head-
quarters**

**Beth Woodin
Vista Trail**
(5.5 miles)

To
Willcox
(29 miles)

GALIURO
MTNS

WINCHESTER
MOUNTAINS

**Muleshoe
Ranch
Preserve**

exit
344

To
New Mexico

exit
340

Airport Rd

Haskell Road

To
Chiricahua
National
Monument

Muleshoe Road

Cascabel Road

exit
336

*Route to
Muleshoe Ranch
Preserve*

10

Willcox

exit
331

191

To
Tucson

To
Cochise

North   0   Miles   5

L. MULESHOE RANCH
COOPERATIVE MANAGEMENT AREA

(110 miles east of Tucson/one or two days)

With five permanently flowing streams and five species of native fishes, the Muleshoe Ranch was a natural for acquisition by The Nature Conservancy. Together with the Bureau of Land Management and the U.S. Forest Service, a Cooperative Management Area (CMA) encompassing 48,200 acres has been set aside since 1982 to protect Arizona's most precious resource: water and its accompanying riparian habitat. The Nature Conservancy estimates that over 80 percent of all the species of flora and fauna in the CMA are dependent on these year-round streams.

That is certainly true of at least two of its trio of Southwest specialty raptors. Muleshoe is famous for its summering Common Black-Hawks and its Gray and Zone-tailed Hawks. Redfield Canyon is the best area in the CMA for Common Black-Hawks, but both Hot Springs and Bass Canyons have hosted one pair each in the shady cottonwood groves near the ranch headquarters. Here, they may consort with two or three pairs of the Ranch's resident Gray Hawks. Zone-tailed Hawks occur throughout. The best way to find these birds of prey, as well as other wildlife, is to hike any one or a combination of the three trails that originate at the headquarters visitor center/guest-cabin area. Only 0.75-mile-long, the Nature Trail is the shortest option. The Bass/Hot Springs Canyon Loop Trail is 3 miles long. A 5.5-mile-long Beth Woodin Vista Trail forms another loop in the hills southwest of the Headquarters.

To reach Muleshoe Ranch, take Interstate 10 east to the second exit for Willcox, #340, Rex Allen Drive. Turn right (east) and go one block to Bisbee Avenue, the street between the shopping center and the truck-stop (0.2 mile). Turn right (south) here and continue past the high school (0.8 mile). Turn right (west) onto Airport Road and go over the interstate. After mile 3.1 the pavement ends and Airport Road turns into a dirt county road. Follow it west to a "Y" intersection with Muleshoe Road at a group of mailboxes (12.3 miles). Bear right (north) here. There are no other major junctions before the road drops into the Headquarters area at Hooker's Hot Springs (14.0 miles). *Be aware, however, that heavy rains can render the last, long hill above the Ranch impassable without four-wheel-drive.* This warning is especially important after the summer monsoons have started, and, again, after winter storms. Call in advance for current road conditions.

Hooker's Hot Springs was originally developed as a health spa just before the turn of the 20th century by Colonel Henry Clay Hooker, whose Sierra Bonita Ranch once covered over 800 square miles—the largest ranch in Arizona in its day. The Nature Conservancy has renovated three buildings with five housekeeping units available for rent to the public. Overnight lodging guests are welcome to use the hot springs for a soak. Set at an elevation of 4,000 feet under big trees, this is a wonderful place both to relax and to bird throughout the year. For further information contact the Muleshoe Ranch Headquarters, R.R. 1, Box 1542, Willcox, AZ 85643; telephone 520/586-7072.

Immature Common Black-Hawk
Narca Moore Craig

M. ARAVAIPA CANYON EAST

(152 miles east of Tucson/one or two days)

The remote east end of the Aravaipa Canyon Wilderness Area is generally regarded as the pretty entrance. The last few miles of road wander through a pastoral setting of big cottonwoods, small orchards, and brilliant green pastures, all butted up against the pocked and pitted adobe-brown walls of the canyon, as if for contrast. One or more Common Black-Hawks ordinarily soar by before you ever reach the designated parking area at Turkey Creek Canyon. Homesteaded over a century ago by the Salazar Family, the property features a family church which makes a photogenic foreground for a herd of Desert Bighorn Sheep that may browse poetically on the slopes above. Meanwhile every field has a resident male Vermilion Flycatcher, snapping up aerial minutiae like a voracious spark and providing an unending distraction for "serious" birders.

Unfortunately, four-wheel-drive vehicles with high clearance are frequently necessary to negotiate the crossings on Aravaipa Creek for the final 3.5 miles of the road. Call the Bureau of Land Management (520/428-4040) for recent road-condition information.

To reach the east entrance of Aravaipa Canyon drive east on Interstate 10 to Willcox and take exit 340 (80 miles). The last inexpensive gasoline and picnic supplies are available at this exit in Willcox, and neither may be available at any price farther on. Take Rex Allen Drive left (west) across Interstate 10, and stay on the pavement until it ends (14.0 miles). The remainder of the road to Bonita (17.0 miles) is well-graded and suitable for passenger cars—except after extremely heavy rains. Both Scaled Quail and Sandhill Cranes (winter) are often sighted from the road between Willcox and Bonita. Turn left at Bonita onto Klondyke Road. The next 10 miles pass through an undeveloped grassland where White-tailed Kites nest in Soaptree Yuccas. In winter watch for Ferruginous Hawk. According to annual Arizona Game & Fish censuses, the herd of Pronghorns that occupies this area numbers between 150 to 250 animals.

Almost without warning, Klondyke Road abruptly drops into the mesquite thickets at the headwaters of Aravaipa Canyon. Mesquite dominates the terrain on both sides of the road for the remaining twenty-odd miles to Klondyke (31 miles from Bonita). A trailer, staffed by the Bureau of Land Management ranger, is located in the center of Klondyke's business district (across the street from the only other structure). You may stop here for information on recent road conditions.

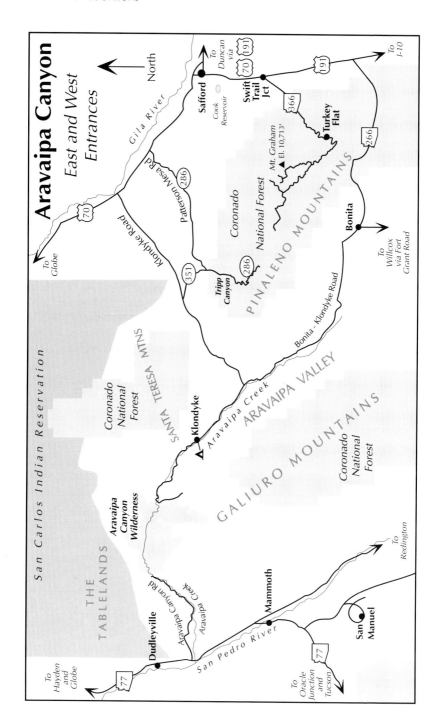

The same regulations apply at the "East End" as at the "West End" of the Wilderness Area. (See also Section C of this chapter.) To wit: only 50 people per day are permitted in the 11-mile-long Aravaipa Canyon Wilderness Area. To obtain a permit contact the Bureau of Land Management, Safford District Office, 711 14th Avenue, Safford, AZ 85546; telephone 520/428-4040. Because of limited availability, the BLM recommends making reservations by phone 13 weeks in advance. There is a charge of $1.50 per person per day. Plan on wearing stout, high-top shoes or boots to wade the stream—you will have to cross it dozens of times. High-top footgear will eliminate some of the gravel sluicing into your socks.

Non-backpackers may wish to use the developed facilities southeast of Klondyke. Fourmile Campground, a BLM fee site, is located one mile up the road which starts across from the ranger's trailer.

Beyond Klondyke the road continues to the first stream-crossing (3.7 miles) and the beginning of a riparian avian community that includes Yellow Warbler and Yellow-breasted Chat. The property on both sides of the road for the remainder of the way to the Turkey Creek Parking Area is owned by the Arizona Chapter of The Nature Conservancy. Birding is not permitted off this road without pre-arrangement or permission from the manager. The manager's house is located just before the second stream-crossing (2.7 miles). The only commercial lodging in Aravaipa Canyon is a guest house maintained by The Nature Conservancy. For more information contact the Aravaipa Canyon Preserve at Box 4, Klondyke, AZ 85643; telephone 520/828-3443.

Unless the stream is exceptionally low, birders are advised *not* to plunge into Aravaipa Creek in a low-slung automobile, especially if it is one of recent vintage. If the creek is high, this may be the end of the road without four-wheel-drive. *Turn back if in doubt—or if it looks as if rain may occur while you're in the canyon.* A short aside here: flash-floods in October 1983 literally swallowed a small pickup truck. Its owner was first incredulous, then suspicious, and finally just plain depressed after learning from the BLM that the truck had vanished. Flash-floods over 10 feet deep occur every decade.

Bear Canyon (2.0 miles) is a dry tributary that feeds into Aravaipa Creek immediately before the third ford. Bear Canyon is known among local birders as perhaps the most reliable site for Gray Vireo in Southeastern Arizona. The BLM has constructed a small parking area at the entrance for use when Aravaipa's lower crossings are impassable. Up the wash the road varies with the season, but it is usually passable with standard transportation if the driver stays out of soft sand. Park at the foot of the obvious switchback (1.1 miles). The vireos stay low in Bear Canyon's dense juniper and mesquite thickets. Other birds here include several species more typical of interior chaparral in Central Arizona: Western Scrub-Jay, Plain Titmouse, and Black-chinned Sparrow.

Common Black-Hawks are usually easy to see between mid-March and mid-October for the remaining distance to the end of the road at the Turkey Creek Parking Area (1.5 miles). Long-term research, conducted since the early 1970s by Jay Schnell, a resident of Aravaipa Canyon, shows that between 10 and 16 pairs of Common Black-Hawks breed annually over a 17-mile-long stretch of the canyon. The stability of this population is probably owing to Aravaipa's protected status.

As the road ends, a Vermilion Flycatcher is ordinarily the first bird that you notice. A male will probably be zooming around the parking lot. Zone-tailed Hawk, however, is the specialty at the Turkey Creek confluence. Up to three pairs nest in this lush feeder-drainage. A four-wheel-drive road on the left leads up along Turkey Creek to primitive campsites approved for overnight use by the BLM.

Birders can see almost all the same species along the road that hikers observe along Aravaipa Creek in the 19,410-acre Wilderness Area. American Dipper (winter) is probably the only species that is restricted to the confines of the inner canyon. But if time allows, a backpack trip into the heart of Aravaipa Canyon will reshape your image of both the Sonoran Desert and the beauty of its birdlife. Once the canyon has been experienced, it is easy to understand why this area was chosen in 1984 as the first Bureau of Land Management Wilderness in the United States.

SPECIALTIES OF
SOUTHEASTERN
ARIZONA

Listed below are the avian specialties found in Southeastern Arizona that are of particular interest to out-of-area birders. Abundance, seasonal status, habitat, and specific locations are given for each species. An effort has been made to list at least three known sites for every bird. Because most visitors begin their tour at Tucson, locations are arranged with those closest to Tucson first, followed by sites that are progressively farther away. All of the suggested areas were selected because they represent good places to observe the birds, usually with reasonable access.

Least Grebe—Very rare straggler to ponds near the Mexican border from Nogales west to the Colorado River, with thirteen records altogether for Arizona. After a hiatus of 17 years, a Least Grebe put in an appearance at Picacho Reservoir from December 1994 through mid-February 1995. Periodic erroneous reports are more frequent. Usually the bird in question turns out to be an Eared Grebe with dull yellow eyes. Least Grebes are substantially smaller than Eared, with proportionately shorter necks, and *bright* yellow eyes. They appear to be more buoyant than other members of the family, and ride high on the water, almost like a "toy grebe." Unless one turns up on the Tucson Audubon Society hotline, your chances of seeing this bird in Arizona are virtually nil.

Neotropic Cormorant—Rare but regular visitor to valley ponds and lakes, primarily in the Nogales area at Patagonia Lake, and less commonly at Kino Springs and Peña Blanca Lake. Care should be used in separating the smaller Neotropic from Double-crested Cormorant, which is uncommon at the same locations. Note that the pale-bordered bare gular patch tapers to a point in Neotropic, but is rounded in Double-crested. Also, some Double-crested Cormorants have an orange supraloral spot, never present in Neotropic Cormorants. Immature Double-cresteds are variably whitish below, while immature Neotropics are Arizona's browner cormorants. In flight note the kinked neck of Double-crested and the noticeably long tail of Neotropic—as long as the head and neck combined.

Ducks and Geese—In winter and migration, up to 15 species can be found on a single visit to such places as Avra Valley Sewage Ponds on Snyder Hill Road, Picacho Reservoir, Peña Blanca Lake, Nogales Sewage Ponds, Patagonia Lake, Sierra Vista Wastewater Ponds, Parker Canyon Lake, and the Willcox Playa area.

Fulvous Whistling-Duck—Strictly a vagrant, although it was fairly common 50 years ago along the lower Colorado River at Yuma. The most recent record in Southeastern Arizona is of one seen at Kino Springs from late April to mid-May 1990. (Other Arizona records in the 1990s have come from the Phoenix area.)

Black-bellied Whistling-Duck—Uncommon resident whose numbers fluctuate with the year. Prefers tree-lined ponds such as Kino Springs and the Patagonia Sewage Pond, but it occasionally uses locations lacking any shoreline cover, such as the Avra Valley Sewage Ponds, the Nogales Sewage Ponds, and the Cochise College Sewage Lagoon west of Douglas. Also try the Nogales Drive-In Theater Ponds.

"Mexican Duck"—This subspecies of Mallard, in which the drake is "female-plumaged," is a fairly common—if local—permanent resident. At present, easiest to find at Willcox Playa, Sierra Vista Wastewater Ponds, and in pools along the San Pedro River, where it is the breeding type. It has also occurred near Tucson, at Buenos Aires National Wildlife Refuge, at San Bernardino National Wildlife Refuge, and on ponds near Rodeo.

Black Vulture—An uncommon permanent resident of the upper Santa Cruz Valley near Nogales and Patagonia, and near Sells on Tohono O'odham lands. During the past few years, it has been seen regularly at the Marana Pecan Grove. Most recently, in the winters of 1993-1994 and 1994-1995, three Black Vultures have roosted on the grounds of the Arizona-Sonora Desert Museum. (Two nests are known from Arizona, both from Organ Pipe Cactus National Monument west of our area.)

White-tailed Kite—Uncommon in summer, rare in winter in valley grassland and desert agricultural areas throughout the southeast corner. Some summers they seem to turn up in all appropriate habitats, but during years when they are scarce, the most reliable areas have been fields south of the Marana Pecan Grove, Buenos Aires National Wildlife Refuge, fields along the upper San Pedro River near Palominas, and fields near Cochise College west of Douglas. The first record of White-tailed Kite in Arizona was in 1972.

Mississippi Kite—Uncommon local summer resident of riparian woodlands, primarily along a 25-mile-long stretch of the lower San Pedro River between Mammoth and Winkelman. The most famous location for this species is near the community of Dudleyville. The first record of Mississippi Kite in Arizona was in 1970.

Bald Eagle—Uncommon winter visitor in the San Rafael Grassland, Parker Canyon Lake, and agricultural areas of the southern Sulphur Springs Valley. Defying conventional wisdom, in southern Arizona it is generally easier to find a Bald Eagle feasting on a deer or a cow carcass, than devouring a fish. Then again, in most of Southeastern Arizona fish are less common than eagles.

Northern Goshawk—Rare permanent resident of the mountains, more widespread in winter. Has nested in the Santa Rita, Huachuca, and Chiricahua Mountains. Watch for it in Madera, Garden, and Cave Creek Canyons. Most often seen soaring over the forests. Occasionally a birder off the beaten track discovers a goshawk nest when a parent bird makes a surprise, hurricane pass at the back of her or his head. Unless you have experienced it, it is hard to convey just how terrifying this feels. Researchers have been seriously maimed by goshawks protecting their young. The blackish-backed "Apache Goshawk" of Mexico is a race which occasionally occurs in the Border Ranges and averages 10 percent larger than the northern subspecies.

Common Black-Hawk—Uncommon summer resident in Aravaipa Canyon, where perhaps a dozen pairs nest, along the San Pedro River near Winkelman (five miles north of Dudleyville), and Redfield Canyon in the Galiuro Mountains. The last nest at Patagonia was in 1976. A lone bird is sighted sporadically along the upper San Pedro River. (Common Black-Hawks remain fairly common in Central Arizona.)

Harris's Hawk—Fairly common permanent resident of Sonoran Desert Saguaro thornscrub northwest of Tucson. Widely scattered populations exist on the Tohono O'odham Nation lands, in the Sulphur Springs Valley, and in the San Simon Valley. Can ordinarily be found along Highway 77/79 somewhere between Tucson city limits and Florence. Look for it off Davis Road and near Elfrida in the Sulphur Springs Valley.

Gray Hawk—Fairly common summer resident of valley riparian cottonwoods, primarily along the upper Santa Cruz River, Arivaca Creek, Sonoita Creek, and the San Pedro River, which has the largest concentration of these birds in the United States. Typically there are three pairs nesting on the Patagonia-Sonoita Creek Preserve, where they are present from mid-March to early October.

Swainson's Hawk—Common summer resident of the valley mesquite grassland. Just a few of the localities where Swainson's Hawk occurs include Highway 82 east of Sonoita, Highway 90 both north and east of Sierra Vista, Highway 92 west of Bisbee, anywhere around Willcox, and Highway 80 both west and east of Douglas—not to mention Interstate 10 from Tucson east to the New Mexico border. You should have little trouble with this one.

Zone-tailed Hawk—Fairly common summer resident, casual in winter. Typically nests in the tallest trees in foothill or mountain canyons, but it may be observed from the desert in and around Tucson all the way up to the summit of Chiricahua Peak. Frequently sighted in Aravaipa Canyon, in Madera Canyon, in the Patagonia-Sonoita Creek Preserve, over the Ramsey Canyon Preserve, and in the main fork of Cave Creek Canyon between Sunny Flat Campground and the Southwestern Research Station. To see this bird double-check every soaring Turkey Vulture.

Ferruginous Hawk—Fairly common winter visitor in the Sulphur Springs Valley and uncommon in winter elsewhere in valley grasslands and deserts. While Ferruginous is widely distributed throughout the Sulphur Springs Valley, the best place to see one is the agricultural area off Highway 191 between Elfrida and Sunizona. Ticking a half-dozen of these beautiful raptors is typical if you stick to the highway, but it is not unusual to see 20 or more if you cruise the farm roads in this vicinity. Watch for them perched on the ground in the fields, as well as on irrigation units and power-poles. Most are the light morph; perhaps one in twenty is a dark-morph. Other locations include the San Rafael Grassland and Avra Valley.

Rough-legged Hawk—Rare winter visitor to valley deserts and grasslands, although in some years none is observed. Rough-legs can occasionally be found in the fields east of San Xavier Mission near Tucson, south of the Marana Pecan Grove at the Trico Road Santa Cruz River crossing, or among the Ferruginous Hawks in the Sulphur Springs Valley.

Golden Eagle—Uncommon permanent resident of valleys and mountains. In years when it is active, there is an eyrie visible on the cliffs above the Ramsey Canyon Preserve. Back roads in the San Rafael Grassland or the Sulphur Springs Valley are frequently productive, especially in winter.

Crested Caracara—Uncommon permanent resident of the Sonoran Desert, particularly on the Tohono O'odham lands. Watch for them along Highway 86 from the Kitt Peak Junction to Sells. Nearly every winter one turns up in Avra Valley west of Tucson, often roaming the area near the Marana Pecan Grove. Caracaras are also recorded very rarely in some winters near Picacho Reservoir, at the Buenos Aires National Wildlife Refuge, in the southern Sulphur Springs Valley, and at the San Bernardino National Wildlife Refuge east of Douglas.

Aplomado Falcon—Locally extirpated. In 1887 H. C. Benson found five nests on Ft. Huachuca, but in three seasons of field work there, beginning in 1896, ornithologist Harry S. Swarth never encountered a single Aplomado Falcon. The last state record accepted by the Arizona Bird Committee was near St. David in the San Pedro Valley in 1940. Misidentified Prairie Falcons and juvenile Swainson's Hawks are thought to account for all subsequent reports of Aplomado Falcon in Arizona. (There are, however, valid recent reports from the nearby Animas Valley in New Mexico.)

Prairie Falcon—Uncommon in summer near mountain cliffs and in winter in valley grasslands. Has nested for years in the Organ Formation at Chiricahua National Monument. Because of falconers, other known breeding sites are not given. During winter, watch power-poles, dead trees, and other conspicuous perches on the back roads along the Santa Cruz River near Tucson, in the San Rafael Grassland, along the San Pedro River, and in the Sulphur Springs Valley.

Peregrine Falcon—Rare in summer near mountain cliffs and locally scarce in winter near Tucson and in valley grasslands. Watch for Peregrines soaring above Lemmon Rock Lookout in the Santa Catalina Mountains, over the cliffs in Cave Creek Canyon, or hunting the Sierra Vista Wastewater Ponds during migration in August and September (also may winter there). A pair of Peregrines nested in downtown Tucson in 1995. Because of falconers, other known breeding sites are not given.

Wild Turkey—Reintroduced into all of the higher mountains. Now an uncommon permanent resident of Sierra Madrean pine/oak woodlands and grassy openings in coniferous forest in the Santa Rita, Huachuca, and Chiricahua Mountains. Recent observations along the San Pedro River and in Guadalupe Canyon seem to be of individuals of the Mexican subspecies, *mexicana*, apparently the result of a natural range-expansion from Sonora. When present, Wild Turkeys in Ramsey Canyon are the best habituated to people.

Montezuma Quail—Fairly common permanent resident of open grassy oak woodlands and glades in coniferous forest in all mountain ranges. The first one can be exasperatingly hard to find. Often seen at the edge of a road, particularly early in the morning and late in the afternoon. Instead of flying when a car approaches, a Montezuma squats. Look for small bumps along the edge of the road. It has been found just above Proctor Road in Madera Canyon, along Ruby Road between

Interstate 19 and California Gulch, at the outlets of Garden, Ramsey, and Miller Canyons in the Huachucas, and near the Southwestern Research Station in Cave Creek Canyon.

Northern Bobwhite—The "Masked Bobwhite" is the native subspecies extirpated in 1897. Reintroduction efforts began at the present-day Buenos Aires National Wildlife Refuge in 1974. The verdict is still out, but recent transplants have had some success. The fall 1994 census showed approximately 500 birds at Buenos Aires. Apparently eliminated by overgrazing, this species is an obligate of grassy swales in wide valley bottomlands. Male Masked Bobwhites have black throats and chestnut breasts and bellies, but females resemble the typical Northern Bobwhite hens of the eastern U.S.

Scaled Quail—Common permanent resident of valley grasslands and the Chihuahuan Desertscrub, primarily east of the Santa Cruz River. The Willcox Playa area by the golf course and the holding ponds is the single best location, but it can also be found in the housing development north of the lower Ramsey Canyon Road, throughout the Sulphur Springs Valley, east of Douglas on Highway 80, and at Willow Tank near Rodeo. Populations fluctuate year by year.

Gambel's Quail—Common to abundant permanent resident of both Sonoran and Chihuahuan desertscrub, particularly in areas of mesquite. Easy to find on the outskirts of Tucson, at the Arizona-Sonora Desert Museum, at the San Pedro House on the San Pedro River, and in the residential area of Portal.

Sandhill Crane—Common winter visitor to the Sulphur Springs Valley, where approximately 10,000 birds occur in two major groups. The northern population forages in the stubble-fields east of Willcox Playa in the area of Kansas Settlement. The southern group frequents the fields southwest of Elfrida between Central Highway and Frontier Road. Both "Lesser" and "Greater" Sandhills are present, but Lessers are by far the more abundant subspecies.

Whooping Crane—Found as a consequence of the Sandhill Crane foster parent program at Grays Lake, Idaho. These wayward (and "non-countable") Whoopers are seen rarely during winter in the Sulphur Springs Valley. They accompany Sandhill Cranes from the Grays Lake, Idaho, flock. The first Arizona sighting was in late December 1980, but Whoopers are not detected every year. Probably they will be even less likely in the future, since the foster parent program using Sandhills to rear Whoopers has been discontinued by the U.S. Fish and Wildlife Service

Shorebirds—A protracted migration period that begins in July and ends in June means that at least some shorebirds are present every month of the year. The only species which actually breed annually are Killdeer and the summering population of American Avocets at Willcox. Snowy Plovers and Black-necked Stilts also nest on occasion. Except for Snowy and Mountain Plovers, all of Southeastern Arizona's regularly occurring shorebirds are widespread and range to both coasts of the United States. They are treated under the bar-graphs. Shorebirds are found at sewage ponds in Tucson, Nogales, Sierra Vista, and Willcox; irrigated fields in the Santa Cruz and Sulphur Springs Valleys; and around lakes, such as Peña Blanca, Patagonia, Parker Canyon, and the Picacho Reservoir.

Snowy Plover—Rare and irregular summer and fall resident at Willcox Lake, where it has bred. Rare migrant at other valley sewage ponds, such as those near Tucson and Sierra Vista, in late April and May, and again in August and September.

Mountain Plover—Uncommon but very local winter visitor to barren valley fields—usually recently plowed—and open desert. There are usually 100 birds or more during winter in the large flock along Rucker Canyon Road at the Spitler Cattle Company in the Sulphur Springs Valley. A smaller group can occasionally be found a few miles away in the fields off Central Highway south and west of McNeal. Mountain Plovers have also been recorded near the Marana Pecan Grove.

Band-tailed Pigeon—Fairly common summer resident of oak, pine/oak, and coniferous forests in the mountains. Rare and irregular in winter. The nesting and feeding habits of Band-tails are erratic, so it is difficult to predict just where and when these birds will be found. The loud clapping of their wings upon take-off is usually the first clue of their presence in areas like Barfoot Park, South Fork Cave Creek, or at the Southwestern Research Station in the Chiricahuas. Also watch for them in tall, dead snags along the Reef Road in the Huachucas, by Proctor Road in Madera Canyon in spring, or along the Catalina Highway above Bear Canyon in the Santa Catalina Mountains.

White-winged Dove—Common summer resident of the Lower Sonoran Life Zone and the lower oak woodlands. A few winter near Tucson, Green Valley, Nogales, and Patagonia. Common from April through September in such areas as the Arizona-Sonora Desert Museum, Saguaro National Park, lower Madera Canyon, Patagonia-Sonoita Creek Preserve, along the San Pedro River, and at Portal.

Inca Dove—Common permanent resident in cities and towns at lower elevations. Avoids unpopulated areas. Easy to find in city parks in Tucson, at the Arizona-Sonora Desert Museum, Patagonia, and the 10th Street Park in Douglas.

Common Ground-Dove—Fairly common permanent resident of better-watered valleys at lower elevations. Avoids town areas but frequents weedy farm-fields. Can be found along the Santa Cruz River, Sonoita Creek, and the San Pedro River. A few specific locations are Kino Springs, Patagonia-Sonoita Creek Preserve, and the San Pedro House.

Ruddy Ground-Dove—Rare, but increasing in recent years, in the same river valleys as Common Ground-Doves. Ironically, Ruddies often ignore the little flocks of closely related Commons and choose to associate with Inca Doves. Distinguishing between female Ruddy and Common Ground-Doves can be difficult. Ruddies have dark-gray bills (never reddish), lack scaling on the neck and breast, have black (not violet or chestnut) markings on the wing coverts and scapulars, and have a longer tail which is warm brown (not short and gray). The Marana Pecan Grove and the Patagonia area have the best track-record for attracting this Mexican stray. Ruddy Ground-Dove was first recorded in Arizona in October 1981.

Thick-billed Parrot—Formerly irruptive to the mountains of southeastern Arizona. The last wild flock was reported from Chiricahua National Monument in 1938. Twenty-six birds were released in the Chiricahua Mountains in 1986, and subsequent efforts to re-establish this species were still underway in 1995. The re-introduced (and currently "non-countable") flock tends to leave the Chiricahuas in summer. Thickbills have attempted to nest several times near Payson in central Arizona, but so far no nests are known to have succeeded. After the breeding season, the parrots return to the Chiricahuas in late summer or fall. Most observations come from the Rustler Park area, but your chances of seeing this bird in the wild are still poor.

Yellow-billed Cuckoo—Fairly common summer resident of valley riparian woodlands. Although individuals show up in May, the bulk of the population does not arrive until the second week of June. The largest concentration of Yellow-billed Cuckoos in the western U.S. breeds along the San Pedro River, and they are also relatively common at the Patagonia-Sonoita Creek Preserve and Arivaca Creek.

Greater Roadrunner—Fairly common permanent resident of open deserts and valley grasslands. Try the back roads in Avra Valley, Marana Pecan Grove, lower Ramsey Canyon Road, Central Highway in Sulphur Springs Valley, and the road between San Simon and Portal.

Groove-billed Ani—Recently an annual visitant from across the Mexican border, primarily in summer and fall, to wet valley areas with rank vegetation. Fewer than 20 records since 1980. Some of the locations where anis have been found include Arivaca Creek, Marana Pecan

Grove, and near the confluence of Escapule Wash with the San Pedro River. Check the Tucson Audubon Society hotline for this bird.

Barn Owl—Fairly common permanent resident of old buildings, abandoned mine-shafts and wells, highway bridge abutments, and dense groves of trees in valleys and foothills. Inquiring minds can usually find this owl during the daytime if they check enough potential roosts—or ask the local owlers. Some of the best areas to search are in Avra Valley west of Tucson, Marana Pecan Grove, and Sulphur Springs Valley north of Douglas. *Ask permission before trespassing on private property or snooping around someone's barn!*

Flammulated Owl—Fairly common but rarely seen summer resident of mountain pine/oak woodland and Ponderosa Pine forest, often along streams where the trees are large. Locations include near the Bear Canyon picnic area in the Santa Catalina Mountains, one-half mile up the trail in Hopkins Fork of Madera Canyon in the Santa Rita Mountains, one mile up Miller Canyon Trail in the Huachuca Mountains, and either Pinery Canyon Campground or the Vista Point pull-out in Cave Creek Canyon in the Chiricahua Mountains. When feeding at dawn or dusk, it is usually silent. During the remainder of the night, when it is less active, it will often sit on the same perch and softly hoot for hours. However, its call is easily missed because it consists of a single low toot given at regular intervals, and the calls may be five seconds or more apart. Although Flammulated will readily answer an imitation of its call, it seldom shows itself. Look for it close to the trunk of a large, dense tree, especially a Douglas-fir or an Alligator Juniper.

Western Screech-Owl—Fairly common permanent resident of Saguaros, valley cottonwoods, and open, lower canyon woodlands. It seems to avoid the dense Sierra Madrean pine/oak woodlands occupied by the Whiskered Screech-Owl. Responds well to either an imitation or a tape-recording of its call. Proven locations include Sabino Canyon, Catalina State Park north of Tucson, the Patagonia-Sonoita Creek Preserve (no tapes permitted), the Hereford Bridge on the San Pedro River, and both Portal and Paradise in the Chiricahua Mountains.

Whiskered Screech-Owl—Common permanent resident of Sierra Madrean pine/oak woodlands in all the major ranges. Its characteristic "Morse Code" call may be heard from April to June in the Santa Catalina Mountains at Bear Canyon picnic area, in Madera Canyon in the Santa Rita Mountains anywhere from the lowest picnic area to the upper end of the road, at the end of the road in Miller Canyon in the Huachuca Mountains, and either in Cave Creek Canyon above the Visitor Information Station or at Pinery Canyon Campground in the Chiricahua Mountains. Occasionally, a male may be found snoozing on a daytime roost at the entrance to its hole during nesting season.

Northern Pygmy-Owl—Uncommon permanent resident throughout the mountains, especially in pine/oak woodlands with big Alligator Juniper trees, but also in Ponderosa Pine. Although this owl responds well to imitations of its call during both day and night—and at almost any season—it has a very large territory of up to a mile in length. Your chances of hearing it are best at dawn. Walk a mountain trail at daybreak and stop every half-mile to try its call. Bog Springs in Madera Canyon, upper Garden Canyon in the Huachuca Mountains, and Cave Creek Canyon anywhere above Sunny Flat Campground in the Chiricahuas are all good locations. "Mountain Pygmy-Owl," the subspecies found in the Border Ranges, uses a fast, double-noted toot. In Southeastern Arizona the slower, single-tooting *Pinicola* form of the Northern Pygmy-Owl is probably limited to the upper elevations of the Santa Catalina Mountains.

Ferruginous Pygmy-Owl—Very rare and local resident in the Lower Sonoran Life Zone from Tucson west. Seen once at the Patagonia Roadside Rest Area and found several times in upper Sycamore Canyon west of Nogales, not far from Hank and Yank Spring. Most records are for the spring or summer. The best way of finding this bird is to ask local birders for information. Some recent sightings have been in northwest Tucson, off the north end of the Tucson Mountains, Dudleyville, and at Organ Pipe Cactus National Monument, west of our area. In June this owl toots monotonously, sometimes throughout the day, and especially at dawn.

Elf Owl—Common summer resident of desert Saguaros, valley and foothill cottonwood groves, and sycamore canyons in the mountains. Since they are noisy little birds between March and June, you should have no trouble locating pairs by their weird, laughing calls at Catalina State Park, Madera Canyon, or Cave Creek Canyon. For years, Elf Owls have nested in telephone poles at the Santa Rita Lodge, and standing vigil to see them emerge at dusk has become a springtime ritual with both local and out-of-area birders.

Burrowing Owl—Uncommon and declining permanent resident of open deserts and valley grassland. Has been found along the Santa Cruz River near San Xavier Mission, the Marana Pecan Grove, and in the desert east of Cochise College near Douglas. Populations of Burrowing Owls collapsed throughout Southeast Arizona in the 1980s.

Spotted Owl—Uncommon permanent resident of dense coniferous forest and cool, shady canyons. "Mexican Spotted Owl," the race that occurs in Southeastern Arizona, nests almost exclusively in pot-holes in cliffs. Roosts, however, are usually in thick groves of trees, 15 feet or less above the ground. Each pair has a large territory of several square miles. Except in Scheelite Canyon in the Huachucas, your chances of finding this bird are not good. Some locations where it has been heard are above the end of the road in Madera Canyon in the Santa Rita Mountains, in Harshaw Canyon east of Patagonia, upper Miller Canyon in the Huachuca Mountains, and along the South Fork Road in the Chiricahua Mountains. Spotted Owl has also wintered at low elevation in Sabino Canyon in the front range of the Santa Catalina Mountains.

Northern Saw-whet Owl—Rare permanent resident in mountain pine/oak woodland and coniferous forest. Almost all sightings occur between mid-March and mid-June when the birds are calling. Most records are from the Chiricahuas—from either near Barfoot Junction or at Pinery Canyon Campground—but there are also reports from Rose Canyon Lake in the Santa Catalina Mountains. If you want to see this bashful owl, check the Tucson Audubon Society hotline.

Lesser Nighthawk—Common summer resident in deserts and valley grasslands. Aggregations of a dozen to over a hundred assemble most evenings over stock-tanks and sewage ponds, around street-lights and parking lots in shopping malls, and along dirt roads in the desert. The Avra Valley Sewage Ponds on Snyder Hill Road, the intersection of Speedway and Anklam Road west of Tucson, the Sierra Vista Wastewater Ponds, Kingfisher Pond near the San Pedro House, Cochise College west of Douglas, and the ford over Cave Creek on the San Simon Road east of Portal are all dependable localities.

Common Nighthawk—Uncommon and local summer resident of the high grassland near Sonoita, south and west of the Huachucas, and west of the Chiricahua Mountains. Lesser Nighthawks outnumber Commons by at least 1,000 to 1 at all other locations in the Southeast corner, and cannot safely be separated simply by how high above the ground they forage.

Common Poorwill—Common summer resident of deserts and foot-hills on dry, warm slopes. A few are active in winter. Poorwill is usually found at lower elevations than Whip-poor-will, although both species may be heard calling from the same clearing. One way to find this bird is to drive back-roads through the desert at night and watch for its bright orange eyeshine. Some good roads to try are Box Canyon Road (which turns off at the base of the Madera Canyon Road), Escapule Road along the San Pedro River, and dirt roads near Portal, such as San Simon Road or Silver Creek Road to Paradise. This is the only bird known to hibernate.

However, on warmer, moonlit nights near Portal a sleepy Common Poorwill may sound off even in midwinter.

Buff-collared Nightjar—Rare summer resident of Foothill Thornscrub canyons with rocky hillsides. Buff-collared Nightjar was first discovered in the United States in Guadalupe Canyon in 1960. Since then it has been detected in virtually every appropriate subtropical habitat in Southeastern Arizona. Its accelerating, ascending, piano-like song sounds like *Presta-me-tu-cuchillo*—or "Lend-me-your-knife" to the people in Mexico, and that is its Spanish name. This inconfusable call is the best way to identify the Buff-collar, since the color of its neck-band is difficult to see after dark, even with powerful lights. Primary locations include the west end parking area at Aravaipa Canyon, Sutherland Wash in Catalina State Park, McCleary Wash just east of the Madera Canyon Road, California Gulch southeast of Ruby, and Guadalupe Canyon east of Douglas.

Whip-poor-will—Common summer resident in Sierra Madrean pine/oak woodland and coniferous forest in the mountains. Easy to hear in major canyons of the Border Ranges, such as Madera, Miller, or Cave Creek. Also common in campgrounds at high elevations in the Santa Catalina, Huachuca, and Chiricahua Mountains. It feeds low among trees, as well as in clearings, and it often lands on a low limb, rather than on the ground. The loud, repetitive songs of Whip-poor-wills in the higher mountains during May and June have caused more insomnia than any actual or imagined incidents involving Black Bears and Mountain Lions combined. Southwestern Whip-poor-wills sing a low-pitched, burry song—*purple-ripp,* that may lead to full-species rank for this race in the future.

Vaux's Swift—Rare spring and uncommon fall migrant through valleys and along mountain crests. Vaux's are reported every year from Tucson, Nogales, and Patagonia. It is most common in the western sector of Southeastern Arizona, although there are a number of valid September reports from the upper San Pedro River and the Chiricahua Mountains.

White-throated Swift—Common summer resident and uncommon in winter around cliffs at all elevations. Less active in cold weather. Once the twittering call is learned, this bird is conspicuous throughout the summer at Sabino Canyon, Gates Pass in the Tucson Mountains, Madera Canyon, the Patagonia Roadside Rest Area, the Reef in upper Carr Canyon, Montezuma Pass in Coronado National Memorial, Chiricahua National Monument, and Cave Creek Canyon. In winter, also look for it in valley areas well removed from the mountains, such as at the Marana Pecan Grove and Kino Springs.

Broad-billed Hummingbird—Common summer resident in mesquite, cottonwood, and sycamore riparian woodlands of foothills and the lower parts of the mountains. A few are resident in the upper desert housing areas around the northern, western, and eastern perimeter of Tucson. Easily found from April through August in Sycamore Canyon west of Nogales, the lower half of Madera Canyon, the Patagonia-Sonoita Creek Preserve, and Guadalupe Canyon, particularly at feeders. In recent years this species has become established in the eastern canyons of the Chiricahua Mountains, but it is still uncommon there.

White-eared Hummingbird—Rare summer visitor to the mountains. Wintered at Ramsey Canyon in 1993, where one to six birds have been present every year since 1989 either at the Preserve or at the Ramsey Canyon Inn Bed & Breakfast just downcanyon. Although most observations come from feeders in Madera, Ramsey, and Cave Creek Canyons, this is a bird of pine/oak forests in the Sierra Madre. Look for it high in the mountains where penstemons are still blooming in late summer, such as Comfort Spring in the upper Huachuca Mountains and feeders at the Iron Door Restaurant in the Santa Catalina Mountains.

Cinnamon Hummingbird—Vagrant to Patons' feeders in Patagonia in July 1992. This dry-tropic species ranges from northwest Costa Rica to northwest Mexico, so it was not entirely unexpected. Birders should be alert for stray Cinnamons in the same Foothill Thornscrub situations used by Buff-collared Nightjars, Black-capped Gnatcatchers, and Five-striped Sparrows. Look for a medium-to-large hummer with cinnamon underparts, a rufous tail, and red on the bill.

Berylline Hummingbird—Very rare but virtually annual visitor to Sierra Madrean pine/oak woodland in the Border Ranges in summer. Recorded from feeders in Madera, Ramsey, and Cave Creek Canyons. Nested successfully in the Ramsey Canyon Preserve in 1978, and near the head of the Natural Bridge Trail in Chiricahua National Monument in 1984. It has also been recorded in the Transition Life Zone at Comfort Spring in the Huachuca Mountains.

Violet-crowned Hummingbird—Locally uncommon summer resident and rare in winter in the riparian woodlands of the foothills and lower mountains. Your best chance of seeing one is at Patons' feeders at Patagonia, where as many as four have been present at once. They are also regular at the Patagonia Roadside Rest Area and in Guadalupe Canyon. After that, they are most likely to be found at feeders in Madera, Ramsey, and Cave Creek Canyons. The nest is in a sycamore tree on a twig with a large overhanging leaf for a roof. In winter, Violet-crowned

Hummingbird is most often seen at private residence feeders in Tucson, Green Valley, Patagonia, Bisbee, and Douglas.

Blue-throated Hummingbird—Fairly common summer resident of sycamore canyons in the border mountains; rare there in winter. Invariably present at feeders in Madera, Ramsey, and Cave Creek Canyons, where up to a few ordinarily overwinter every year. Has also wintered at feeders in Tucson. It usually announces its arrival with loud, piercing *seep* notes. This is the largest hummingbird in the United States, and it is dominant over all other related species.

Magnificent Hummingbird—Common summer resident of sycamore canyons and open glades in coniferous forest up to 9,000 feet in all the mountains of the southeast corner. Rare in sycamore canyons in winter. Common at feeders in Madera, Ramsey, and Cave Creek Canyons, where a few ordinarily overwinter every year. As the second-largest U.S. hummingbird, Magnificents are dominated only by Blue-throats.

Plain-capped Starthroat—Very rare summer visitor to arid, lower mountain canyons with agaves, almost annual since 1985. Records since then have come from Sabino Canyon, McCleary Wash, Atascosa Mountains, Patagonia, Stump Canyon and Coronado National Memorial in the Huachucas, and the east side of the Chiricahuas at Portal, Silver Creek, and Whitetail Canyon. Altogether there are about 12 records since 1985.

Lucifer Hummingbird—Rare summer resident in arid, lower mountain-canyons with agaves. Most likely to be seen at canyon feeders in April and May and again in August and September, before and after the peak agave blossoming-period. Some recent records are from northeast Tucson, the Santa Rita Lodge in Madera Canyon, Sonoita, Ramsey Canyon Preserve, Coronado National Memorial, and now annually at the Spoffords' feeders in Portal.

Black-chinned Hummingbird—Common summer resident of the desert, foothills, and lower mountain canyons. From April through September Black-chins are the most abundant and widespread hummingbird in this area. Invariably at feeders in Tucson and Madera, Ramsey, and Cave Creek Canyons.

Anna's Hummingbird—Common winter resident and uncommon summer visitor in the western deserts and western foothills. In late summer and early fall squadrons of Anna's invade the lower canyons of the Huachuca and Chiricahua Mountains. In fact, since the early 1980s this has become one of the most abundant hummingbirds in the Ramsey Canyon Preserve from August through mid-October. During winter Anna's can be found at flowers and feeders in Tucson, the Arizona-Sonora Desert Museum, and the Marana Pecan Grove. From spring through midsummer a few birds are likely to be seen at the Patons' feeders in Patagonia, at the Ramsey Canyon Preserve, and at the Spoffords' feeders in Portal.

Costa's Hummingbird—Fairly common in winter and spring on the low deserts around Tucson, where it nests; uncommon in summer and very rare in fall in foothill and valley riparian thickets. After nesting it begins to disperse in May, and most are gone by July. In winter and spring, it can usually be found at Tucson feeders, the Arizona-Sonora Desert Museum, and Florida Canyon where it intersects the Madera Canyon Road. In early summer look for this species at the head of Sycamore Canyon west of Nogales, Kino Springs, the Patagonia-Sonoita Creek Preserve, the Ramsey Canyon Preserve, and feeders at Portal. In September and October document any Costa's sighting anywhere except at the Arizona-Sonora Desert Museum.

Calliope Hummingbird—Rare spring and uncommon fall migrant in the mountain canyons and meadows. From September through October females also exploit gardens and ornamental plantings in the valleys. Feeders at the Ski Valley area in the Santa Catalina Mountains and at Portal Store, and the agave stand at Silver Creek Spring four miles northwest of Portal, have proven to be reliable locations for males of the smallest avian species in the U.S. In fall apricot-bellied little females are fairly common on flowers at Cochise College west of Douglas, as well as at the sites mentioned above.

Bumblebee Hummingbird—This species is included in the Specialties listing because two females were collected in July 1896 from Ramsey Canyon. Since then there have been no other accepted records. The nearest Mexican population is 300 miles southeast in the Sierra Madre of Chihuahua, where the species prefers low brambles in pine/oak woodland. Females resemble female Calliopes, but they average one-half inch shorter, have shorter bills, have short wings that do not project beyond the tail, have bright cinnamon sides that contrast with a white collar, have more densely spotted throats, and have extensively rufous-based tails that usually feature white or buff outer-tail feather-tips. Tiny male Bumblebees have elongate purple-red gorgets and extensive rufous-cinnamon at the base of the tail.

Broad-tailed Hummingbird—Common summer resident of the coniferous forests of the higher mountains. Less common along streams in the Sierra Madrean pine/oak woodlands. During spring and fall Broad-tails can also be found at flower patches anywhere from desert oases to the summits of all major ranges. The high-pitched trill generated by the wings of the male is heard more frequently than the bird is seen. Although the species occurs throughout the mountains of Southeastern Arizona, in midsummer it is most common at feeders in the high Santa Catalina Mountains and at Ramsey Canyon. The shrill wing-trills of fighting males are a serious threat to the serenity of meadows such as Rustler Park when the Rocky Mountain Iris blossoms in June.

Rufous Hummingbird—Uncommon spring migrant in the Sonoran Desert near Tucson, and almost rare in lower mountain canyons; common fall migrant in the mountains at all elevations, and at desert oases such as Tucson. From late July until October, it may be seen at feeders at the Ski Valley area in the Santa Catalinas, and in Madera, Ramsey, and Cave Creek Canyons. Agave stands like the one at Silver Creek Spring in the Chiricahuas are heavily patronized by returning Rufous. When the delphinium and salvia are in bloom from late July till mid-September, the mountain meadows may swarm with these golden fighters.

Allen's Hummingbird—Recent banding studies have shown that female and immature Allen's are uncommon migrants in the mountain canyons in July and August. Adult males are rare migrants in the same areas, primarily in July. Most records are from the Huachuca Mountains westward. Since female and immature Allen's and Rufous are impossible to separate in the field, only adult males of this species can be safely identified. Watch for full adult male Allen's at feeders in Sonoita and Patagonia, and at Madera and Ramsey Canyons.

Elegant Trogon—Fairly common summer resident of deep sycamore canyons within Sierra Madrean pine/oak woodland in the Border Ranges. Trogons are frequently heard (a croaking *co-ah*) before being seen, as males patrol up and down riparian corridors every morning, advertising for mates or maintaining territorial boundaries. After the young fledge in July or August, however, adult trogons are largely silent. Territories average one-half-mile long in prime habitat such as Sycamore Canyon west of Nogales, Madera and Josephine Canyons in the Santa Ritas, Sunnyside and Garden Canyons in the Huachucas, and Cave Creek and South Fork Canyons in the Chiricahua Mountains. Trogons in Madera, Garden, and Cave Creek Canyons are ordinarily the most accessible. But, in both 1994 and 1995, a pair successfully fledged young in Ramsey Canyon Preserve, and the families were often observed on the edge of the visitor center parking lot. Probably at least one or two trogons overwinter in Arizona every year. Although in some years none is detected, winter reports have come from lower Sonoita Creek, Josephine Canyon, Sycamore Canyon west of Nogales, and Sunnyside Canyon in the Huachucas, all south-draining canyons.

Eared Trogon—Very rare resident of upper pine/oak woodland and coniferous forest in the Huachuca and Chiricahua Mountains, most often descending into sycamore canyons during fall. Also recorded in the Josephine and Hopkins Forks of Madera Canyon in July and August of 1991. Since their first appearance October 1977 in the South Fork of Cave Creek Canyon, Eared Trogons have been observed during most of the intervening years, usually between August and November. In October 1991 a nest found high in Ramsey Canyon failed when an early freeze killed the nestlings. Eared Trogons have also been observed in Scheelite, Carr, and Miller Canyons in the Huachucas, and the North Fork, Snowshed Fork, and Main Fork of Cave Creek in the Chiricahuas. Listen for its *squee-chuck* call.

Green Kingfisher—Uncommon resident of valley tree-lined ponds and sluggish waters along Arivaca and Sonoita Creeks, and the Santa Cruz and San Pedro Rivers. The first known successful nesting of Green Kingfisher in Arizona was in the San Pedro Riparian National Conservation Area in 1989. Since then, Bureau of Land Management biologists have noted up to 15 kingfishers using the NCA. The most reliable place to look for this species is at the appropriately named Kingfisher Pond, one-half mile south of the San Pedro House, and along the river trail that runs north from the pond almost to the Highway 90 Bridge. Other proven sites are Kino Springs east of Nogales and the north railroad bridge abutment in the Patagonia-Sonoita Creek Preserve. Intermittent sites include Arivaca Cienaga and the Nogales Drive-In Theater Ponds.

Acorn Woodpecker—Common and conspicuous permanent resident of canyons within oak woodlands. An important component of Acorn Woodpecker habitat is standing dead timber in which the birds can store acorns. It's tough to miss this species in places like Bear Canyon in the Santa Catalina Mountains, Madera Canyon, Ramsey Canyon, or Cave Creek Canyon.

Gila Woodpecker—Common resident in Saguaro forests of the Sonoran Desert and valley cottonwood groves. Gilas are a conspicuous feature of the avian landscape at the Arizona-Sonora Desert Museum, Sabino Canyon, Tubac, Patagonia-Sonoita Creek Preserve, the San Pedro River, and Guadalupe Canyon.

Red-naped Sapsucker—Fairly common winter visitor to desert oases with deciduous trees, valley groves, and wooded mountain canyons, especially in pecan and apple orchards. Numbers peak in March and October, when it is usually easy to find in the ash trees by the Otter Pool at the Arizona-Sonora Desert Museum, Sabino Canyon, Kino Springs,

Madera Canyon, Ramsey Canyon, and in the old apple orchard at the Southwestern Research Station in Cave Creek Canyon.

Williamson's Sapsucker—Uncommon migrant and rare winter visitor in mountain Ponderosa Pines. Most common in the Chiricahua Mountains and in the months of September and April. Rustler and Barfoot Parks and the meadow edges along the crest in the Chiricahua Wilderness Area are the best areas. During some winters, a Williamson's Sapsucker assumes quarters in a valley grove or desert oasis such as at the Arizona-Sonora Desert Museum or the pecan grove at Continental. These birds usually make the Tucson Audubon Society rare-bird tape.

Ladder-backed Woodpecker—Fairly common permanent resident of the mesquite deserts, Soaptree Yucca valley grasslands, and the more arid oak woodlands. Usually found in pairs in such areas as Saguaro National Park, Sabino Canyon, Marana Pecan Grove, Patagonia Roadside Rest Area, San Pedro House, below Portal, and at the outlets of all of the canyons of the larger mountains.

Strickland's Woodpecker—Fairly common permanent resident of the Sierra Madrean pine/oak woodlands of all the mountain ranges. Look for it at Bear Canyon in the Santa Catalinas, Madera Canyon in the Santa Ritas, Ramsey Canyon in the Huachucas, and South Fork Cave Creek in the Chiricahua Mountains. In the Chiricahuas, Strickland's Woodpecker is also fairly common on the dry hillsides along the Trans-mountain Road between the Southwestern Research Station and Onion Saddle.

Strickland's has a reputation for being difficult to find. This is true partly because birders spend little time in its preferred habitat after breeding season—the arid oak woodlands where other Sierra Madrean specialties are not so common. During spring, listen for its sharp *Peek* call note, very similar to that of a Hairy Woodpecker.

Gilded Flicker—Common resident in Saguaro forests and valley cottonwood groves east to the upper San Pedro Valley. Gilded Flicker is easily separated in Arizona by the yellow undersurfaces on the tail and flight feathers. Perched, note that Gilded has a bright cinnamon crown. Look for Gilded Flicker at Saguaro National Park west of Tucson, Kino Springs, the Patagonia-Sonoita Creek Preserve, and at the San Pedro House on the San Pedro River east of Sierra Vista.

Northern Beardless-Tyrannulet—Uncommon to fairly common summer resident in riparian thickets of mesquite, hackberry, and cottonwoods in foothills and canyon mouths. Rare in winter. Hard to find and even harder to identify. Look—and *listen*— for it at Catalina State Park, Agua Caliente Park northeast of Tucson, Florida Wash, Sycamore Canyon west of Nogales, the Patagonia-Sonoita Creek Preserve, the Patagonia Road-side Rest Area, and Guadalupe Canyon.

This tiny bird is so nondescript that it is often passed off as a Verdin or something else. Its bushy little crest, distinct eyebrow, and more horizontal posture should separate it from *Empidonax* flycatchers. The surest means of identification is its song, a short series of four to five loud, clear *Peer* notes.

Greater Pewee—Fairly common summer resident of the pines and pine/oak woodlands of the higher mountains. Rare in winter at the outlets of major canyons and in valley pecan and cottonwood groves. Its large nesting territory may include riparian woodland and adjacent slopes. Usually feeds from a tree top in typical pewee fashion, but it seems to prefer taller trees than those used by the Western Wood-Pewee. Once its very distinctive and dulcet *José María* (Ho-SAY Mah-REE-ah) call is learned, the voice of Greater Pewee is easy to pull out of the dawn chorus in appropriate habitat. During summer listen for it in such areas as along the Catalina Highway from Bear Canyon up, one-half mile up the Hopkins Fork of Madera Canyon, the staff residence at the end of the nature trail in Ramsey Canyon, Sawmill Campground in the upper end of Garden Canyon in the Huachucas, and at the Herb Martyr parking lot and at the Barfoot Junction on the Rustler Park Road in the Chiricahuas. The distinctive *pip* note used by overwintering pewees has led to the discovery of birds in Tucson, at the Marana Pecan Grove, lower Madera Canyon, and at Patagonia, far below the mountains where they breed.

Western Wood-Pewee—Abundant summer resident of the pines, oaks, and riparian woodlands of the mountains and river valleys. Nesting at 100-yard intervals in appropriate habitat, this bird is so common, conspicuous, and noisy that it is almost impossible to miss in the proper season, particularly in early morning and late afternoon. On the other hand, Western Wood-Pewees are so nondescript that they are occasionally mistaken for practically anything else.

Willow Flycatcher—Uncommon migrant in late May and early June and again in August and September. Watch for it in dense willows, cattails, and reeds in the canal behind the Marana Pecan Grove, at the Patagonia-Sonoita Creek Preserve, at Willcox Lake by the golf course, and near the swimming pool at the Southwestern Research Station in the Chiricahua Mountains. Several pairs of Willow Flycatchers breed along the lower San Pedro River near Dudleyville.

Hammond's Flycatcher—Fairly common spring and fall migrant through mountain canyon trees, and uncommon winter visitor in valley cottonwood groves. Look for it in migration in Madera, Ramsey, and

Cave Creek Canyons. In winter watch for it at Kino Springs, Patagonia-Sonoita Creek Preserve, and along the San Pedro River.

Dusky Flycatcher—Fairly common spring and fall migrant through mountain canyon thickets, and uncommon winter visitor in valley hackberry, mesquite, and elderberry thickets. Look for it in migration in Madera, Ramsey, and Cave Creek Canyons. In winter watch for it at Kino Springs, Patagonia-Sonoita Creek Preserve, and the San Pedro River.

Gray Flycatcher—Fairly common spring and fall migrant through valley mesquite and foothill juniper stands, and uncommon winter visitor in valley thickets. Look for it in migration and in winter at Catalina State Park, Redington Pass, the Buenos Aires National Wildlife Refuge, Tubac, Patagonia-Sonoita Creek Preserve, and the San Pedro River.

Pacific-slope Flycatcher—Fairly common spring and fall migrant through valley cottonwood groves and dense mesquite thickets. When "Western Flycatcher" was split into this and the next species in 1990, the new taxonomy created an identification problem. Positive identification of migrants is possible only if the bird is calling. Male Pacific-slope Flycatchers give a slurred, ascending *sweeet* vocalization, while male Cordilleran Flycatchers use a bi-syllabic *wee-seet!* Habitat is a good clue to the identity of yellow-throated *Empidonax* flycatchers in Southeastern Arizona. Mountain birds, during the summer, are Cordillerans. Most valley birds are Pacific-slopes. Places to look and listen for Pacific-slope Flycatcher are the Marana Pecan Grove, along Arivaca Creek, at the Patagonia-Sonoita Creek Preserve, and along the San Pedro River.

Cordilleran Flycatcher—Common summer resident of moist forests at higher elevations, and in deep, shady canyons. Often nests under the eaves of cabins, as in Rustler Park, or in niches in large, streamside boulders. Dependable locations include the Corkbark Fir forest on Mount Lemmon, the spring one-half mile above the end of the road in the Hopkins Fork of Madera Canyon, the huge cliffs in Scheelite Canyon just above the one-half mile marker, and the "Bathtub" pool at the fourth stream-crossing three-quarters of a mile up South Fork Cave Creek.

Buff-breasted Flycatcher—Locally fairly common summer resident of open pine-forest, primarily in the Huachuca Mountains, but a breeding enclave also exists in the Chiricahuas, and there are records for both the Santa Catalina and Santa Rita Mountains. In favorable habitat in Mexico, this bird often nests in loose colonies of four or five pairs. Two such groups exist in the Huachuca Mountains—one at the Sawmill Canyon Campground above the Boy Scout Cabin on Fort Huachuca, and the other by the pond in lower Scotia Canyon. A similar cluster of Buff-breasteds is located near the outlet of Saulsbury Canyon in West Turkey Creek in the Chiricahua Mountains. All three of these colonies are in Chihuahua Pines. Other areas in the Huachucas that have proven reliable for this species include lower Carr Canyon 2.2 miles from Highway 92, Ramsey Vista Campground, and Comfort Spring one-half mile beyond the end of the same road. In the Chiricahuas Buff-breasteds breed every few years behind the Southwestern Research Station in Cave Creek Canyon and in the burn area east of the Ranger cabins at Rustler Park.

Black Phoebe—Common, permanent resident near permanent water in deserts, valleys, and lower mountain canyons. Although the species is ecologically tied to water, the exact form of the water may range from a horse-trough to a river. Frequently nests under bridges. Has been found at all sewage ponds and recreational lakes around Tucson and throughout the southeast corner, as well as at Sycamore Canyon west of Nogales, the Patagonia-Sonoita Creek Preserve, San Pedro River, Willcox golf-course pond, and Cave Creek Canyon in the Chiricahuas.

Say's Phoebe—Common permanent resident of deserts, valley grassland, and artificial clearings in the mountain canyons. Most nests are placed under the eaves of buildings. More abundant and widespread in winter, when northern migrants augment the resident population. Often nests at the Kino Springs golf course, Sierra Vista Wastewater Ponds, near the club house at the Willcox golf course, and at the Southwestern Research Station in Cave Creek Canyon.

Vermilion Flycatcher—Common summer resident in weedy openings and pastures near water in deserts, valleys, and broad foothill canyons with mesquite, willow, and cottonwood groves. Less common in winter, especially in the higher eastern sector. In summer this bird is probably more numerous along Sonoita Creek and the San Pedro River than at any other location in the United States. It is also found at Woodland and Wentworth Roads in northeast Tucson, Marana Pecan Grove, Aravaipa Canyon, upper Sycamore Canyon, Peña Blanca Lake, Kino Springs, Sierra Vista Wastewater Ponds, Guadalupe Canyon, and Willow Tank near Rodeo. During most winters literally dozens use the Arivaca Creek Cienaga; a few may also be present at Kino Springs.

Dusky-capped Flycatcher—Common summer resident of Sierra Madrean pine/oak woodland canyons in all of the border foothills and mountain ranges. Its long-drawn, descending "mournful Pierre" whistle is a familiar call in Sycamore, Madera, Ramsey, and Cave Creek Canyons. It is also common at the Patagonia-Sonoita Creek Preserve. Most Dusky-caps depart from Arizona before the end of August.

Ash-throated Flycatcher—Common summer resident of the deserts, valley grasslands, arid foothills, and lower mountain canyons. Nests in holes in Saguaros, cottonwoods, sycamores, and other trees, as well as in fence-posts. Places to look for this bird include the Arizona-Sonora Desert Museum, Sycamore Canyon west of Nogales, Coronado National Memorial, Cochise College west of Douglas, and Silver Creek near Portal. Ash-throateds are not hard to find, but they can be difficult to separate from the Brown-cresteds if neither heard nor seen well. Rare in winter in the western lowlands and foothills.

Brown-crested Flycatcher—Fairly common summer resident in desert Saguaros, valley cottonwoods, and in the sycamores of the foothills and lower mountain canyons. Can be found in Saguaro National Park, Sabino Canyon, lower Madera Canyon, the Patagonia-Sonoita Creek Preserve, along the San Pedro River, lower Cave Creek Canyon, and Guadalupe Canyon.

Nutting's Flycatcher—Vagrant from Pacific-slope dry season deciduous forest south of the border. Recorded from the Research Ranch near Elgin in July 1985. This species resembles Ash-throated Flycatcher, but can be distinguished by its orange mouth-color and sharp *week* call-notes. It usually lacks the dark tail-corners of Ash-throated. Significantly, the only record ever accepted for Southeastern Arizona was of a bird that was mist-netted, measured, and photographed.

Sulphur-bellied Flycatcher—Common summer resident in the sycamore canyons of the Border Ranges, and uncommon in Bear Canyon in the Santa Catalina Mountains. Substantial numbers usually do not arrive until mid-May. It occurs in Sycamore Canyon west of Nogales, Madera Canyon in the Santa Ritas, Garden Canyon in the Huachucas, and Cave Creek Canyon in the Chiricahuas. Both Ramsey Canyon and South Fork Cave Creek harbor about six pairs of Sulphur-bellies per mile. Listen for the squeaky "rubber-ducky" calls.

Tropical Kingbird—Uncommon local summer resident of ponds and streams edged with cottonwoods and willows in river valleys near the border. Most records are from the Santa Cruz Valley or the San Pedro Valley. Regular at Arivaca Cienaga, at the larger pond at Kino Springs, and since 1993, at Kingfisher Pond near the San Pedro House. Breeding pairs reach as far north as the Marana Pecan Grove and Winkelman. Listen for the twittering *pip-pip-pip-pip* calls.

Cassin's Kingbird—Common summer resident in riparian woodlands, most abundant in lower mountain canyons, but also present at desert oases such as the campus of Cochise College west of Douglas. With its loud *chi-bew* call, hard to miss in such areas as Madera Canyon, Patagonia-Sonoita Creek Preserve, Garden Canyon, the San Pedro River, and Cave Creek Canyon. You will soon be saying, "It's just another Cassin's."

Thick-billed Kingbird—Locally uncommon summer resident of riparian woodlands in the foothills. Nests in sycamores or cottonwoods. Areas where it occurs regularly include Dudleyville, lower Sycamore Canyon, Arivaca Creek, the Patagonia-Sonoita Creek Preserve, and the Patagonia Roadside Rest Area. It was first discovered in the U.S. in Guadalupe Canyon in 1958, and that is still a reliable place to find it.

Western Kingbird—Common summer resident of open desert and valley grassland with a few trees or telephone poles for nesting. Often found perched on roadside fences or utility wires. This is the common kingbird at San Xavier Mission south of Tucson, at the Marana Pecan Grove, in the desert grassland along the lower Madera Canyon Road, in the Sonoita Grassland, on the outskirts of Sierra Vista, throughout the Sulphur Springs Valley, including the Willcox Playa, and in downtown Portal.

Rose-throated Becard—Rare and local summer resident. Nearly everyone's life bird comes from Sonoita Creek across Highway 82 from the north end of the Patagonia Roadside Rest Area. Watch for traffic as you cross this busy highway, and descend the embankment with care. *Do not cross the fence.* There are usually one or two huge, football-shaped nests hanging from the tips of sycamore branches directly over the stream in this 100-yard stretch. If you time your visit between mid-May to mid-August, there is a pretty good chance that you'll see the becards entering and leaving their nests. Other recent nesting sites have been on the Patagonia-Sonoita Creek Preserve, Circle Z Guest Ranch, Arivaca Creek, and about 3.5 miles downstream from the Sycamore Canyon parking area. Ask the local birders.

Purple Martin—Common summer resident of Saguaro stands near Tucson and west to Organ Pipe Cactus National Monument. This Saguaro-nesting race is endemic to southern Arizona, and is closely associated with Arizona Upland Sonoran Desertscrub. A larger, coniferous-forest-nesting subspecies confined to the Chiricahua Mountains was last recorded in August 1985. Purple Martins east of the Tucson area are rare in migration in May and June, and again in August and September, and are often just single birds. During late August and September, by way of contrast, Purple Martins on the periphery of Tucson join collective roosts that number in the thousands and cause utility wires to sag. Dependable locations for martins include the Shannon-Broadway Desert and the intersection of Anklam Road and Speedway in west Tucson, and the Arizona-Sonora Desert Museum.

Violet-green Swallow—Common summer resident of the Rocky Mountain pines and firs of the higher mountains, descending into the major canyons that drain them. Migrating Violet-greens arrive in western lowland valleys as early as January during some years. This is the only swallow likely in the coniferous forests. Areas in which to look for them include Rose Canyon Lake and Lemmon Rock Lookout in the upper Santa Catalina Mountains, Ramsey Vista Campground and Carr Peak in the high Huachucas, and Rustler Park and Barfoot Lookout on top of the Chirica-hua Mountains. They also pay daily visits to all major canyons, and are common flying as low as Portal at the mouth of Cave Creek Canyon early in the morning.

Cave Swallow—First detected in 1979, a single bird spent most of the 1980s consorting with Cliff Swallows from mid-April through July at the Main Library at the University of Arizona in Tucson, even nesting among the Cliffs with another Cave Swallow in 1983. The most recent records were at Kino Springs in mid-August 1991 and at Tucson in late October 1991.

Jays—The three species of jays found in Southeastern Arizona are rather restricted to particular habitats, reducing competition which might otherwise exist. Steller's Jay occurs in coniferous forests and moist canyons, usually above 7,000 feet. Mexican Jay is found in Sierra Madrean pine/oak woodland between 4,500 and 7,500 feet. Western Scrub-Jay prefers hillside chaparral below 6,000 feet.

Steller's Jay—Common permanent resident of mountain coniferous forests and shady, moist canyons. Usually conspicuous at Rose Canyon Lake and around Ski Valley in the Santa Catalina Mountains, Reef Townsite and Ramsey Vista Campgrounds in the Huachucas, and at Rustler Park and Pinery Canyon Campgrounds in the Chiricahuas. During winter a few Steller's Jays descend to the Santa Rita Lodge in Madera Canyon, to the visitor center in the Ramsey Canyon Preserve, and to Stewart Campground in Cave Creek Canyon. During some winters, Steller's Jays even reach the valley lowlands, such as Evergreen Cemetery in Tucson.

Western Scrub-Jay—Fairly common and local permanent resident of interior chaparral on dry hillsides and mixed hackberry/mesquite thickets in foothill canyons. Lower and more widespread in winter. Lack of chaparral, as well as competition from the Mexican Jay, makes the Western Scrub-Jay quite local in the Border Ranges. It is more numerous in the mountains of central Arizona, where there is more brush and fewer Mexican Jays. In Southeastern Arizona it can be found at Molino Basin in the Santa Catalinas, in Scheelite Canyon of the Huachucas, along the

Silver Creek Road and at Portal in the Chiricahua Mountains, and in Guadalupe Canyon.

Mexican Jay—Common resident of Sierra Madrean pine/oak woodland in all of the mountains, north sparingly to the Mogollon Rim in central Arizona. One of the noisiest birds in Bear Canyon in the Santa Catalinas, upper Sycamore Canyon west of Nogales, Madera Canyon in the Santa Ritas, Ramsey Canyon in the Huachucas, and Cave Creek Canyon in the Chiricahua Mountains.

Mexican Jays travel throughout the year in flocks that average a dozen or so birds, consisting of a nucleus pair and two or more generations of offspring. One jay acts as a sentinel while the others feed. The nests are tended by three or more birds, usually including older siblings, and any member of the flock may feed the young. In this way young birds gain parenting experience that enhances their own future nesting success. A long-term research project conducted in Cave Creek Canyon by Dr. Jerram Brown has shown how altruistic behavior benefits these jays.

Chihuahuan Raven—Common permanent resident of valley grasslands and the Chihuahuan Desertscrub from the Santa Cruz Valley eastward. Nests on tall yuccas, mesquites, windmills, and telephone poles. Easy to find at the Sierra Vista Wastewater Ponds, at Cochise College between Bisbee and Douglas, the Willcox area, and at the Rodeo Town Dump east of the Chiricahua Mountains.

Finding this bird is not difficult, but seeing the white on its neck is. Unless the conditions are windy enough to reveal a patch of white at the base of the neck feathers, visitors to the area may not be certain if they have seen a Chihuahuan Raven or a Common. Clues include habitat preferences and number. Typically Common Ravens prefer the mountains or the cottonwoods along the rivers, while Chihuahuans keep strictly to the open, broad, level valleys that resemble the arid plains of west Texas. Typically, Commons come in twos and threes, while the more social little Chihuahuan is generally in a flock of a dozen or more outside the breeding season; during winter at Willcox there may actually be several hundred. The Chihuahuan's smaller size, when that can be judged, and flatter call, when heard, can also lead to a probable identification. Birders should be aware, however, that the *sinuatus* race of Common Raven breeding in the Southwest averages smaller than ravens in most other areas of the U.S. And, given the large vocal repertoire of both species, voice may be simply a source of confusion. Some locals swear that there are actually three species present, including one that is intermediate in size and sound. This third species gets listed as "Raven spp." on Christmas Bird Counts throughout the southeast corner. American Crow is a vagrant in Southeastern Arizona, although it has been found near agricultural areas at Safford, St. David, and Elfrida.

Mexican Chickadee—Fairly common permanent resident of the coniferous forest and upper Sierra Madrean pine/oak woodland of the Chiricahua Mountains. During spring, Mexican Chickadees seem to descend into the major canyons to breed. At that time of year they are generally easier to find in Pinery Canyon Campground than in Rustler Park. By the onset of the rainy season in July, Mexican Chickadees are all over the crest of the Chiricahuas, including both Rustler and Barfoot Parks, and throughout the Chiricahua Wilderness Area. They are also permanent fixtures at Massai Point in Chiricahua National Monument.

Mountain Chickadee—Common permanent resident of the coniferous forests of the Santa Catalina Mountains and northward. Lower and more widespread in winter. Easiest to find along the Catalina Highway from Rose Canyon Lake upward. Look for it at the Bear Wallow Picnic Area and at the Ski Valley area. Responds well to squeaks and owl calls.

Bridled Titmouse—Common permanent resident of the oak and pine/oak woodlands in all mountain ranges. Less common and localized in the riparian woodlands at lower elevations. Lower and widespread in winter. Present in Sycamore Canyon, Madera Canyon, Patagonia-Sonoita Creek Preserve, Ramsey Canyon, upper San Pedro River (winter only), and in Cave Creek Canyon. Responds well to squeaks and owl calls. You should have little trouble finding and savoring this handsome bird.

Plain Titmouse—Uncommon permanent resident of One-seed Juniper and Border Pinyon Pine in the northeastern foothills of the Chiricahua Mountains and locally near the Bellota Ranch Pond in the Redington Pass area of the Santa Catalina Mountains. Lying in the rainshadow of the higher peaks, the foothills from Portal north along the eastern base of the Chiricahuas depend on winter rainfall, the same weather pattern as in the Great Basin. Along with Western Scrub-Jay and Black-chinned Sparrow, Plain Titmouse exploits this unique Southeastern Arizona habitat. The easiest place to see this species is at feeders in Portal, or especially at the George Walker House Bed and Breakfast in Paradise, but Plain Titmouse occurs throughout the length of Silver Creek in between these two Chiricahua communities.

Verdin—Common permanent resident of desert thornscrub thickets. Locations include the Arizona-Sonora Desert Museum, Saguaro National Park, Sabino Canyon, Florida Canyon below Madera Canyon, the Patagonia Roadside Rest Area, the San Pedro River, and in the desert east of Portal. Responds well to pishing.

Bushtit—Fairly common permanent resident of canyon groves and of chaparral and oak/juniper woodlands on dry mountain slopes. Usually occurs at higher elevations than the Verdin, although wandering flocks may descend to the desert in winter. Also highly responsive to pishing, Bushtits are usually easy to observe once a flock is located. Look for them in Molino Basin, Madera Canyon, Peña Blanca Lake, Patagonia-Sonoita Creek Preserve, all canyons in the Huachuca and Chiricahua Mountains, and in Guadalupe Canyon.

Red-breasted Nuthatch—Common resident in upper canyon groves and mountain coniferous forest. A few descend to valley pecan groves and desert oases in winter. Road-accessible Red-breasted Nuthatches occur at Bear Wallow in the Santa Catalinas and at the East Turkey Creek crossing on Trans-mountain Road in the Chiricahua Mountains, as well as Rustler Park on top. Birders who hike will encounter this species near the one-half mile marker in Scheelite Canyon and near the Hamburg Mine in Ramsey Canyon of the Huachuca Mountains.

Pygmy Nuthatch—Common permanent resident of the Ponderosa Pines. Prefers mature trees. Easy to find at Rose Canyon Lake and Mt. Bigelow in the Santa Catalina Mountains, Reef Townsite Campground in the Huachucas, and at Barfoot Junction and Rustler Park in the Chiricahua Mountains. Usually first located by its little piping call notes.

Brown Creeper—Fairly common permanent resident of riparian timber in the major mountain canyons and coniferous forest high in the mountains. In some winters can be found in Tucson. Creepers occur from Bear Canyon up in the Santa Catalinas, Madera Canyon, Ramsey Canyon, South Fork Cave Creek, and at Rustler Park in the Chiricahuas.

Cactus Wren—Common permanent resident of desert thornscrub and valley acacia and mesquite thickets. This conspicuous, noisy species can be found anywhere on the perimeter of Tucson, at the Arizona-Sonora Desert Museum, Saguaro National Park, Sabino Canyon, Florida Wash on the Madera Canyon Road, along lower Ramsey Canyon Road, and at Portal.

Rock Wren—Fairly common permanent resident of arid, open, rocky areas in the foothills. Winters down to Tucson. Look for it in Aravaipa Canyon, Molino Basin, Sabino Canyon, along Ruby Road, at the Patagonia Roadside Rest Area, at the Lavender Pit parking area at Bisbee, along Silver Creek Road near Portal, and at Guadalupe Canyon. In winter also frequents the grounds of the Arizona-Sonora Desert Museum and the little hill east of San Xavier Mission.

Canyon Wren—Common permanent resident of rocky canyons and cliffs, ranging above 9,000 feet along the Chiricahua Crest Trail near Paint

Rock. Its loud, descending cascade of whistles fills such rock-walled locations as Aravaipa Canyon, Sabino Canyon, Sycamore Canyon west of Nogales, Patagonia Roadside Rest Area, Scheelite Canyon, Cave Creek Canyon, and Chiricahua National Monument.

Bewick's Wren—Common permanent resident of valley and canyon groves, including mesquite bosques, and of oak and pine/oak woodlands in the foothills and lower mountains. Widespread in winter, when it reaches the desert. Responds well to squeaking and owl calls. This is the most common wren in Molino Basin, Madera Canyon, Sycamore Canyon west of Nogales, at the Patagonia-Sonoita Creek Preserve, along the San Pedro River, and throughout all lower canyons in the Huachuca and Chiricahua Mountains.

American Dipper—Rare but reported in some winters from Aravaipa Canyon, Sabino Canyon in the Santa Catalina Mountains, the Proctor Road area of Madera Canyon, Ramsey Canyon in the Huachuca Mountains, and South Fork Cave Creek in the Chiricahua Mountains. (More common along mountain streams in central Arizona.)

Black-tailed Gnatcatcher—Fairly common permanent resident of the Sonoran Desertscrub west of Tucson, uncommon in Chihuahuan Desertscrub farther east. Prefers dry washes in creosote flats, but also occurs in foothill acacia and cactus thickets. Easiest to find at Tucson Mountain Park, Sabino Canyon, the Arizona-Sonora Desert Museum, Saguaro National Park, and in Florida Wash. Farther east it can be found along the Charleston Road east of the San Pedro River, in Silver Creek near Portal, and in Guadalupe Canyon.

Black-capped Gnatcatcher—Formerly and possibly still a very rare summer resident of Foothill Thornscrub canyons in the border foothills. In 1981 a pair nested three times in Chino Canyon on the west side of the Santa Rita Mountains, and nested yearly through 1985. The species, however, has not been seen in the canyon since 1991. This Mexican species was first recorded in the United States in 1971 from near the Patagonia Roadside Rest Area, and there have been several documented sightings along Sonoita Creek since then. Sycamore Canyon west of Nogales hosted a nesting pair in 1986. Black-capped closely resembles Black-tailed Gnatcatcher, but the underside of its tail is largely white, similar to that of Blue-gray Gnatcatcher. There are also a few winter records; however, it is extremely difficult to separate Black-caps from the numerous Blue-grays at that season. Look for the Black-capped Gnatcatcher's slightly longer bill and—compared to Blue-gray—more strongly graduated tail. Also listen for the mewing call, similar to that of California Gnatcatcher.

Eastern Bluebird—Uncommon permanent resident in grassy pine/oak woodlands and open pine forests of the Border Ranges. The Mexican subspecies, *fulva,* sometimes called "Azure Bluebird," is at the northern limits of its distribution in Southeastern Arizona. Look for it at Hank and Yank Spring at the head of Sycamore Canyon, in Harshaw Canyon near Patagonia, at the confluence of Sawmill and Garden Canyons in the Huachucas, and in North Fork Cave Creek in the first mile above the Southwestern Research Station in the Chiricahua Mountains.

Western Bluebird—Uncommon summer resident of the Ponderosa Pines in the Santa Catalina and Chiricahua Mountains. Lower and usually more common in winter, when it is found in areas with abundant berries, especially junipers, hackberries, and any trees with mistletoe. In summer watch for Westerns at Rose Canyon Lake and Rustler Park. During most winters they can be found in Molino Basin, along the Ruby Road near Peña Blanca Lake, in Harshaw Canyon near Patagonia, in the oaks of the San Rafael Valley, and along the road to Paradise in the Chiricahua Mountains. During invasion winters it is common in agricultural areas such as the Marana Pecan Grove.

Mountain Bluebird—Irregular winter visitor to open valleys and open foothill scrub. Sometimes Mountain Bluebirds are almost non-existent in Southeastern Arizona; in other years there are flocks of hundreds. Watch for it in open deserts, pastures, and particularly in plowed fields. Locations include the Santa Cruz River at San Xavier Mission, Arivaca, Kino Springs, Sonoita Grassland, Palominas Road in the San Pedro Valley, at the Spitler Cattle Company in the Sulphur Springs Valley, and in the Whitetail Prairie north of Paradise in the Chiricahuas.

Townsend's Solitaire—Fairly common winter visitor, primarily to juniper woodlands and riparian groves in foothills and lower mountain canyons. Numbers vary from one year to the next. The most dependable locations include Redington Pass east of Tucson, Box Canyon on the north end of the Santa Ritas, Harshaw Canyon near Patagonia, Garden Canyon in the Huachucas, along the road to Paradise from Portal, and Guadalupe Canyon.

Rufous-backed Robin—Rare and reclusive winter visitor from Mexico in damp, dense valley, foothill, and lower mountain canyon thickets. This bird may mingle with flocks of American Robins, but skulks in the background. It is often found in dense groves of hackberries. Recent sightings are from the Arizona-Sonora Desert Museum, Kino Springs, the Patagonia-Sonoita Creek Preserve, Harshaw Canyon, Ramsey Canyon, and along the San Pedro River at Hereford and Palominas. There are only four summer records: one from Madera Canyon, one from Sonoita, another from Whitetail Canyon in the Chiricahuas, and one from Guadalupe Canyon. Your best bets are to ask local birders about recent sightings and to stay tuned to the Tucson Audubon Society rare-bird tape.

Aztec Thrush—Very rare summer visitor to wet canyon riparian woods in the Border Ranges. There is one winter record from January 1991 of a bird feasting on Pyracantha berries at Portal in the Chiricahua Mountains. Since the first Aztec Thrush was discovered in Madera Canyon in May 1978, there have been almost annual sightings, especially in August. Madera Canyon has produced more records than any other location, but Aztecs have also been reported from Huachuca, Garden, upper Carr near Comfort Spring, and Ramsey Canyons in the Huachucas, and from South Fork Cave Creek in the Chiricahuas. Birders inexperienced with this species may confuse a black-and-white juvenile Spotted Towhee for an Aztec Thrush, but the bill shape should be diagnostic. Watch for a nervous adult Spotted Towhee in close proximity. (If it feeds the bird in question, that's a very good clue!) The Aztec Thrush is one species that always makes the Tucson Audubon Society rare-bird tape.

Sage Thrasher—Uncommon winter visitor in sparse vegetation in the deserts, valley mesquite grasslands, and open foothills. Sometimes common in migration. Most often found at San Xavier Mission, Redington Pass, along Mile Wide Road in Avra Valley, Box Canyon Road near Madera Canyon, Harshaw Canyon near Patagonia, Charleston Road east of the San Pedro River, Double Adobe Road in the Sulphur Springs Valley, and the Paradise Road in the Chiricahua Mountains.

Bendire's Thrasher—Uncommon to fairly common resident in desert mesquite and valley mesquite grasslands, especially in hedgerows along fence-lines. Hard to find and to identify. Easiest when singing in January and February. Good locations include Thornydale Road in northwest Tucson, San Xavier Mission, along Central Highway in the Sulphur Springs Valley, Stateline Road near Rodeo, and along the Guadalupe Canyon Road.

Curve-billed Thrasher—Very common permanent resident of desert and valley mesquite grasslands. Unlike other members of its clan, this thrasher is not shy. It is often seen perched in the top of trees or utility poles, giving a sharp, human-like *Whit-wheet!* whistle, as if to attract your attention. Easy to find at the Arizona-Sonora Desert Museum, Tucson Mountain Park, Sabino Canyon, Saguaro National Park, along the Santa Cruz and San Pedro Rivers, at the Patagonia Roadside Rest Area, in the patches of Chihuahuan Desert near Tombstone and Douglas, and at Portal. This is the thrasher that inhabits Tucson and all other towns in Southeastern Arizona.

Crissal Thrasher—Fairly common but difficult-to-see permanent resident of dense thickets along dry washes in the deserts, valley mesquite grasslands, and in interior chaparral in the foothills. Crissals are almost as bold as Curved-bills from January through March, when birds tee up on the tallest brush in their territories to sing their long-drawn ballads that end with *chee-ry! chee-ry! toit toit.* Watch for this species at San Xavier Mission, Molino Basin, Florida Wash, on desert terraces along the San Pedro River, in Silver Creek near Portal, and in Guadalupe Canyon.

Le Conte's Thrasher—Rare and local resident of open, sandy creosote flats in the Colorado River Sonoran Desertscrub west and north of Tucson. This retiring bird is easiest to find when singing in January and February. Responds well to recordings of its call, particularly in late winter. Known locations in Avra Valley include south on the dirt track from the end of Mile Wide Road, and west on Emigh Road from its junction with Sandario Road at Marana High School. Watch for this pale thrasher to run between the shrubs, rather than fly.

Blue Mockingbird—Casual winter visitor to hackberry groves in foothill riparian canyons along the Mexican border. There are at least two U.S. records, one from the Circle Z Guest Ranch south of the Patagonia-Sonoita Creek Preserve from late December 1991 through early March 1992, and another from lower Cave Creek Canyon near Portal from January through early April 1995. Neither bird was particularly shy and both vocalized fairly frequently as they foraged thrasher-style under shrubs or clambered around small trees searching for dried fruits. Calls include a rich, inquisitive *querp?* and a burbling, well-spaced series of characteristic mimic-thrush notes. A third bird was seen briefly in desertscrub in Tucson in late September 1992, but that individual may have been an escapee. Blue Mockingbird is known to use thorn forest streams just 125 miles south of the border in Sonora; deeper into the Sierra Madre it follows deciduous growth up watercourses into pine/oak woodlands.

Sprague's Pipit—Rare winter visitor to tall, valley grasslands. Its distinctive flight-style, an abrupt climb followed by a plummeting descent back into the grass, is probably the best give-away to its presence. It may also give a loud *squeet* alarm note at take-off. Most birders looking for this species in Southeastern Arizona gravitate to the San Rafael Grassland. Other proven locations are on the Buenos Aires National Wildlife Refuge, in the Sonoita Grassland, and near McNeal off Leslie Canyon Road in the Sulphur Springs Valley.

Phainopepla—Common permanent resident of desert mesquites, river valley elderberries, and foothill canyons with juniper, especially where the trees are laden with mistletoe. Uncommon in the eastern sector in winter. Easy to find in the desert at Arizona-Sonora Desert Museum, the west unit of Saguaro National Park, Sabino Canyon, Kino Springs, Patagonia-Sonoita Creek Preserve, along the San Pedro River, and in Guadalupe Canyon.

Bell's Vireo—Fairly common summer resident in dense riparian thickets in the foothills, especially in mesquite/hackberry associations. Look for it at Sabino Canyon, along the Santa Cruz River at Continental and Tubac, in the Patagonia-Sonoita Creek Preserve, along the San Pedro River at Charleston and Hereford, along Cave Creek Canyon below Portal, at the east entrance to Aravaipa Canyon near Klondyke, and at the entrance to Guadalupe Canyon. This bird generally goes undetected unless its distinctive call is learned. It usually consists of two parts of three notes each: *cheedle cheedle chee—cheedle cheedle cher.* The first phrase ends with a rising inflection, as if the bird were asking a question. The second phrase, which is given after a short pause, ends with a downward turn, as if in answer to the first part. Some birds ask a lot of questions; others have mostly answers.

Gray Vireo—Rare and local summer resident of arid Pinyon Pine/juniper hillsides in the foothills. A scattering of winter records, primarily in desert mesquite. Gray Vireo is rarely seen in migration away from its breeding localities. Summer records come from Redington Pass east of Tucson, the Muleshoe Ranch in the Galiuro Mountains, and the east end of Aravaipa Canyon, especially from its Bear Canyon tributary. During some years, it is also reported from Silver Creek in the Chiricahuas.

Both in song and plumage pattern, the common "Plumbeous" race of the Solitary Vireo is easily mistaken for Gray Vireo. The Gray Vireo, however, usually shows a single faint wing-bar on a brownish wing, and the way it flicks its long tail is reminiscent of a gnatcatcher. When feeding, Gray Vireo stays low in chaparral.

Solitary Vireo—The gray-backed, white-bellied "Plumbeous" form found in the Rocky Mountains and Great Basin is a common summer resident in mountain canyon groves, pine/oak woodland, and Ponderosa Pine forest. "Plumbeous Vireo" is the only form that breeds here. During winter it is rare in valley and foothill mesquite and cottonwood woodlands, and is a vagrant in lower-canyon sycamores. The greenish-backed "Cassin's Vireo" race is a fairly common migrant through wooded habitats from desert oases up through pine forest. It is rare in western valley mesquite bosques and cottonwood groves in winter. Only hypothetical in Arizona, "Blue-headed Vireo," the breeding race of eastern North

America, was reported twice from the upper San Pedro River in September and November of 1987.

Hutton's Vireo—Common permanent resident of mountain oak and Sierra Madrean pine/oak woodland, especially in canyons. Look for it in Madera Canyon, Garden Canyon, and Cave Creek Canyons in the Chiricahuas. What may appear to be a vaguely annoyed expression of its face, a deliberate foraging strategy, and a lack of a black posterior wing-bar, all help to distinguish it from the similar Ruby-crowned Kinglet, which shares its habitat in winter. The vireo responds well to squeaks and owl calls.

Yellow-green Vireo—A summer vagrant to valley and foothill cottonwood groves along the border in June and July, with a possible sighting in early September 1989. No more than five records altogether, and no documented records since a bird was taped near the Patagonia-Sonoita Creek Preserve in 1969. With a gray cap, distinct whitish eye-brow, dull red eye, greenish back, yellow flanks, and white underparts, this bird should not be easily confused with any other vireo. (Red-eyed Vireo, a rare migrant, is more expected.)

Migrant Warblers—Because of the mild weather in Arizona, large concentrations of migrants are uncommon. You may find them almost anywhere from the mesquite thickets on the deserts to the wooded canyons of the mountains. A few of the spots that are often visited by the local birders during early spring are the Marana Pecan Grove, Sabino Canyon, Kino Springs, Patagonia-Sonoita Creek Preserve, and Highway 90 Bridge and Charleston on the San Pedro River. By May, warblers and other migrant landbirds are as likely to be found in mountain canyons as in the desert oases. During the fall migration, from late July through October, many migrants move through the mountains. Some of the spring sites (e.g., Marana Pecan Grove) are particularly productive in fall.

Some of the warblers that are found here only as migrants are Nashville, Townsend's, Hermit, Northern Waterthrush, MacGillivray's, and Wilson's. There are also records for many Eastern vagrants, such as Golden-winged, Tennessee, Black-and-white, Northern Parula, Magnolia, Black-throated Blue, Chestnut-sided, Prairie, Ovenbird, Kentucky, Hooded, and American Redstart.

Virginia's Warbler—Fairly common summer resident of interior chaparral and oak/juniper woodland on dry hillsides in the mountains. Often comes down to canyon bottoms on brushy slopes. Look for it near the upper end of the Oracle Road in the Santa Catalina Mountains, in Madera Canyon in the Santa Ritas, Scheelite Canyon in the Huachucas, and in South Fork Cave Creek and along the road between Onion Saddle and Rustler Park in the Chiricahua Mountains.

Lucy's Warbler—Common summer resident in dense stands of mesquite and hackberry in desert washes and valley cottonwood groves, but often hard to see well. Some good locations are near San Xavier Mission, Florida Wash, Kino Springs, Patagonia-Sonoita Creek Preserve, the San Pedro River, and Portal. Nests in tree cavities. The first summer warbler to arrive and depart, Lucy's is uncommon at best from the beginning of July to the end of September. The Marana Pecan Grove is an excellent fall location for Lucy's Warbler.

Tropical Parula—There is only one record of this Mexican vagrant, a bird that summered in Madera Canyon from mid-July through mid-September 1984. It was possibly joined by a female for a single day soon after it arrived. Tropical Parulas use subtropical thorn forest and lower pine/oak woodland canyons in southern Sonora. They can be separated from Northern Parulas, which are rare annual migrants through the same habitats, by the lack of white eye-crescents and more extensive yellow on the lower face and lower belly.

Crescent-chested Warbler—Mexican vagrant to wet canyons within Sierra Madrean pine/oak woodland in the Huachuca Mountains, and cottonwood groves in the Patagonia-Sonoita Creek Preserve. After this southern species made its U.S. debut in Garden Canyon in the Huachucas in early September 1983, a pair appeared in Ramsey Canyon the following spring from late April to mid-May 1984. No further Crescent-chesteds were seen until a bird was discovered at the Patagonia-Sonoita Creek Preserve in mid-September 1992. This bird entertained hundreds of birders throughout the winter, and it—or a wandering kinsman—returned to Patagonia from mid-November 1993 through mid-January 1994. Crescent-chested Warblers in Arizona have thus far been found in mixed flocks containing Bridled Titmice and Yellow-rumped Warblers.

Black-throated Gray Warbler—Common summer resident in oak, pine/oak, and pinyon/juniper woodlands in the mountains. Not hard to find in Molino Basin, Sycamore Canyon, Madera Canyon, Ramsey Canyon Preserve, and Cave Creek Canyon. This bird likes to feed on the sunny slopes. Responds well to squeaks and owl toots. A few winter in riparian areas around Tucson.

Grace's Warbler—Common summer resident of tall Sierra Madrean pine/oak woodland and Ponderosa Pine forest in the mountains. Follows the conifers down canyonbottoms, and is usually found gleaning among the needles at the top of a pine tree. Sings its accelerating trill frequently. Look for it at Rose Canyon Lake in the Santa Catalinas, above the end of the road in Madera Canyon, at Sawmill Canyon and Ramsey Vista Campgrounds in the Huachucas, and in South Fork Cave Creek and Rustler Park in the Chiricahuas.

Red-faced Warbler—Common summer resident of Gambel's Oak and aspen groves within mountain coniferous forest, and upper canyons with maples or other deciduous trees. Occurs lower in major wet canyons during migration periods in April and August. Nests on the ground under a small tree or grass clump. This handsome bird can be found at Rose Canyon Lake, Bear Wallow, Marshall Gulch, and at the Ski Valley area in the Santa Catalinas; usually one-half mile or higher above the road end in the Hopkins Fork of Madera Canyon; at the one-half-mile marker and above in Scheelite Canyon, upper Ramsey Canyon, and at Comfort Spring in the Huachucas; and at Pinery Canyon Campground, Rustler Park, and beginning about 2 miles up South Fork Cave Creek in the Chiricahua Mountains. Responds well to owl toots and pishing (for the toot-challenged).

Painted Redstart—Common summer resident in Sierra Madrean pine/oak woodlands in the mountains, most common along streams. Easy to find at Rose Canyon Lake in the Santa Catalina Mountains, in Sycamore Canyon west of Nogales, Madera Canyon in the Santa Ritas, Ramsey Canyon in the Huachucas, and Cave Creek Canyon in the Chiricahuas. A few winter, especially at canyon homes with humming-bird feeders, such as the Spoffords' in Portal and Santa Rita Lodge in Madera Canyon.

This little jewel actually seems to come out to twist, turn, flutter, and spread its white outer-tail feathers as if to say, "Look at me! Look at me!" If you give an owl call, you may get mobbed. You will undoubtedly see many of these flashing beauties, but you will never get to the point of saying, "It's just a redstart." Each one is too pretty and too animated to pass up.

Slate-throated Redstart—A vagrant from south of the border; the only definite record came from pine/oak woodland canyon thickets in Miller Canyon of the Huachuca Mountains in April 1976. There are additional sight reports from Portal in May 1978, Sawmill Canyon in the Huachucas in July 1988, and from South Fork Cave Creek in the Chiricahuas in March 1993. This species can be readily distinguished from the common Painted Redstart by the absence of a white crescent under the eye, lack of white markings on the wings, and reduced white in the tail.

Fan-tailed Warbler—Mexican vagrant to shady, cliff-walled canyon thickets, usually near water, within Sierra Madrean pine/oak woodland in the Border Ranges. The first record for both Arizona and the U.S. came from Baker Canyon, a tributary of Guadalupe Canyon, in late May 1961. The next sighting was in Scheelite Canyon in May 1983, followed by an observation in nearby Garden Canyon in May 1984. A Fan-tail discovered in Sycamore Canyon west of Nogales was seen by numerous birders in June and July 1987. The most recent sighting in Guadalupe Canyon in September 1990 is supported by photographs. Fan-tails forage near or on the ground, expressively fanning a long, white-tipped tail, especially in response to pygmy-owl toots. They are known to nest approximately 10 miles south of Guadalupe Canyon in Cajón Bonito, Sonora.

Rufous-capped Warbler—Mexican summer vagrant to cliff-walled canyon thickets within Sierra Madrean pine/oak woodland in the Border Ranges. The first Arizona record was of a female that nested unsuccessfully midway between Sunny Flat Campground and the Southwestern Research Station in Cave Creek Canyon of the Chiricahuas in May 1977. Probably the same bird returned to this location in April 1978. Rufouscaps have since been observed at Coronado National Memorial in August 1983, and Comfort Spring in the Huachuca Mountains in April 1985, and from California Gulch in July 1993 and Sycamore Canyon west of Nogales from mid-March through June 1994. There were also sightings of up to three birds in spring/summer of 1995 in French Joe Canyon in the Whetstone Mountains north of Sierra Vista. Both the long, cocked tail and the behavior of this understory species are reminiscent of a Bewick's Wren.

Olive Warbler—Fairly common summer resident of mountain coniferous forests. Rare in winter in canyon riparian, occasionally descending to valley groves. This bird can be hard to spot as it feeds in a deliberate manner among the needles at the top of a pine. Good locations include Rose Canyon Lake in the Santa Catalina Mountains, Sawmill and Ramsey Vista Campgrounds in the Huachuca Mountains, and Barfoot Junction on the road to Rustler Park in the Chiricahua Mountains. One of the easiest places to find this bird is the Chiricahua Crest Trail to Barfoot Lookout, which offers tree-top-level views of the canopy.

Hepatic Tanager—Common summer resident of canyon groves, pine/oak woodlands, and pine forests in the mountains. Rose Canyon Lake, Sycamore Canyon, Madera Canyon, Scheelite Canyon in the Huachucas, and South Fork Cave Creek are all proven locations for Hepatic Tanagers. Rarely winters in Southeastern Arizona, with recent reports from the Patagonia-Sonoita Creek Preserve, and Madera, and Sycamore Canyons. Compared to the brilliant red of a Summer Tanager, the male Hepatic is dull brick-red. Both sexes have blackish bills and gray cheeks and flanks that serve to distinguish them from either sex of the

Summer. Their call notes are also distinctive—the Hepatic utters a single
chuck note, while the Summer gives a tri-syllabic *Kit-ty-tuck!*

Summer Tanager—Common summer resident of valley and foothill
riparian groves, particularly in cottonwoods. Can be found at Kino
Springs, Patagonia-Sonoita Creek Preserve, the San Pedro River, and at
Portal.

Western Tanager—Common summer resident in mountain coniferous forests. During the prolonged spring and fall migrations Western
Tanagers are common in virtually all Southeastern Arizona habitats,
including desert washes, valley cottonwoods, and canyon sycamores.
The Ski Valley area in the Santa Catalina Mountains, Reef Townsite
Campground in the Huachucas, and Rustler Park in the Chiricahuas are
breeding areas. In migration Western Tanagers are common at such
lowland locations as the Arizona-Sonora Desert Museum, Marana Pecan
Grove, Kino Springs, and the San Pedro River.

Flame-colored Tanager—Very rare summer resident of tall canyon
timber within Sierra Madrean pine/oak woodland in the Border Ranges.
After the first U.S. record of a male in South Fork Cave Creek from
mid-April through mid-July 1985, there was a seven-year hiatus until
March 1992 when Flame-colored Tanagers appeared in both Madera
Canyon and in the Ramsey Canyon Preserve. A report from Miller
Canyon in May 1994 expanded into another Huachuca drainage the
areas where they are known to have occurred. Beginning with the Cave
Creek bird that mated with a Western Tanager (and successfully fledged
two hybrid young), Flame-colored Tanagers have attempted to nest in
both Madera Canyon and the Ramsey Canyon Preserve. Like Western
Tanagers—and unlike Hepatics or Summers—Flame-colored Tanagers
have wing-bars. They can be separated from Westerns, however, by the
large, charcoal-colored bill and dark-bordered cheek-patch. The stripes
on its back are also diagnostic—if they are visible. Young males have
flecks of orange on the face; as they mature the orange-red coloration
spreads back over the entire body. Females of any age are bright yellow.
They can be separated from female Westerns by their dark bill, dark ear
outline, thick white wingbars, and streaked back.

Northern Cardinal—Common permanent resident of thickets and
riparian woodlands in deserts, valley mesquite grasslands, and foothill
canyons. Usually easy to find at Sabino Canyon, San Xavier Mission,
Saguaro National Park, Kino Springs, Patagonia-Sonoita Creek Preserve,
San Pedro River at the San Pedro House, and Portal.

Pyrrhuloxia—Fairly common to common permanent resident in
thickets and riparian woodlands in deserts, valley mesquite grasslands,

and foothill canyons. More common from the San Pedro Valley westward to about Ajo. Pyrrhuloxias have the peculiar habit of moving up in elevation into the canyon outlets of the Border Ranges during winter. Locations include San Xavier Mission, Marana Pecan Grove, Tubac, Patagonia-Sonoita Creek Preserve, the lower Ramsey Canyon Road, Sulphur Springs Valley, and—during winter—Portal.

Yellow Grosbeak—Approximately 15 summer records exist for this Mexican vagrant since its first appearance in the United States near Patagonia in 1971. Most records are "one-day wonders." Virtually all records fall in either June or July. It seems to prefer major sycamore canyons with streams in the border ranges and river valley cottonwood groves with permanent water. Madera Canyon has had the most records, but this species has also been reported from the Patagonia Roadside Rest Area, Ramsey Canyon Preserve, Sycamore Canyon, the San Pedro River at Fairbank, and Cave Creek Canyon at the Southwestern Research Station. Yellow Grosbeak is sure to get top billing on the Tucson Audubon Society rare-bird tape if one strays into the Southeastern corner.

Black-headed Grosbeak—Common summer resident of canyon riparian groves, pine/oak woodland, and open Ponderosa Pine forest in the mountains. Migrates through desert oases and valley groves. Easy to find at Rose Canyon Lake, and Sycamore, Madera, Ramsey, and Cave Creek Canyons. Common during migration at the Patagonia-Sonoita Creek Preserve and along the San Pedro River.

Blue Grosbeak—Common summer resident of mesquite valley grassland and foothill canyon thickets. Very rare in winter. Probably reaches its greatest density in the weedy edges of irrigated fields. Reliable locations are Kino Springs, Patagonia-Sonoita Creek Preserve, San Pedro River, Cochise College campus in the Sulphur Springs Valley, Stateline Road near Rodeo, and the big mesquite thicket between Portal and the USFS boundary.

Lazuli Bunting—Common spring and fall migrant in valley riparian thickets, tall weeds on the edge of irrigated fields and ponds, and foothill canyon thickets. Uncommon winter visitor. Rare in summer. Can be found at the Marana Pecan Grove, Kino Springs, Patagonia-Sonoita Creek Preserve, Sierra Vista Wastewater Ponds, San Pedro House, Willcox golf-course pond, and at Portal.

Varied Bunting—Fairly common local summer resident in foothill canyon mesquite thickets and thornscrub. Proven locations are lower Sycamore Canyon west of Nogales, Florida Wash and Proctor Road on the road into Madera Canyon, the first pond at Kino Springs, Patagonia Roadside Rest Area, Fairbank on the San Pedro River, Sulphur Draw one mile west of Willow Tank near Rodeo, and the entrance at Guadalupe Canyon. This bird can be hard to find unless you hear the male singing from an exposed perch early in the morning before the temperature climbs.

Green-tailed Towhee—Fairly common migrant and uncommon winter visitor to desert and valley field hedgerows and thickets, and dense brush in foothill canyons. Numbers fluctuate from year to year. Green-tailed Towhees can be found at San Xavier Mission, Marana Pecan Grove, Florida Wash, Kino Springs, Patagonia-Sonoita Creek Preserve, San Pedro River at Fairbank, and Portal.

Spotted Towhee—Common permanent resident in foothill and mountain thickets. A few descend into desert and valley thickets during winter. Locations to look for Spotted Towhees include Rose Canyon Lake in the Santa Catalinas, Madera Canyon in the Santa Ritas, Miller Canyon in the Huachucas, and Cave Creek Canyon in the Chiricahuas.

Canyon Towhee—Common permanent resident of the thickets in deserts, valleys, foothills, and lower mountain canyons. This bird may not be colorful, but it is confiding. Often seen about cabins, picnic areas, and parking areas. Easy to find at San Xavier Mission, Molino Basin, Florida Wash, Peña Blanca Lake, Patagonia Roadside Rest Area, San Pedro House, and Portal. If you miss it at any of these spots, check under your car before you drive off.

Abert's Towhee—Fairly common permanent resident of the undergrowth in valley mesquite thickets and riparian woodlands, usually near permanent water. Abert's has one of the smallest ranges of any species that lives primarily in the U.S. Can be found at San Xavier Mission, Marana Pecan Grove, Kino Springs, Patagonia-Sonoita Creek Preserve, the San Pedro House, and—since the early 1990s—just downstream from Portal along Cave Creek.

Botteri's Sparrow—Fairly common summer resident of valley mesquite grasslands, especially in stands of tall Sacaton Grass. Difficult to find and to identify except when it sings its "bouncing ball" song during the rainy season from July through September. Has been found along the Box Canyon Road below Madera Canyon, at the Nogales Airport, the Research Ranch near Elgin, the grassland below Garden Canyon in the Huachucas, at the San Pedro House, in fields west of Rodeo, and along the Guadalupe Canyon Road.

Cassin's Sparrow—Fairly common summer resident July through September, when its song can be heard in valley mesquite grasslands. In wet years it also sings from March to mid-May. Rare at other seasons. Cassin's occurs in the same areas and sings in the same season—fortunately, for identification purposes—as the similar Botteri's Sparrow. Proven locations include Florida Wash, Nogales Airport, Highway 82 east of Sonoita, lower Garden Canyon Road in the Huachuca Mountains, the San Pedro House, and at the junction of the San Simon and Portal Roads.

Rufous-winged Sparrow—Fairly common but local permanent resident of desertscrub and desert grasslands mixed with cholla near the Santa Rita Mountains, on the Tohono O'odham Nation lands, and in the Tucson area. Search for this species at the junction of Speedway and Anklam west of Tucson, San Xavier Mission, on Wilmot Road about one-half mile north of Interstate 10 in Tucson, at Sells, Florida Wash, Chino Canyon, and Santa Gertrudis Lane.

Rufous-crowned Sparrow—Common permanent resident on rocky slopes in the foothills and in interior chaparral in the mountains. Fairly easy to find in such areas as Sycamore Canyon, Peña Blanca Lake, Florida Wash, Patagonia Roadside Rest Area, Scheelite Canyon and Coronado National Memorial in the Huachucas, Chiricahua National Monument, Silver Creek near Portal, and Guadalupe Canyon.

Brewer's Sparrow—Common to abundant winter visitor in desert, weedy fields, valley mesquite grasslands, and lower canyon outlets. Fairly easy to find off Sandario Road in Avra Valley west of Tucson, Marana Pecan Grove, Kino Springs, Palominas Road west of the San Pedro River, Cochise College west of Douglas, in the Sulphur Springs Valley, and along Portal Road.

Black-chinned Sparrow—Uncommon permanent resident of interior chaparral in the Santa Catalina Mountains, the Mule Mountains north of Bisbee, and the northeastern quarter of the Chiricahua Mountains. In winter, it uses mesquite thickets in desert washes and foothills. Summer locations are Molino Basin in the Santa Catalinas and Silver Creek in the Chiricahuas. In winter Black-chins can be found in King Canyon across Kinney Road from the entrance to the Arizona-Sonora Desert Museum, Florida Wash, and in good numbers between Portal and the USFS boundary in Cave Creek Canyon. Some winters they are also at Catalina State Park and below Proctor Road in lower Madera Canyon.

Black-throated Sparrow—Common permanent resident in both Sonoran and Chihuahuan desertscrub. Easy to find in the desert surrounding Tucson, Florida Wash, along the San Pedro River at Charleston, in the desert between Portal and Rodeo, and along the road into Guadalupe Canyon.

Five-striped Sparrow—Rare summer resident of Foothill Thornscrub on steep-walled foothill canyons along the Mexican border. Occasional in winter. Since the discovery of a lone bird in 1957 in lower Madera Canyon, Five-stripes have been found regularly at a few canyons in the region. Most birders try California Gulch four miles from the Ruby Road west of Nogales. Sycamore Canyon is another location, beginning about three miles down. There are also records from both Chino Canyon on the west side of the Santa Ritas and along Sonoita Creek below the Patagonia Roadside Rest Area.

Lark Bunting—Common to abundant winter visitor to open desert flats and valley fields and grasslands. Lark Buntings arrive in August and do not depart till early June. Fields along the Santa Cruz River at San Xavier Mission, Sierra Vista Wastewater Ponds, Willcox golf course, west of Cochise College in the Sulphur Springs Valley, and along the Stateline Road near Rodeo usually host dozens, if not hundreds, of buntings.

Baird's Sparrow—Uncommon but rarely-seen winter visitor to high valley grasslands along the border. Seems to prefer areas where the grass is fairly tall or mixed with a few weeds on rolling hills. Most Tucson birders look for Baird's in the San Rafael Valley. It also occurs on the Buenos Aires National Wildlife Refuge, in the Sonoita Grassland, along the Palominas Road in the upper San Pedro Valley, and east of McNeal off Leslie Canyon Road in the Sulphur Springs Valley.

Yellow-eyed Junco—Common permanent resident of grassy areas within mountain coniferous forests. Easy to find in summer at Rose Canyon Lake and Ski Valley in the Santa Catalinas, at the Ramsey Vista Campground in the Huachucas, and at Rustler Park in the Chiricahua Mountains. When populations are high, Yellow-eyed Junco also breeds in grassy areas of major canyons such as Madera, Ramsey, and South Fork Cave Creek. Look for it at the Santa Rita Lodge, Ramsey Canyon Preserve, Portal, and other canyon outlets during winter.

McCown's Longspur—Rare winter visitor in bare valley fields, stubble, and sparse grasses. This hard-to-see species has been found in the Sonoita Grassland, in the San Rafael Valley, at the Sierra Vista Wastewater fields, and in fields along Highway 191 north of Elfrida on the Spitler Cattle Company land and at Seven Leagues Ranch. Look for it amid flocks of Horned Larks.

Chestnut-collared Longspur—Common winter visitor in tall valley grasslands near Sonoita, in the San Rafael Valley, in the Sulphur Springs Valley at Spitler Cattle Company, and at Willow Tank near Rodeo. Sometimes abundant in migration.

Eastern Meadowlark—Common permanent resident of valley grasslands from Arivaca and the Santa Rita Mountains eastward. Less common westward and in winter. Easy to find near Sonoita, in the San Rafael

Valley, at the San Pedro House, lower Ramsey Canyon Road, Spitler Cattle Company in the Sulphur Springs Valley, and along the Portal Road. The race of Eastern Meadowlark that breeds in Southeastern Arizona, *lilianae,* has virtually pure-white outer-tail feathers, slightly whiter than those of Western Meadowlark. The only useful visible field character is a distinct blackish post-ocular stripe that contrasts with *lilianae's* pale cheek. In Western Meadowlark, the stripe behind the eye blurs into a darker-streaked cheek. Voice is always preferable to nuances of plumage when separating the two meadowlark species.

Western Meadowlark—Fairly common winter resident of valley grasslands and irrigated fields near Tucson and west of the Santa Rita Mountains. In winter it can usually be found near San Xavier Mission or in the fields adjacent to the Marana Pecan Grove. Less common farther east during winter at such locations as the Sierra Vista Wastewater fields and at Spitler Cattle Company fields in the Sulphur Springs Valley. Western Meadowlarks are rare and irregular breeders on the Santa Cruz River near Tucson and in Avra Valley during exceptionally wet years. The last documented nest in the Sulphur Springs Valley was found in 1941.

Yellow-headed Blackbird—Common to abundant winter visitor and uncommon summer resident in the valleys near permanent water with tall reeds. Also winters at cattle pens and in irrigated fields. The most reliable sites are at Picacho Reservoir, Sierra Vista Wastewater Ponds, farm ponds and fields along the Hereford Road east of the San Pedro River, and the Willcox golf-course pond.

Great-tailed Grackle—Common permanent resident in cities, on farms, and at tree-lined ponds in the deserts and valleys. The first record of this bird in Southeastern Arizona was in 1935 at Safford. Now it is common in every city and town below 4,500 feet in elevation.

Bronzed Cowbird—Common summer resident of irrigated fields, golf courses, and lawns, and uncommon in mountain canyons with syca- mores. Rare in winter at livestock pens in the Santa Cruz Valley. In summer some good locations include the Arizona-Sonora Desert Mu- seum, Madera Canyon, Kino Springs golf course club-house, the Patago- nia city park, and Portal. In winter, Bronzed Cowbirds can occasionally be found at the cattle pens north of Tucson just east of Cortaro.

Black-vented Oriole—Mexican vagrant in spring and possibly sum- mer to canyon riparian in foothills thickets and mountains along the border. This beautiful oriole is superficially similar to Scott's, but it lacks any white in the wing and has an all-black tail, including the undertail coverts. The only accepted Arizona record is from Patagonia Lake State

Park on April 18, 1991. There is also another possibly valid record from Cave Creek Canyon in the Chiricahuas dating back to July 1971.

Hooded Oriole—Common summer resident in desert oases, valley groves, and sycamore canyons in foothills and lower mountains. Increasingly common in the cities, particularly around hummingbird-feeders. Occasionally winters in Tucson. Nests in palm trees in the cities, and in walnuts, sycamores, and cottonwoods elsewhere. Can be found in Tucson, at the Arizona-Sonora Desert Museum, Sycamore Canyon, Madera Canyon, Patagonia Roadside Rest Area, San Pedro House, and at Portal.

Streak-backed Oriole—Very rare Mexican resident along the lower San Pedro and the lower Santa Cruz River Valleys, but seen mainly in fall and winter. Nearly annual now at Dudleyville. Nesting pairs successfully fledged young at Dudleyville in 1993 and 1994, and were nesting there again in 1995. Another pair nested unsuccessfully near the Marana Pecan Grove in 1994. In Sonora, Mexico, it is found in river valley riparian woodland thickets, where it builds large pendulous nests on the ends of dangling limbs. Has wintered sporadically in Tucson, Green Valley, and Arivaca. This bird usually tops the Tucson Audubon Society rare-bird tape when it is present.

Bullock's Oriole—Common summer resident in desert oases, valley groves, and sycamore canyons in foothills and lower mountains. Rarely winters in Tucson. Proven locations include the Santa Rita Lodge in Madera Canyon, Patagonia-Sonoita Creek Preserve, San Pedro House on the San Pedro River, and at private-residence feeders in Portal. (In Southeastern Arizona Baltimore Oriole is strictly a vagrant.)

Scott's Oriole—Common summer resident of upper valley yucca grasslands, foothill oak savanna, and mountain pine/oak woodlands. Very rare in winter at feeders in the Santa Cruz Valley and lower mountain canyons. Usually nests in yucca, but occasionally in small trees. Can be found in Molino Basin, in the agaves along Highway 82 just east of Sonoita, in the yuccas along Highway 92 south of Sierra Vista, along Highway 181 west of Chiricahua National Monument, and in the mountain canyons such as Madera, Ramsey, Miller, and Cave Creek. Visits canyon hummingbird-feeders in Madera Canyon, Ramsey Canyon, and at Portal in the spring, but much less often in summer. Somewhat regular but local during winter at private-residence feeders in Tucson and Nogales, and in Ash and Stump Canyons near Sierra Vista.

Cassin's Finch—Irregular but sometimes fairly common winter visitor in canyon riparian groves in mountain pine/oak woodlands and open pine-forest. During major invasions occasionally descends to Tucson.

Cassin's quickly becomes a habitué of seed-feeding stations in major canyons such as Madera, Ramsey, and Cave Creek.

Red Crossbill—Fairly common but irregular permanent resident of major canyons with tall pines and mountain coniferous forests. During some winters, crossbills descend to Tucson parks and cemeteries with conifers, where they have even been recorded breeding and lingering into summer. Sporadic, but possible, at Bear Canyon Picnic Area and Rose Canyon Lake in the Santa Catalinas, upper Madera Canyon in the Santa Ritas, Sawmill Canyon in the Huachucas, and at Rustler Park in the Chiricahuas. In many years, there is a flock between the Southwestern Research Station and Herb Martyr Recreation Site in Cave Creek Canyon.

Lesser Goldfinch—Common permanent resident of riparian thickets and river groves in the deserts, valleys, foothills, and mountain canyon outlets. Can be found at Aravaipa Canyon, the Marana Pecan Grove, Arivaca Creek, Kino Springs, Patagonia-Sonoita Creek Preserve, Upper Picnic Area in Garden Canyon in the Huachuca Mountains, Kingfisher Pond on the San Pedro River, and at Portal.

Lawrence's Goldfinch—Irregular and uncommon fall and winter visitor in desert and river valley weedy fields, pecan groves, and riparian woodlands. Most common in the lowlands and agricultural areas near Tucson. Proven locations are the Marana Pecan Grove, Tanque Verde Wash east of Tucson, Tubac, and Arivaca Creek. Every three to ten years there are invasions as far east as the upper San Pedro River at Hereford, and, very infrequently, to Portal.

Evening Grosbeak—Irregular and uncommon summer resident in mountain coniferous forests, usually near deciduous trees such as maples and Box Elders. Unpredictable but often found near Bear Wallow in the Santa Catalina Mountains, in Sawmill Canyon in the Huachucas, and at Rustler Park in the Chiricahuas. Rare in winter, usually at canyon feeders such as the Santa Rita Lodge in Madera Canyon, Ramsey Canyon Preserve, and at the Spoffords' home in Portal.

BIRDS OF SOUTHEASTERN ARIZONA

Bar-Graphs

All of the birds regularly occurring in Southeastern Arizona in an average year are represented in the following graphs, which are intended to give you a conservative idea of your chance of finding each of these species in a given season. Yearly population fluctuations, extremely early or late dates, and unusual occurrences are addressed in the species accounts found in the Specialties Section, not in these graphs. Birds that occur less than annually, are possible escapees, or are of dubious authenticity are listed in a separate appendix at the end.

The bar-graphs reflect the probability of your actually seeing the bird, rather than that bird's relative abundance. Thus a large raptor such as the Red-tailed Hawk is graphed as "Hard to Miss", while a shy, hard-to-identify, and smaller species such as Crissal Thrasher is shown as "May See"—even though it occurs within appropriate habitat in greater numbers than the ubiquitous Red-tail. The categories used in the bar-graphs are:

▬▬▬▬▬▬▬▬	HARD TO MISS = Abundant/Conspicuous
▬▬▬▬▬▬	SHOULD SEE = Common
══════	MAY SEE = Fairly Common
═════	LUCKY TO FIND = Uncommon
───────	HOW LUCKY CAN YOU GET = Rare
··············	IRREGULAR = Very Rare or Sporadic

If you are in the CORRECT HABITAT in a SUGGESTED LOCATION at the PROPER SEASON, you should be able to find the "**Hard to Miss**" birds on nearly every field trip, the "**Should See**" on at least 3 out of 4 trips, the "**May See**" 1 or 2 times every 4 trips, and the "**Lucky to Find**" on 1 out of every 10 trips or less often. The "**How Lucky Can You Get**" species occur at infrequent intervals or take an expert to identify.

For a few species, either of very "**Irregular**" occurrence or which sporadically arrive far earlier or linger far later than it was possible to represent using the above categories, a dotted line is used to show either their extreme rarity or the irruptive nature of their visits. This symbol is only used when a species exhibits a pattern of vagrancy that is possible to graph.

Many local people and others who bird the area frequently were consulted in determining the status of each bird. Since these birders are familiar with the birds, their songs, habits, and habitats, they are good at finding the more elusive species. On your first trip to the area, you may think that some species are harder to find than is indicated!

Habitat Categories

The habitat categories on the left half of each Bar-Graph are designed to tell you where to look for any regularly occurring bird. Of the ten different habitats included, four are riparian, underscoring the importance of water and its associated plants in determining bird distribution and abundance in Southeastern Arizona. The role of elevation and topography in shaping the vegetative community also limits the species of birds that may occur in any given location. In the habitat chart the elevational limits of the habitats are indicated in feet.

Seasonal "pie charts" indicate the times of the year when each species is most likely to be found in any given habitat. Yellow-rumped Warblers, for example, breed in the coniferous forest on the mountain peaks during summer, and they winter in desert and foothill habitats. The bar-graph represents them only as common year-round. Using the seasonal pie charts in conjunction with the habitat checklist should enable you to predict exactly where you ought to invest your time and energy when searching for any given species.

The following locations within each habitat type are described in the text. They are listed with those nearest to Tucson first, followed by those progressively farther away. Remember that the locations cited below are *not* comprehensive; there are other possible areas within each habitat category that may be equally productive. Also remember that birds are the most mobile of all wildlife. Most birds can and do occur outside of their "preferred" habitats.

Rivers, Ponds, and Lakes: Open water with or without associated marsh vegetation is the most limited habitat in Southeastern Arizona. Yet all of the pelagic and near-shore birds, herons and egrets, waterfowl, shorebirds, and gulls and terns in this region are dependent on it. With few exceptions, all large bodies of water in this area lie below 4,000 feet in elevation. Areas to visit to see open-water and marsh birds are: Avra Valley Sewage Ponds, Picacho Reservoir, Nogales Sewage Ponds, Aguirre Lake at Buenos Aires National Wildlife Refuge, Peña Blanca Lake, Big Pond at Sells, Kino Springs, Patagonia Lake, Parker Canyon Lake, Sierra Vista Wastewater Ponds, Kingfisher Pond, Willcox Playa, and Willow Tank east of Portal.

Desertscrub: Two distinct arid land biomes meet at elevations below 4,500 feet in Southeastern Arizona: the Sonoran and the Chihuahuan Deserts. Most desert birds, however, occur in both. Cactus Wren and Curve-billed Thrasher are examples of species which range across the lowlands of the entire area. Areas which harbor typical desert species include: Tucson, Sabino Canyon, the Arizona-Sonora Desert Museum, Saguaro National Park, the west entrance of Aravaipa Canyon, Sells, Fairbank on the San Pedro River, Douglas, and the Big Thicket east of Portal.

Valley Grassland and Desert Fields: This habitat includes vast tracts of unbroken savanna as well as the enormous fields at agricultural developments, also usually below 4,500 feet in elevation. Grasshopper Sparrows and Eastern Meadowlarks share this habitat with wintering Mountain Plovers and Chestnut-collared Longspurs. The best grasslands are those at the Buenos Aires National Wildlife Refuge, the Sonoita Grassland, the San Rafael Grassland, near Palominas in the San Pedro Valley, the Sulphur Springs Valley, and the upper San Bernardino Valley southeast of the Chiricahuas. Major agricultural areas are found in Avra Valley west of Tucson, near Picacho Reservoir, Kansas Settlement near Willcox, and in the southern Sulphur Springs Valley surrounding Elfrida.

Valley Groves and Pecan Farms: Tall groves of Fremont Cottonwoods and isolated stands of pecans in Southeastern Arizona's broad, arid valleys are magnets for breeding birds, migrants, and rarities that are often far out of range. Gray Hawks and Tropical Kingbirds are among the birds that prefer this habitat. Some of the areas to check for these species include city parks in Tucson, the Marana Pecan Grove, Tubac, the Patagonia-Sonoita Creek Preserve, Arivaca Cienaga, Dudleyville, Kino Springs, San Pedro House, Kingfisher Pond, and the San Bernardino National Wildlife Refuge.

Foothill Groves: Ordinarily, foothill groves occur at slightly higher elevations than valley groves, usually between 3,500 and 4,500 feet. Sycamore trees intertwine with cottonwoods in the canopy that shades foothill streams. They also have steep canyon walls that create a completely different "edge habitat" from the ecotone that separates river valley groves from the adjacent deserts, grassland, or agricultural fields. Many species are shared with valley groves but many others are not. Highly-restricted Thick-billed Kingbirds and Rose-throated Becards are good symbols for this habitat. Some of the foothill grove locations discussed in the text include: Patagonia Roadside Rest Area, Arivaca Creek, Aravaipa Canyon, Sycamore Canyon, Muleshoe Ranch Preserve, and Guadalupe Canyon.

Foothill Thornscrub: A subtropical thicket of spiny shrubs grows on sunny slopes above some foothill groves, generally between the same elevations of 3,500 and 4,500 feet. This limited habitat attracts a group of species that are more common in arid situations on the Pacific slope of western Mexico. Buff-collared Nightjar, Varied Bunting, and Five-striped Sparrow represent these species. Some areas with foothill thornscrub are Sutherland Wash in Catalina State Park, McCleary Wash below Madera Canyon, Chino Canyon, Patagonia Roadside Rest Area, the west entrance of Aravaipa Canyon, Sycamore Canyon and California Gulch west of the Atascosa Mountains, and Guadalupe Canyon.

Mountain Interior Chaparral: Where nights are too cold for the frost-sensitive species that grow in the foothill thornscrub, normally between elevations of 4,500 and 6,500 feet, a structurally similar set of plants covers the slopes.   In Southeastern Arizona, the primary plant constituents are frequently manzanita and Mountain Mahogany. Where soils are deeper, however, and there is adequate precipitation, a short woodland of Pinyon Pine and One-seed Juniper replaces the chaparral, but the birds are much the same. Breeding species include Western Scrub-Jay and Virginia's Warbler. Mountain Interior Chaparral and pinyon/juniper woodland can be found at Molino Basin in the Santa Catalina Mountains, in Scheelite Canyon in the Huachuca Mountains, in Coronado National Memorial, at Chiricahua National Monument, and in Silver Creek near Portal.

Mountain Pine/oak Woodland: Sierra Madrean pine/oak woodland is the largest single habitat type in Mexico. Here it reaches its northernmost outposts in the Border Ranges at mid-elevations between 5,000 and 7,000 feet. Dominant plants include a variety of spring deciduous oaks, Alligator Juniper, and both Chihuahua and Apache Pines. Strickland's Woodpecker and Mexican Jay are typical in this habitat. Areas with mountain pine/oak woodland include slopes adjacent to Madera Canyon, Sycamore Canyon (well below its usual altitudinal limits), Garden and Ramsey Canyons in the Huachucas, and Cave Creek and South Fork Canyons in the Chiricahua Mountains.

Mountain Canyon Groves: Owing to the presence of permanent water near or on the surface, strands of Arizona Sycamore flourish in some canyons between 5,000 and 6,500 feet. Tall conifers follow the water and the cool-air drainage down these narrow defiles. Elegant Trogon is perhaps the most eloquent symbol of this habitat along the border in Southeastern Arizona, but this is also the center of abundance for Painted Redstart. Locations with Mountain Canyon Groves include the actual canyon beds of Madera Canyon, Sycamore Canyon, Garden and Ramsey Canyons in the Huachucas, and Cave Creek and South Fork Canyons in the Chiricahua Mountains.

Mountain Coniferous Forest: The high ranges above 7,000 feet in Southeastern Arizona have isolated stands of Ponderosa Pine, Douglas-fir, and other trees typical of the Rocky Mountains farther north. With them come Hairy Woodpecker, Steller's Jay, and Red-breasted Nuthatch. In Southeastern Arizona there is paved access to the high Santa Catalina Mountains and dirt roads that climb to the forests of the Huachuca and Chiricahua Mountains. Trails provide access to this habitat type in the upper Santa Rita and Galiuro Mountains.

	December
	November
	October
	September
	August
	July
	June
	May
	April
	March
	February
	January

over 7,000 feet — Mountain Coniferous Forest
5,000 to 6,500 — Mountain Canyon Groves
5,000 to 7,000 — Mountain Pine/Oak Woodland
4,500 to 6,500 — Mountain Interior Chaparral
3,500 to 4,500 — Foothill Thornscrub
3,500 to 4,500 — Foothill Groves
up to 4,500 — Valley Groves and Pecan Farms
up to 4,500 — Valley Grasslands, Desert Fields
up to 4,500 — Desertscrub
up to 4,000 — Rivers, Ponds, Lakes

Common Loon
Usually on larger lakes such as Parker Canyon.

Pied-billed Grebe *

Horned Grebe

Eared Grebe *
Nesting at Willcox since 1992.

Western Grebe

Clark's Grebe

American White Pelican

Brown Pelican

Double-crested Cormorant
Especially at Picacho Reservoir and Patagonia Lake.

Neotropic Cormorant
Patagonia Lake.

Magnificent Frigatebird
Soaring birds can be blown in after violent storms in the Sea of Cortez.

American Bittern
Especially at Picacho Reservoir.

☐ Least Bittern *
Breeding resident at Picacho Reservoir.
Very rare wanderer to other ponds.

☐ Great Blue Heron *

☐ Great Egret
Always rare away from Picacho Reservoir.

☐ Snowy Egret
Nested at Picacho Reservoir in 1973.

☐ Little Blue Heron

☐ Tricolored Heron

☐ Cattle Egret
Prefers irrigated fields and farm ponds.

☐ Green Heron *

☐ Black-crowned Night-Heron *

☐ White-faced Ibis

☐ Black-bellied Whistling-Duck *

☐ Tundra Swan

☐ Greater White-fronted Goose

☐ Snow Goose

☐ Ross's Goose

☐ Canada Goose

☐ Wood Duck

☐ Green-winged Teal

* Nesting   ⊗ Spring ⊗ Summer ⊗ Fall ⊗ Winter

	December	November	October	September	August	July	June	May	April	March	February	January

over 7,000 feet — Mountain Coniferous Forest
5,000 to 6,500 — Mountain Canyon Groves
5,000 to 7,000 — Mountain Pine/Oak Woodland
4,500 to 6,500 — Mountain Interior Chaparral
3,500 to 4,500 — Foothill Thornscrub
3,500 to 4,500 — Foothill Groves
up to 4,500 — Valley Groves and Pecan Farms
up to 4,500 — Valley Grasslands, Desert Fields
up to 4,500 — Desertscrub
up to 4,000 — Rivers, Ponds, Lakes

Mallard *

Mallard "Mexican Duck" *
San Pedro and Sulphur Springs Valleys.

Northern Pintail *
Has nested at Willcox.

Blue-winged Teal

Cinnamon Teal *

Northern Shoveler *

Gadwall

Eurasian Wigeon

American Wigeon

Canvasback

Redhead *
Nests sporadically at Picacho Reservoir.

Ring-necked Duck

Greater Scaup

Lesser Scaup

Species	Notes
Common Goldeneye	
Bufflehead	
Hooded Merganser	
Common Merganser	Larger lakes.
Red-breasted Merganser	Larger lakes.
Ruddy Duck *	
Black Vulture *	From Patagonia, Nogales, and Sells area.
Turkey Vulture *	Uncommon in winter at Nogales and on Tohono O'odham Nation lands.
Osprey	Can occur in any habitat during migration.
White-tailed Kite *	Marana and Buenos Aires.
Mississippi Kite *	San Pedro River, especially near Dudleyville.
Bald Eagle	San Rafael and Sulphur Springs Valleys.
Northern Harrier *	
Sharp-shinned Hawk *	
Cooper's Hawk *	
Northern Goshawk *	Some winters a few Goshawks invade lowlands.

Spring ⊗ Summer ⊗ Fall ⊗ Winter

* Nesting

Months (top to bottom): December, November, October, September, August, July, June, May, April, March, February, January

Habitat columns:
- over 7,000 feet — Mountain Coniferous Forest
- 5,000 to 6,500 — Mountain Canyon Groves
- 5,000 to 7,000 — Mountain Pine/Oak Woodland
- 4,500 to 6,500 — Mountain Interior Chaparral
- 3,500 to 4,500 — Foothill Thornscrub
- 3,500 to 4,500 — Foothill Groves
- up to 4,500 — Valley Groves and Pecan Farms
- up to 4,500 — Valley Grasslands, Desert Fields
- up to 4,500 — Desertscrub
- up to 4,000 — Rivers, Ponds, Lakes

Species:

☐ Common Black-Hawk *
Aravaipa, Redfield, and Bass Canyons in Galiuro Mtns, and near Winkelman on San Pedro River.

☐ Harris's Hawk *
More common north of Tucson.

☐ Gray Hawk *
More common in valley cottonwood groves.

☐ Swainson's Hawk *

☐ Zone-tailed Hawk *

☐ Red-tailed Hawk *
Harlan's form is extremely rare in winter.

☐ Ferruginous Hawk
Fairly common in Sulphur Springs Valley; light-morph outnumber dark-morph birds by 20:1.

☐ Rough-legged Hawk

☐ Golden Eagle *
Soars over all habitats; nests on foothill and mountain cliffs.

☐ Crested Caracara *
Tohono O'odham Nation lands.

☐ American Kestrel *
Hunts open areas, fields, meadows, and burns.

Merlin

Peregrine Falcon *

Prairie Falcon *

Wild Turkey *
"Mexican" race turkeys occur in Huachuca Mtns; rarely San Pedro River & Guadalupe Canyon.

Montezuma Quail *
Grassy glades from oak savannah to top of Chiricahua Peak.

Northern Bobwhite *
Extirpated in 1897; efforts at reintroduction of the "Masked Bobwhite" subspecies began in 1974.

Scaled Quail *
Primarily Chihuahuan Desert grassland.

Gambel's Quail *

Clapper Rail
Picacho Reservoir.

Virginia Rail *
Cattail and tule marshes.

Sora
Cattail and tule marshes.

Common Moorhen *
Picacho Reservoir, Kino Springs, and Kingfisher Pond.

American Coot *

Sandhill Crane
Sulphur Springs Valley.

Black-bellied Plover

⊗ Spring   ⊗ Summer   ⊗ Fall   ⊗ Winter

* Nesting

	December
	November
	October
	September
	August
	July
	June
	May
	April
	March
	February
	January

over 7,000 feet — Mountain Coniferous Forest
5,000 to 6,500 — Mountain Canyon Groves
5,000 to 7,000 — Mountain Pine/Oak Woodland
4,500 to 6,500 — Mountain Interior Chaparral
3,500 to 4,500 — Foothill Thornscrub
3,500 to 4,500 — Foothill Groves
up to 4,500 — Valley Groves and Pecan Farms
up to 4,500 — Valley Grasslands, Desert Fields
up to 4,500 — Desertscrub
up to 4,000 — Rivers, Ponds, Lakes

Snowy Plover *
Occasionally nests at Willcox Sewage Ponds.

Semipalmated Plover

Killdeer *

Mountain Plover
Primarily in barren fields in Sulphur Springs Valley.

Black-necked Stilt *

American Avocet *
Especially Willcox Sewage Ponds and Sierra Vista Wastewater Ponds.

Greater Yellowlegs

Lesser Yellowlegs

Solitary Sandpiper

Willet

Spotted Sandpiper

Whimbrel

Long-billed Curlew
Large flocks use freshly tilled fields in Sulphur Springs Valley and rest at ponds.

☐ Marbled Godwit
Hudsonian Godwit appears in May some years at Willcox Sewage Ponds.

☐ Sanderling

☐ Semipalmated Sandpiper
Most fall records are of juveniles.

☐ Western Sandpiper

☐ Least Sandpiper

☐ Baird's Sandpiper

☐ Pectoral Sandpiper

☐ Dunlin
Has wintered at Picacho Reservoir.

☐ Stilt Sandpiper

☐ Short-billed Dowitcher
Easily confused with and far outnumbered by next species; use call notes.

☐ Long-billed Dowitcher

☐ Common Snipe

☐ Wilson's Phalarope

☐ Red-necked Phalarope

☐ Red Phalarope

☐ Franklin's Gull

☐ Bonaparte's Gull

☐ Ring-billed Gull

* Nesting

⊗ Spring ⊗ Summer ⊗ Fall ⊗ Winter

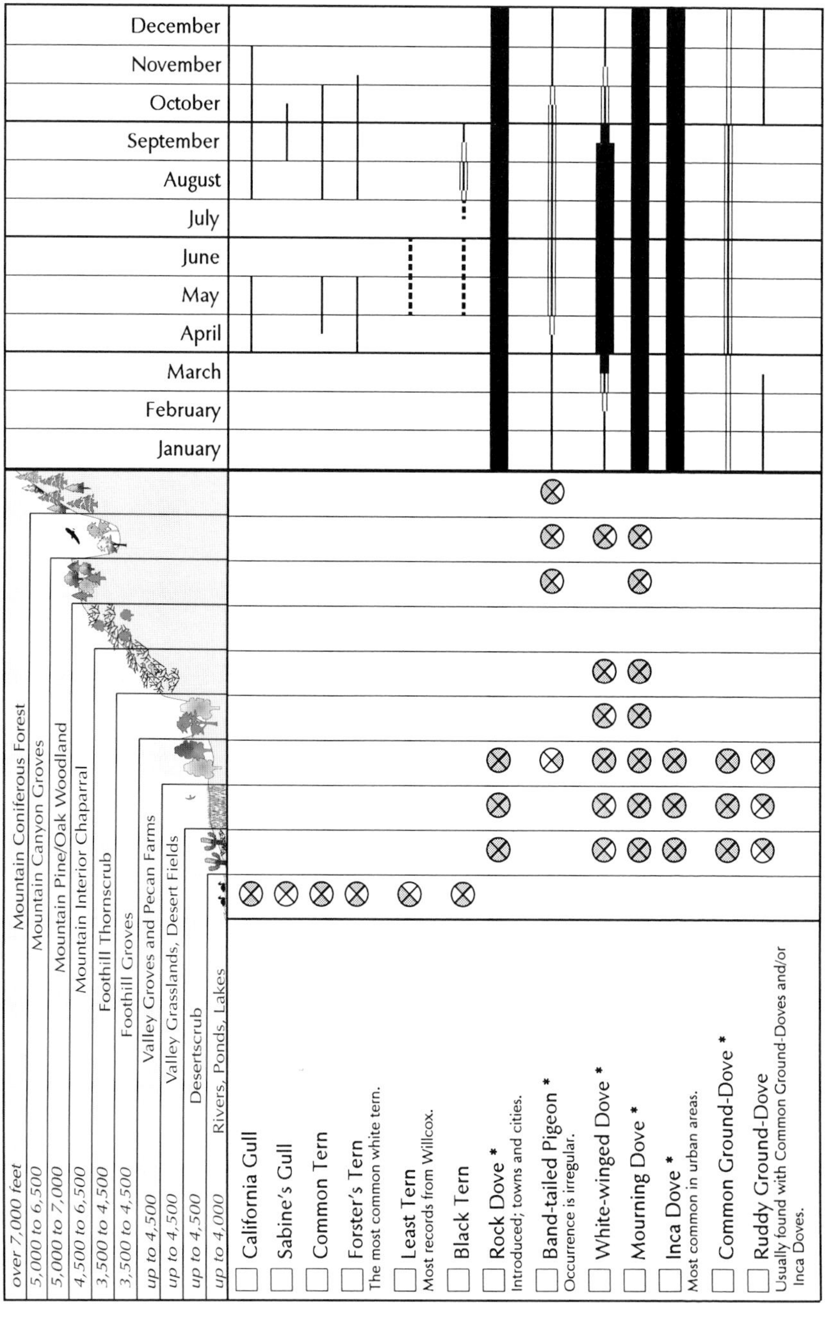
December
November
October
September
August
July
June
May
April
March
February
January
over 7,000 feet
Mountain Coniferous Forest
5,000 to 6,500
Mountain Canyon Groves
5,000 to 7,000
Mountain Pine/Oak Woodland
4,500 to 6,500
Mountain Interior Chaparral
3,500 to 4,500
Foothill Thornscrub
3,500 to 4,500
Foothill Groves
up to 4,500
Valley Groves and Pecan Farms
up to 4,500
Valley Grasslands, Desert Fields
up to 4,500
Desertscrub
up to 4,000
Rivers, Ponds, Lakes
California Gull
Sabine's Gull
Common Tern
Forster's Tern
The most common white tern.
Least Tern
Most records from Willcox.
Black Tern
Rock Dove *
Introduced; towns and cities.
Band-tailed Pigeon *
Occurrence is irregular.
White-winged Dove *
Mourning Dove *
Inca Dove *
Most common in urban areas.
Common Ground-Dove *
Ruddy Ground-Dove
Usually found with Common Ground-Doves and/or Inca Doves.

Species			
☐ Yellow-billed Cuckoo *			
☐ Greater Roadrunner *			
☐ Groove-billed Ani			
☐ Barn Owl * Rare in other habitats up to Ponderosa Pine forest.			
☐ Flammulated Owl * Difficult to find after midsummer when not calling.			
☐ Western Screech-Owl * Difficult to find after midsummer when not calling. Prefers more open habitat than Whiskered Screech-Owl.			
☐ Whiskered Screech-Owl * Difficult to find after midsummer when not calling. Ordinarily at higher elevations than Western Screech-Owl.			
☐ Great Horned Owl * Difficult to find after midsummer when not calling.			
☐ Northern Pygmy-Owl * Difficult to find after midsummer when not calling. Likes large juniper trees.			
☐ Ferruginous Pygmy-Owl * Western part of area only.			
☐ Elf Owl * Difficult to find after midsummer when not calling.			
☐ Burrowing Owl * Local.			
☐ Spotted Owl *			
☐ Long-eared Owl * Has nested in sparse oak woodland.			

⊗ Spring ⊗ Summer ⊗ Fall ⊗ Winter

* Nesting

Months (top to bottom): December, November, October, September, August, July, June, May, April, March, February, January

Habitat elevation zones:
- over 7,000 feet — Mountain Coniferous Forest
- 5,000 to 6,500 — Mountain Canyon Groves
- 5,000 to 7,000 — Mountain Pine/Oak Woodland
- 4,500 to 6,500 — Mountain Interior Chaparral
- 3,500 to 4,500 — Foothill Thornscrub
- 3,500 to 4,500 — Foothill Groves
- up to 4,500 — Valley Groves and Pecan Farms
- up to 4,500 — Valley Grasslands, Desert Fields
- up to 4,500 — Desertscrub
- up to 4,000 — Rivers, Ponds, Lakes

Species:

Short-eared Owl
Farmlands and marshes.

Northern Saw-whet Owl *
Almost all sightings occur between March 10 and June 10 when birds are calling.

Lesser Nighthawk *
Often near ponds, rivers, streetlights, and large parking areas.

Common Nighthawk *
Sonoita, San Rafael Grassland, and near Huachuca Mountains.

Common Poorwill *

Buff-collared Nightjar *

Whip-poor-will *

Chimney Swift
Almost all records from Univ. of Arizona in Tucson. No records since 1985.

Vaux's Swift
Aerial.

White-throated Swift *
Cliffs in summer; widespread in winter.

☐ **Broad-billed Hummingbird ***
More common west of San Pedro.

☐ **White-eared Hummingbird ***
Annual since 1989 at Ramsey Canyon.

☐ **Berylline Hummingbird ***
Has fledged young as late as mid-September.

☐ **Violet-crowned Hummingbird ***
Especially at Patagonia. Has wintered at feeders from Tucson to Bisbee.

☐ **Blue-throated Hummingbird ***
Winters at feeders.

☐ **Magnificent Hummingbird ***
Winters at feeders.

☐ **Plain-capped Starthroat**
Primarily near flowering agaves; enters pine/oak and mountain canyon groves only when they occur below 6,000 feet.

☐ **Lucifer Hummingbird ***
Wooded canyons and agave slopes near Mexican border.

☐ **Black-chinned Hummingbird ***

☐ **Anna's Hummingbird ***
More common west of San Pedro and below 6,000 ft.

☐ **Costa's Hummingbird ***
Most common west of San Pedro and below 5,000 ft. Year-round at Arizona-Sonora Desert Museum.

☐ **Calliope Hummingbird**
Males precede females and immatures; most adult males pass through in fall by August 15.

Spring ⊗ Summer ⊗ Fall ⊗ Winter

* Nesting

December
November
October
September
August
July
June
May
April
March
February
January

over 7,000 feet — Mountain Coniferous Forest
5,000 to 6,500 — Mountain Canyon Groves
5,000 to 7,000 — Mountain Pine/Oak Woodland
4,500 to 6,500 — Mountain Interior Chaparral
3,500 to 4,500 — Foothill Thornscrub
3,500 to 4,500 — Foothill Groves
up to 4,500 — Valley Groves and Pecan Farms
up to 4,500 — Valley Grasslands, Desert Fields
up to 4,500 — Desertscrub
up to 4,000 — Rivers, Ponds, Lakes

Broad-tailed Hummingbird *
Migrates through lowlands.

Rufous Hummingbird
Males precede females and immatures; most adult males pass through in fall by August 15.

Allen's Hummingbird
Most adult males pass through in July.

Elegant Trogon *
Primarily sycamore-wooded mountain canyons in the border ranges.

Eared Trogon *
Upper canyons in border ranges.

Belted Kingfisher

Green Kingfisher *

Lewis's Woodpecker

Acorn Woodpecker *
Rare in valley groves.

Gila Woodpecker *

Red-naped Sapsucker
Confined to riparian and orchards in deserts and valleys.

Williamson's Sapsucker

Ladder-backed Woodpecker *

Hairy Woodpecker *
Rare in mountain canyons below 6,000 feet.

Strickland's Woodpecker *
Nests in mountain canyon groves. Some move upslope into dry pine/oak woodland after breeding.

Northern "Red-shafted" Flicker *
Some winter in lowland riparian and orchards.

Gilded Flicker *
Sonoran desert Saguaro stands and western cottonwood riparian only.

Northern Beardless-Tyrannulet *
Prefers mesquite thickets.

Olive-sided Flycatcher *
Perches on dead treetops.

Greater Pewee *
Often perches on dead treetops in spring; winters in valley groves and orchards.

Western Wood-Pewee *
Migrates through lowlands.

Willow Flycatcher *
Prefers more open habitats than Hammond's or Dusky. Several pairs breed near Dudleyville.

Hammond's Flycatcher

Dusky Flycatcher

Gray Flycatcher
Mesquite thickets and arid juniper hillsides.

* Nesting

⊗ Spring   ⊗ Summer   ⊗ Fall   ⊗ Winter

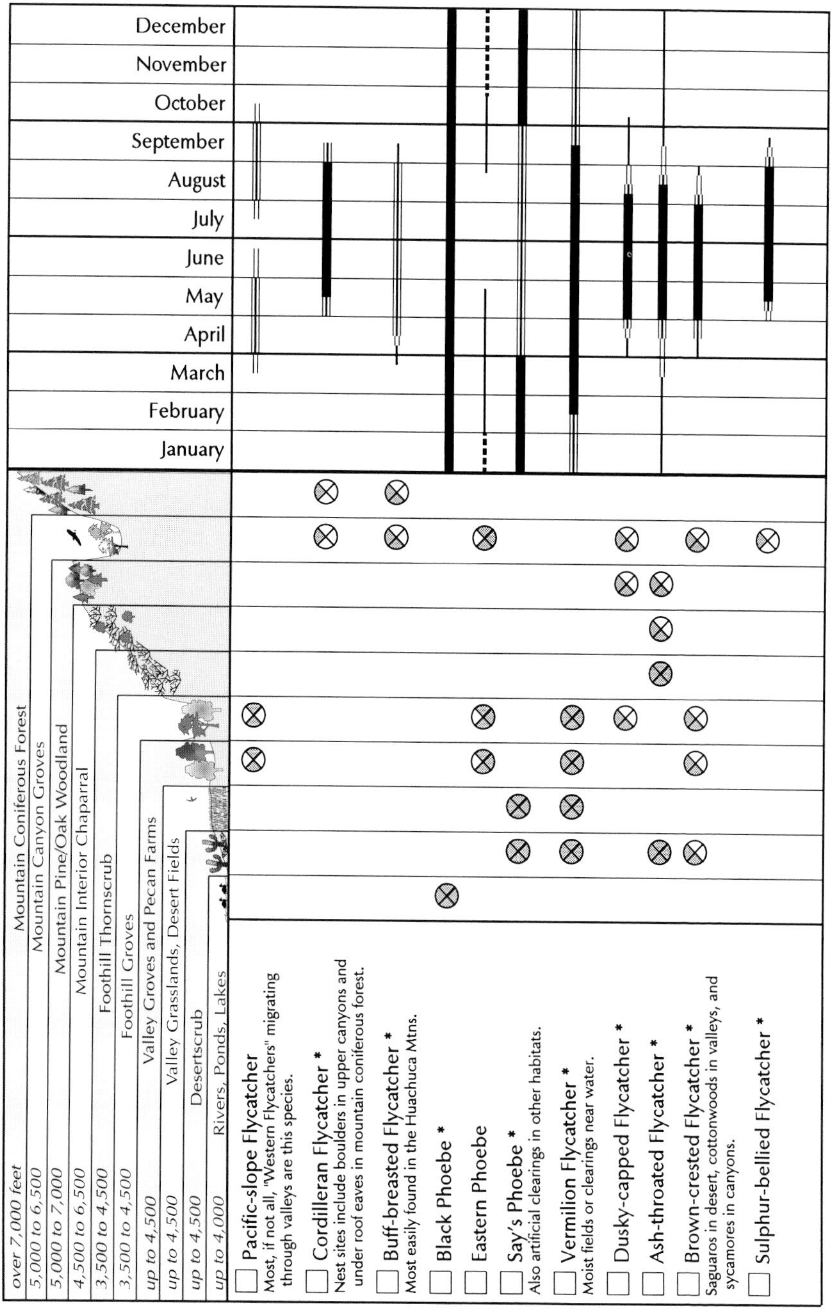

Months (top axis): December, November, October, September, August, July, June, May, April, March, February, January

Habitat rows (left labels):
- over 7,000 feet — Mountain Coniferous Forest
- 5,000 to 6,500 — Mountain Canyon Groves
- 5,000 to 7,000 — Mountain Pine/Oak Woodland
- 4,500 to 6,500 — Mountain Interior Chaparral
- 3,500 to 4,500 — Foothill Thornscrub
- 3,500 to 4,500 — Foothill Groves
- up to 4,500 — Valley Groves and Pecan Farms
- up to 4,500 — Valley Grasslands, Desert Fields
- up to 4,500 — Desertscrub
- up to 4,000 — Rivers, Ponds, Lakes

Species:
- Pacific-slope Flycatcher
  Most, if not all, "Western Flycatchers" migrating through valleys are this species.
- Cordilleran Flycatcher *
  Nest sites include boulders in upper canyons and under roof eaves in mountain coniferous forest.
- Buff-breasted Flycatcher *
  Most easily found in the Huachuca Mtns.
- Black Phoebe *
- Eastern Phoebe
- Say's Phoebe *
  Also artificial clearings in other habitats.
- Vermilion Flycatcher *
  Moist fields or clearings near water.
- Dusky-capped Flycatcher *
- Ash-throated Flycatcher *
- Brown-crested Flycatcher *
  Saguaros in desert, cottonwoods in valleys, and sycamores in canyons.
- Sulphur-bellied Flycatcher *

☐ Tropical Kingbird *

☐ Cassin's Kingbird *
Generally higher elevations and more heavily wooded habitats than Western Kingbird.

☐ Thick-billed Kingbird *
Foothill riparian woodland near Mexican border.

☐ Western Kingbird *

☐ Eastern Kingbird
Open woodlands/riparian edges.

☐ Scissor-tailed Flycatcher
Most strays are during rainy season; August is peak month.

☐ Rose-throated Becard *
Foothill riparian woodland near Mexican border.

☐ Horned Lark *
Primarily valley grasslands and fields. Within desertscrub, only in large flat openings.

☐ Purple Martin *
Saguaro stands and formerly forest openings in Chiricahuas; flocks of 100s, occasionally 1000s mass on N and W sides of Tucson in Sept.

☐ Tree Swallow
Most common at valley ponds and rivers.

☐ Violet-green Swallow *

☐ Northern Rough-winged Swallow *
Especially near ponds and rivers.

☐ Bank Swallow
Especially near ponds.

⊗ Spring   ⊗ Summer   ⊗ Fall   ⊗ Winter

* Nesting

Months (columns): January, February, March, April, May, June, July, August, September, October, November, December

Elevation / Habitat rows:

over 7,000 feet	Mountain Coniferous Forest
5,000 to 6,500	Mountain Canyon Groves
5,000 to 7,000	Mountain Pine/Oak Woodland
4,500 to 6,500	Mountain Interior Chaparral
3,500 to 4,500	Foothill Thornscrub
3,500 to 4,500	Foothill Groves
up to 4,500	Valley Groves and Pecan Farms
up to 4,500	Valley Grasslands, Desert Fields
up to 4,500	Desertscrub
up to 4,000	Rivers, Ponds, Lakes

Species:

Cliff Swallow *
Nests at Univ. of Arizona/Tucson and Cochise College near Douglas.

Barn Swallow *
In the desert, only at ponds and irrigated fields.

Steller's Jay *
Sporadic in valley groves and city parks some winters.

Western Scrub-Jay *

Mexican Jay *

Pinyon Jay
Years or decades may separate major invasions.

Clark's Nutcracker
Years or decades may separate invasions. During invasions usually not found in summer.

American Crow
Agricultural areas only, especially Safford, St. David, Elfrida.

Chihuahuan Raven *
Prefers open habitats.

Common Raven *
Prefers wooded habitats and mountains.

Mexican Chickadee *
Chiricahua Mtns only.

Mountain Chickadee *
Breeds in Santa Catalina and Rincon Mtns only.

Bridled Titmouse *
Less common in valley riparian.

Plain Titmouse *

Verdin *

Bushtit *
Wanders down to desert washes and up to coniferous forest after breeding.

Red-breasted Nuthatch *
Rare in valley and town groves in winter.

White-breasted Nuthatch *

Pygmy Nuthatch *

Brown Creeper *
Rare in valley and foothill groves in winter.

Cactus Wren *
The Arizona State Bird.

Rock Wren *
Rocky areas; pronounced shift to W deserts from mid-Sept. through mid-April.

Canyon Wren *
Canyon cliffs, occasionally to above 9,000 feet.

Bewick's Wren *
Also mesquite thickets and pinyon/juniper woodlands.

House Wren *

Spring   Summer   Fall   Winter

* Nesting   ⊗ Nesting

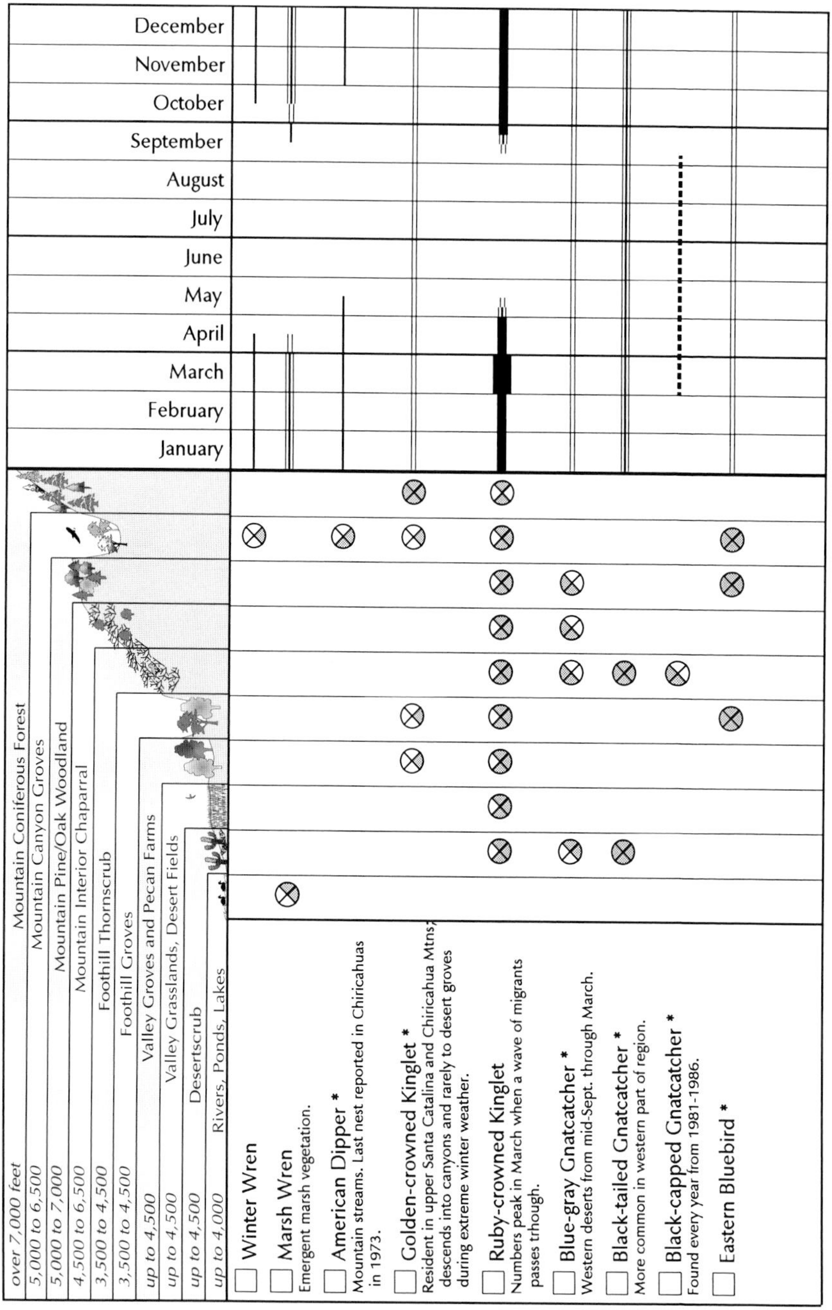
December
November
October
September
August
July
June
May
April
March
February
January
over 7,000 feet
Mountain Coniferous Forest
5,000 to 6,500
Mountain Canyon Groves
5,000 to 7,000
Mountain Pine/Oak Woodland
4,500 to 6,500
Mountain Interior Chaparral
3,500 to 4,500
Foothill Thornscrub
3,500 to 4,500
Foothill Groves
up to 4,500
Valley Groves and Pecan Farms
up to 4,500
Valley Grasslands, Desert Fields
up to 4,500
Desertscrub
up to 4,000
Rivers, Ponds, Lakes
Winter Wren
Marsh Wren
Emergent marsh vegetation.
American Dipper *
Mountain streams. Last nest reported in Chiricahuas in 1973.
Golden-crowned Kinglet *
Resident in upper Santa Catalina and Chiricahua Mtns; descends into canyons and rarely to desert groves during extreme winter weather.
Ruby-crowned Kinglet
Numbers peak in March when a wave of migrants passes trhough.
Blue-gray Gnatcatcher *
Western deserts from mid-Sept. through March.
Black-tailed Gnatcatcher *
More common in western part of region.
Black-capped Gnatcatcher *
Found every year from 1981-1986.
Eastern Bluebird *

☐ **Western Bluebird** *
Breeds only in Santa Catalina and Chiricahua Mtns. Winters throughout region in Upper Sonoran Life Zone. During invasion years, flocks also occur in desert Oct. 15–March 15.

☐ **Mountain Bluebird** *
Graph represents invasion year; some winters almost none present. Nested once in Sonoita, 1981.

☐ **Townsend's Solitaire**
Numbers fluctuate. Vagrant to coniferous forest in summer.

☐ **Swainson's Thrush**
Also city thickets and ranch yards.

☐ **Hermit Thrush** *

☐ **Rufous-backed Robin**

☐ **American Robin** *
Lowlands only in winter.

☐ **Varied Thrush**
Dense riparian groves; not reported some winters.

☐ **Aztec Thrush** *
Also one winter record: Portal Jan–Feb 1991. Presence of immature birds in late summer suggests nesting.

☐ **Gray Catbird**
Also city parks and desert oases.

☐ **Northern Mockingbird** *

☐ **Sage Thrasher**
Graph represents average winter; some years fairly common.

* Nesting

⊗ Spring   ⊗ Summer   ⊗ Fall   ⊗ Winter

December
November
October
September
August
July
June
May
April
March
February
January

over 7,000 feet — Mountain Coniferous Forest
5,000 to 6,500 — Mountain Canyon Groves
5,000 to 7,000 — Mountain Pine/Oak Woodland
4,500 to 6,500 — Mountain Interior Chaparral
3,500 to 6,500 — Foothill Thornscrub
3,500 to 4,500 — Foothill Groves
up to 4,500 — Valley Groves and Pecan Farms
up to 4,500 — Valley Grasslands, Desert Fields
up to 4,500 — Desertscrub
up to 4,000 — Rivers, Ponds, Lakes

Brown Thrasher

Bendire's Thrasher *

Curve-billed Thrasher *

Crissal Thrasher *
Dense thickets; sings January through March.

Le Conte's Thrasher *
Open Creosote Bush desert in Avra Valley.

American Pipit
Pond and stream edges, open fields, and golf courses.

Sprague's Pipit
Tall grasses.

Cedar Waxwing
Also exploits Pyracantha plantings and tall trees in towns. Numbers fluctuate.

Phainopepla *
Especially near trees with mistletoe. Range extends only to lower mountain canyon groves. Very common in western Soronan Desert mesquite in winter.

Loggerhead Shrike *

European Starling *
Towns, farms, and ranches.

Bell's Vireo *

Gray Vireo *
Pinyon/juniper hillsides; western lowlands only in winter.

Solitary "Plumbeous" Vireo *
Within desertscrub prefers dense mesquite thickets.

Solitary "Cassin's" Vireo
Within desertscrub prefers dense mesquite thickets.

Hutton's Vireo *
Rare in valley riparian in winter.

Warbling Vireo *
Common migrant through all wooded habitats, desert oases.

Red-eyed Vireo
Some years not reported.

Tennessee Warbler

Orange-crowned Warbler *

Nashville Warbler

Virginia's Warbler *

Lucy's Warbler *

Northern Parula

Yellow Warbler *
Also migrates through desert oases and towns.

Chestnut-sided Warbler
Especially during fall at desert oases near Tucson.

⊗ Spring   ⊗ Summer   ⊗ Fall   ⊗ Winter

* Nesting

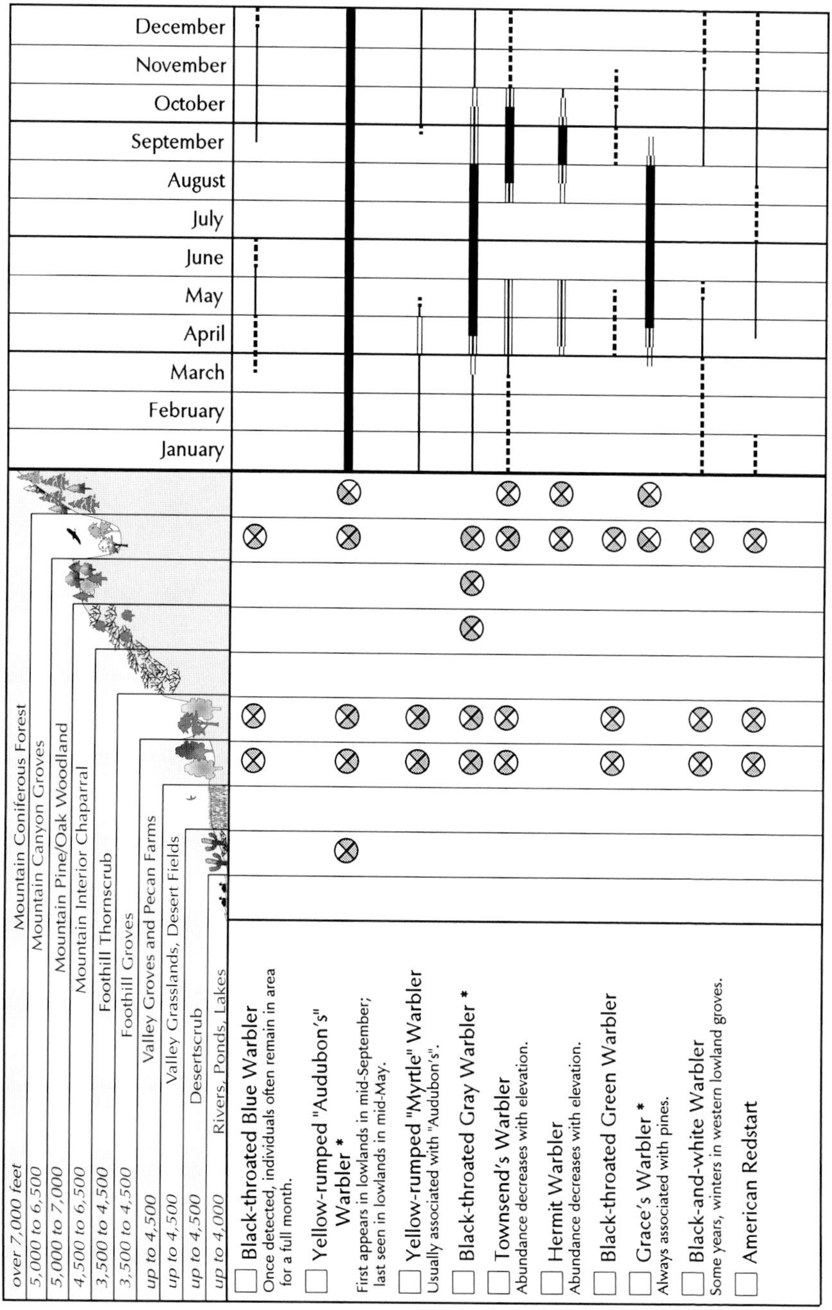

December
November
October
September
August
July
June
May
April
March
February
January
over 7,000 feet Mountain Coniferous Forest
5,000 to 6,500 Mountain Canyon Groves
5,000 to 7,000 Mountain Pine/Oak Woodland
4,500 to 6,500 Mountain Interior Chaparral
3,500 to 4,500 Foothill Thornscrub
3,500 to 4,500 Foothill Groves
up to 4,500 Valley Groves and Pecan Farms
up to 4,500 Valley Grasslands, Desert Fields
up to 4,500 Desertscrub
up to 4,000 Rivers, Ponds, Lakes
Black-throated Blue Warbler
Once detected, individuals often remain in area for a full month.
Yellow-rumped "Audubon's" Warbler *
First appears in lowlands in mid-September; last seen in lowlands in mid-May.
Yellow-rumped "Myrtle" Warbler
Usually associated with "Audubon's".
Black-throated Gray Warbler *
Townsend's Warbler
Abundance decreases with elevation.
Hermit Warbler
Abundance decreases with elevation.
Black-throated Green Warbler
Grace's Warbler *
Always associated with pines.
Black-and-white Warbler
Some years, winters in western lowland groves.
American Redstart

☐ Prothonotary Warbler
Valley groves, lower mountain canyons only.

☐ Northern Waterthrush
In mountain canyons below 5,500 feet.

☐ Louisiana Waterthrush
Only in canyons with permanent streams.

☐ Kentucky Warbler

☐ MacGillivray's Warbler
Thickets within all habitats.

☐ Common Yellowthroat *

☐ Hooded Warbler

☐ Wilson's Warbler *
Winter records from western lowlands.

☐ Red-faced Warbler *
Breeds in or near groves of deciduous trees above 6,000 feet.

☐ Painted Redstart *
Post-breeding wanderers occur rarely from river valleys to coniferous forests. Winters in mtn canyons only.

☐ Yellow-breasted Chat *

☐ Olive Warbler *
A few winter birds descend to river groves.

☐ Hepatic Tanager *
Western sector only in winter.

☐ Summer Tanager *
Western sector only in winter.

⊗ Spring ⊗ Summer ⊗ Fall ⊗ Winter

* Nesting

December	
November	
October	
September	
August	
July	
June	
May	
April	
March	
February	
January	

over 7,000 feet — Mountain Coniferous Forest
5,000 to 6,500 — Mountain Canyon Groves
5,000 to 7,000 — Mountain Pine/Oak Woodland
4,500 to 6,500 — Mountain Interior Chaparral
3,500 to 4,500 — Foothill Thornscrub
3,500 to 4,500 — Foothill Groves
up to 4,500 — Valley Groves and Pecan Farms
up to 4,500 — Valley Grasslands, Desert Fields
up to 4,500 — Desertscrub
up to 4,000 — Rivers, Ponds, Lakes

Western Tanager *
Confined to breeding areas in coniferous forest in late June-early July.

Flame-colored Tanager *

Northern Cardinal *
Below 5,500 feet in mountain canyon groves.

Pyrrhuloxia *
Below 5,500 feet in mountain canyon groves. Sometimes forms flocks in winter.

Yellow Grosbeak

Rose-breasted Grosbeak

Black-headed Grosbeak *
A few lowland winter records.

Blue Grosbeak *
Most common in mesquite grassland.

Lazuli Bunting
Especially weedy fields.

Indigo Bunting *

Varied Bunting *

Painted Bunting
Most birds are greenish females or immatures. Below 5,500 feet in mountain canyon groves.

Dickcissel

Green-tailed Towhee
Numbers fluctuate from year to year.

Spotted Towhee *
Brushy habitats.

Canyon Towhee *
Lower mtn canyons only.

Abert's Towhee *
Dense thickets along streams and ponds.

Botteri's Sparrow *

Cassin's Sparrow *

Rufous-winged Sparrow *

Rufous-crowned Sparrow *

Chipping Sparrow *

Clay-colored Sparrow *
Very rare in winter.

Brewer's Sparrow

Black-chinned Sparrow *

Vesper Sparrow

Lark Sparrow *

Black-throated Sparrow *
Winters in mountain canyon groves below 5,000 feet.

* Nesting

⊗ Spring ⊗ Summer ⊗ Fall ⊗ Winter

December
November
October
September
August
July
June
May
April
March
February
January

Elevation	Habitat
over 7,000 feet	Mountain Coniferous Forest
5,000 to 6,500	Mountain Canyon Groves
5,000 to 7,000	Mountain Pine/Oak Woodland
4,500 to 6,500	Mountain Interior Chaparral
3,500 to 4,500	Foothill Thornscrub
3,500 to 4,500	Foothill Groves
up to 4,500	Valley Groves and Pecan Farms
up to 4,500	Valley Grasslands, Desert Fields
up to 4,500	Desertscrub
up to 4,000	Rivers, Ponds, Lakes

Sage Sparrow

Five-striped Sparrow *
Easiest to find in California Gulch and Sycamore Canyon. Possibly a few winter.

Lark Bunting

Savannah Sparrow

Baird's Sparrow
Tall and dense grasslands.

Grasshopper Sparrow *
Grassy flats within desertscrub.

Fox Sparrow

Song Sparrow *
Rare in lowland hedgerows in winter.

Lincoln's Sparrow

Swamp Sparrow

White-throated Sparrow
Probably easiest to find at Patagonia-Sonoita Creek Preserve.

Golden-crowned Sparrow
Usually associates with White-crowned Sparrows.

White-crowned Sparrow

Harris's Sparrow
Usually associates with White-crowned Sparrows.

Dark-eyed Junco, "Slate-colored"

Dark-eyed Junco, "Oregon"

Dark-eyed Junco, "Gray-headed"

Dark-eyed Junco, "Pink-sided"

Yellow-eyed Junco *

McCown's Longspur

Chestnut-collared Longspur

Red-winged Blackbird *
Feedlots in winter, even those on grasslands.

Eastern Meadowlark *

Western Meadowlark *
Has bred after wet winters.

Yellow-headed Blackbird
Also uses desert and valley feedlots.
Winter populations fluctuate.

Brewer's Blackbird

Great-tailed Grackle *

Bronzed Cowbird *
Tucson feedlots in winter.

Brown-headed Cowbird *
Feedlots in winter, even those on grasslands.

⊗ Spring ⊗ Summer ⊗ Fall ⊗ Winter

* Nesting

December
November
October
September
August
July
June
May
April
March
February
January

over 7,000 feet — Mountain Coniferous Forest
5,000 to 6,500 — Mountain Canyon Groves
5,000 to 7,000 — Mountain Pine/Oak Woodland
4,500 to 6,500 — Mountain Interior Chaparral
3,500 to 4,500 — Foothill Thornscrub
3,500 to 4,500 — Foothill Groves
up to 4,500 — Valley Groves and Pecan Farms
up to 4,500 — Valley Grasslands, Desert Fields
up to 4,500 — Desertscrub
up to 4,000 — Rivers, Ponds, Lakes

Hooded Oriole *
Most winter records from Tucson feeders.

Streak-backed Oriole *
Has nested near Marana Pecan Grove and Dudleyville.

Bullock's Oriole *
Most winter records from Tucson feeders.

Scott's Oriole *
Most winter records from canyon and valley feeders.

Purple Finch
Small numbers occur every 5-10 years at desert and valley oases and lower mtn canyons.

Cassin's Finch
Present nearly every winter but numbers fluctuate.

House Finch *

Red Crossbill *
Numbers fluctuate; some winters at Tucson's Evergreen Cemetery.

Pine Siskin *
Confined to coniferous forest from mid-May to mid-August.

☐ **Lesser Goldfinch** *
In the desert only at oases. In mountain canyons below 5,500 feet.

☐ **Lawrence's Goldfinch**
Fields and desert oases; numbers fluctuate, but more common in western valleys.

☐ **American Goldfinch**
Wet fields and riparian trees. In mountain canyons below 5,000 feet.

☐ **Evening Grosbeak** *
Numbers fluctuate; descends into mtn canyons from mid-Oct. through mid-May.

☐ **House Sparrow** *
Towns, farms, and ranches below 5,000 feet.

⊗ Spring ⊗ Summer ⊗ Fall ⊗ Winter

* Nesting

SELDOM SEEN

Although "forget it" is the answer that you will probably receive when inquiring about your chances of seeing an unusual species, do not stop looking. This listing of "Seldom Seen" birds includes rare birds, about a dozen hypothetical species, and two identifiable forms. Adding one of these to your list is what puts the topping on any birding trip. If you are positive of your identification, take careful notes or photos and report your find to the Regional Editor of *National Audubon Society Field Notes*, c/o Tucson Audubon Society, 300 E. University Blvd. #120, Tucson, AZ 85705. A Rare Bird Report form is included on page 318 for your convenience.

Pacific Loon *Vagrant to large lakes in migration and winter.*
Least Grebe *Discussion in Specialties Section.*
Least Storm-Petrel *Hypothetical; 1 possible record from August 1992 at Patagonia Lake.*
Red-billed Tropicbird *3 records: September 1927 in Apache Pass, Chiricahua Mountains, June 1990 near Tucson, and May 1992 in Green Valley.*
Anhinga *1 record from Tucson September 1893.*
Yellow-crowned Night-Heron *4 records: May 1968 in Tucson, May-June 1984 and June-July 1985 at Dudleyville, and May 1992 at Picacho Reservoir.*
White Ibis *2 records: June-September 1986 at Picacho Reservoir and August 1988 at Tucson.*
Roseate Spoonbill *Last record: June-October 1973 at Picacho Reservoir.*
Wood Stork *Last record: December 1972 at Tombstone.*
Trumpeter Swan *Hypothetical; reported December 1994–January 1995 at Willow Tank near Rodeo.*
Fulvous Whistling-Duck *Discussion in Specialties Section.*
Brant *2 records: December 1972 in Tucson and May 1993 at Willcox Playa.*
Garganey *2 records: April 1988 at Buenos Aires NWR and March 1992 in Tucson.*
Oldsquaw *Winter vagrant, primarily in November-December.*
Black Scoter *2 records: November 1975 in Tucson and December 1978 in Nogales.*
Surf Scoter *Vagrant, primarily in October and November.*
White-winged Scoter *Vagrant in late October and November.*
Barrow's Goldeneye *2 records: March 1973 in Tucson and January-February 1982 at Willcox Playa.*
California Condor *Extirpated; last recorded March 1881.*
American Swallow-tailed Kite *Hypothetical; 1 record in August 1980 near Dudleyville.*
Great Black-Hawk *Hypothetical; 1 record from July 1987 on upper San Pedro River.*
Red-shouldered Hawk *Vagrant throughout the year.*
Broad-winged Hawk *Vagrant, primarily in April-May and July-October, especially to Chiricahua and Huachuca Mountains.*
Short-tailed Hawk *Hypothetical; sight records during the summer rainy season near the crests of the Chiricahuas (1985) and the Huachucas (1988).*
White-tailed Hawk *Hypothetical; reported January-February 1971 in San Rafael Grassland.*
Aplomado Falcon *Last record October 1940; discussion in Specialties Section.*
Blue Grouse *Hypothetical; at least 4 records from May-July 1973 through 1985 from Chiricahua Mountains; possibly an unauthorized attempt to introduce this species.*
Black Rail *Hypothetical; 2 records in April 1881 at Tucson and April 1977 at Willcox Playa.*

Purple Gallinule *Summer and early fall vagrant to ponds and canals; most recent records from Picacho Reservoir and upper San Pedro River.*

Whooping Crane *Discussion in Specialties Section.*

American Golden-Plover *Vagrant in spring and fall, primarily at Willcox Playa.*

Northern Jacana *1 record from June 1985 to January 1986 at Kino Springs and Guevavi Ranch Ponds, upper Santa Cruz Valley.*

Upland Sandpiper *2 records since 1900: September 1988 at Avra Valley Sewage Ponds and May 1989 at Buenos Aires NWR.*

Hudsonian Godwit *3 records: all in May, 1976, 1986, and 1988, all from Willcox.*

Ruddy Turnstone *Vagrant in April-May and August-September.*

Red Knot *Vagrant from August-September.*

White-rumped Sandpiper *3 records: June 1977 and 1990 from Willcox Playa and May 1993 from Buenos Aires NWR.*

Long-tailed Jaeger *2 records: September 1980 from Tucson and September 1989 from north of Sierra Vista.*

Laughing Gull *Vagrant in spring and fall, primarily from Willcox.*

Heermann's Gull *Vagrant, primarily in fall.*

Herring Gull *Vagrant, primarily in late fall.*

Thayer's Gull *1 record in December 1968 at Bowie north of Dos Cabezas Mountains.*

Black-legged Kittiwake *2 records: November 1980 on Highway 83 to Sonoita and April-May 1989 at Willcox.*

Gull-billed Tern *1 record in April 1976 at Nogales.*

Caspian Tern *Vagrant, primarily in late September and October, in western half of area.*

Elegant Tern *2 records in May and July 1990 in and near Tucson.*

Arctic Tern *3 records: September 1965, October 1968, and May 1982, all from Tucson.*

Black Skimmer *1 record in August 1984 at Willcox Playa.*

Thick-billed Parrot *Discussion in Specialties Section.*

Black-billed Cuckoo *Hypothetical; 3 fall sight records: October 1966 at Peña Blanca Lake, August 1972 at Patagonia, and October 1984 at Silver Creek near Portal. There is still no documentation of this species in Arizona.*

Black Swift *Hypothetical; sight records fall between May and August at upper Cave Creek Canyon (multiple reports) and by Hereford.*

Cinnamon Hummingbird *1 record in July 1992; discussion in Specialties Section.*

Bumblebee Hummingbird *1 record in July 1896; discussion in Specialties Section.*

Red-headed Woodpecker *5 records: 3 from the Chiricahuas, 1 from Huachucas, and recently from Continental from November 1991-May 1992.*

Yellow-bellied Sapsucker *Vagrant from September through May in desert oases and valley groves.*

Red-breasted Sapsucker *Winter vagrant in desert oases, valley groves, and canyon outlets.*

Downy Woodpecker *Approximately 5 records since 1980 for the Chiricahua Mountains and 1 record for the Huachuca Mountains in July 1994, all in coniferous forest, all between April and July.*

Northern "Yellow-shafted" Flicker *Vagrant between October and May to valley groves.*

Eastern Wood-Pewee *2 records: October 1953 at Tucson and October 1972 near Nogales.*

Yellow-bellied Flycatcher *2 records: September 1956 at Tucson and December 1992–February 1993 at Patagonia.*

Acadian Flycatcher *1 record in May 1886 at Tucson.*

Least Flycatcher *Hypothetical; 3 sight records: May 1985 at South Fork in the Chiricahua Mountains, November 1986 and May 1988 on the upper San Pedro River.*

Nutting's Flycatcher *Discussion in Specialties Section.*

Great Crested Flycatcher *1 record in June 1901 from the Huachuca Mountains; other sight reports have yet to be accepted by Arizona Bird Committee.*

Great Kiskadee *2 records: March 1978 at Sabino Canyon and December 1979–May 1980 at Canoa Ranch in the upper Santa Cruz Valley.*
Cave Swallow *Discussion in Specialties Section.*
Blue Jay *2 records: December 1989–May 1990 at St. David and November 1993 at Kansas Settlement.*
Sinaloa Wren *Hypothetical; 1 reported in June 1989 from Highway 90 Bridge on San Pedro River.*
Sedge Wren *Hypothetical; 1 reported in December 1979 from San Simon Cienaga.*
Veery *Hypothetical; 2 records: May 1984 from Portal and May 1989 from Fairbank on the upper San Pedro River.*
Gray-cheeked Thrush *1 record in September 1932 in Cave Creek Canyon near Portal.*
Wood Thrush *Vagrant, primarily in May and October-November in desert oases and lower canyon and foothill river groves.*
Blue Mockingbird *Discussion in Specialties Section.*
Red-throated Pipit *Hypothetical; 1 sight report in May 1989 at Avra Valley Sewage Ponds.*
Bohemian Waxwing *Vagrant with flight years separated by decades; the last sighting was May 1974 in Carr Canyon, Huachuca Mountains.*
Northern Shrike *Vagrant to valley grasslands between early December and mid-March with years between sightings.*
White-eyed Vireo *Vagrant, primarily from May through July, to valley and canyon thickets.*
Black-capped Vireo *Hypothetical; 1 record in April 1970 from Tanque Verde Wash east of Tucson.*
Yellow-throated Vireo *Vagrant from May through September in desert oases, valley groves, and lower mountain canyons.*
Philadelphia Vireo *Vagrant in spring and fall to desert oases and valley groves.*
Yellow-green Vireo *Discussion in Specialties Section.*
Blue-winged Warbler *3 records: May 1986 from Sycamore Canyon, September 1992 from Portal, and May 1993 from Sonoita.*
Golden-winged Warbler *Vagrant, primarily in spring and fall, but also in winter to desert oases, city parks, and riparian timber.*
Tropical Parula *Discussion in Specialties Section.*
Crescent-chested Warbler *Discussion in Specialties Section.*
Magnolia Warbler *Vagrant in May and in October-November in desert oases, valley groves, and lower mountain canyons.*
Cape May Warbler *Vagrant from October through mid-April to desert oases, city parks, and riparian timber.*
Blackburnian Warbler *Vagrant in May and June and again in October to desert oases, city parks, and valley groves.*
Yellow-throated Warbler *Vagrant from January through September in desert oases, valley groves, and mountain canyons.*
Pine Warbler *Hypothetical; 3 records: November 1987–January 1988 at Benson, March 1991 at the Southwestern Research Station, and October 1994 in Tucson.*
Prairie Warbler *3 records: December 1952, January 1965, and December 1974–January 1975, all from Tucson.*
Palm Warbler *Vagrant from September through May to desert oases, valley groves, and mountain canyons.*
Bay-breasted Warbler *Vagrant, primarily in May to desert oases, valley groves, and mountain canyons.*
Blackpoll Warbler *Vagrant, primarily in September-October, but with a few spring appearances to desert oases, valley groves, and mountain canyons.*
Cerulean Warbler *2 records: May 1970 in Cave Creek Canyon and May 1979 in Madera Canyon.*
Worm-eating Warbler *Vagrant, primarily in April and May, but scattered throughout year to desert oases, valley groves, and mountain canyons.*
Ovenbird *Vagrant, primarily in May and June and October to desert oases, valley groves, and mountain canyons.*
Connecticut Warbler *1 record in September 1979 from Tucson.*

Mourning Warbler *Hypothetical; 2 sight records in September 1988 from near Charleston on the upper San Pedro River and August 1993 from Florida Wash.*
Canada Warbler *4 records: September 1975 from Sabino Canyon, August and October 1979 from Tucson, and September 1993 from Ida Canyon, Huachuca Mountains.*
Slate-throated Redstart *Discussion in Specialties Section.*
Fan-tailed Warbler *Discussion in Specialties Section.*
Rufous-capped Warbler *Discussion in Specialties Section.*
Scarlet Tanager *Vagrant, primarily in October, to desert oases, valley groves, and lower mountain canyons.*
Dark-eyed "Red-backed" Junco *Vagrant, from October through April, in mountain canyons. (This subspecies breeds in Central Arizona.)*
Lapland Longspur *5 records: February-March 1984 at Elfrida, October 1989 at Arivaca Cienaga, January and November-December 1991 and March 1995 at San Rafael Grassland.*
Smith's Longspur *Hypothetical; 1 record in November 1986 from near Charleston on the upper San Pedro River.*
Bobolink *Vagrant, primarily in August and September, to sewage ponds, wet pastures, and fields.*
Rusty Blackbird *Vagrant from November through March at valley, ponds, farms, pastures, and cattle pens.*
Common Grackle *Vagrant from November through May, primarily from valley agricultural areas, but also from Portal, April 1992.*
Black-vented Oriole *Discussion in Specialties Section.*
 Orchard Oriole *Vagrant from May through September, primarily in May and June, to desert oases, valley groves, and mountain canyons.*
Baltimore Oriole *Vagrant from April through June to Tucson and Portal.*
Pine Grosbeak *3 records: November 1972 from Bear Wallow, Santa Catalina Mountains, and November 1978 and January 1982 from Rustler Park, Chiricahua Mountains.*

Amphibians and Reptiles
of Southeastern Arizona

Most desert and foothill reptiles are nocturnal and are seldom seen unless a special effort is made to find them. Those unexpectedly found during the day frequently give both the observer and the animal quite a fright. As a rule, the best way to find reptiles with minimal stress to either their or your nervous system is to drive back-country roads at night—particularly after rains. The best roads are those that have vegetation growing close to the edges. The following appendix is complete. You'll be fortunate to find even a small fraction of the species listed, and it's entirely possible to bird Southeast Arizona for a week or a month without seeing a snake at all, let alone a rattler.

SALAMANDER

Arizona Tiger Salamander Rare; oak woodland streams. The only salamander in Arizona. Parker and Scotia Canyons in the Huachuca Mountains.

FROGS and TOADS

Western Barking Frog Rare; rocky hillsides in canyons, Santa Rita and Pajarito Mountains. Found after summer rains.
Couch's Spadefoot Abundant after first summer rains; deserts and grasslands .
Southern Spadefoot Abundant after summer rains; primarily desert.
Plains Spadefoot Abundant after summer rains; Upper Sonoran grasslands.
Sonoran Desert Toad Along tributaries of the Río Yaqui (San Bernardino Ranch and Guadalupe Canyon) and the Río de la Concepción (Sycamore Canyon).
Southwestern Woodhouse's Toad Permanent streams and irrigation ditches, mostly Lower Sonoran.
Red-spotted Toad Localized; pools and seeps in rocky canyons. Upper Sonoran.
Great Plains Toad Irrigation ditches and rain-pools of the deserts and grasslands, Lower and Upper Sonoran.
Green Toad Abundant after summer rains; grasslands, Cochise and Santa Cruz Counties.
Sonoran Green Toad Breeds after the summer rains in deserts west of Tucson.
Canyon Treefrog Common; rocky streams from the desert to the pines.
Mountain Treefrog Known only from Miller Canyon, Huachuca Mountains, where last sighted in 1970.
Tarahumara Frog Possibly now locally extirpated. Formerly found in the United States only along the tributaries of the Río de la Concepción (Sycamore, Peña Blanca, and Alamo Canyons) and Josephine Canyon in the Santa Rita Mountains.
Chiricahua Leopard Frog Rocky streams in oak and pine/oak woodlands.
Plains Leopard Frog Ponds and pools in the Sulphur Springs Valley and West Turkey Creek in the Chiricahua Mountains.
Lowland Leopard Frog Desert and foothill ponds and streams in the Santa Rita and Atascosa Mountains.
Subaquatic Singing Leopard Frog Accorded species status in 1993, this interesting species sings its courtship songs only underwater in pools in Ramsey and Brown Canyons in the Huachuca Mountains.
Bullfrog Introduced, primarily in valley ponds and lakes.
Sinaloa Narrow-mouthed Toad Rare; found after summer rains in pools and streams, Pajarito and Patagonia Mountains.

TURTLES

Yellow Mud Turtle Streams and ponds in the grasslands, Cochise and Pima Counties.
Sonoran Mud Turtle Streams of the Gila River drainage, chiefly in the woodlands.
Western Box Turtle Grasslands, mainly Cochise County.
Desert Tortoise Sonoran Desert from near Benson westward.
Spiny Softshell Introduced; now established in ponds and streams in the Santa Cruz and San Pedro watersheds.

LIZARDS

Tucson Banded Gecko Rocky areas protected from frost and around houses, Lower Sonoran.
Mediterranean Gecko Introduced in Tucson.
Desert Iguana Creosote flats in the Sonoran Desert west of Tucson.
Arizona Chuckwalla Rocky outcrops in the Sonoran Desert west of Avra Valley.
Lesser Earless Lizard Grasslands and areas of low brush, Upper Sonoran.
Greater Earless Lizard Washes and stream-beds in areas of low brush and open oak woodlands, Lower and Upper Sonoran.
Zebra-tailed Lizard Sandy plains, and deserts, Lower Sonoran.
Common Collared Lizard Rocky areas of deserts and foothills.
Large-spotted Leopard Lizard Brush grasslands and deserts, Lower Sonoran.
Bunch Grass Lizard Grassy slopes in coniferous forests of the border ranges.
Mountain Spiny Lizard Cliffs and talus slopes in oak and coniferous forests of the border ranges.
Northern Crevice Spiny Lizard Rocky areas in Guadalupe Canyon, Peloncillo Mountains.
Desert Spiny Lizard Desert scrub, mesquite thickets, cottonwood groves, and rocky areas, Lower Sonoran. Usually on the ground.
Clark's Spiny Lizard Mainly in wooded areas along streams on the slopes of the border ranges, Upper Sonoran. Usually found in trees.
Southern Prairie Lizard Many habitats, Upper Sonoran and Transition.
Striped Plateau Lizard Wooded streams within pine/oak woodland in the Chiricahua Mountains.
Side-blotched Lizard Many habitats, deserts and grasslands, Lower and Upper Sonoran.
Tree Lizard Trees and large rocks, from the deserts to the pines.
Texas Horned Lizard Plains with scrubby vegetation, Chihuahuan Desert in Cochise County.
Short-horned Lizard Primarily mountains. Not a desert species.
Round-tailed Horned Lizard Plains with scrubby vegetation, Chihuahuan Desert in Cochise County.
Regal Horned Lizard Rocky areas of desert foothills, Sonoran Desert in Pima and Santa Cruz Counties.
Great Plains Skink Under rocks and litter along water-courses, from the deserts to the mountains.
Mountain Skink Under rocks and litter in wooded areas of the border ranges.
Giant Spotted Whiptail Dense brush along water-courses, from the deserts and grasslands into the oak woodlands up to 4,500 feet.
Little Striped Whiptail Grasslands; known only from vicinity of Willcox Playa in Cochise County.
Desert Grassland Whiptail Plains and slopes of deserts and mesquite grasslands, Lower and Upper Sonoran.
Chihuahuan Spotted Whiptail Canyon bottoms in oak and oak/pine woodlands and in riparian woodlands and rocky areas of grasslands and deserts, mostly Upper Sonoran.
Sonoran Spotted Whiptail Oak woodland along the border.
Gila Spotted Whiptail Upper Sonoran chaparral and woodland in the Santa Catalina and Chiricahua Mountains.

Arizona Desert Whiptail Many habitats, but usually fairly open areas. From the deserts to the lower oak woodlands up to 4,500 feet.
Checkered Whiptail From creosote brush to pinyon pine. Known only from Peloncillo Mountains.
Madrean Alligator Lizard Under rocks and litter, primarily in pine/oak woodlands; rarely in coniferous forest or riparian woodlands in the deserts.
Gila Monster Rare; rocky areas from the deserts to lower edge of oak woodlands. Venomous.

SNAKES

Western Blind Snake Deserts and arid grasslands, Sonoran and Chihuahuan Deserts, Lower Sonoran.
Texas Blind Snake Deserts and grasslands, particularly in moist areas. Chihuahuan Deserts and surrounding grasslands.
Regal Ring-necked Snake Moist areas in oak grasslands and riparian woodlands, mostly Upper Sonoran.
Western Hog-nosed Snake Mainly grasslands, Upper Sonoran.
Spotted Leaf-nosed Snake Sandy soils, west of Tucson; nocturnal.
Saddled Leaf-nosed Snake Rocky soils, west of Tucson.
Coachwhip Many habitats, deserts and grasslands. Often very pink.
Sonoran Whipsnake From the brushy deserts to the oak/pine woodlands.
Western Patch-nosed Snake Open scrub of deserts, Lower Sonoran.
Graham Patch-nosed Snake Open oak and pine/-oak woodlands, Upper Sonoran.
Green Rat Snake Rare; canyons of the border ranges.
Glossy Snake Many habitats, deserts and grasslands; nocturnal.
Sonoran Gopher Snake Many habitats, from the deserts to the mountains. Probably the most commonly seen snake.
Common Kingsnake Many habitats in the deserts and grasslands. A black form with few or no light dorsal markings may be found south of Tucson.
Sonoran Mountain Kingsnake Scrub, woodlands, and coniferous forests of the mountains.
Western Long-nosed Snake Deserts and grasslands; nocturnal.
Western Black-necked Garter Snake Streams from the desert to the pines.
Mexican Garter Snake Streams, mainly on the grasslands.
Checkered Garter Snake Usually along streams and ponds in the deserts and grasslands.
Western Ground Snake Sandy plains and rocky hillsides of the deserts and grasslands.
Banded Sand Snake Sandy soils, Sonoran Deserts from lower San Pedro Valley westward.
Chihuahuan Hook-nosed Snake Known only from the deserts and grasslands in Cochise County.
Thornscrub Hook-nosed Snake Known only from the grasslands of Santa Cruz County.
Southwestern Black-headed Snake Under rocks and litter from the desert canyons to the oak woodlands.
Plains Black-headed Snake Under rocks and litter in the grasslands. Usually in moist areas.
Huachuca Black-headed Snake Rare; under rocks and litter in the grasslands and oak woodlands of the Huachuca, Santa Rita, and Patagonia Mountains.
Yaqui Black-headed Snake Streamside woodlands in the Chiricahua, Mule, and Atascosa Mountains.
Brown Vine Snake Rare; brush and trees along canyon bottoms. Known only from the area west of Nogales in the headwater tributaries of the Río de la Concepción.
Sonoran Lyre Snake Rocky canyons and hillsides from the deserts to the pines.
Night Snake Many habitats, from the desert to the oak woodlands.
Arizona Coral Snake Rare; arid habitats, from the deserts to the lower oak woodlands.
Massasauga Rare; grasslands of Cochise County.
Western Diamond-backed Rattlesnake Many habitats, from the deserts and grasslands to the lower oak woodlands. The most common valley rattlesnake.

Banded Rock Rattlesnake Rocky areas of the oak and pine/oak woodlands of the border ranges.
Black-tailed Rattlesnake Rocky areas from the deserts to the pines. The most common rattlesnake in the mountains.
Tiger Rattlesnake Rocky areas, Sonoran Desert west of Tucson.
Western "Arizona Black" Rattlesnake Many habitats, from the foothills to the pines. Found only in the Rincon and Santa Catalina Mountains and northward.
Mojave Rattlesnake Non-rocky plains of the open deserts and grasslands; rarely in the mountains.
Twin-spotted Rattlesnake Rocky areas within the coniferous forests of the border ranges.
Ridge-nosed Rattlesnake Rare; rocky areas in wooded canyons in the Santa Rita and Huachuca Mountains; two reports from the Chiricahua Mountains.

MAMMALS OF SOUTHEASTERN ARIZONA

Virginia "Sonoran" Opossum Possibly introduced: primarily in valley farming areas, but also recorded in canyons of the Huachuca Mountains.
Vagrant Shrew Meadows and grassy areas in the higher mountains.
Desert Shrew River woodlands at lower elevations.
Leaf-chinned Bat Known only from mines in Santa Cruz County.
California Leaf-nosed Bat Mines and caves at lower elevations.
Mexican Long-tongued Bat Small groups in mines, caves, and abandoned buildings at mid to high elevations in mountains. Endangered.
Lesser Long-nosed Bat Moist caves and mines. Colonial roosts. Endangered.
Yuma Myotis Mines, caves, tree hollows.
Cave Myotis Caves at lower elevations.
Southwestern Myotis Primarily in Ponderosa Pine and dense canyon woodlands.
Fringed Myotis Caves and buildings at higher elevations.
Long-legged Myotis Open forests at higher elevations.
California Myotis Caves and hollows; all elevations.
Small-footed Myotis Mines, caves, hollows; all elevations.
Silver-haired Bat Solitary; forested areas in the mountains.
Western Pipistrelle Crevices and buildings; all elevations.
Big Brown Bat Buildings and caves; all elevations.
Red Bat Solitary; forested areas in the mountains.
Southern Yellow Bat Roosts in Washington Fan Palms near Tucson, and probably sycamores and hackberry trees farther east.
Hoary Bat Solitary; hangs in trees, forested areas.
Allen's Lappet-browed Bat Usually at mid to high elevations in mountains.
Townsend's Western Big-eared Bat Caves, usually at higher elevations.
Mexican Big-eared Bat Colonial in mines and caves in the oak woodlands.
Pallid Bat Many habitats, all elevations.
Mexican Free-tailed Bat Mines, caves, buildings, low to mid elevations.
Pocketed Free-tailed Bat Mines and caves at lower elevations.
Big Free-tailed Bat Mines and caves at lower elevations.
Western Mastiff Bat Rock crevices at lower elevations.
Underwood's Mastiff Bat Rock crevices at lower elevations in the Baboquivari Mountains, primarily seen over ponds in the evenings.
Grizzly Bear Locally extirpated about 1901; formerly primarily in oak and pine/oak woodlands.
Black Bear Higher mountains. Crosses valleys from one mountain range to the next.
Ring-tail Rocky areas at all elevations; nocturnal.
Raccoon Streams at all elevations.
Coati Fairly common in oak and pine/oak woodlands.
Long-tailed Weasel Many habitats; all elevations.

Badger Valley grasslands and deserts.
Western Spotted Skunk Woodlands; all elevations.
Striped Skunk Many habitats; all elevations.
Hooded Skunk Common, brush and woodlands, Lower and Upper Sonoran.
Hog-nosed Skunk Common, brush and woodlands, Lower and Upper Sonoran.
Coyote Many habitats; all elevations.
Mexican Gray Wolf Probably extirpated; formerly throughout.
Kit Fox Desertscrub.
Gray Fox Scrub, Upper and Lower Sonoran.
Jaguar Straggler from Mexico, primarily in foothill canyons. Last recorded in the Dos
    Cabezas Mountains near Willcox in 1987 after a 49-year hiatus.
Mountain Lion Mountains, mid- to high elevations.
Ocelot One definite record from near Patagonia in 1960 and a sight record from Cave
    Creek in the Chiricahua Mountains in 1982. Usually found near foothill streams.
Jaguarundi Hypothetical; one seen in March 1938 in Canelo Hills. Scrub or deserts
    and lower mountain slopes.
Bobcat Primarily mountain and foothill edges, especially along water-courses.
Spotted Ground-Squirrel Grasslands, Sulphur Springs and San Pedro Valleys.
Rock Squirrel Rocky areas, Lower and Upper Sonoran.
Harris's Antelope Ground-Squirrel Deserts and grasslands.
Round-tailed Ground-Squirrel Deserts, lower elevations.
Cliff Chipmunk Scrub and woodlands, mountains. Not in Huachuca or Santa Rita
    Mountains.
Black-tailed Prairie-Dog Locally extirpated about 1938; formerly in valley grasslands
    surrounding the Chiricahua and Huachuca Mountains.
Abert's Tassel-eared Squirrel Introduced from Central Arizona into the Catalina
    Mountains.
Arizona Gray Squirrel Oaks and pines in all the mountains in the southeast corner
    except the Chiricahuas; also in the Patagonia-Sonoita Creek Preserve.
    Taxonomically, the Arizona Gray Squirrel is a true fox squirrel closely related
    to the Apache Fox Squirrel.
Apache Fox Squirrel Primarily pine/oak woodlands, but also regular in coniferous
    forest on the summit of Fly Peak at 9,666 feet elevation; in the U.S. endemic to
    the Chiricahua Mountains.
Southern Pygmy Pocket-Gopher Meadows and stream-banks, from Huachuca
    Mountains westward, Upper Sonoran.
Valley Pocket-Gopher Meadows and valleys, all elevations.
Bailey Pocket-Gopher Meadows at high elevations in the Huachuca and Chiricahua
    Mountains.
Silky Pocket-Mouse Grasslands, Upper Sonoran.
Arizona Pocket-Mouse Deserts, south and west of Tucson.
Bailey's Pocket-Mouse Deserts, south and west of Tucson.
Desert Pocket-Mouse Deserts and grasslands, Lower Sonoran.
Rock Pocket-Mouse Lava flows and rocky areas, Lower Sonoran.
Hispid Pocket-Mouse Grasslands, Upper Sonoran.
Banner-tailed Kangaroo-Rat Grasslands, Upper Sonoran.
Merriam's Kangaroo-Rat Deserts and grasslands, Lower Sonoran.
Ord's Kangaroo-Rat Grassland, Upper Sonoran.
Beaver Extirpated by 1900; formerly in cottonwood groves along the upper Santa
    Cruz and San Pedro Rivers.
Northern Pygmy-Mouse Grasslands, Upper Sonoran.
Southern Grasshopper-Mouse Weedy fields and grasslands, Lower Sonoran.
Plains Harvest-Mouse Grasslands, Cochise County.
Western Harvest-Mouse Weedy fields and grasslands, Lower and Upper Sonoran.
Fulvous Harvest-Mouse Grasslands, western Cochise and Santa Cruz Counties.
Pygmy Mouse Grasslands, Upper Sonoran.
Cactus Mouse Cactus, Lower Sonoran.
Merriam's Mouse Deserts, Pinal, Pima, and Santa Cruz Counties.
Deer Mouse Many habitats; all elevations.

White-footed Mouse Brush and woodlands; all elevations.
Brush Mouse Scrub; all elevations.
Pinyon Mouse Rocky pinyon/juniper areas, Chiricahua Mountains.
Rock Mouse Rocky areas, Chiricahua Mountains.
Hispid Cotton-Rat Open riparian and grassy areas, Lower Sonoran.
Least Cotton-Rat Grasslands, Lower and Upper Sonoran.
Yellow-nosed Cotton-Rat Foothills and mountains, Cochise and Santa Cruz Counties.
White-throated Woodrat Cactus and scrub, Lower and Upper Sonoran.
Mexican Woodrat Rocky scrub, Upper Sonoran.
Norway Rat Introduced; cities.
House Mouse Introduced; cities.
Porcupine Mesquite and cottonwood woods and aspen groves within coniferous forests, Lower Sonoran through Canadian.
Antelope Jackrabbit Brush, grasslands, foothills of the Santa Rita Mountains.
Black-tailed Jackrabbit Open deserts and grasslands, Lower and Upper Sonoran.
Eastern Cottontail Woodlands, Chiricahua Mountains.
Desert Cottontail Deserts and brush lands, Lower Sonoran.
Collared Peccary Deserts and oak woodlands, Lower and Upper Sonoran.
Merriam's Elk Extirpated from the Chiricahua Mountains in 1906. This race extinct.
Rocky Mountain "Desert" Mule Deer Desert scrub, foothills, and valley edges.
Coues White-tailed Deer River bottom groves, all woodlands and forested mountains.
Pronghorn Extirpated before 1900; present populations stem from re-introductions since 1949. Grasslands on the Buenos Aires Wildlife Refuge, near Sonoita, in the San Rafael Valley, on Fort Huachuca, in the upper Sulphur Springs Valley, and the San Bernardino Valley southeast of the Chiricahua Mountains harbor approximately 600 Pronghorns altogether, according to the Arizona Game and Fish Department.
Desert Bighorn Sheep Rocky, cliff-walled mountains in the Sonoran Desert north and west of Tucson. Pusch Ridge on the west end of the Santa Catalina Mountains and Aravaipa Canyon are the best areas in which to see this reclusive species. The Arizona Game and Fish Department estimated the total population in Southeastern Arizona was approximately 100-150 wild sheep in 1995.

SUGGESTED REFERENCES

Birds

Brown, David E. 1985. *Arizona Wetlands and Waterfowl.* University of Arizona Press.

_____. 1989. *Arizona Game Birds.* University of Arizona Press and Arizona Game and Fish Department.

Monson, Gale and Allan R. Phillips. 1981. *Annotated Checklist of the Birds of Arizona.* University of Arizona Press.

Phillips, Allan, Joe Marshall, and Gale Monson. 1964. *The Birds of Arizona.* University of Arizona Press.

Rosenberg, Gary H. and Dave Stejskal. 1994. *Field Checklist of the Birds of Arizona.* Arizona Bird Committee.

Taylor, Richard Cachor. 1993. *Location Checklist to the Birds of the Chiricahua Mountains.* Borderland Productions.

_____. 1995. *Location Checklist to the Birds of the Huachuca Mountains and the Upper San Pedro River.* Borderland Productions.

_____. 1994. *Trogons of the Arizona Borderlands.* Treasure Chest Publications.

Tucson Audubon Society. 1995. *Davis and Russell's Finding Birds in Southeast Arizona.*

Geology & History

Chronic, Halka. 1994. *Roadside Geology of Arizona.* Mountain Press Publishing Co.

Trimble, Marshall. 1994. *Roadside History of Arizona.* Mountain Press Publishing Co.

Plants

Arnberger, Leslie P. 1982. *Flowers of the Southwest Uplands.* Southwest Parks and Monuments Association.

Bowers, Janice. 1993. *Shrubs & Trees of the Southwest Deserts.* Southwest Parks and Monuments Association.

Brown, David E., editor. 1994. *Biotic Communities of the Southwest United States & Northwest Mexico.* University of Utah Press.

Craighead, John, Frank Craighead, and Ray Davis. 1991. *Field Guide to Rocky Mountain Wildflowers.* Houghton Mifflin Company.

Dodge, Natt. 1985. *Flowers of the Southwest Deserts.* Southwest Parks and Monuments Association.

Elmore, Frances and Jeanne Janish. 1976. *Shrubs & Trees of the Southwest Uplands.* Southwest Parks and Monuments Association.

Kearney, Thomas H. and Robert H. Peebles. 1963. *Arizona Flora.* University of California Press.

Insects

Bailowitz, Richard A. and James P. Brock. 1991. *Butterflies of Southeastern Arizona.* Sonoran Arthropod Studies.

Werner, Floyd and Carl Olsen. 1994. *Insects of the Southwest.* Fisher Books.

Reptiles

Lowe, Charles, Cecil Schwalbe and Terry Johnson. 1989. *The Venomous Reptiles of Arizona.* Arizona Game and Fish Department.

Stebbins, Robert C. 1985. *A Field Guide to Western Reptiles and Amphibians.* Houghton Mifflin Company.

Mammals

Cockrum, E. Lendell and Yar Petryszyn. 1992. *Mammals of the Southwest.* Treasure Chest Publications.

Hoffmeister, Donald F. 1986. *Mammals of Arizona.* University of Arizona Press and Arizona Game and Fish Department.

Native Americans

Arnold, Elliot. 1979. *Blood Brother.* University of Nebraska Press. (novel)

Opler, Morris Edward. 1965. *An Apache Life-Way.* University of Chicago Press.

Preston, Douglas. 1992. *Cities of Gold.* Simon & Schuster.

Spicer,Edward H. 1976. *Cycles of Conquest.* University of Arizona Press.

Natural History

Heald, Weldon. 1993. *The Chiricahua Sky Island.* Marguerite Bantlin Publishing.

Krutch, Joseph Wood. 1952. *The Desert Year.* University of Arizona Press.

Nabhan, Gary Paul. 1987. *Gathering the Desert.* University of Arizona Press.

Hiking

Cowgill, Pete and Eber Glendening. 1975. *Trail Guide to the Santa Catalina Mountains* by Rainbow Expeditions.

Leavengood, Betty. 1991. *Tucson Hiking Guide* by Pruett Publishing Company.

_____ and Mike Liebert. 1994. *Hiker's Guide to the Santa Rita Mountains.* Pruett Publishing Company.

Taylor, Leonard. 1991. *Hiker's Guide to the Huachuca Mountains.* Thunder Peak Productions.

Taylor, Richard Cachor. 1977. *Hiking Trails and Wilderness Routes of the Chiricahua Mountains.* Rainbow Expeditions.

Newsletter

Tucson Audubon Society. *The Vermilion Flycatcher* (monthly bulletin). 300 E. University Blvd., #120, Tucson, AZ 85705.

Tape

Keller, Geoffrey. 1988. *Bird Songs of Southeastern Arizona & Southern Texas.* Sora Record Company.

Video

Godfrey, Michael. 1988. *Hummingbirds Up Close.* Nature Science Network.

Godfrey, Michael. 1990. *Owls Up Close.* Nature Science Network.

Gates, Larry and Terri Gates. 1993. *Birds of Southeastern Arizona.* Portal Productions.

ABA

The Organization Devoted to North American Birders

ABA is *the* organization of North American birders and its mission is to bring all the excitement, challenge, and wonder of birding to you. As an ABA member you will get the information you need to increase your birding skills so you can make the most of your time in the field.

Each year members receive six issues of ABA's award-winning magazine, *Birding,* and twelve issues of *Winging It,* a monthly newsletter. ABA's periodicals put you in touch with the birding scene across the continent. ABA conducts regular conferences and biennial conventions in the continent's best birding areas, publishes a yearly *Membership Directory/Yellow Pages* to help you keep in touch, offers discount prices for bird books, optical gear, and other birding equipment through ABA Sales, and compiles an annual *Directory of Volunteer Opportunities* for members. The organization's *ABA/Lane Birdfinding Guides* set the standard for accuracy and excellence.

ABA is engaged in bird conservation through such activities as Partners in Flight and the American Bird Conservancy. ABA encourages birding among young people through youth birding camps and other activities, and publishes *A Bird's-Eye View,* a newsletter by and for its younger members. The organization promotes ethical birding practices. In short, the American Birding Association works to insure that birds and birding have the healthy future they deserve.

"ABA is the best value in the birding community today."
Roger Tory Peterson

The American Birding Association gives active birders what they want. Consider joining today. You will find a membership application in the other side of this page.

American Birding Association
PO Box 6599
Colorado Springs,
Colorado 80934-6599

AMERICAN BIRDING ASSOCIATION
Membership Application

All memberships include six issues of **Birding** magazine, monthly issues of **Winging It,** ABA's newsletter, member discounts offered by ABA Sales, and full rights of participation in all ABA activities.

Membership classes and dues:

❑ Individual - US	$36.00 / yr	❑ Family - US	$43.00 / yr
❑ Individual - Canada	$38.52 / yr	❑ Family - Canada	$46.01 / yr
❑ Individual - Int'l	$45.00 / yr	❑ Family - Int'l	$52.00 / yr
❑ Century Club	$100.00 / yr	❑ Life Membership	$1,200.00

US Funds only, please

Application Type

❑ New Membership   ❑ Renewal

Member Information

Name _____

Address _____

_____

_____

Phone _____

Payment Information

❑ Check or Money Order enclosed (US funds only)

❑ Charge to VISA / MasterCard (circle one)

Account Number _____

Exp Date _____

Signature _____

Sent this completed form with payment to: **ABA Membership**
PO Box 6599
Colorado Springs, CO 80934

SEAZ 7/95

OTHER BIRDFINDING GUIDES IN ABA/LANE SERIES

A Birder's Guide to Arkansas
new format, 1995, $16.95
A Birder's Guide to Eastern Massachusetts
new format, 1994, $16.95
A Birder's Guide to Churchill (Manitoba)
new format, 1994, $14.95
A Birder's Guide to Wyoming
new format, 1993, $16.95
A Birder's Guide to the Texas Coast
new format, 1993, $14.95
A Birder's Guide to the Rio Grande Valley of Texas
new format, 1994, $16.95
A Birder's Guide to Southern California
new format, 1990, $14.95
A Birder's Guide to Florida
under revision
A Birder's Guide to Colorado
under revision
A Birder's Guide to New Hampshire
in preparation
After the Birds: A Birder's Guide to Planning Major Trips
in preparation

These and many other birdfinding and bird identification publications are available from:

ABA Sales
PO Box 6599
Colorado Springs, CO 80934
Toll-free (US and Canada): phone 800-634-7736
fax 800-590-2473
International: phone 719-578-0607 — fax 719-578-9705

Write, call, or fax to order or to request a free *ABA Sales Annotated Catalog* containing hundreds of publications and other items of interest to birders.

Dealer inquiries invited.

ARIZONA BIRD REPORT

Species: Date:

Number: Age: Sex:

Locality (Exact address or other specific information to describe location, such as *x miles north of x intersection*):

County: City: Elevation:
Time: Length of time observed:
Habitat:

Distance to bird: Light conditions:
Optical equipment:
Observer:
Other observers who independently identified this bird:

Description. Write a detailed description of the bird's appearance, including size, shape, plumage, pattern, color, and any unique features:

Voice and/or call notes:

Behavior:

Describe what specific feature(s) you saw and/or heard that caused you to come to your conclusions:

What similar species might it have been, and how were these eliminated?

What experience have you had with this and similar species?

Books, illustrations, and advice consulted, and how these influenced this description:

Significance of record in the area and/or state:

Additional information (attach drawing, photograph, tape-recording if available):

Signature:

Address: Date Prepared:

Phone:

NOMENCLATURE CHANGES

The bird names used in this book basically follow those of the American Ornithologists' Union (AOU) and the American Birding Association (ABA). Below are some names which differ from those used in older field guides, or which have yet to appear in even the most recent field guides.

Current Name	Former Name or Derivation
Neotropic Cormorant	Neotropical or Olivaceous Cormorant
Tricolored Heron	Louisiana Heron
Green Heron	Green-backed Heron
Black-bellied Whistling-Duck	Black-bellied Tree Duck
Fulvous Whistling-Duck	Fulvous Tree Duck
Tundra Swan	Whistling Swan
"Mexican Duck"	now conspecific with Mallard
Northern Pintail	Common Pintail
Black Scoter	Common or American Scoter
Northern Harrier	Marsh Hawk
Common Black-Hawk	Lesser Black Hawk
Common Moorhen	Common Gallinule
Red-necked Phalarope	Northern Phalarope
American Golden-Plover	split from Lesser Golden-Plover
Western Screech-Owl	split from Common Screech Owl
Northern Saw-whet Owl	Saw-whet Owl
Common Poorwill	Poor-will
Buff-collared Nightjar	Ridgeway's Whip-poor-will
Magnificent Hummingbird	Rivoli's Hummingbird
Elegant Trogon	Coppery-tailed Trogon
Red-naped Sapsucker	split from Yellow-bellied Sapsucker
Strickland's Woodpecker	Arizona or Brown-backed Woodpecker
Gilded Flicker	split from Northern Flicker
Northern Beardless-Tyrannulet	Northern Beardless Flycatcher
Greater Pewee	Coues Flycatcher
Western Wood-Pewee	Western Pewee
Pacific-slope Flycatcher	split from Western Flycatcher
Cordilleran Flycatcher	split from Western Flycatcher
Dusky-capped Flycatcher	Olivaceous Flycatcher
Brown-crested Flycatcher	Wied's Crested Flycatcher
Western Scrub-Jay	split from Scrub Jay
Mexican Jay	Gray-breasted Jay
Chihuahuan Raven	White-necked Raven
Common Raven	Northern Raven
Marsh Wren	Long-billed Marsh Wren
American Pipit	Water Pipit
Northern Parula	Northern Parula Warbler
Spotted Towhee	split from Rufous-sided Towhee
Canyon Towhee	split from Brown Towhee
Dark-eyed Junco	Northern Junco
Yellow-eyed Junco	Mexican Junco
Streak-backed Oriole	Scarlet-headed Oriole
Bullock's Oriole	split from Northern Oriole
Lesser Goldfinch	Dark-backed Goldfinch
House Sparrow	English Sparrow

NOTES

Tear-Out Trail Map:
Scheelite Canyon, Fort Huachuca

● = Spotted Owl sighting locations since 1978
From data recorded by Robert T. Smith

Contour Interval: 100 feet

.... = foot trail

Garden Canyon

To Entrance Gate
Fort Huachuca

North

P

x El. 5,500'

To
Sawmill
Canyon

1/8 mile

1/4 mile

bedrock

3/8 mile

El. 7,200' x

1/2 mile

cliff

"Jaws"
eye-level
cave

Original Lower
Roosting Area

5/8 mile

bedrock

Middle
Roosting
Area

3/4 mile

Upper
Roosting
Area

talus

7/8 mile

Shiprock

To Crest Trail
(2.8 miles from
junction)

Birding in Scheelite Canyon

Look for Painted Redstarts in Bigtooth Maple grove by parking area. Trail starts behind enormous boulders across the road. It is steep and mined with rolling rocks. *There is no drinking water in the canyon.* A walking stick might help you keep your balance. Take and use sunscreen.

Scheelite is most famous for its Spotted Owls, but it is also a good location for other pine/oak woodland birds. Watch for Strickland's Woodpecker, Red-naped Sapsucker (winter), Bridled Titmouse, Virginia's Warbler (summer), and Rufous-crowned Sparrow in the lower drainage. This is also the best stretch for Montezuma Quail, Hammond's and Dusky Flycatchers (migration), Dusky-capped Flycatcher (summer), Western Scrub-Jay (screeching from the brushy slopes above), Hutton's Vireo, Black-throated Gray Warbler (summer), Black-headed Grosbeak, and Spotted Towhee. After ½ mile, the trail approaches an area with a towering cliff on the right side. This is the start of the "Lower Area" commonly used by the owls for roosting (although they can occur as low as ¼ mile). Listen for Canyon Wrens here. In summer, Painted Redstarts are invariably here, as well as a pair of Red-faced Warblers. Summering Cordilleran Flycatchers nest in this cool, shady zone.

"Jaws," a rock formation to the left is set amidst tall timber. Listen for Northern Pygmy-Owl, Whip-poor-will (occasionally even in the daytime during summer), Red-breasted Nuthatch, House Wren, and Hepatic Tanager (summer).

Ordinarily, Spotted Owls take perches under 20 feet in height, preferably on a major limb in the lower half of a tree. In large oaks, they may park well out on a bough, but look for them to sit near the trunk in small trees and conifers. The pair is often side by side, and usually within 300 feet of one another if both are present, but they may be in different roosting areas. The code of self-restraint which Smitty asks birders to exercise is simple:

Do not approach within 50 feet of the birds—Do not talk loudly—Do not point at the birds or wave your arms— Photographers should not use flash or make noise to get the birds' attention— Do not use tape recordings or try to imitate the calls of Spotted Owls. (Spotted Owl calls are specifically prohibited on Fort Huachuca.)

Approximately 100 yards beyond the 5/8-mile marker, Scheelite narrows to a rocky chute with a small spring, except in extremely dry years. Platter-sized pools attract warblers. You may spot a Montezuma Quail on the slopes above the pools. White-throated Swifts and Violet-green Swallows (summer) zoom overhead, and an occasional Golden Eagle floats across the narrow slit of sky. Check here for Greater Pewee (summer) and the "Plumbeous" form of Solitary Vireo. Mexican Jays occur throughout Scheelite, but above the chute Steller's Jays are common, also. At mile-marker ¾, approximately 150 paces beyond the seep, Scheelite splits into two major canyons. Elevation here is 6,350 feet, some 850 feet above the parking area.

The main trail continues up the left fork another 2.8 miles, climbing steeply 2,000 feet before it joins the Crest Trail. The Spotted Owls sometimes roost near the junction—and, infrequently, in the first 200 yards up the left fork, but usually the birds are up the unmaintained track ascending the right-hand fork. Look for them in dense stands of maple or oak, especially between 200 and 650 yards upcanyon from the junction. The trail peters out 200 yards or so beyond "Shiprock", a prow-shaped boulder in the center of the dry creek-bed.

Take your time on the trip downcanyon—and stay quiet until you are back to your vehicle.

Tear-Out Trail Map: Sycamore Canyon

The darker the shading, the higher the elevation.

The darkest areas have elevations above 4,800 feet.

The lightest areas have elevations between 3,400 and 3,600 feet. Contour interval is 200 feet.

See reverse for birding and trail information, as well as precautions about birding this remote canyon.

© 1995, American Birding Association, *A Birder's Guide to Southeastern Arizona*

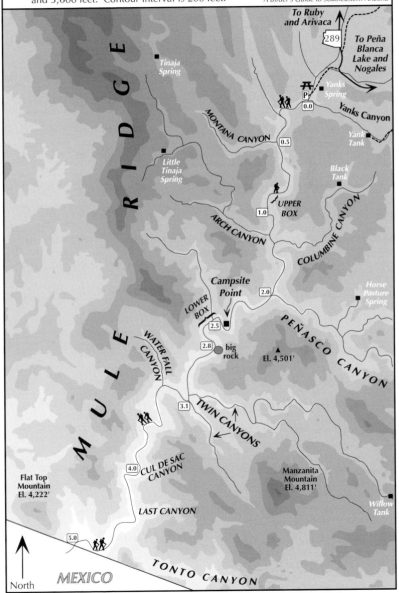

To Ruby and Arivaca

To Peña Blanca Lake and Nogales

289

Tinaja Spring

MONTANA CANYON

Yanks Spring

P 0.0

Yanks Canyon

0.5

Yank Tank

Little Tinaja Spring

1.0

UPPER BOX

Black Tank

ARCH CANYON

COLUMBINE CANYON

R I D G E

Campsite Point

2.0

Horse Pasture Spring

LOWER BOX

2.5

2.8 big rock

El. 4,501'

PEÑASCO CANYON

WATER FALL CANYON

M U L E

3.1

TWIN CANYONS

4.0

CUL DE SAC CANYON

Manzanita Mountain El. 4,811'

Flat Top Mountain El. 4,222'

LAST CANYON

Willow Tank

5.0

North

MEXICO

TONTO CANYON

No one should hike down **Sycamore Canyon** without water. From April - October, take 3 to 4 quarts *per person*. Depart well before sunrise—carry lunch—add a first aid kit to your knapsack—take *(and use)* both hat and sunscreen. This is not a well-traveled area—*bird with a companion* who could go for assistance. Sudden weather changes, that may not be apparent to you down in the canyon are possible, as are flash-floods.

After wet winters, Parry Penstemon along trail leading to the stream host Costa's Hummingbird (April and May). Broad-billed and Black-chinned Hummingbirds (summer) are the common species beyond where the trail drops into the streambed. Ferruginous Pygmy-Owl is a remote possibility just above Montana Canyon. Big ash trees at confluence of Montana Canyon (0.5 mile) on the right (west) side ordinarily mark upper limits patrolled by Elegant Trogons.

One mile downstream from parking area, the canyon twists around a waterfall—best negotiated by climbing over a small spur on the left (east) side. A pair of Sulphur-bellied Flycatchers often nests here. The waterfall signals the beginning of Upper Box area. For the next 0.25 mile, the water threads its way through a tortuous stone vise. At the bottom end of the Upper Box, the stream plunges across polished granite through a gap only 10 feet wide. Unless you are *very sure* of your footing, plan on getting wet. Acrobatic birders may be able to pass this pool by spidering along the right (west) wall of the stream.

A series of plunge-pools carved out of solid rock on the right (west) side right below Upper Box indicate the confluence of Arch Canyon. A short distance beyond, a little brook trimmed with Golden Columbine trickles in from the left (east) side (Columbine Canyon). Stay on the right side of Sycamore Canyon to negotiate the next few canyon bends and boulder fields. The canyon suddenly widens and sycamore trees shade the canyon floor for the remaining 0.25 mile down to the Peñasco Canyon tributary, which joins Sycamore from the left (east) side.

Pause here to bird. All the Madrean pine/oak woodland species of the border ranges occur in this area, many 1,000 feet below their usual altitudinal limits. **In summer:** Zone-tailed Hawk, Montezuma Quail, Band-tailed Pigeon, Elegant Trogon, Strickland's Woodpecker, "Red-shafted" Northern Flicker, Western Wood-Pewee, Dusky-capped, Brown-crested, and Sulphur-bellied Flycatchers, Cassin's Kingbird, Violet-green Swallow, Mexican Jay, Bridled Titmouse, Bushtit, White-breasted Nuthatch, Bewick's Wren, Hermit Thrush, "Plumbeous" Solitary Vireo, Painted Redstart, Hepatic and Summer Tanagers, Black-headed Grosbeak, Spotted and Canyon Towhees, Rufous-crowned Sparrow, Hooded, Bullock's, and Scott's Orioles, House Finch, and Lesser Goldfinch. **In migration:** Warbling Vireo and Western Tanager. **In winter:** Red-naped Sapsucker and Yellow-rumped Warbler (mostly "Audubon's", but mixed with "Myrtle"). Louisiana Waterthrush is very rare from mid-July through mid-March.

A trail-of-use generally hugs the base of the left (east) wall of Sycamore Canyon down to Campsite Point, a spur with a natural flat top about 15 feet above stream level that projects into canyon from the right (west) side at about mile 2.5. Just beyond, the canyon takes a sudden jog to the north, then to the west, as it negotiates the Lower Box. Wading may be unavoidable.

A Fan-tailed Warbler hung out (1987) behind "Big Rock", a huge boulder on the left (east) side at mile 2.8. The mile or so of Sycamore Canyon below Big Rock is probably more likely to shelter overwintering trogons than any other area in Arizona. In summer Varied Buntings are common below Big Rock.

"Twin Canyons" come in from the left (east) only a few yards apart at mile 3.1—this is the upper end of Rose-throated Becard, Thick-billed Kingbird, and Five-striped Sparrow zone. Some summers Rose-throated Becards are found. Five-stripes are probably present every year—in an average summer there are about 50 adults (mid-April through August). Slopes used by the sparrows are matted with impenetrable thickets of thornscrub; males usually sing from exposed perches.

There is ordinarily no reason to continue downcanyon beyond "Cul de Sac Canyon" at mile 4.0. Saguaros now dominate and the birds are similar to those found near Tucson. The trip back to your car will take at least as long as the hike down, even without birding. Watch your footing! Drink your water! Refresh your sunscreen!

Tear-Out Trail Map:
Mt. Wrightson Area Trails
Madera Canyon

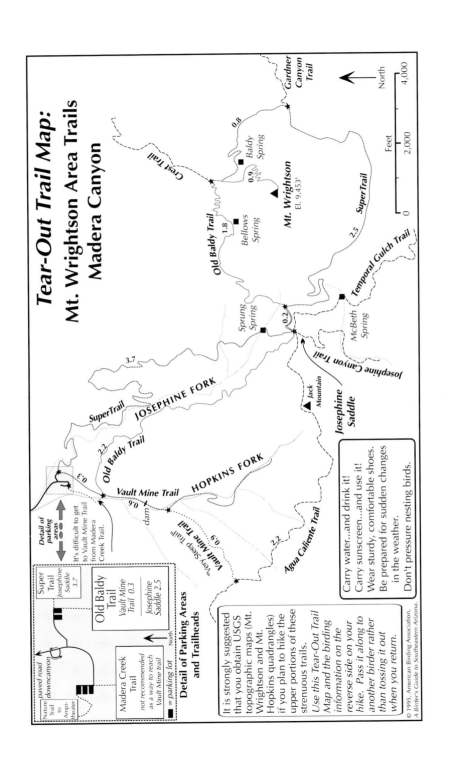

Gardner Canyon Trail

North

4,000

Feet

2,000

0

0.8

Baldy Spring

Crest Trail

0.9

Mt. Wrightson
El. 9,453'

Old Baldy Trail

1.8

Bellows Spring

SuperTrail

2.5

Sprung Spring

0.2

Temporal Gulch Trail

McBeth Spring

Josephine Canyon Trail

3.7

SuperTrail

JOSEPHINE FORK

Old Baldy Trail

2.2

Jack Mountain

Josephine Saddle

Detail of parking areas

It's difficult to get to Vault Mine Trail from Madera Creek Trail.

0.3

Vault Mine Trail

0.6

dam

HOPKINS FORK

"Very Steep Trail"

Vault Mine Trail

0.9

Agua Caliente Trail

2.2

Nature Trail to Amphitheater

paved road downcanyon

North

Detail of Parking Areas and Trailheads

Super Trail
Josephine Saddle 3.7

Old Baldy Trail
Vault Mine Trail 0.3
Josephine Saddle 2.5

Madera Creek Trail
not recommended as a way to reach Vault Mine trail

■ = parking lot

It is strongly suggested that you obtain USGS topographic maps (Mt. Wrightson and Mt. Hopkins quadrangles) if you plan to hike the upper portions of these strenuous trails.

Use this Tear-Out Trail Map and the birding information on the reverse side on your hike. Pass it along to another birder rather than tossing it out when you return.

Carry water...and drink it!
Carry sunscreen...and use it!
Wear sturdy, comfortable shoes.
Be prepared for sudden changes in the weather.
Don't pressure nesting birds.

Hopkins Fork: From trailhead on upper tier of Josephine Fork parking lot, a dirt road contours 0.3 mile across ridge dividing Josephine Fork from Hopkins Fork. Trail joins Hopkins Fork near beginning of Old Baldy Trail (0.3 mile), which is a steep short-cut to Josephine Saddle (2.2 miles long instead of the 3.7-mile alternative). Birders should ignore Old Baldy Trail and take route continuing straight up the bottom of Hopkins Fork.

The upper branches of Madera Canyon have a large number of House Wrens. One of several Aztec Thrushes found in Madera Canyon used the stretch of Hopkins Fork right above the Old Baldy Trail junction (Aug 1989). Elegant Trogons have tried to nest just below trail junction, but photographers invariably cause these nests to fail. *Under no circumstances should you disturb or knowingly approach an active nest tree.*

Most reliable area for Elegant Trogons is in the basin ¼ mile farther upcanyon. The trail follows the left side of the stream for 200 or so yards, then climbs a steep, rocky hill. Links of an old pipeline are frequent up to a concrete spring-box on the right side of the path. This marks the lower end of the trogon-nesting zone, although pairs patrol the whole length of Hopkins Fork. Other summering species here include Cooper's Hawk, Flammulated Owl, Magnificent Hummingbird, Greater Pewee, Cordilleran, Dusky-capped, and Sulphur-bellied Flycatchers, Solitary and Hutton's Vireos, Grace's Warbler, Painted Redstart, and Hepatic Tanager. Common in migration are Warbling Vireo, and Western Tanager. One or two Red-faced Warblers are often here in April and May. Look for Painted Redstarts near a permanent spring that cascades between a pair of slab-like boulders just 100 yards above the spring-box. Two Aztec Thrushes were discovered above the spring-box in August 1994.

Trail crosses the stream in ¼-mile, then divides 200 yards beyond. The Vault Mine Trail up to the Agua Caliente Trail is the "very steep trail" mentioned on the sign at the trailhead. It leads 0.5 mile to the abandoned Vault Mine, over 600 feet above, and is *not* recommended above this junction. Birders who still need the trogon should veer left

another 200 yards up the bottom of Hopkins Fork to where trail disappears into the rocks of the stream channel itself. The ¼-mile stretch above the stream-crossing to where the trail ends in the streambed is just as good for trogons as the ¼-mile stretch below the stream-crossing. If the trogons are nesting you may have to wait *patiently* all morning for a nest-exchange before a bird passes by. *No tapes are allowed in the canyon*. From here back to the Josephine Fork parking area is 0.9 mile.

At the left (NE) end of **Josephine Fork** parking area is the start of the 8-mile-long Super Trail to Mount Wrightson. This scenic path is great for birding. *Don't forget to carry plenty of water.* At first, you will be in the oak belt, where the birds will be about the same as those in the middle canyon near Santa Rita Lodge. Elegant Trogons occasionally nest in sycamores along the stream, approximately one mile up Josephine.

After one mile, trail makes a sharp switchback to the left to climb a dry hillside. Hutton's Vireo, Black-throated Gray Warbler, and Scott's Oriole are typical birds. About 3 miles above parking area, trail enters Ponderosa Pine, home of Greater Pewee, Grace's Warbler, and Yellow-eyed Junco. Watch for Red-faced Warbler at Sprung Spring (3.8 miles above parking area). Eared Trogon was sighted here in July/Aug 1991. Josephine Saddle (El. 7,100') is only 0.2 mile beyond, 1,700 feet above the parking lot.

In the forested glades of the remaining four miles on the Super Trail to the 9,453-foot-high summit of Mt. Wrightson, look for Broad-tailed Hummingbird, Hairy Woodpecker, Steller's Jay, Red-breasted and Pygmy Nuthatches, Brown Creeper, House Wren, Yellow-rumped, Grace's, Red-faced, and Olive Warblers, Hepatic and Western Tanagers, Yellow-eyed Junco, Red Crossbill (irregular), and Pine Siskin. The Baldy Saddle area (elevation 8,800 feet; 0.9 mile below Mt. Wrightson summit) is a particularly good location for most of these species. In May 1993, a Buff-breasted Flycatcher was reported from the saddle.

INDEX

Whooping 228, 303
Creeper
Brown 37, 86, 91, 113, 118, 124, 168, 170, 173, 177, 249, 289
Crossbill
Red 37, 40, 91, 172, 177, 266, 300
Crow
American 248, 288
Cuckoo
Black-billed 303
Yellow-billed 8, 52, 57, 65, 67, 96, 98, 127, 131, 134, 156, 230, 281
Curlew
Long-billed 145, 148, 153, 278

D

Deer
Desert Mule 24, 62, 83, 96
White-tailed 68
White-tailed Coues 37, 172
Dickcissel 146, 297
Dipper
American 42, 170, 222, 250, 290

Dos Cabezas Mountains 303
Douglas 213, 224, 226-229, 236-237, 252, 269
Dove
Inca 7, 23, 27, 30, 52, 65, 164, 229-230, 280
Mourning 20, 30, 42-43, 52, 280
Rock 280
White-winged 8, 20, 30, 42-43, 50, 52, 61, 67, 86, 96, 134, 162, 187, 195, 215, 229, 280
Dowitcher
Long-billed 29, 100, 132, 146, 279
Short-billed 132, 146, 279
Drive-In Theater Ponds (Nogales) 56, 224, 239
Duck
Black-bellied Tree 319
Fulvous Tree 319
Ring-necked 54, 57, 146, 274
Ruddy 54, 133, 146, 148, 275
Wood 45, 273
Dudleyville 189, 225, 232, 241, 245, 265, 270, 302
Dunlin 146, 279

E

Eagle
Bald 9, 136, 150, 152, 207, 225, 275
Golden 70, 86, 101-102, 112, 115, 124, 133, 144, 149-152, 154, 160, 163, 205, 207, 211, 213, 226, 276
Egret
Cattle 136, 153, 273
Great 153, 185, 273
Snowy 130, 133, 153, 185, 273
Elfrida 152, 225-226, 228, 248, 263, 269, 305
Elgin 261
Escapule Wash (Sierra Vista) 137, 231

F

Fairbank 140, 260-261, 269, 304
Falcon
Aplomado 154, 227, 302
Peregrine 37, 41, 76, 101, 150, 168, 170, 188, 227, 277
Prairie 28, 31, 70, 97, 101, 133, 150, 182, 207, 211, 227, 277
Finch
Cassin's 37, 87, 167, 265, 300
House 20, 30, 42-43, 55, 78, 87, 144, 162, 167, 195, 199, 215, 300
Purple 300
Flicker
Gilded 20, 42-43, 46, 52, 58, 67, 129, 134, 191, 240, 285
Northern 319
Northern "Red-shafted" 20, 27, 31, 36, 58, 67, 86, 96, 119, 123, 129, 179, 198, 215, 285
Northern "Yellow-shafted" 303

Blue 46, 52, 54, 57, 68, 76, 83, 100, 109, 113, 129, 134, 151, 156, 162-163, 167, 195, 215, 260, 296
Evening 38, 113, 167, 180, 266, 301
Pine 305
Rose-breasted 296
Yellow 8, 61-62, 140, 171, 260, 296
Ground-Dove
Common 30, 58, 67-68, 96, 130, 134, 215, 230, 280
Ruddy 3, 7, 27, 30, 60, 70, 132, 230, 280
Ground-Squirrel
Harris's Antelope 24, 68, 79
Spotted 154
Grouse
Blue 302
Guadalupe Canyon 2, 213, 227, 234-235, 239, 241, 243-245, 247, 249-254, 258, 261-262, 270
Guevavi Ranch Ponds (Nogales) 303
Gull
Bonaparte's 146, 279
California 280
Franklin's 132, 146, 279

Heermann's 303
Herring 303
Laughing 303
Ring-billed 146, 279
Sabine's 146, 156, 280
Thayer's 303

H
Hamburg Meadow (Huachuca Mtns) 116
Harrier
Northern 8, 26, 31, 55, 70, 76, 97, 101, 107, 129, 136, 144, 150, 275
Harshaw Canyon (Patagonia) 233, 251-252
Harshaw Creek (Patagonia) 205
Hawk
Broad-winged 302
Cooper's 24, 27, 31, 42, 52, 90, 101, 113, 118-119, 123, 150, 162, 168, 187, 215, 275
Ferruginous 8, 134, 136, 149-151, 206, 219, 226, 276
Gray 7, 50, 52-53, 55, 57, 59-62, 65, 67-68, 96, 98, 105, 127, 131, 137-138, 141, 188-189, 217, 225, 270, 276
Harris's 25, 144, 152-153, 225, 276
Lesser Black 319
Marsh 319
Red-shouldered 302
Red-tailed 8, 26, 31, 41-42, 76, 78, 101, 107, 112-113, 123-124, 133, 144, 149-150, 168, 183, 276
Rough-legged 26, 31, 136, 149, 153, 226, 276
Sharp-shinned 27, 30, 52, 101, 150, 275
Short-tailed 302
Swainson's 8, 70, 101, 113, 129, 133-134, 144, 151, 154, 163, 213, 226, 276
White-tailed 302
Zone-tailed 7, 27, 37, 41, 59, 62, 65, 68, 76, 86, 102, 112, 116, 123-124, 168, 171-172, 179, 182, 198, 205, 210, 215, 217, 222, 226, 276
Herb Martyr Campground (Chiricahua Mtns) 172
Herb Martyr Road (Chiricahua Mtns) 171
Hereford 251, 254, 266, 303
Hereford Bridge (Sierra Vista) 134, 231
Hereford Road 264
Heron
Great Blue 29, 45, 52, 55, 57, 65, 69, 96, 100, 131, 146, 156, 164, 185, 195, 273
Green 45, 57, 59, 96, 130, 136, 185, 273
Green-backed 319
Little Blue 134, 273
Louisiana 319
Tricolored 136, 164, 273
Hooker's Hot Springs (Muleshoe Preserve) 217
Hopkins Fork of Madera Canyon 231, 239, 241-242, 257
Huachuca Canyon 252

Abbreviated Table of Contents

Abbreviated Table of Contents

Abbreviated Table of Contents

Abbreviated Table of Contents

Abbreviated Table of Contents

Southeastern Arizona Mileage Chart

Location index (diagonal labels):

1. Amado/Arivaca Jct.
2. Arivaca
3. Aravaipa East
4. Aravaipa West
5. Ariz.-Sonora Desert Museum
6. Bisbee
7. Buenos Aires NWR HQ
8. Chiricahua National Monument
9. Coronado National Memorial
10. Douglas
11. Dudleyville
12. Elfrida
13. Green Valley
14. Madera Canyon
15. Muleshoe Ranch Preserve
16. Nogales
17. Patagonia
18. Picacho Reservoir
19. Portal
20. Ramsey Canyon Preserve
21. Rustler Park
22. Sabino Canyon Visitor Center
23. San Pedro House
24. San Simon
25. Sierra Vista
26. Ski Valley, Santa Catalina Mtns
27. Sonoita
28. Sycamore Canyon, Atascosa Mtns
29. Tombstone
30. Tucson: I-10 and I-19
31. Willcox

Mileage matrix (each row lists distances from that location to the lower-numbered locations, in order):

From	1	2	3	4	5	6	7	8	9	10	11	12	13	14	15	16	17	18	19	20	21	22	23	24	25	26	27	28	29	30
2 Arivaca	23																													
3 Aravaipa East	185	208																												
4 Aravaipa West	101	124	139																											
5 Ariz.-Sonora Desert Museum	40	73	169	78																										
6 Bisbee	129	152	159	164	112																									
7 Buenos Aires NWR HQ	41	19	212	128	57	156																								
8 Chiricahua National Monument	144	167	103	179	128	65	171																							
9 Coronado National Memorial	119	142	162	162	110	19	154	84																						
10 Douglas	154	177	160	197	146	24	189	61	43																					
11 Dudleyville	93	116	122	16	70	156	120	171	154	189																				
12 Elfrida	138	161	115	165	121	27	161	38	46	23	164																			
13 Green Valley	11	34	177	90	39	140	53	133	81	115	82	124																		
14 Madera Canyon	22	45	190	104	51	88	65	145	78	112	95	73	12																	
15 Muleshoe Ranch Preserve	143	166	97	178	127	61	170	61	82	101	170	120	132	125																
16 Nogales	37	60	186	88	65	145	79	155	82	117	79	48	60	73	144															
17 Patagonia	51	74	168	127	76	74	97	127	64	98	82	16	64	74	126	18														
18 Picacho Reservoir	74	97	127	74	127	209	100	209	120	130	60	48	65	38	18	126	144													
19 Portal	94	117	213	109	75	157	121	172	155	190	101	165	83	97	186	99	131	171												
20 Ramsey Canyon Preserve	110	133	152	153	102	30	145	113	16	54	145	59	72	69	110	55	73	146	189											
21 Rustler Park	161	184	120	196	145	82	188	17	115	72	188	55	186	143	78	189	131	15	65	146										
22 Sabino Canyon Visitor Center	50	73	157	70	30	101	77	116	99	134	61	109	39	53	87	64	52	90	64	110	154									
23 San Pedro House	108	131	150	150	90	36	142	109	26	57	142	57	69	66	108	71	52	126	17	45	117	90								
24 San Simon	155	178	114	190	139	129	182	52	83	182	85	144	158	72	156	138	183	183	27	183	72	143	138							
25 Sierra Vista	101	124	143	143	92	29	135	102	19	53	135	59	101	64	45	101	64	119	110	10	119	136	45	136						
26 Ski Valley, Santa Catalina Mtns	79	102	186	111	59	130	106	145	128	163	103	68	82	93	144	104	116	162	119	104	162	38	93	104	109					
27 Sonoita	39	62	156	114	63	62	109	115	52	86	115	71	29	26	128	30	12	132	43	107	132	51	30	107	40	116				
28 Sycamore Canyon, Atascosa Mtns	40	63	212	143	92	118	105	171	108	142	135	128	63	62	171	26	38	188	99	136	200	92	44	136	89	182	56			
29 Tombstone	105	128	132	135	94	24	128	90	35	48	128	33	67	76	89	107	73	92	26	61	99	17	26	107	7	96	75	121		
30 Tucson: I-10 and I-19	33	56	152	68	17	96	60	111	94	129	104	43	22	36	94	59	24	73	128	80	107	17	59	128	46	73	38	17	46	
31 Willcox	113	136	72	148	97	30	114	31	43	102	95	56	102	95	141	114	101	48	80	141	30	69	96	30	109	141	102	84	68	80

342